Addiction Treatment

Addiction Treatment

Theory
and
Practice

Sandra Rasmussen

Sage Publications, Inc.
International Educational and Professional Publisher
Thousand Oaks ▪ London ▪ New Delhi

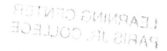

For information:

 Sage Publications, Inc.
2455 Teller Road
Thousand Oaks, California 91320
E-mail: order@sagepub.com

Sage Publications Ltd.
6 Bonhill Street
London EC2A 4PU
United Kingdom

Sage Publications India Pvt. Ltd.
M-32 Market
Greater Kailash I
New Delhi 110 048 India

Printed in the United States of America

Library of Congress Cataloging-in-Publication Data

Rasmussen, Sandra.
    Addiction treatment: Theory and practice / by Sandra Rasmussen.
        p. cm.
Includes bibliographical references and index.
    ISBN 0-7619-0842-0 (cloth: alk. paper) — ISBN 0-7619-0843-9 (pbk.: alk. paper)
    1. Substance abuse—Treatment. 2. Addicts—Rehabilitation. I. Title.
    HV4998 .R37 2000
    362.29'18—dc21   00-008183

This book is printed on acid-free paper.

00   01   02   03   04   05   06   7   6   5   4   3   2   1

Acquisition Editor:	Jim Brace-Thompson
Editorial Assistant:	Anna Howland
Production Editor:	Elly Korn and Sanford Robinson
Editorial Assistant:	Cindy Bear
Typesetter:	Rebecca Evans
Indexer:	Jean Casalegno
Cover Designer:	Michelle Lee

In memory of Slim H.

Contents

Part I. Addiction

Part II. Addiction Treatment

Part III. Treatment Process

Part IV. Client Diversity and Treatment Matching

Part V. Treatment Collaboration for Coexisting Medical, Psychological, and Social Problems

Preface

This book is a comprehensive text that provides a foundation for addiction practice by health and human service professionals. It is broad in scope and inclusive in content. It builds upon generic concepts and skills of caring and helping. The text is divided into five parts comprising 20 chapters. Each chapter begins with a list of objectives and a chapter outline and ends with a summary, a checklist of skills related to the chapter topic, some suggested areas for further study, and references. Each also includes a challenge to practitioners to affirm and advance addiction treatment in this new century, a concept I call *addiction practice 2000*. Throughout, the text emphasizes the knowledge considered essential for general addiction practice. An appendix containing examples of treatment tools and other resources for clients and clinicians completes the book.

Part I: Addiction

Addiction jeopardizes the health and well-being of individuals, families, and communities. Chapter 1 defines addiction, depicts the many faces of addiction, asserts that treatment works, and describes effective prevention programs. Addiction practice terms and concepts are also defined. Chapter 2 examines the origins, characteristics, adequacy, and relevance of conventional, contemporary, and comprehensive theories and models of addiction. Addiction practitioners use theories and models of addiction to ground and guide their practice. Chapter 3 reviews substances of abuse, including central nervous system depressants, central nervous system stimulants, opioids, and hallucinogens. It describes use and abuse of marijuana, inhalants, anabolic steroids, designer drugs, and herbs. Because addiction includes both chemical and nonchemical addictive disorders, Chapter 4 discusses pathological gambling, compulsive shopping, sex and love addiction, eating disorders, and other addictive behaviors. Chapter 5 describes the multidisciplinary group of health professionals, paraprofessionals, volunteers, and recovering people who work in addiction treatment.

Part II: Addiction Treatment

Treatment works! Chapter 6 compares and contrasts different treatment methodologies, describing the client and clinician roles associated with each treatment approach. Chapter 7 discusses short-term, intermediate, and long-term client goals. Treatment goals reflect desired client change. Chapter 8 addresses the concepts of addiction severity and treatment intensity. It describes the *Addiction Severity Index (ASI)* and the *American Society of Addiction Medicine Patient Placement Criteria for the Treatment of Substance-Related Disorders 2 (ASAM PPC-2)*. Clinicians use addiction severity to determine treatment intensity. They place clients in appropriate levels of care and specify the number, type, and frequency of interventions and services.

Part III: Treatment Process

Addiction treatment is a collaborative process between clinicians and client, a process of assessment, diagnosis, treatment planning, intervention, and evaluation. Chapter 9 explains *assessment*—how clinicians and client collect and organize data about the substance abuse or addictive behavior, the client, and the environment. Chapter 10 describes *diagnosis*—how clinicians and client validate, cluster, and interpret assessment data to denote or name the client's problem. This chapter includes *DSM-IV* diagnoses for substance-related disorders and other addictive disorders. Chapter 11 discusses *treatment planning*—the way clinicians and client establish and prioritize treatment goals, specify objectives or expected outcomes, select interventions, and designate services. Treatment plans reflect level of care and intervention dose. Chapter 12 reviews intervention—the actions clinicians and client use to reach outcomes, achieve treatment goals, meet client needs and ultimately resolve client problems. Intervention with individual clients includes medical management, nursing, counseling, medication, spiritual care, social services, and psychological services. Many interventions utilize groups, the family, and the community. Chapter 13 examines *evaluation*—the way clinicians, client, and providers evaluate client treatment and the treatment program. Total Quality Management (TQM) is the continuous monitoring and evaluation of the treatment program to improve both process and outcome.

Part IV: Client Diversity and Treatment Matching

Clients differ in age, ethnocultural characteristics, gender, and sexual orientation. Effective treatment respects and reflects client diversity. Chapter 14 highlights addiction across the lifespan from perinatal addiction to prescription drug abuse by older adults. Treatment needs of addicted infants, adolescents, and older adults are examined. Chapter 15 discusses multiculturalism and addiction. It challenges clinicians to develop treatment initiatives for clients with diverse ethnocultural characteristics. In Chapter 16 clinicians confront the many dilemmas posed by women and addiction, especially the great disparity between treatment needs and access to effective services. Chapter 17 urges clinicians to develop sensitive treatment for gay, lesbian, bisexual, and transgender clients and to accept the challenge for prevention and early intervention with gay and lesbian youth.

Part V: Treatment Collaboration for Coexisting Medical, Psychological, and Social Problems

Medical, psychological, and social problems that coexist with addictive disorders increase addiction severity and confound treatment. Chapter 18 reviews alcohol-related medical problems, adverse medical effects of drug abuse, HIV/ AIDS, pain, and physical disabilities. Chapter 19 notes the prevalence of dual disorders. Clients with dual disorders experience more severe and chronic medical and social problems. They relapse with alcohol and other drugs more frequently, decompensate psychiatrically more often, have more crises, and progress more slowly in treatment. Barriers to treatment are legion! Chapter 20 shows how social problems such as unemployment, poverty or excess, homelessness, unsafe neighborhoods, and legal problems contribute to the development of addictive disorders, influence treatment planning, and impact recovery. The book concludes with a challenge to addiction practitioners to affirm and advance addiction practice 2000.

Acknowledgments

In *Memoirs of Childhood and Youth,* Albert Schweitzer avows: "Sometimes our light goes out but is blown again into flame by an encounter with another human being. Each of us owes the deepest thanks to those who have rekindled this inner light." *Addiction Treatment* reflects the expectations and encouragement of colleagues and clients, students and sponsors, friends and family, the fellowship, and Sage Publications.

Colleagues include nurses, counselors, social workers, physicians, psychologists, educators, and administrators from The NORCAP Center of Southwood Community Hospital, Brown University Center for Alcohol and Addiction Studies, and AdCare Hospital and Recovery Services. Clients like "steady Eddie," Serine M. and her family, Michelle R., and Tom F. showed me that recovery is a journey, not a destination. Hundreds of students challenged me, especially those concentrating in addiction studies or conducting research with special addiction populations. The lives, and in some cases deaths, of Ella, Charlotte, Ann, Eileen, and Judy taught me the meaning of survival, beauty, genuineness, courage, and fidelity.

Thanks to my special friends Barbara and Francis who were always there. Appreciation to my family who reminded me, that even though I am a busy nurse, counselor, and teacher, I am first and foremost a caring mother and loving grandmother. And finally, abiding gratitude to the fellowship of recovering men and women who willingly shared "their experience, strength, and hope."

Special thanks to Francis D. Doucette, Ph.D., J.D., who edited the draft manuscript with rigor and red pen. Sincere appreciation to the staff of the Office of Publishing Services of Rhode Island College and the many editors and assistants from Sage who expedited publication.

Part I

Addiction

1

Addiction

Objectives

- Recognize the many faces of addiction.
- Acknowledge that treatment works.
- Support effective prevention programs.
- Utilize standard addiction terminology.
- Employ addiction concepts.
- Understand addiction practice concepts, client concepts, and treatment concepts.
- Identify primary, secondary, and tertiary levels of prevention.
- Support effective prevention program.

Outline

- **Faces of Addiction**
- **Treatment Works!**
- **Definitions**
  - Words and Meanings
  - Standard Terminology
  - Addiction
  - Alcoholism
  - Psychoactive Substances
  - Controlled Substances
  - Substance-Related Disorders
       Substance Use Disorders
       Substance-Induced Disorders
  - Other Addictive Disorders

- **Addiction Concepts**
  - Craving
  - Tolerance
  - Cross-Tolerance
  - Cross-Addiction
  - Progression
  - Relapse
  - Abstinence
  - Harm Reduction
  - Moderate Drinking
  - Remission
  - Recovery
- **Addiction Practice Concepts**
  - Practice
  - Practitioners
  - Treatment
  - Clinicians
- **Client Concepts**
  - Clients
  - Client Diversity
  - Comorbidity
  - Addiction Severity
- **Addiction Treatment Concepts**
  - Treatment Methodology
  - Treatment Goals
  - Treatment Intensity
  - Treatment Matching
  - Treatment Collaboration
  - Treatment Process
- **Prevention Concepts**
  - Primary Prevention
  - Secondary Prevention
  - Tertiary Prevention
- **Effective Prevention Programs**
- **Summary**
- **Related Skills Checklist**
- **Special Topics for Further Study**
- **Addiction Practice 2000**

Faces of Addiction

Substance abuse jeopardizes the health and well-being of individuals, families, and communities. Other addictive disorders, such as pathological gambling, compulsive shopping, sex and love addiction, eating disorders, and other addictive behaviors devastate the lives of many people. Addiction wears many faces:

- *An infant* born 4 weeks premature to a mother who is addicted to cocaine and alcohol

- *Four teens* admitted to a hospital emergency room, two of them dead on arrival, following injection of heroin

- *A young mother* under investigation for neglect of her three small children related to her abuse of alcohol and other drugs

- *A truck driver* who purchases a nicotine patch to help him kick his three-pack-a-day habit after his best buddy, also a heavy smoker, drops dead from a heart attack

- *A hospice nurse,* employee of the year, who has been suspended from work because she diverted narcotics to self-medicate her back pain

- *A high school teacher* who finds herself in bankruptcy court, promising herself that she will curb her compulsive shopping

- *An immigrant woman,* who survived the killing fields of Cambodia but cannot accept her daughter's marriage to an American or understand the lack of respect her grandchildren show her, who feels such shame that she isolates herself and begins to drink

- *An inmate* transferred from a prerelease work program to higher security because of a positive urine test for cocaine

- *An executive vice president* of a major insurance company who is indicted for embezzlement related to gambling debts

- *A retired postal worker* who drinks himself into a stupor every evening to cope with his depression related to the recent death of his wife

- *A 10-year-old boy* so obsessed with Pokémon cards, games, toys, videos, TV show, and movie that he bullies his friends when they refuse to trade cards with him

Treatment Works!

Dr. A. Thomas McClellan and his colleagues (1997) underscore the social costs of addiction:

Problems of alcohol and drug dependence produce dramatic costs to society in terms of lost productivity, social disorders, and avoidable health-care utilization. Reports from the Robert Wood Johnson Foundation suggest that alcohol abuse costs society approximately $99 billion annually; that abuse of other drugs costs approximately $67 billion annually; and that one-eighth to one-sixth of all deaths here in America are associated in some way with alcohol or drug use. Perhaps more subtle but no less significant is the fact that more than three-fourths of all foster children in the country are the products of alcohol- and/or drug-addicted parents. (pp. 7-8)

McClellan and his colleagues evaluated the effectiveness of addiction treatment and found that "treatment works!" Not only does addiction treatment work, but it is cost-effective when compared with treatment for such medical diseases as high blood pressure, asthma, and diabetes. The effectiveness of substance abuse treatment can be judged using three outcome expectations: (a) reduction in substance use, (b) improvement in personal health and social function, and (c) reduction in public health and safety risks. Furthermore, substance abuse treatment has been and can be evaluated in a scientific manner.

Yet, according to opinion polls conducted by the Harvard School of Public Health, public support for drug treatment declined from a high of 65% in 1990 to 53% in 1996 (Knox, 1998). Spending for mental health and alcohol and drug abuse treatment also declined over the past decade, with a shift of expenditures from the private to the public sector. Currently, the majority of treatment costs for mental health and substance abuse problems are paid for by federal, state, and local governments. (For an analysis of these treatment costs, see Exhibit A in the appendix to this volume.) Addiction practitioners recognize this dilemma and understand how misguided views regarding morality and legal sanctions, rather than treatment outcome studies, tend to determine public policy and influence funding for addiction treatment. One positive note, however, can be found in the fact that the March 1998 public television series *Moyers on Addiction: Close to Home* drew a large audience. Series installments included "Portrait of Addiction," "The Hijacked Brain," "Changing Lives," "The Next Generation," and "The Politics of Addiction."

Definitions

Words and Meanings

Language and discourse about addiction have changed over the years, yet today people still use many words with inexact meanings to describe addiction. Unfortunately, many of these terms reflect attitudes of disapproval, disdain, and disgust. Addiction is called a habit, use, abuse, dependency, alcoholism, or addiction per se. A person with an addiction is referred to as an inebriate, a dipsomaniac, a rummy, a drunk, a drunkard, a druggie, a junkie, an alcoholic, a user, or an addict. An overweight child is called "fatty." People with sex addictions are labeled perverts. To add to the confusion, addiction terminology is used frequently in casual conversation: "I am addicted to chocolate." "Bill is an Internet junkie."

Clients in addiction treatment often use these pejorative labels: "What do you expect? I'm a street addict." "Supportive family? My father is a junkie and my mother is a drunk." Following an assessment interview, a young adult client exclaimed with abject horror to the clinician, "Does that mean I'm an alcoholic?"

Standard Terminology

As addiction practice developed into a distinct discipline, practitioners identified concepts and defined terms relevant to the field. A shared vocabulary enhances communication among practitioners and between practitioners and the general public. Current usage as articulated by the following three primary sources informs the terminology and definitions used in this book:

- *The Alcohol and Other Drug Thesaurus: A Guide to Concepts and Terminology in Substance Abuse and Addiction,* second edition (1995), four volumes developed jointly by the National Institute on Alcohol Abuse and Alcoholism, the Center for Substance Abuse Prevention, the National Institutes of Health, the Substance Abuse and Mental Health Services Administration, and the Public Health Service

- The American Psychiatric Association's *Diagnostic and Statistical Manual of Mental Disorders,* fourth edition (*DSM-IV;* 1994)

- The American Society of Addiction Medicine's *Patient Placement Criteria for the Treatment of Substance-Related Disorders,* second edition (*ASAM PPC-2;* 1996)

Addiction

Addiction is a broad term that embraces both substance-related (chemical) and behavioral (nonchemical) problems. Addictive disorders include (a) *substance use disorders,* more specifically substance dependence and substance abuse, and (b) *substance-induced disorders,* such as intoxication, withdrawal, and flashbacks. Because nonchemical disorders such as pathological gambling, compulsive shopping, sex and love addictions, and eating disorders resemble substance-related disorders in etiology, expression, and treatment, it is useful to include these problems in addiction practice.

Addiction is dependence on a substance or behavior. It is characterized by (a) tolerance, (b) preoccupation with obtaining and using the substance or engaging in the behavior, (c) use of the substance or engaging in the behavior despite actual or potential adverse biopsychosocial consequences, (d) repeated efforts to cut down or control the use or behavior, and (e) withdrawal symptoms when the substance or behavior is removed.

Alcoholism

The Joint Committee to Study the Definition and Criteria for the Diagnosis of Alcoholism of the National Council on Alcoholism and Drug Dependence and the American Society of Addiction Medicine have defined alcoholism as follows:

> Alcoholism is a primary, chronic disease with genetic, psychosocial, and environmental factors influencing its development and manifestations. The disease is often progressive and fatal. It is characterized by continuous or periodic: impaired control over drinking, preoccupation with the drug alcohol, use of alcohol despite adverse consequences, and distortions in thinking, most notably denial.

(For an explanation of the key terms used in this definition, see Exhibit B in the appendix.)

Psychoactive Substances

Psychoactive substances are licit or illicit substances that, when ingested, affect the central nervous system and alter mood, perception, cognition, memory, or consciousness. Users experience pleasure or diminished pain. Psychoactive substances include *central nervous system depressants* such as alcohol and other sedative, hypnotic, and anxiolytic drugs; *central nervous system stimulants,* including cocaine, amphetamines, nicotine, and caffeine; *opioids* in any form, including heroin and prescription analgesics; *hallucinogens,* such as lysergic acid diethylamide (LSD) and phencyclidine hydrochloride (PCP); *marijuana;* and *inhalants, anabolic steroids, designer drugs,* and *some herbs.*

Controlled Substances

Controlled substances are drugs classified by the U.S. Drug Enforcement Agency (DEA) according to their potential for abuse, ability to produce dependence, and medical utility. The classifications range from Schedule I drugs, which have potential for abuse so high as to be unacceptable for licit use, to

Schedule V drugs, which have minimal abuse potential. Heroin and LSD are Schedule I controlled substances; buprenorphine (Buprenex), an opioid analgesic, is a Schedule V drug. New substances are added to the schedules every year, and drugs may be moved from one schedule to another. For example, several years ago propoxyphene (Darvon) was listed as a Schedule V drug; because of increased abuse, it is now classified as Schedule IV. Most states' laws concerning controlled substances are stricter than the federal statutes.

Substance-Related Disorders

DSM-IV and *ASAM PPC-2* classify disorders caused by psychoactive substances as substance-related disorders. *DSM-IV* further divides these disorders into substance use and substance-induced disorders.

Substance Use Disorders

Substance dependence is a maladaptive pattern of substance use that leads to clinically significant impairment or distress. Dependence is characterized by tolerance, withdrawal, the need to ingest a larger amount of substance or ingestion over a longer period of time than was intended, and unsuccessful attempts to control use. Individuals who meet substance dependence criteria often lead drug-dependent lifestyles characterized by neglect of family, work, or leisure activities. They continue to use despite knowledge of their physical or psychological problems. (Note that it is preferable for treatment practitioners to use the clinical term *substance dependence* instead of *addiction* or *alcoholism* when describing addiction to alcohol or other drugs.)

Substance abuse is a maladaptive pattern of substance use that leads to clinically significant impairment or distress. Such use is physically hazardous, may result in the user's failure to fulfill role expectations, and may cause legal problems or precipitate interpersonal and social problems for the user.

Substance-Induced Disorders

As noted above, psychoactive substances affect the central nervous system. During or shortly after use of a psychoactive substance, individuals may develop *substance intoxication*. Clinically significant maladaptive biopsychosocial changes characterize intoxication. Intoxication is reversible. Cessation or reduction in substance use may cause *substance withdrawal*. Clinically significant biopsychosocial distress or impairment characterizes withdrawal. Other substance-induced disorders include delirium, dementia, amnestic disorder, and psychotic disorders. Mood and anxiety disorders, sleep disorders, and sexual dysfunction can occur.

Other Addictive Disorders

Pathological gambling, compulsive shopping, sex and love addiction, eating disorders, and other addictive behaviors meet many of the descriptive criteria of addiction. Pathological gambling meets *DSM-IV* diagnostic criteria for an impulse-control disorder. Compulsive shopping resembles impulse-control disorders, with elements of obsessive-compulsive disorder. Sex and love addictions may meet *DSM-IV* criteria for sexual and gender identity disorders, relational problems, or sexual abuse. Eating disorders constitute a separate *DSM-IV* diagnostic category.

Addiction Concepts

Craving

Craving is an intense, strong desire, a powerful urge beyond reason for a drink, a drug, or an addictive activity ("I don't want to use, but I just can't help it"). Currently, researchers are trying to explain the craving phenomenon and to develop treatment modalities to curb this addictive process. For example, it appears that the antiepilepsy medication gammavinyl GABA or GVG (Vigabatrin) may help control cravings for cocaine, heroin, amphetamines, and even nicotine. The anticraving drug acamprosate (Campral), which is used in Europe to increase abstinence in alcohol dependence, is undergoing clinical trials in the United States.

Tolerance

Tolerance is present when increased amounts of a substance or activity are needed to achieve the desired effects, or when diminished effects are experienced with use of the same amount of substance or same level of activity ("I use more and more and it does less and less for me"). Tolerance is one of the defining criteria of addiction.

Cross-Tolerance

Cross-tolerance is the development of tolerance to a new substance because of previous use of a similar substance. Cross-tolerance is apparent when the new substance fails to produce the expected effect. The two substances usually have similar pharmacological effects—for example, alcohol and barbiturates are both central nervous system depressants, and cross-tolerance for the two is common.

Cross-Addiction

Cross-addiction is the predisposition to multiple addictions. For example, Joan M. is dependent on nicotine, alcohol, and cocaine; Tom C. meets diagnostic criteria for pathological gambling and compulsive overeating; Ian B. abuses cocaine and is facing charges of exhibitionism.

Progression

Progression in an addictive disorder is the increasing extent or severity of the disorder over time. Progression characterizes the addictive process.

Relapse

Relapse is the recurrence of substance use or other addictive behavior following a period of abstinence. Relapse prevention is a critical treatment goal.

Abstinence

Abstinence is the voluntary avoidance of a substance or behavior previously used or abused. Abstinence is the usual treatment goal for clients with diagnoses of substance dependence and/or pathological gambling. Clients will remain alcohol-free, drug-free, and/or free from all wagering.

Harm Reduction

Harm reduction is a term used to describe programs or policies that focus on reducing the harm resulting from substance use or other addictive behavior without necessarily affecting the underlying drug dependence or addiction. For example, designated driver programs reduce injury and death from motor vehicle accidents as a result of drinking and driving. Needle exchange programs for intravenous drug users reduce the spread of HIV. Methadone maintenance programs replace addicts' need for street heroin and thereby decrease illicit drug activities.

Moderate Drinking

Moderate drinking is an inexact term that denotes drinking that is moderate in amount and does not cause problems. Moderate drinking is defined by addiction experts as no more than one drink a day for most women and no more than two drinks a day for most men. The concept of moderate drinking is often confused with "social drinking" or "controlled drinking."

Remission

An addictive disorder is considered in remission when symptoms of the addiction lessen or abate. *DSM-IV* divides remission into four types: early full remission, early partial remission, sustained full remission, and sustained partial remission.

Recovery

Recovery includes optimal client health, well-being, and functioning. Recovery is a long-term, comprehensive treatment goal. For example, Mark L. reports with pride sustained full remission from all use of cocaine and alcohol for 2 years, no symptoms of anxiety or depression, and a desired weight gain of 20 pounds. His family and home life have never been better, and he recently received a promotion at work with a raise. Mark declares, "I have a life second to none and this is only the beginning!" He is experiencing recovery.

Addiction Practice Concepts

Practice

Addiction practice is a broad concept that includes all aspects of addiction work: prevention and treatment, theory and research, policy and politics. Federal government agencies, state health departments, colleges and universities, and hospitals and other treatment providers engage in addiction practice. A great variety of clinicians and other practitioners work in the addiction field.

Practitioners

Professionals from many diverse disciplines contribute to addiction practice, including health, mental health, and public health; education, evaluation, law, and public policy; and biology, chemistry, pharmacology, psychology, sociology, and economics. In this text, I use the term *practitioner* to refer to clinicians, health care administrators, government officials, university faculty, researchers, and any other professionals involved in addiction practice.

Treatment

Addiction treatment is a collaborative process between clinicians and clients, a process of assessment, diagnosis, treatment planning, intervention, and evaluation. Client diversity and comorbidity influence treatment. Addiction severity determines treatment intensity. Treatment helps clients manage actual and potential problems related to their addictions.

Clinicians

In this text, I use the term *clinician* to refer to persons who provide treatment, care, and other direct services for clients. Clinicians include nurses, physicians, counselors, social workers, psychologists, clergy, educators, and other professionals who care for clients directly.

Client Concepts

Clients

In this text, I use the term *client* to refer to individuals, groups, families, or communities who demonstrate a need for addiction treatment, care, or services. The term *patient* is often used synonymously with *client,* especially by staff in inpatient treatment settings.

Client Diversity

Clients differ in their ages, ethnocultural characteristics, genders, and sexual orientations. These differences influence clients' needs and preferences. Effective treatment processes respect and reflect client diversity.

Comorbidity

Medical, psychological, and social problems often coexist with addictive disorders. *Comorbidity* refers to the coexistence of a second disease with the primary disease. Major medical problems such as heart disease, cancer, and diabetes may coexist with addictive disorders. Alcohol-related medical problems, adverse medical effects of drug abuse, HIV/AIDS, pain, and physical disabilities increase addiction severity and confound treatment.

The term *dual disorders* refers to clients who have a primary addiction diagnosis plus a second mental health diagnosis, such as alcohol dependence and major depressive disorder, cocaine dependence and posttraumatic stress disorder, pathological gambling and bipolar disorder, or bulimia nervosa and narcissistic personality disorder. Compared with clients who have no second diagnosis, those with dual disorders relapse with alcohol and other drugs more frequently, decompensate psychiatrically more often, have more crises, and progress more slowly in treatment.

Social problems such as unemployment, poverty, homelessness, unsafe neighborhoods, and legal problems often coexist with addictive disorders, increasing addiction severity, challenging treatment, and affecting recovery.

Addiction Severity

The seriousness of client symptoms and the degree of impairment related to an addiction may be moderate to severe. Coexisting medical, psychological, and social problems contribute to greater addiction severity. Clinicians use standardized tools such as the Addiction Severity Index (ASI) to determine the level of severity of clients' addictions.

Addiction Treatment Concepts

Treatment Methodology

The explicit, purposeful, organized way in which clinicians and clients conduct treatment is referred to as the *treatment methodology*. Clinicians employ a variety of approaches to addiction treatment, including 12-step recovery methods, the Minnesota model, psychodynamic approaches, cognitive therapies, motivational enhancement therapy, the stages-of-change model, problem-oriented treatment, and solution-focused treatment. The treatment methodology used may emphasize group therapy, family as treatment, or community as treatment.

Treatment Goals

Treatment goals reflect desired client change. Short-term, immediate goals include safe withdrawal, abstinence, harm reduction, and moderate drinking. Relapse prevention and remission are intermediate treatment goals. Recovery is a comprehensive, long-term client goal.

Treatment Intensity

The intensity of treatment varies with the number, types, and frequency of interventions and services; treatment intensity is often associated with level of care. Addiction severity determines treatment intensity. Clinicians use standardized tools such as *ASAM PPC-2* to place clients in the appropriate level of care and to select interventions.

Treatment Matching

No single treatment approach is effective for all clients. Clinicians match treatment methodologies with client variables. Treatment matching involves assigning clients to different treatments based on the clients' characteristics, special needs, and expressed preferences—"Different strokes for different folks."

Treatment Collaboration

Addiction clinicians work together with teams of health and human service providers and other professionals to treat clients. Treatment collaboration is especially important for clients from nonmajority ethnic and cultural backgrounds and for clients who are adversely affected by coexisting medical, psychological, and social problems.

Treatment Process

The step-by-step way in which clinicians provide addiction treatment is referred to as the *treatment process.* Effective treatment takes the form of a collaborative process between clinicians and client, a process of assessment, diagnosis, treatment planning, intervention, and evaluation.

During *assessment,* clinicians and client collect and organize data about the client's substance use or other addictive behavior, the client him- or herself, and the client's environment. A comprehensive assessment begins with screening, which is followed by a history and physical examination, substance use/addiction assessment, mental status examination, psychosocial assessment, family assessment, toxicology testing, and specialized testing if indicated.

Clinicians and client then validate, analyze, and interpret the assessment data to *diagnose* or name the client's problem. Clinicians use *DSM-IV* diagnoses for substance-related disorders and other addictive disorders.

Treatment planning is the process through which clinicians and client develop an individualized, written description of planned treatment, including goals, expected outcomes, interventions, and services. The treatment plan builds upon the comprehensive assessment of the client and the *DSM-IV* diagnoses. The plan reflects addiction severity and treatment intensity, the client's needs in regard to any specific ethnic or cultural factors, and treatment matching. The treatment plan identifies client problems or needs as well as the client's strengths and preferences.

Intervention describes the actions and services clinicians and client use to reach outcomes, achieve goals, and ultimately resolve the client's problems and meet his or her needs. Intervention with individual clients may include medical and pharmacological management, nursing, counseling, self-help groups, family support, community care, spiritual care, and psychological services. Intervention may involve groups, clients' families, or the community.

Treatment providers, clinicians, and client must also *evaluate* the client's treatment and the treatment program. Specific concepts, licensing rules and regulations, accreditation standards and criteria, and special program requirements guide evaluation. Total quality management involves the continuous monitoring and evaluation of the treatment program to improve both process and outcome.

Prevention Concepts

Addiction prevention is a public health concept that includes health promotion, prompt treatment, and rehabilitation.

Primary Prevention

Primary prevention is true prevention in that it precedes onset of the problem—that is, before an individual abuses substances or develops addictive behavior. Primary prevention activities include addiction education, health promotion, and specific alternatives to use. Primary prevention frequently targets individuals who are at risk of developing addiction problems. Programs often involve groups of clients in schools or work sites, or elsewhere in the community.

Secondary Prevention

Secondary prevention emphasizes early intervention and prompt treatment with individuals who have addiction problems. Screening and case finding are secondary prevention techniques. The aim of secondary prevention is to check the addictive process early and thus limit disability, arrest progression, and prevent death.

Tertiary Prevention

Tertiary prevention occurs when the addictive disorder is severe or chronic. The aim of tertiary prevention is to minimize the effects of the addiction with interventions to prevent further disability or reduced functioning. Tertiary prevention strategies include remotivation, retraining, restoration, and rehabilitation.

Effective Prevention Programs

Addiction practice 2000 includes prevention. Effective prevention programs and practices are based on sound theoretical principles; they have undergone rigorous evaluation, and there is high confidence in the results. The Center for Substance Abuse Prevention describes seven such programs in its publication *Understanding Substance Abuse Prevention: Toward the 21st Century: A Primer on Effective Programs* (1999b):

- *Across Ages:* The Across Ages program is a research-based mentoring initiative in Philadelphia, Pennsylvania, that successfully improved adolescents' social competence and enhanced their ability to resist alcohol, tobacco, and drug use. The unique and highly effective feature of Across Ages is the pairing of older adults with middle school children to provide the children with positive, nurturing role models.

- *Child Development Project:* The Child Development Project (CDP) is a research-based school-improvement initiative designed by the Developmental Studies Center of Oakland, California. By transforming elementary schools into "caring communities of learners," CDP significantly reduced children's use of alcohol and illicit drugs while dramatically increasing the children's resilience to substance use. CDP scientifically demonstrates that nurturing a student's intrinsic desire to learn, cultivating supportive relationships, and promoting the child's sense of common purpose and commitment to prosocial values are effective protections against the risk of substance use.

- *Creating Lasting Connections:* The Creating Lasting Connections (CLC) program, a 5-year demonstration project in the city of Louisville, Kentucky, and six surrounding counties, scientifically demonstrates that families in high-risk environments can be helped to become strong, healthy, and supportive families, which in turn significantly increases the children's resilience to substance use and dramatically reduces their use of alcohol and illicit drugs. CLC provides parents and children with strong defenses against environmental risk factors by teaching appropriate skills for personal growth, family enhancement, and interpersonal communication.

- *Dare to Be You:* The Dare to Be You program is a 5-year demonstration project that, by dramatically improving parent and child resilience factors—particularly in the areas of communication, problem solving, self-esteem, and family skills—significantly lowers the risk of future substance abuse and other high-risk activities. The multilevel prevention program is an adaptation of the Dare to Be You community and school training programs.

- *Residential Student Assistance Program:* The Residential Student Assistance Program (RSAP), a 5-year demonstration project in Westchester County, New York, has dramatically reduced substance use among institutionalized adolescents at risk. RSAP is adapted from the county's highly successful Student Assistance Program, which is similar to the employee assistance programs effectively used by industry to identify and aid employees whose jobs and lives have been harmed by substance abuse.

- *SMART Leaders:* SMART Leaders is a 2-year, sequential program for youth who have completed Stay SMART, a component of Boys & Girls Clubs of America's SMART Moves program. Evaluation results show the effectiveness of this multiyear approach in promoting refusal skills and creating drug-free peer leaders.

- *Family Advocacy Network (FAN) Club:* The FAN Club program directly involves parents of youth participating in Boys & Girls Clubs of America's SMART Moves program, including the SMART Leaders booster program. The FAN Club strengthens families and promotes family bonding, thereby increasing the resistance of youth to drug use.

Summary

Addiction wears many faces. Treatment works! The use of standard terminology enhances practitioners' communication with clients, with other practitioners, and with the general public. Addiction concepts help to explain addiction. Treatment concepts clarify client variables and treatment terms. Prevention activities reflect primary, secondary, and tertiary levels of prevention. Research grounds effective prevention programs.

Related Skills Checklist

Practitioner skills related to the overall topic of addiction as discussed in this chapter include the ability to do the following:

- Use accurate standard terminology with clients, colleagues, and the community at large.

- Define addiction concepts in ways that can be observed and measured.

- Individualize treatment concepts.

- Employ prevention concepts.

- Support effective prevention programs.

Special Topics for Further Study

Addiction practice suggests many questions for further study. What constitutes treatment effectiveness? What are the dimensions and dynamics of relapse? What are the incidence and prevalence of cross-addiction? Why is harm reduction such a controversial treatment goal? Is moderate drinking an appropriate treatment goal for some clients? How can treatment process respect and respond to the needs of racially, ethnically, and otherwise diverse clients? What is the role of addiction clinicians in the care of clients with coexisting medical, psychological, and social problems? What is a realistic primary prevention program for teens at risk?

Addiction Practice 2000

Addiction practice 2000 challenges practitioners to affirm and advance the forward movement of the discipline on all fronts: practice, policy, research, and theory. More specifically, addiction practitioners must explain the depth and scope of addiction practice to other health and human service providers, business interests, and public officials—anyone and everyone with a vested interest in addiction. Addiction practice embraces both treatment and prevention.

References

American Psychiatric Association. (1994). *Diagnostic and statistical manual of mental disorders* (4th ed.). Washington, DC: Author.

American Society of Addiction Medicine. (1996). *Patient placement criteria for the treatment of substance-related disorders* (2nd ed.). Chevy Chase, MD: Author.

Center for Substance Abuse Prevention. (1999). *Understanding substance abuse prevention: Toward the 21st century: A primer of effective programs* (DHHS Publication No. SMA 99-3302). Rockville, MD: Author.

Knox, R. A. (1998, March 19). Addiction treatment works, doctors say. *Boston Globe,* p. A3.

McClellan, A. T., Woody, G. E., Metzer, D., McKay, J., Durrell, J., Alterman, A. I., & O'Brien, C. P. (1997). Evaluating the effectiveness of addiction treatments: reasonable expectations, appropriate comparisons. In J. A. Egertson, D. M. Fox, & A. I. Leshner (Eds.), *Treating drug abusers effectively* (pp. 7-40). Malden, MA: Blackwell.

National Institute on Alcohol Abuse and Alcoholism, Center for Substance Abuse Prevention, National Institutes of Health, Substance Abuse and Mental Health Services Administration, & Public Health Service. (1995). *The alcohol and other drug thesaurus: A guide to concepts and terminology in substance abuse and addiction* (2nd ed., 4 vols.). Washington, DC: U.S. Department of Health and Human Services.

Other Sources

Center for Substance Abuse Prevention. (1994). *Prevention primer: An encyclopedia of alcohol, tobacco, and other drug prevention terms* (DHHS Publication No. SMA 94-2060). Rockville, MD: Author.

Center for Substance Abuse Prevention. (1999). *Here's proof prevention works* (DHHS Publication No. SMA 99-3300). Rockville, MD: Author.

Doweiko, H. E. (1999). *Concepts of chemical dependency* (4th ed.). Pacific Grove, CA: Brooks/Cole.

Johnson, M. (1991). *Cross-addiction: The hidden risk of multiple addictions.* New York: Rosen.

Lenson, D. (1995). *On drugs.* Minneapolis: University of Minnesota Press.

Milgram, G. G. (1996, May/June). Alcohol and other drugs in the American society: Part I. An overview. *Counselor,* pp. 30-32.

Milgram, G. G. (1996, July/August). Alcohol and other drugs in the American society: Part II. Significant issues for the '90s. *Counselor,* pp. 27-32.

Miller, N. W., & Swift, R. M. (1999). *Addictive disorders.* Philadelphia: J. B. Saunders.

National Institute on Alcohol Abuse and Alcoholism. (1996). *Alcoholism: Getting the facts* (NIH Publication No. 96-4153). Bethesda, MD: Author.

National Institute on Drug Abuse. (1995). *Assessing client needs using the ASI: Resource manual* (NIH Publication No. 95-3620). Rockville, MD: Author.

National Institute on Drug Abuse. (Ed.). (1997). *Problems of drug dependence, 1996: Proceedings of the 58th Annual Scientific Meeting of the College on Problems of Drug Dependence, Inc.* (NIH Publication No. 97-4236). Rockville, MD: Author. (NTIS No. PB 97-160295)

Sheerer, L., Kimball, C., Ungerleider, S., Meyer, G., & Zevnik, B. L. P. (1999). *Health resources online: A guide for mental health and addiction specialists* (2nd ed.). Eugene, OR: Integrated.

Singer, J. A. (1997). *Message in a bottle: Stories of men and addiction.* New York: Free Press.

Substance Abuse and Mental Health Services Administration. (1996). *Trends in the incidence of drug use in the United States, 1919-1992* (DHHS Publication No. 96-3076). Rockville, MD: Author.

Substance Abuse and Mental Health Services Administration. (1997). *The prevalence and correlates of treatment for drug problems* (DHHS Publication No. SMA 97-3135). Rockville, MD: Author.

Substance Abuse and Mental Health Services Administration. (1999). *National household survey on drug abuse population estimates 1998* (DHHS Publication No. SMA 99-3327). Rockville, MD: Author.

Substance Abuse and Mental Health Services Administration. (1999). *Summary of findings from the 1998 National Household Survey on Drug Abuse* (DHHS Publication No. SMA 99-3328). Rockville, MD: Author.

Thomas, C. L. (Ed.). (1997). *Taber's cyclopedic medical dictionary* (18th ed.). Philadelphia: F. A. Davis.

Wilson, J. J., & Wilson, J. A. (1999). *Addictionary: A primer of recovery terms and concepts from abstinence to withdrawal.* Center City, MN: Hazelden.

2

Theories and Models
of Addiction

Objectives

- Distinguish the properties of theories and models.
- Appreciate the value of addiction theories and models.
- Compare and contrast conventional, contemporary, and comprehensive theories and models of addiction.
- Identify the origins, assumptions, characteristics, and skills associated with different addiction theories and models.
- Evaluate the adequacy and relevance of various theories and models of addiction.
- Recognize that conventional, contemporary, and comprehensive theories and models of addiction influence current addiction practice.

Outline

- **Theories and Models**
- **Theories and Models of Addiction**
  - Conventional Models
    - The Moral Model
    - The Legal Model
    - The Disease Concept or Medical Model
    - The Pharmacological Model
  - Contemporary Theories
    - Biological Theories

Theories and Models

Theories and models help practitioners to describe, explain, predict, and control phenomena. Theories and models are made up of concepts and propositions. Concepts are abstract properties of the phenomena that are being studied. Examples of addiction concepts include craving, relapse, remission, and abstinence. Propositions are statements that indicate relationships—for example, Substance use relieves tension. Models are usually broad and general. They are extremely useful in the early development of the knowledge base of a discipline. Theories address phenomena with much greater specificity than do models. Theories and models are neither true nor false; rather, they are useful.

Theories and Models of Addiction

Theories and models of addiction reflect prevailing attitudes, practice, and knowledge. For the sake of description, addiction theories and models are organized broadly here according to these attributes. *Conventional models* of addiction include the moral model, the legal model, the disease concept or medical model, and the pharmacological model. *Contemporary theories* of addiction include biological, psychological, sociocultural, and transcendental/spiritual theories. *Comprehensive models* of addiction include the biopsychosocial model and the public health agent-host-environment model. It should be noted that there is overlap among the elements of many models.

Addiction theories and models provide frames of reference that help practitioners understand the etiology, expression, and course of addiction. Practitioners use theories to guide treatment, promote prevention, conduct research, and develop policy. Each addiction practitioner typically grounds his or her practice in one dominant theory or model. To utilize a theory or model effectively, a practitioner must understand its origins, examine its characteristics, critique its adequacy (strengths and limitations), and determine its clinical and social relevance. What assumptions support the theory or model? What is its knowledge base? What practice skills are associated with the theory or model?

Conventional Models

The Moral Model

From the 1620s until the 1770s, alcohol had personal, social, and commercial value in colonial America. The colonists from Europe appreciated alcoholic beverages, and people of all classes drank frequently and heavily. Wine and sugar were consumed at breakfast, workers broke during the day for their "bitters," cider and beer were drunk at lunch, and toddies were consumed at supper and during the evening. Alcoholic drinks were used to quench thirst and to fortify the body; liquor was seen as an invigorating food. Alcohol was used as a medicine to kill pain, fight fatigue, soothe indigestion, and prevent fever. Water was often considered dangerous to drink and too low-class to serve to guests. Drinking was believed to contribute to social well-being; it played an essential part in collective community activities, from barn raising to the harvesting of crops to the mustering of the militia.

Trade in liquor provided an important source of revenue for the early colonists. Taxes levied on wines and spirits provided money to educate children, care for widows and orphans, and defend the frontier. In the latter part of the 17th century, large quantities of West Indian molasses arrived in New England. The domestic distilling trade burgeoned, and people amassed fortunes trading rum for African slaves. The whiskey trade also became an indispensable element of the economic expansion westward.

Overindulgence in liquor, however, was understood to be the abuse of a God-given gift; drinking to excess was seen as personal indiscretion. Drink itself was not seen as the culprit, any more than food deserved blame for the sin of gluttony. Drunkenness was condemned and was punished by fines, whipping, stocks, or even banishment. Drunkenness was seen as deliberate, informed self-abuse and the expression of a sinful nature.

Many people today still consider alcohol abuse a sin and see alcohol abusers as immoral. Some individuals and groups view drug abuse, gambling, and overeating, as well as masturbation, pornography, prostitution, and homosexuality, as morally wrong. From their perspective, addicts are depraved, dissolute degenerates and should be punished, not treated. A strictly moral model of addiction denies scientific theory and research; it rejects a holistic concept connecting human and environment.

The Legal Model

Following the Revolutionary War, the United States experienced a sudden and dramatic growth in population. Alcohol production and consumption changed. People drank more and in places designed exclusively for drinking: saloons. Stable colonial towns that policed themselves gave way to an open, lawless frontier. Drinking and public drunkenness increased. Drinking led to neglect of families and crimes against persons and property. In addition, many packaged remedies for illnesses contained alcohol and other drugs; it was difficult to control mail-order sales or to check drug traffic across state lines.

Heightened awareness of the harmful effects and addictive properties of drugs eventually prompted the enactment of many laws to control the possession and distribution of drugs. Beginning in 1875 and continuing until about 1915, states and cities passed legislation outlawing opium and cocaine. Increasingly, the public mind associated drug use with the urban, criminal underworld and with minority populations. The Harrison Narcotic Act of 1914, the first such act passed by any nation, established the word *narcotic* as a legal term. The law regulated the importation, manufacture, sale, and use of opium and cocaine, and their compounds and by-products, as well as other synthetic compounds capable of producing physical or psychological dependence. In 1919, decisions of the U.S. Supreme Court allowed federal and state governments to fight drugs through repressive legislation, strict control of addicts, and increased interdiction measures. The Narcotic Drugs Import and Export Act of 1922 created the Narcotics Control Board to regulate the uses of opium, cocaine, and their derivatives.

In 1919, Congress ratified the 18th Amendment, which prohibited the manufacture, sale, or transportation of intoxication liquors within the United States; this amendment was repealed in 1933 (I discuss Prohibition later in this chapter, in the subsection on the pharmacological model). In 1932, the federal government passed the Uniform Narcotics Act, which was an attempt to standardize the varied state approaches to the drug problem. By 1937, 46 of 48 states had passed antimarijuana legislation and Congress passed the Marijuana Tax Act, which made the use and sale of marijuana federal offenses.

Following World War II, the Boggs Act of 1951 imposed severe mandatory sentences for narcotic offenses. President Eisenhower called for a new war on narcotic addiction at the local, national, and international levels. The Narcotic Control Act of 1956 increased sentences, and thousands of offenders were prosecuted.

The most significant drug legislation of the latter half of the 20th century was the Comprehensive Drug Abuse Prevention and Control Act of 1970, also known as the Controlled Substances Act. This law provided for increased research into drug abuse prevention and treatment for drug dependency; it strengthened existing law enforcement and established drug schedules (discussed below in the subsection on the pharmacological model). In 1988, Congress passed the Anti-Drug Abuse Act.

In 1992, the President's Commission on Model State Drug Laws was formed, with the mission "to develop comprehensive model state laws to significantly reduce, with the goal to eliminate, alcohol and other drug abuse in America through effective use and coordination of prevention, education, treatment, enforcement, and corrections" (President's Commission, 1993, p. 2). The commission asserted that tough sanctions are necessary to punish individuals who refuse to abide by the laws. According to the commission, sanctions will deter abuse. In addition, sanctions can serve to leverage alcohol and other drug abusers into treatment, rehabilitation, and recovery. The commission developed 44 model state drug laws and recommendations in the areas of economic remedies against drug traffickers, community mobilization, crime code enforcement, alcohol and other drug treatment, and drug-free families, schools, and workplaces. The scope of the commission's work exemplifies the commanding influence the legal model of addiction currently holds.

Regulation versus legalization of addictive substances in the United States remains controversial. Although alcohol, nicotine, and caffeine are recognized as psychoactive substances, caffeine is entirely unregulated and use of alcohol and nicotine is legal for persons of specified ages. Although Americans show no interest in returning to the days of Prohibition, many adults favor stricter regulation of smoking and drinking, including zero-tolerance policies concerning underage smoking and drinking, control of advertising and sales of tobacco products and alcoholic beverages, and higher taxes on alcohol and tobacco products to deter purchase, with the revenues raised going for prevention and treatment. States are passing tougher laws concerning drinking and driving, and municipalities are designating smoke-free facilities, curbing public drinking, and prohibiting home delivery of alcohol.

Some people advocate the legalization of currently illicit substances, claiming that we have lost the "war on drugs." Illicit drugs are widely available and affordable. International drug trade is big business, and a vast infrastructure exists for laundering drug money. In 1999, a congressional committee debated the legalization issue. Robert Stewart, a spokesman for the Drug Policy Foundation in Washington, D.C., suggested that legalization of marijuana should at least be considered. Joseph A. Califano, Jr., founder of the National Center on Addiction and Substance Abuse (CASA) at Columbia University, argued vehemently against the legalization of marijuana. He cited a recent CASA study that found that in 1996 more teens entered treatment for marijuana use than for any other substance, including alcohol. Califano reviewed the harmful effects of marijuana use on teens as well as its potential danger as a gateway drug (see Harris, 1999). Reliance on laws alone to confront drug problems, whether through control or legalization, however, externalizes responsibility and minimizes individual accountability.

The Disease Concept or Medical Model

Disease literally means lack of ease: a pathological condition of the body that presents a group of clinical signs and symptoms and laboratory findings peculiar to it. Disease may be acute, chronic, local, or systemic. *Illness* refers to the state of being sick; illness is highly individual and often associated with distress, pain, and suffering. Disease is a medical concept, whereas illness is a more holistic concept.

The idea that drunkenness is a disease was common among doctors in the 18th century. In 1790, Dr. Benjamin Rush described a disease syndrome caused by alcohol and characterized by individual moral and physical decay. According to Rush, the diseased condition of dependence could be cured by total abstinence from hard liquor. The American Association for the Study and Cure of Inebriates, organized in 1870, confirmed a commitment to the disease model and campaigned for institutional care based on the following beliefs:

1. Inebriety is a disease.

2. It is curable as other diseases are.

3. The constitutional tendency to this disease may be either inherited or acquired.

4. The disease is often induced by the habitual use of alcohol or other narcotic substances.

5. Hence, the establishing of hospitals for the special treatment of inebriety, in which such conditions are recognized, becomes a positive need of the age. (Edwards, 1997, p. 22)

The British Society for the Study and Cure of Inebriety, founded in 1884, recognized inebriety as a true disease. In his inaugural address to the society, Dr. Norman Kerr stated: "What is inebriety? We may define it as a diseased state of brain and nerve centers, characterized by an irresistible impulse to indulge in intoxicating liquors or other narcotics for the relief which they afford at any peril." According to Kerr:

■ Inebriety is a disease caused by an abnormality in brain function and characterized by craving.

■ The causes of this disease are multiple: genetic predisposition, adverse life events or fatigues, and "drinking long continued."

■ Total abstinence is the treatment goal.

■ Inebriety must be studied with the same scientific method as other forms of disease to "acquire a more exact acquaintance with the phenomena, causation and condition of inebriety" (Edwards, 1997, pp. 18-21).

By the 1890s, there were more than 30 inebriate treatment institutions in the United States.

Unfortunately, the disease concept gained little ground in late-19th- and early-20th-century America because of the influence of the temperance movement and Prohibition. In Britain, too, stringent licensing controls, together with prevailing social attitudes and conditions, brought alcohol consumption to an all-time low, and support for the disease concept waned.

In the 1940s, and especially after World War II, the disease concept of alcoholism reemerged as a dominant explanation of etiology and guide for treatment. The disease concept was championed by Alcoholics Anonymous, the Yale Center on Alcohol Studies, the National Council on Alcoholism, and Jellinek's prestigious 1960 publication *The Disease Concept of Alcoholism.* Subsequently, the American Medical Association, American Psychiatric Association, American Public Health Association, World Health Association, National Institute on Alcohol Abuse and Alcoholism, and National Institute on Drug Abuse recognized alcoholism and other drug addictions as diseases.

Reimbursement by insurers for addiction treatment exists in large part today because substance-related disorders and other addictive disorders meet medical criteria to be considered diseases. In 1997, the city of Baltimore began to treat addiction more as a medical problem than a criminal problem, pouring money into treatment and prevention rather than enforcement and incarceration. Officials increased funding for programs and treatment facilities—approaching, although not achieving, treatment on demand—as well as a publicly funded needle exchange program, job training, housing aid, a "drug court," and other social programs for recovering addicts.

Thomas Szasz (1961) has criticized the disease model of addiction, as well as disease models of other mental disorders, because a disease concept diminishes individual and social responsibility for the problem and its management. Norman Zinberg (1981) has acknowledged the benefits a disease model may have for treatment, but asserts that such a model offers an oversimplified explanation of etiology that is counterproductive for prevention (see also the discussion in Milkman & Shaffer, 1985). According to James Prochaska, the disease model of addiction is predicated on the idea that something happened to the individual (see, e.g., Prochaska & DiClemente, 1983). This puts the person into a passive-reactive model that does not help to prevent or solve the problem and in part may explain why so many treatment programs have high failure rates. Prochaska argues for a biobehavioral model in which therapists explore with clients why they like to drink and then set up a process of gradual change that requires clients to take responsibility for their behavior.

The Pharmacological Model

In 1785, Dr. Benjamin Rush published the influential tract *An Inquiry Into the Effects of Ardent Spirits Upon the Human Body and Mind.* Rush helped to overthrow beliefs that alcoholic spirits are good for health and stamina. His theory of addiction had great appeal to Americans, who were ready to reject the puritanical view of drunkenness as deliberate, informed self-abuse, an expression of a sinful nature. According to Rush, an alcoholic is a person compelled and controlled, a victim of a substance extraneous to him- or herself.

By the 1800s, many Americans believed alcohol to be a serious threat to the social order, a menace as great as the gin epidemic in London between 1720 and 1750. In addition to the widespread use of alcohol, increasing numbers of people were using and becoming addicted to drugs. Doctors universally prescribed opium to relieve pain; it was cheap and easily obtainable and regarded with little more suspicion than brandy. Laudanum (tincture of opium) was the faithful companion of many women. In 1821, Thomas De Quincey published *Confessions of an English Opium Eater,* in which he vividly charted the course of his dependence on opium and the pleasure and pain that made up an addict's life. By the middle of the 19th century, however, the effects of opium and its addictive properties were recognized. Concern about addiction to morphine surfaced in the United States following the Civil War (1861-1865). The Opium Wars between China and Great Britain (1839-1842 and 1856-1860) were fought because China opposed British importation of opium. China lost those conflicts. Not only had China become a nation of opium users, but Britain forced China to expand trade opportunities and to cede Hong Kong to Britain.

There was growing belief among Americans that the government must protect U.S. citizens from the consuming ravages of distilled spirits and drugs by adopting a public health approach to control the epidemic of addiction. These propositions became the central constructs of the temperance movement that began in the early 1800s, burgeoned 20 years later, and gained nationwide momentum between 1875 and the early 1900s, culminating with the passage of the 18th Amendment, which prohibited the manufacture, sale, and transportation of intoxicating liquors within the United States. As mentioned earlier, the political ascendancy of the temperance movement in large part led to the short-lived popularity of the disease concept of alcoholism and addiction in the late 19th and early 20th centuries.

As noted above, the United States has passed many laws to regulate the use and sale of alcohol and drugs, beginning with the Harrison Narcotic Act in 1914. Of special relevance to the pharmacological model of addiction is the Comprehensive Drug Abuse Prevention and Control Act of 1970, also known as the Controlled Substances Act. This act established a classification system to categorize drugs according to their abuse potential. Classes, or schedules, are determined by the Drug Enforcement Agency, an arm of the U.S. Justice Department, and

TABLE 2.1 Schedule of Controlled Substances

Schedule I	potential for abuse very high; all non-research use forbidden; heroin, cocaine, LSD, MDA, marijuana
Schedule II	high potential for abuse: extreme liability for physical and psychological dependence: opioid analgesics (morphine, codeine, oxycodone), certain barbiturates, amphetamines.
Schedule III	intermediate potential for abuse; intermediate liability for physical and psychologicial dependence: limited dosages of certain opioid analgesics, certain non-barbiturate sedatives, certain non-amphetamine central nervous system stimulants, anabolic steriods.
Schedule IV	less abuse potential with minimal liability for physical and psychological dependence: certain sedative/hypnotics, certain anti-anxiety agents, benzodiazepines.
Schedule V	minimal abuse potential: cough suppressants with small amounts of codeine, antidiarrheals containing paregoric.

are based on individual drugs' potential for abuse and liability for physical and/ or psychological dependence. Prescription and dispensing restrictions are specified (see Table 2.1). Drugs may be added or deleted from the schedules or moved from class to class. For example, after years of reports that people were becoming addicted, and after at least 41 reported deaths, the widely prescribed migraine drug butophanol (Stadol) was classified as a Schedule IV agent in 1997.

Of note is a 1997 Massachusetts law that requires tobacco manufacturers to identify the additives in each brand of cigarettes or smokeless tobacco and to reveal how much nicotine these products yield. Public health advocates believe that such required disclosure will prompt the tobacco industry to modify its products, much as nutritional labeling requirements have motivated food manufacturers to offer lower-sodium and lower-cholesterol alternatives. Some health officials advocate the classification of nicotine as a controlled substance.

In 1998, five states and the District of Columbia voted to make marijuana legal for certain medical uses, including chronic pain; more states are expected to follow. Yet in 1999, while a congressional committee discussed the possible decriminalization of certain illegal drugs, the National Center on Addiction and Substance Abuse at Columbia University released a study arguing that the decriminalization of marijuana could threaten millions of American children. The study found that more teens enter treatment for abuse of marijuana than for any other drug, including alcohol.

Today, the use of various licit and illicit drugs can lead to abuse and dependence. Warnings about the potential for abuse appear on the bottles or package inserts of many prescription drugs. The warnings imply that these drugs, owing to their pharmacological properties, are habit-forming. The threshold theory holds that if people ingest enough of a habit-forming drug, they can become addicted. Abuse and dependence are attributed primarily to the drug, and to a much lesser degree to the individual or environment. The pharmacological model of substance abuse is current. It contributes to our understanding of the development of abuse and dependence; knowledge of particular drugs is useful in prevention programs.

Contemporary Theories

Biological Theories

Recent research has demonstrated neurobiological, neurobehavioral, and genetic bases for addictive disorders. *Neurobiological theory* focuses on neuro-adaptive processes and the role they play in the etiology of substance use disorders. Genetic predisposition plays a large role in this theory. *Neurobehavioral theory* attributes alcohol and other drug use disorders to a link between certain behavioral disturbances and neural system dysfunction, interpreted within a neuropsychological framework. Genetic predisposition also plays a large role in neurobehavioral theory.

Genetic theory emphasizes the role of heredity in the development of addictive disorders. The apparent vulnerability of some people to addictions has prompted researchers to search for factors that may contribute to heightened susceptibility. Genograms often reveal the history of alcoholism in families. Among certain ethnic groups, genetic factors are theorized to increase individuals' likelihood of becoming alcohol dependent. Individuals within other ethnic groups appear to have protective genetic factors that make it doubtful they will ever abuse alcohol. Molecular biology techniques have isolated and identified genes that may confer vulnerability for alcohol dependence and other addictive processes. It is possible that the enzymes monoamine oxidase and adenylate cyclase are biochemical markers to predisposition to alcoholism. Genetic factors alone, however, do not account for the development of alcohol abuse. A host of environmental factors shape individuals' thinking about alcohol and affect use, including family dynamics, peer influences, everyday stress, and cultural values. Drinking, let alone drinking to states of abuse or dependence, represents a complex interplay between genetic and environmental factors.

Alcohol and other drugs produce brain changes. As the research examined in the 1998 public television series *Moyers on Addiction: Close to Home* emphasizes, addiction is a chronic and relapsing brain disease. A sight or a smell can trigger brain circuits altered by drug abuse and spur a relapse. Yale School of Medicine scientists have found that the protein delta-fosB stimulates mice brain genes that intensify the craving for cocaine. If a similar process occurs in humans, this could help explain why cocaine addiction is so difficult to arrest. Brain changes have also been identified in individuals with pathological gambling, compulsive shopping, sex addiction, and eating disorders. Some of these changes compromise the individual's decision-making ability, including the capacity to make rational choices about substance use and its consequences. Addicts experience dysphoria and craving; craving is relieved with another drink, drug, or behavior.

Brain reward helps explain why a drug or addictive behavior is self-administered. The effects are pleasant: The individual experiences a feeling of well-being or reduced anxiety. Researchers have identified a D_2 dopamine receptor for alcoholism in mice. Alcohol and other drug use and addictive behaviors such as gambling, shopping, sex, or eating increase pleasure and/or reduce pain. Heroin addicts often report they use "just to feel normal." Neuroscience theory helps clinicians and clients understand that the intense drug seeking, profound denial, and extreme manipulation that characterize addictive behavior may in part be caused by drug-induced brain changes. Biological research is trying to discover the precise neurotransmitters and processes associated with specific substance use. Related research seeks to develop medications to treat withdrawal, reduce craving, and prevent relapse.

Psychological Theories

For many years, psychologists considered alcoholism and other drug problems as symptoms of mental illness, not as diseases or disorders in themselves. Today, both the American Psychiatric Association and the American Psychological Association recognize addiction as a disease. Many psychological theories extend our understanding of addiction and expand treatment skills.

Conditioning theory addresses the relevance and implications of classical conditioning with respect to preferences for and aversion to alcohol, other drugs, and addictive behaviors. Conditioning theory helps clinicians and clients to understand tolerance, craving, and withdrawal. *Operant conditioning* underscores the significant role reinforcement plays in the development and maintenance of addiction. Substance abuse and dependence, as well as other addictive behaviors, are primarily learned behaviors.

Psychodynamic theory helps explain addiction. First, addiction develops when individuals use alcohol, drugs, or behaviors to experience pleasure or escape pain. Second, conflicts among the id, ego, and superego can lead to use and abuse of substances to relieve anxiety. Third, self-care and self-preservation are ego tasks; self-care disturbances and self-destruction characterize addiction and signal an impaired ego. The ego also regulates feelings. According to psychodynamic theory, deficiencies in self-care, self-esteem, and sense of well-being, together with the incapability to control affect, contribute to the dependency that addicts experience and exhibit. Other psychodynamic manifestations of addictive disorders include impulsivity, self-centeredness, self-destructiveness, irresponsibility, poor judgment, regression, irritability, and labile mood. Denial helps clinicians understand how clients can persist in such self-defeating behaviors. Clients also employ other defense mechanisms, especially rationalization, projection, and minimization, to reject diagnoses of addictive disorders and resist treatment. In addition, infantile narcissism (self-pathology) typifies addiction. What Alcoholics Anonymous calls "character defects," psychodynamic theory views as infantile narcissism. A.A. suggests replacing the "big ego" with a more humble self. Even the "Twelve Traditions" of A.A. emphasize avoiding the egocentric pitfalls of individual leaders. Psychodynamic clinicians recognize that psychopathology can precede the development of addiction or predispose the individual to addiction. They were some of the first mental health professionals to treat clients with dual disorders. Psychopathology can coexist with or follow addiction.

Trait theory suggests that there are certain personality traits that predispose individuals to addiction. There is no evidence of a preaddiction personality structure per se; experimental studies have been unable to distinguish the personality traits of addicts from those of the general population. The phrase *addictive personality* is often used to describe an individual who is immature, dependent, impulsive, and easily frustrated. A recently published report describes a Canadian study that followed 1,034 boys beginning in kindergarten and continuing for more than a decade to assess personality traits and report on use of cigarettes, alcohol, and drugs. *High novelty seeking* and *low harm avoidance* significantly predicted the onset of cigarette smoking, getting drunk, and using drugs. High novelty seeking described children who could not keep still and often acted without thinking; these children demonstrated hyperactivity and impulsivity. Low harm avoidance described children who showed little caution and were anxious to experiment. The authors of the report urge parents and teachers to pay special attention to children with these two predictive traits, as the research indicates that early intervention is promising. Other researchers have acknowledged the renewed interest in personality traits as predictors of substance use. Use, however, does not always lead to abuse and dependence (Tye, 1997).

Cognitive-behavioral factors such as self-awareness, expectancy, and attribution help clinicians and clients to understand addiction. *Self-awareness theory* examines the effects of psychoactive substances on self-awareness, especially cognitive processes. Contrary to popular belief among many teens, smoking marijuana actually impairs short-term memory, decreases attention span, and alters cognition, motivation, sensory perception, and sense of time. *Expectancy theory* describes the anticipation of a relationship between substance use and personal behavior and social functioning. Expectancy theory helps explain initial use (especially by teens), continued use, and relapse. *Attribution theory* is concerned with the way in which individuals interpret the causes of their own addictive behavior. The individual looks to a variety of internal and external sources of information. Attribution may be positive (e.g., accepting responsibility for one's addiction) or negative (e.g., blaming other people, places, and things).

Stress-management theory recognizes the need for people to reduce the tension and anxiety that is often associated with stress. People with addictive disorders report high stress levels and may, in fact, be more vulnerable to stress than other individuals. Alcohol and other drugs (or gambling, shopping, eating, or sex) reduce tension and stress for many people. Individuals can address the sources of their stress—the difficult job, the dysfunctional marriage, a delinquent child—but it is usually quite difficult and time-consuming to do so. Most people with stress-related tension and anxiety want more immediate relief. Many self-medicate to relieve tension and manage stress. Even relaxation exercises, meditation, and other nonpharmacological techniques take longer to provide relief than a drug. In the United States, the pharmaceutical industry aggressively markets products that promise quick relief for tension-related problems. Fortunately, clinicians and clients are beginning to use more nonpharmacological therapies to prevent and manage stress.

Social learning theory is a self-efficacy paradigm that posits personal factors, environment, and behavior as interlocking determinants of one another. The principles of learning, cognition, and reinforcement are important. Substance use and other addictive behaviors are socially learned, purposeful behaviors resulting from an interplay between socioenvironmental factors and personal perceptions. What is the individual's social learning history? What is his or her cognitive set, such as expectations or beliefs about the effects of use or behavior? What are the physical and social settings in which use or behavior occurs?

Sociocultural Theories

What is the role of the family, environment, culture, and other socioeconomic factors in the development and expression of addiction? *Family theory* challenges the premise that addiction is an individual problem or disease. Family theory examines how the family contributes to the addiction, how the problem affects each family member, and the impact of the addiction on the family as a whole. Addiction is one way a family attempts to adapt to life's needs and challenges. Addiction is a coping mechanism. Enabling behavior on the part of the family sustains the addiction. Over time, family "rituals" and "rules" develop that determine behavior and define roles for all family members vis-à-vis the addiction. Ineffective communication and limited expression of feelings characterize families with addiction. Parental interactions and expectations are inconsistent, and vicarious behavior by children is common. Negativity, denial, and anger are high, and self-medication is common.

Codependence develops. As addiction progresses, codependence becomes rampant. Family responses become more out of control, and the need to control increases. Stress and dysfunction within the family escalate. For example, Helen M., the wife of an alcoholic, believes that everything inside her and around her is out of control, so she takes charge and tries to control her husband and his drinking behavior. This enabling often alternates between rescue and blame. Helen calls in sick for her drunk husband and then lashes out at him for "being a drunken bum." Codependence perpetuates addiction and family dysfunction. In early recovery it contributes to relapse. Children in family systems with addiction may be forced into dysfunctional family roles of hero, scapegoat, lost child, or mascot. There is an extensive body of literature on family theory and treatment of addiction,

Systems theory posits systems and their environments. Organization, interaction, interdependency, and integration of parts and elements characterize systems theory. According to von Bertalanffy (1968), all living organisms are open systems. An open system maintains a continuous input and output of energy with its environment. The open system becomes more differentiated, complex, and ordered. A closed system is isolated from its environment and moves toward increasing disorder. Systems theory views people as primarily social beings rather than as biological or psychological entities. The interaction between individual and environment is critical. For example, detoxification of a homeless addict is poor treatment if the client is discharged back to the street.

If systems theory is applied to the "addicted family," it becomes clear that substance abuse or other addictive behavior serves some purpose, albeit a dysfunctional or pathological one, within the family system. Addiction signals family dysfunction. The family is a system, and as such it plays a critical role in the onset, development, and treatment of addiction. Individuals within the family represent interactive, component subsystems of the whole. How does the client's addiction affect the family? How does the family contribute to the client's addiction? How can the family aid in treatment and recovery? What treatment does the family need? Removing the addiction, however, creates a major void in the family system. Systems theory holds that if this functional void is not filled, risk for relapse is high and family dysfunction heightens. Recovery requires new roles and responsibilities for all family members.

Anthropological theory emphasizes the values, attitudes, beliefs, and norms that a population holds with respect to substance use and other addictive behaviors. Primitive societies know and use many kinds of drugs, yet addiction is rare. Cross-cultural research suggests that the primary function of alcohol in all societies is tension reduction, which is often related to social instability, dysfunction, or change.

Gateway theory suggests that the use of certain drugs, whether licit or illicit, opens the way to more serious drug use. Many studies, particularly among adolescents, have found that the use of tobacco, and then alcohol, tends to precede the use of and dependence on other drugs. The order of progression is from tobacco to alcohol, then marijuana, then other pills, and finally "hard drugs."

Availability theory maintains that the greater the access to substances (or gambling, shopping, or sex), the greater the prevalence and severity of addiction. Despite the prevailing belief that the 18th Amendment was a mistake and a national joke, Prohibition did reduce the overall rate of alcohol consumption in the group most vulnerable to the devastating effects of drinking: the working class. Data from that period show declines in the incidence of tuberculosis, admissions to state mental hospitals for alcoholic psychosis, and death rates from cirrhosis. Arrests for drunkenness and disorderly conduct decreased. Welfare agencies reported dramatic reductions in alcohol-related family problems. Today, taxes help to reduce the total consumption of alcohol and tobacco products. Massachusetts, for example, credits a drop in adult smoking in part to an increase in the tax on cigarettes of 25 cents per pack 1992 and another 25 cent increase in 1996. Raising the age at which it is legal for individuals to buy tobacco products or alcohol, or to gamble, has helped to control use and behavior. The law setting 21 as the minimum age for drinking has reduced teenage alcohol consumption and saved thousands of lives.

Economic theories of addiction are concerned with the social costs of excessive addiction and the economic dimensions of government policies aimed at changing consumption habits. Economic theorists study the factors that influence substance consumption/addictive behavior and how addiction-related problems are linked to consumption levels. Modeling of consumption and linking consumption with abuse, dependence, and addiction are two key elements of economic models.

Transcendental/Spiritual Theories

Spirituality is an important aspect of a person's well-being. *DSM-IV* recognizes that a "religious or spiritual problem" can be the focus of clinical attention (American Psychiatric Association, 1994, V62.89). Jung (1933) views the spiritual dimension as the essence of human nature. According to Frankl (1963), a religious sense is deeply rooted in each and every person's unconscious depths. Rogers (1980) emphasizes the importance of the spiritual dimension and sees individual consciousness as a figment of cosmic consciousness. Maslow (1964) considers human beings to be capable of transcending the limitations of personal identity and achieving a deeper sense of eternity and of the sacred. Transpersonal psychology, sometimes called the fourth force in Western psychology, reaches beyond dynamic, behavioral, and humanistic theories and seeks to incorporate higher states of consciousness and spiritual connection.

The psychiatrist Gerald May writes convincingly in his book *Addiction and Grace* (1991) that all human beings have an inborn desire for God. Whether we are religious or not, this desire is our deepest longing. We long for wholeness, completion, or fulfillment. We hunger to love, to be loved, and to move closer to the source of love. This longing gives meaning to our lives. This yearning is the essence of the human spirit; it is the origin of our highest hopes and most noble dreams. But according to May, something gets in the way. Modern experience creates a sense of aloneness, alienation, and pain for many people. Addiction offers temporary relief; it can transport people out of their aloneness and pain into a world of the extraordinary. Psychoactive substances and addictive behaviors can help people transcend reality. According to Oliveira (1995), individuals experience a sense of incompleteness or void that they attempt to fill. Through addiction, individuals replace what is missing in their lives; psychoactive substances or addictive behaviors fill this void. The addictive process is the result of an unconscious desire to become whole.

People may search for a sense of belonging or an unfettered expansiveness. Craving is a nonspecific hunger for something that is missing in people's lives; this hunger originates at the very core of being. Craving represents a need for completion, a desire for inner truth and comfort. Jung (1933) describes the craving for alcohol as equivalent to the spiritual thirst of our being for wholeness. According to Grof (1993), craving is the universal thirst to become whole. People also crave release from pain, a desire for joy, a "rush" or "high."

Spirituality has been a critical component of 12-step recovery programs for decades. Increasingly, medicine and psychology are recognizing the healing power of the mind-body and body-soul connections. In 1997, the New York Open Center presented "Psyche, Spirit, and Addiction," an international conference devoted to the exploration of the cultural, psychological, and spiritual roots of substance abuse and its treatment.

Comprehensive Models

Biopsychosocial Model

Rather than viewing addiction from a single perspective, many addiction practitioners employ a biopsychosocial model to understand the etiology, expression, treatment, and prevention of addiction. They see addiction as a synthesis of biological, psychological, and sociocultural variables. A biopsychosocial perspective includes and integrates aspects of current biological, psychological, and sociocultural theories. A biopsychosocial model is consonant with a holistic view of the client.

Sederer (1985) identifies several limitations inherent in the biopsychosocial model. First, the model does not provide a method for making a hierarchy of causation. Furthermore, expression of the addiction and its meaning may cloud the search for causation. Finally, it is difficult to stage treatment using a biopsychosocial model. Despite Sederer's criticisms, the biopsychosocial model is widely used. Assessment, diagnosis, treatment planning, intervention, evaluation, and related documentation address biopsychosocial variables. Accreditation standards and criteria reflect the biopsychosocial model. Specific tools such as *DSM-IV* and *ASAM PPC-2* (American Society of Addiction Medicine, 1996) incorporate the biopsychosocial model.

Public Health Agent-Host-Environment Model

Thus far, we have observed that many factors contribute to the development of addiction: individual vulnerability, drug properties, and environmental factors. The public health agent-host-environment model is a comprehensive model of health and illness that originated in community health work in the 1960s. The model has been expanded to describe the causes of diseases and disorders in many health areas. According to this model, the level of health or disorder depends on the dynamic interaction among three elements: agent, host, and environment.

The *agent* is any internal or external factor that by its presence or absence can lead to a disease or disorder. For example, the virus varicella-zoster must be present for a child to contract varicella (chicken pox). A diet deficient in lean meat or liver, whole-grain enriched breads and cereals, and green leafy vegetables contributes to iron-deficiency anemia, fatigue, weakness, lethargy, and lowered immunity. In the case of addiction, an agent can be a substance such as alcohol or some other drug or a behavior such as gambling, shopping, eating, or sex. The agent must be present for an addiction to develop ("If you don't drink, you can't get drunk"). Yet the presence of the substance or behavior (agent) alone does not lead directly to addiction.

The *host* is the individual who may be susceptible to a particular disease or disorder, in this case addiction. Host factors are biopsychosocial factors that put an individual or group at risk for the disorder. Host factors that increase susceptibility for addiction include a family history of substance abuse, past sexual abuse, and a self-destructive lifestyle. *Resilience* describes protective factors of the host that increase the likelihood the individual can resist use, abuse, or addiction. Certain genetic factors, a functional family, personal competence, and healthy coping mechanisms increase the likelihood the host can resist use, abuse, or addiction.

The *environment* consists of all physical and social conditions external to the host: climate, housing, the family, school, neighborhood, transportation, workplace, and so on. Major environmental stressors include inadequate health services, poverty, homelessness, unemployment, incarceration, exposure to war and other hostilities, and exposure to natural or other disasters.

The agent-host-environment model emphasizes the dynamic interactions among these three variables as determinants of health or illness. The public health model supports a theory of multiple causation; the model helps practitioners explain complex phenomena such as heart disease, cancer, homelessness, and addiction. Addiction practitioners engaged in prevention, treatment, research, and public policy find the public health-agent-host-environment model very useful. The model is congruent with diagnostic tools such as *DSM-IV* and *ASAM PPC-2*.

Summary

Addiction practitioners use theories and models of addiction to ground and guide their practice. Theories and models represent relationships between concepts and propositions. Models are broad and general, whereas theories tend to be more formal and specific. Theories and models help practitioners describe, explain, predict, and control phenomena. Conventional models of addiction include the moral model, the legal model, the disease concept or medical model, and the pharmacological model. Contemporary theories of addiction encompass biological, psychological, sociocultural, and transcendental/spiritual theories. Comprehensive models of addiction include the biopsychosocial model and the public health agent-host-environment model. Addiction practitioners examine the origins, characteristics, adequacy, and relevance of various theories and models of addiction. They identify the assumptions, knowledge bases, and skills associated with different theories and models and then choose and use particular theories or models to guide their practice.

Related Skills Checklist

Practitioner skills related to theories and models of addiction include the ability to do the following:

- Examine personal attitudes and beliefs about addiction.
- Identify the origins, assumptions, characteristics, knowledge bases, and skills associated with different addiction theories and models.
- Evaluate the adequacy and relevance of various theories and models of addiction.

- Review agency mission, philosophy, and program goals.

- Choose and use a dominant addiction theory or model to ground and guide practice.

Special Topics for Further Study

What theories and models of addiction help to explain the "many faces of addiction" noted in Chapter 1? Explain how you can use the same theory or model to explain binge drinking by college students and chronic alcohol abuse by many homeless people.

Addiction Practice 2000

Addiction practice 2000 requires a scientific knowledge base. When will science inform policy? When will theory and research guide practice? Enlightened policy, sound theory, and action research ground responsive and responsible practice. In turn, practice stimulates theory construction, supports action research, and prompts policy development. Addiction practitioners must develop and test theories and models of addiction. Biological research and theory development will further understanding of genetic, pharmacological, neurobiological, and neurobehavioral factors that determine addiction. Researchers continue to examine craving. Biopsychosocial research will help clinicians learn more about client variables. What is the role of spirituality in the development and treatment of addiction? Social scientists are exploring the contexts or environments in which addiction develops and in which recovery occurs: the family, school, workplace, community, and society itself. How do we confront the moral barriers and legal sanctions that block acceptance of addiction and addiction treatment?

References

American Psychiatric Association. (1994). *Diagnostic and statistical manual of mental disorders* (4th ed.). Washington, DC: Author.

American Society of Addiction Medicine. (1996). *Patient placement criteria for the treatment of substance-related disorders* (2nd ed.). Chevy Chase, MD: Author.

De Quincey, T. (1966). *Confessions of an English opium eater.* New York: Signet. (Original work published 1821)

Edwards, G. (1997). Lunch with Dr. Kerr: Nathan B. Eddy Award lecture. In National Institute on Drug Abuse (Ed.), *Problems of drug dependence, 1996: Proceedings of the*

58th Annual Scientific Meeting of the College on Problems of Drug Dependence, Inc. (NIH Publication No. 97-4236) (pp. 17-27). Rockville, MD: National Institute on Drug Abuse. (NTIS No. PB 97-160295)

Frankl, V. (1963). *Man's search for meaning.* New York: Simon & Schuster.

Grof, C. (1993). *The thirst for wholeness.* San Francisco: Harper.

Harris, K. (1999, July 14). Study urges against legalizing marijuana. *Boston Globe,* p. 10.

Jellinek, E. M. (1960). *The disease concept of alcoholism.* New Haven, CT: College & University Press.

Jung, C. (1933). *Modern man in search of a soul.* New York: Harcourt Brace.

Maslow, A. (1964). *Religions, values, and peak experiences.* New York: Viking.

May, G. G. (1991). *Addiction and grace: Love and spirituality in the healing of addictions.* San Francisco: Harper.

Milkman, H. B., & Shaffer, H. J. (Eds.). (1985). *The addictions: Multidisciplinary perspectives and treatments.* Lexington, MA: D. C. Heath.

Oliveira, M. D. (1995). *Is the addictive process an unconscious desire to become whole?* Unpublished master's thesis, Cambridge College.

President's Commission on Model State Drug Laws. (1993). *Report of the President's Commission on Model State Drug Laws: Executive summary.* Washington, DC: Government Printing Office.

Prochaska, J. O., & DiClemente, C. C. (1983). Transtheoretical therapy: Toward a more integrative model of change. *Psychotherapy: Theory, Research, and Practice, 20,* 161-173.

Rogers, C. (1980). *A way of being.* Boston: Houghton Mifflin.

Sederer, L. I. (1985). Diagnosis, conceptual models, and the nature of this book. In H. B. Milkman & H. J. Shaffer (Eds.), *The addictions: Multidisciplinary perspectives and treatments* (pp. 185-195). Lexington, MA: D. C. Heath.

Szasz, T. S. (1961). *The myth of mental illness.* New York: Harper & Row.

Tye, L. (1997, February 4). Addictive personalities formed early, a study finds. *Boston Globe,* p. 1.

von Bertalanffy, L. (1968). *General system theory.* New York: George Braziller.

Zinberg, N. E. (1981). Alcohol addiction: Toward a more comprehensive definition. In M. H. Bean & N. E. Zinberg (Eds.), *Dynamic approaches to the understanding and treatment of alcoholism* (pp. 97-127). New York: Free Press.

Other Sources

Baskys, A., & Remington, G. (1996). *Brain mechanisms and psychotropic drugs.* Boca Raton, FL: CRC.

Bean, M. H., & Zinberg, N. E. (Eds.). (1981). *Dynamic approaches to the understanding and treatment of alcoholism.* New York: Free Press.

Blaine, J. J., & Demetrios, A. J. (1993). *Psychodynamics of drug dependence.* Northvale, NJ: Jason Aronson.

Bonner, A., & Waterhouse, J. M. (1996). *Addictive behaviour: Molecules to mankind: Perspectives on the nature of addiction.* New York: St. Martin's.

Brick, J., & Erickson, C. K. (1998). *Drugs, the brain, and behavior: The pharmacology of abuse and dependence.* New York: Haworth Medical Press.

Fawcett, J. (1990). *Analysis and evaluation of conceptual models of nursing* (2nd ed.). Philadelphia: F. A. Davis.

Freeman, E. M. (1993). *Substance abuse treatment: A family systems perspective.* Newbury Park, CA: Sage.

Gomberg, E. L., White, H. R., & Carpenter, J. A. (Eds.). (1984). *Alcohol, science, and society revisited.* Ann Arbor: University of Michigan Press/Rutgers Center of Alcohol Studies.

Gottheil, D., Druley, K. A., Skolodo, T. E., & Waxman, H. M. (Eds.). (1993). *Etiologic aspects of alcohol and drug abuse.* Springfield, IL: Charles C Thomas.

Green, J. (Ed.). (1997). *Faith communities* (NCADI Publication No. 98-05043). Rockville, MD: Center for Substance Abuse Prevention.

Karch, S. B. (1998). *A brief history of cocaine.* Boca Raton, FL: CRC.

Knapp, C. (1997). *Drinking: A love story.* New York: Delta.

Kus, R. J. (1995). *Spirituality and chemical dependency.* New York: Haworth.

Leonard, K. E., & Blane, H. W. (1999). *Psychological theories of drinking and alcoholism* (2nd ed.). New York: Guilford.

Leshner, A. I. (1998, October). Addiction is a brain disease—and it matters. *National Institute of Justice Journal,* pp. 2-6.

Marlatt, G. A., & VandenBos, G. R. (Eds.). (1997). *Addictive behaviors: Readings on etiology, prevention, and treatment.* Washington, DC: American Psychological Association.

Mollenkamp, C., Levy, A., Menn, J., & Rothfeder, J. (1998). *The people vs. big tobacco: How the states took on the cigarette giants.* Princeton, NJ: Bloomberg.

Moore, M. H., & Gerstein, D. R. (1981). *Alcohol and public policy: Beyond the shadow of prohibition.* Washington, DC: National Academy Press.

Nakken, C. (1996). *The addictive personality: Understanding the addictive process and compulsive behaviors* (2nd ed.). Center City, MN: Hazelden.

Nash, J. M. (1997, May 5). Addicted. *Time,* pp. 68-73, 76.

Pegram, T. R. (1998). *Battling demon rum: The struggle for a dry America, 1800-1933.* Chicago: Ivan R. Dee.

Pringle, P. (1998). *Cornered: Big tobacco at the bar of justice.* New York: Holt.

Tighe, L. C. (1997, Winter). The six stages of change to a healthier you. *Your Health,* pp. 6-9.

Vaillant, G. E. (1995). *The natural history of alcoholism revisited.* Cambridge, MA: Harvard University Press.

3

Substance Abuse

Objectives

- Grasp the concept of substance abuse.
- Understand the pharmaceutics, pharmacokinetics, and pharmacodynamics of drug use.
- Identify the properties of drugs.
- Recognize patterns of substance use.
- Understand the desired effects of alcohol and other drugs.
- Recognize the signs and symptoms of substance abuse, especially intoxication and withdrawal.
- Comprehend the adverse effects of alcohol and drug abuse. (Note: The chapters in Part V discuss the medical, psychological, and social effects of addiction in greater detail.)

Outline

- **Substance Abuse**
- **Pharmacology**
- **Central Nervous System Depressants**
  - Alcohol
  - Sedative, Hypnotic, and Anxiolytic Drugs
    - Barbiturates
    - Benzodiazepines
    - Rohypnol
    - Ketamine
- **Central Nervous System Stimulants**
  - Cocaine

- Amphetamines
    Methamphetamine
- Nicotine
- Caffeine
■ **Opioids**
- Opioid Analgesics
- Heroin
■ **Hallucinogens**
- Lysergic Acid Diethylamide
- Phencyclidine Hydrochloride
- Peyote and Mescaline
■ **Marijuana**
■ **Inhalants**
■ **Anabolic Steroids**
■ **Designer Drugs**
- Fentanyl Analogs
- Meperidine Analogs
- Methamphetamine Analogs
- Other Designer Drugs
■ **Herbs**
■ **Summary**
■ **Related Skills Checklist**
■ **Special Topics for Further Study**
■ **Addiction Practice 2000**

Substance Abuse

Use of a substance is considered to be abuse when the substance is used in excess, when use of the substance is contraindicated, or when its use is illegal. For example, Alan M. drinks three six-packs of beer while watching a football game on TV; he falls down in his bathroom, lacerates his head, and requires 17 stitches. Three sixth-grade boys steal and sniff glue during recess and feel "different." Rose M. blames her boyfriend for turning her on to crack cocaine. Her boyfriend is long gone, and Rose now works the streets to support her daily habit.

Substances of abuse include prescription drugs, over-the-counter (OTC) drugs, and "social" drugs such as alcohol, nicotine, and caffeine; illicit drugs such as marijuana, cocaine, heroin, LSD, and Ecstasy; and compounds sold for other purposes but used for psychoactive effects, such as aerosol sprays, certain glues, and paint thinner. Drugs may be classified by their expected actions, as central nervous system depressants, central nervous system stimulants, analgesics, and hallucinogens. Other kinds of drugs of abuse include inhalants, anabolic steroids, "designer" drugs, and herbs.

Pharmacology

Addiction clinicians need to understand the properties, routes of use, and desired and adverse effects of particular drugs. *Pharmaceutics* is the science of making substances into forms suitable for entrance into the body: powders, tablets, capsules, lotions or ointments, liquids, and gases. For example, meperidine (Demerol), a Schedule II opioid analgesic, is available in tablet, syrup, and injectable forms. "Crack" is cocaine that has been processed from cocaine hydrochloride to a freebase form for smoking.

Pharmacokinetics is the process of absorption, distribution, metabolism, and excretion of drugs from the body. Absorption is a complex phenomenon. The local or systemic action of a drug depends on the site and method of administration plus the properties of the drug. Route of administration is the way in which the drug reaches the action sites in the body: by mouth or injection, via mucous membrane or skin. In the past, most heroin addicts injected heroin intravenously. In the 1990s, however, the purity of heroin and fear of AIDS prompted many heroin users to shift from injecting to smoking or sniffing the drug.

In addition to the administration routes and action sites of drugs, clinicians need to know whether particular drugs act locally (where they are ingested or applied) or whether they reach their destinations through systemic circulation. Does a given drug reach the bloodstream directly or does it first pass through the liver, where it is metabolized? Drugs taken by mouth are absorbed in the stomach and intestines and then pass into the liver for biotransformation or metabolism. Drugs that enter the bloodstream directly miss this first-pass effect. Thus, for example, oral doses for propranolol (Inderal) range from 40 to 160 mg; parenteral (intravenous) doses range from 1 to 2 mg.

Pharmacodynamics refers to the actions or effects of drugs that users experience. Some drugs have both local and systemic effects; this is particularly true when drugs are applied to mucous membranes. Effects depend upon the agent, the host, and the environment as well as the drug, the dose, and the route of ingestion. The user's general physical health and psychological state, especially feelings and expectations at time of use, together with the environment in which the drug is consumed, influence pharmacodynamics.

Central Nervous System Depressants

Alcohol suppresses, inhibits, or decreases central nervous system (CNS) activity, as do prescription sedative, hypnotic, and anxiolytic drugs. The potential for tolerance and dependence is high with these drugs: stupor, coma, and death can occur. Cross-tolerance between alcohol and other CNS depressant drugs is common. Opioids also depress the central nervous system, a subject that I address later in this chapter.

Alcohol

Ethanol (C_2H_5OH), the main psychoactive ingredient in alcoholic beverages, is produced during the fermentation of sugar by yeast. Cultural norms, religious sanctions, social mores, and availability are but a few of the factors that influence patterns of alcohol use by particular societies and their people. In the United States, per capita consumption of alcohol has declined since 1980. However, heavy drinking remains constant. Young people are beginning to drink at earlier ages, especially teenage girls.

Many myths and misinformation surround alcohol use. For example, one often hears remarks such as "I can't be an alcoholic; I only drink beer." The alcohol content in 12 ounces of beer is equivalent to that in 5 ounces of wine or 1.5 ounces of 80-proof distilled spirits. People drink to "feel good." Individuals who ingest alcohol report feeling relaxed, warm all over, less inhibited, and more sociable. However, for individuals, families, and society, the adverse effects of alcohol use are legion.

Signs and symptoms of excessive alcohol use include slurred speech, unsteady gait, and impaired motor coordination. An intoxicated person may fall; bruising is common. People who drive under the influence of alcohol may be arrested. Intoxication contributes to accidents at work and to many injuries and deaths during recreational activities. Persons who drink may experience states of euphoria, altered judgment, inability to concentrate, impaired attention, and memory loss (the alcoholic blackout). Some people demonstrate inappropriate sexual or aggressive behaviors when they drink.

Signs of simple alcohol withdrawal include sweating, nausea or vomiting, tremors, weakness, psychomotor agitation, anxiety, confusion, and insomnia, as well as transient hallucinations, delusions, and illusions. Delirium tremens (DTs) is a much more serious withdrawal state. Signs and symptoms of DTs include profuse sweating, fever, tachycardia, hypertension, agitation, restlessness, gross tremors, and grand mal seizures. This acute psychotic state is characterized by confusion, distractibility, disorientation, paranoid ideation, delusions, illusions, and visual or tactile hallucinations. Signs of simple alcohol withdrawal usually precede DTs.

Alcohol can cause profound respiratory and cardiovascular depression, stupor, coma, and death. Heavy, chronic alcohol consumption causes major medical, psychological, and social problems. Fetal alcohol syndrome, caused by alcohol consumption during pregnancy, is the leading cause of mental retardation in children.

Sedative, Hypnotic, and Anxiolytic Drugs

Sedative, hypnotic, and anxiolytic drugs are prescription drugs, usually taken orally, that depress the central nervous system, producing muscle relaxation and feelings of contentment. These drugs reduce tension, induce sleep, and alleviate anxiety. Sedatives have a calming effect, reduce activity, and thus reduce tension. Hypnotics induce or produce sleep. Anxiolytics reduce anxiety. Sedative and anxiolytic drugs produce sleep when the dose is increased.

The effects of these CNS depressants are similar to those of alcohol. Small amounts of the drug relax muscles and produce a calm feeling. With larger doses, users may exhibit slurred speech, staggering gait, and altered perception. Very large doses can cause respiratory depression, coma, and death. The combination of CNS depressant drugs and alcohol multiplies the effects of the drugs and increases risk. Babies born to mothers who abuse depressants may be physically dependent and show withdrawal symptoms. The use of CNS depressants during pregnancy may cause birth defects and subsequent behavior problems in the children.

Barbiturates

Barbiturates constitute one group of CNS depressants; these include such drugs as amobarbital (Amytal), amobarbital/secobarbital (Tuinal), pentobarbital (Nembutal), phenobarbital (Luminal), primidone (Sertan), secobarbital (Seconal), thiopental (Pentothal), and barbiturate-like methaqualone (Quaalude). Barbiturates are usually taken orally. Desired effects include sedation, feeling of escape, loss of inhibition, reduction of aggressive and sexual drives, and sleep. Barbiturates are used medically to control seizures, for anesthesia, and, less commonly, to reduce anxiety. Acute and chronic use induces effects similar to those of alcohol. Potential for tolerance and dependence is high. Barbiturates have a narrow therapeutic-to-toxic dosage ratio and are often lethal in overdose.

Signs and symptoms of barbiturate intoxication include rapid and weak pulse, decreased respirations or respiratory paralysis, cyanosis, slurred speech, poor coordination, unsteady gait, involuntary movement of the eyeballs, and abnormal dilation of pupils. Individuals may exhibit emotional instability, impaired judgment, decreased attention, or diminished memory; inappropriate sexual or aggressive behavior may occur. A barbiturate overdose can result in stupor, coma, and death.

People who suddenly stop taking large doses of barbiturates can experience such withdrawal symptoms as elevated pulse rate, sweating, weakness, tremors, headache, insomnia, nausea, vomiting, cramping, anorexia, anxiety, confusion, psychomotor agitation, disorientation, and hallucinations, as well as psychosis with delirium, seizures, and death.

Benzodiazepines

Benzodiazepines are minor tranquilizers that are relatively safe when used as prescribed. However, tolerance and dependence are common; ingestion of benzodiazepine drugs may be fatal when taken with alcohol, barbiturates, or narcotics. Tranquilizers have a quieting or dampening effect on the psychomotor processes without interfering with consciousness (except at high doses). Commonly used and abused benzodiazepines include alprazolam (Xanax), chlordiazepoxide (Librium), clonazepam (Klonopin), diazepam (Valium), lorazepam (Ativan), oxazepam (Serax), temazepam (Restoril), and triazolam (Halcion).

Busiprone (BuSpar) is often prescribed for addicts with severe anxiety because tolerance and dependence are rare with this drug. Nonbenzodiazepine sedative-hypnotic drugs include chloral hydrate (Noctect), ethchlorvynol (Placidyl), glutethimide (Doriden), hydroxyzine pamoate (Vistaril), meprobamate (Equanil, Miltown), propranolol (Inderal), and zolpidem (Ambien). Paraldehyde is a potent, nonbarbiturate sedative-hypnotic used to manage dangerously agitated clients. Many substance abuse clients use OTC drugs for sleep, such as doxylamine (Unisom) and diphenhydramine (Benadryl), a hypnotic and antihistamine.

Rohypnol

Rohypnol, sometimes called the "forget pill" or "forget me pill," is Hoffman-LaRoche's registered trade name for flunitrazepam, a benzodiazepine agonist legally available by prescription and used to treat severe sleep disorders. During the mid-1990s, however, Rohypnol (called Roofies on the street) became the date-rape drug of choice because of its disinhibiting effect, especially when combined with even a moderate amount of alcohol. Users experience relief from anxiety and tension, muscle relaxation, and a slowing of psychomotor performance, which is greatly increased with alcohol consumption. Sedation, sleep, and amnesia occur. Sedation can last for 8 hours, with psychomotor impairment lasting up to 12 hours after ingestion. Users of Rohypnol may develop physical and psychic dependence; risk of dependence increases with dose and duration of use and is greater in users with a history of alcohol or drug abuse. Once physical dependence occurs, withdrawal symptoms may include extreme anxiety, tension and restlessness, confusion, and irritability; headache, muscle pain, numbness and tingling of extremities; hypersensitivity to light, noise, and physical contact; disorientation, derealization, and depersonalization; and hallucinations and delirium. Convulsions, shock, and cardiovascular collapse can also occur.

Ketamine

Recently, adolescents and young adults have discovered ketamine hydrochloride (Ketalar), a synthetic nonbarbiturate used primarily as an animal tranquilizer. On the street, ketamine is called Special K, K, vitamin K, or Kit Kat. Users quickly feel dissociated and detached from their environment; disturbing dreams and hallucinations may occur when the drug wears off.

Central Nervous System Stimulants

CNS stimulants activate, enhance, or increase CNS activity. They include cocaine, amphetamines, nicotine, caffeine, and certain synthetic diet suppressants. Potential for tolerance and dependence is high.

Cocaine

Cocaine is a white crystalline powder extracted from the leaves of the coca plant. It is a powerful CNS stimulant. Users snort, inject, or smoke cocaine to experience feelings of well-being, excitement, wakefulness, and euphoria. Users report enjoying feelings of elation, grandiosity, and limitless power and energy. Cocaine is an appetite suppressant, and users may show evidence of weight loss. It is also a sexual stimulant for many people.

Freebasing is the process of extracting pure cocaine alkaloid and inhaling heated vapors through a cigarette or water pipe; freebasing increases cocaine's potency. Crack cocaine got its name from the crackling sound it makes when it is heated. The physical effects of crack are felt within 10 seconds and may last 10-15 minutes. In both powder and crack forms, cocaine is highly addictive. Users who snort, inject, or smoke cocaine develop dependence very quickly. Cocaine users often go on "runs" where they do not eat or sleep but just use repeatedly and then "crash." First-time users may experience seizures or heart attacks, which can be fatal.

Ingestion of cocaine elevates blood pressure, heart rate, respiratory rate, and body temperature; it also dilates the pupils. Serious physiological effects of cocaine use may be immediate, including respiratory failure, cardiovascular collapse, and death. Occasional use can cause a stuffy or runny nose; chronic use can ulcerate the mucous membranes of the nose. Sharing needles to inject cocaine increases users' risk of contracting hepatitis and HIV. Preparation of freebase involves the use of volatile solvents and can result in injury or death from fire or explosion. Chronic or heavy use of cocaine can lead to paranoia—users become highly nervous and suspicious.

Signs and symptoms of cocaine intoxication include respiratory depression, tachycardia or bradycardia, elevated or lowered blood pressure, cardiac arrhythmias, chest pain, perspiration or chills, nausea and vomiting, psychomotor agitation or retardation, muscular weakness, undesirable voluntary muscle contractions and movements, and seizures. Individuals may demonstrate restlessness, verbosity, inability to concentrate, and compulsive behaviors. Anxiety, tension, confusion, impaired judgment, disturbed concentration, and hypervigilance are common. Interpersonal hypersensitivity, anger with violent outbursts, and antisocial behavior are frequent. Paranoid thinking, hallucinations (especially "coke bugs"—a sensation of imaginary insects crawling over the skin), and psychosis can develop.

Withdrawal from cocaine is characterized by fatigue and increased appetite, psychomotor retardation or agitation, insomnia or hypersomnia, and vivid, unpleasant dreams. Cocaine users are at increased risk of suicide, burns, falls, car crashes, and drowning. Cocaine addicts often become unable to function sexually. They experience distress and demonstrate functional impairment related to neglect of their health, family and other relationships, and work. They lose interest in friends, family, sports, hobbies, and other activities. Chronic users develop myriad medical, psychological, and social problems. They may spend hundreds, even thousands, of dollars on powder cocaine or crack each week. They may sell drugs, prostitute themselves, or commit other crimes to support their habits. Cocaine use during pregnancy can damage the fetus and cause developmental delays and deficits in the infants and children of using mothers.

Amphetamines

Amphetamines, often called uppers, are sympathomimetic drugs that stimulate or excite the central nervous system. Drugs in this class include amphetamine, dextroamphetamine, and methamphetamine. The amphetamines vary in their degrees of potency and effects. Amphetamines are taken orally, snorted, smoked, or injected. Potential for abuse, tolerance, and dependence is high.

Amphetamines increase heart and respiratory rates, elevate blood pressure, and decrease appetite. Users may experience sweating, headache, dizziness, blurred vision and dilated pupils, and insomnia. Users report feeling restless, anxious, and moody; they may demonstrate irritability, impulsiveness, confusion, hostility, and aggressiveness. Extremely high doses can cause rapid or irregular heart rate, increased blood pressure, hyperreflexivity tremors, loss of coordination, convulsions, and even physical collapse.

Amphetamine intoxication is similar to cocaine intoxication and is characterized by chest pain, respiratory depression, tachycardia or bradycardia, elevated or lowered blood pressure, and cardiac arrhythmias. Clients may perspire profusely; chills, nausea, and vomiting are common. Psychomotor agitation or retardation, together with muscular weakness and undesirable voluntary muscle contractions and movements may also result. Individuals may demonstrate euphoria; anxiety, tension, and hypervigilance are heightened; affect is distorted. Impaired judgment, confusion, and interpersonal hypersensitivity may follow. Amphetamine use can cause seizures and coma. Chronic amphetamine users often experience negative consequences stemming from neglect of their health, family and other relationships, and work.

Withdrawal from amphetamines is characterized by fatigue, muscle pain, lethargy, depression, and increased appetite. Clients may demonstrate psychomotor retardation or agitation and insomnia or hypersomnia with vivid, unpleasant dreams.

Individuals use amphetamines to suppress fatigue, increase alertness, enhance psychomotor performance, increase wakefulness, decrease appetite, and induce a temporary state of excitation and feeling of well-being. Amphetamines have been used medically as appetite suppressants, as energizers and euphoriants, and as antidepressants. They also have been used to combat narcolepsy (involuntary sleep), to reduce hyperkinesis (increased muscular movement), and to promote alertness, retention, and wakefulness. Although their effects are paradoxical, dextroamphetamine (Dexedrine) and the related substance methylphenidate (Ritalin) are widely used to treat attention deficit hyperactivity disorder in children and young adults. Both drugs are commonly sold on the streets, where Ritalin is often mixed with heroin.

Methamphetamine

Methamphetamine, a drug that came into prominence in the 1990s, is significantly more potent than amphetamines. Street methamphetamine (known as speed, meth, or crank) is made in illegal laboratories. Meth is a popular drug at raves (all-night dancing parties) and is one of a number of drugs used by college students. It is ingested in pill form or in powdered form through snorting or injecting. Crystallized methamphetamine, known as ice, crystal, or glass, is a smokable, very powerful form of the drug. Immediately after smoking or shooting up, users experience a "rush" or "flash" that lasts a few minutes and is described as extremely pleasurable, almost orgasmic. Oral or intranasal use produces euphoria (a high), but not a rush. Users experience wakefulness, insomnia, and heightened physical activity. Because methamphetamine elevates mood, people who experiment with it tend to use it with increasing frequency and in increasingly higher doses. Euphoria and physical activity escalate. After several days, however, the person "crashes," becoming exhausted and lapsing into long periods of sleep and depression. Methamphetamine is often used in combination with alcohol, heroin, or cocaine.

Methamphetamine increases heart rate and blood pressure; over time it can cause irreversible damage to blood vessels in the brain, producing strokes. Other serious effects include respiratory distress, hyperthermia, convulsions, and cardiovascular problems that can lead to death. Decreased appetite is common; extreme anorexia can develop. Irritability, anxiety, confusion, tremors, paranoia, and violent behavior often occur.

Nicotine

Nicotine is a mild CNS stimulant; however, in high doses it has a depressant effect. Individuals ingest nicotine by smoking cigarettes, cigars, or pipe tobacco or by using smokeless tobacco in the form of snuff, plug, dipping tobacco, or chewing tobacco. Nicotine use is associated with many pleasurable individual, interpersonal, and social activities, such as driving a car, relaxing after a meal, drinking with friends at a bar, and resting after sexual intercourse. Nicotine is the substance in tobacco that reinforces and strengthens the desire to smoke or use. Nicotine is highly addictive; tobacco use is a powerful habit and is very difficult to stop. According to Mark H., "I had a harder time giving up cigarettes than heroin."

Cigarette smoking is considered the world's most devastating, preventable cause of disease and premature death. It is linked to more than 400,000 deaths annually in the United States. As of 1997, the Centers for Disease Control and Prevention reported that some 48 million Americans smoked regularly, or about 24.7% of the nation's adult population, an estimated 27.6% of men and 22.1% of women. This rate remained steady during the 1990s, primarily due to an increase in smoking rates among young adults, with the highest rates found in individuals between the ages of 18 and 48. The lowest smoking rate, 12%, was found among adults 65 and older. In 1997, about 44.3 million adults described themselves as smokers who had quit, a fairly constant figure since 1995. The survey found that 26.7% of Blacks, 25.3% of Whites, and 20.4% of Latinos smoked regularly. Adults who lived below the poverty line were more likely to smoke than were those living above the poverty level. The smoking rate for adults with 9 to 11 years of education was 35.4%, compared with 11.5% for college graduates. High school dropouts were three times more likely to smoke than college graduates.

Smoking is particularly dangerous for teenagers because their bodies are still developing and changing, and the 4,000 chemicals (including 200 known toxins) in cigarette smoke can adversely affect development. Because nicotine is so addictive, one-third of young people who begin using tobacco in their teens become addicted by the time they are 20, accounting for the increase in smoking rates among young adults noted above. As rising numbers of adults have begun to quit smoking, Joe Camel and other tobacco advertising campaigns have targeted teens, especially minority youth. Marketing tobacco to women is paying off as well, as more women begin and continue to smoke. Lung cancer is now the leading cause of cancer deaths in women. Smoking during pregnancy adversely affects fetal development, and smoking by mothers contributes to the development of asthma in their children.

People who use tobacco may experience excitement, restlessness, psychomotor agitation, and insomnia. Chronic smoking or use of smokeless tobacco diminishes or extinguishes the user's senses of smell and taste. Smokers have frequent colds and often a "smoker's cough." Gastrointestinal distress and cardiac arrhythmias are common. Diuresis and flushed face occur. Signs and symptoms of nicotine intoxication include shortness of breath, fine tremor, decreased appetite, nervousness, raised arousal level, rambling flow of thoughts, decreased attention to extraneous stimuli, periods of inexhaustibility, sedation, and decreased aggressiveness.

Symptoms of nicotine withdrawal include craving, irritability, anxiety, restlessness, difficulty concentrating, lethargy, drowsiness, disruption in sleep, insomnia, headaches, increased appetite with excessive eating, gastrointestinal distress, and constipation. Physical discomfort usually abates within 72 hours of stopping tobacco use.

Nicotine is an extremely toxic substance. It irritates lung tissues, constricts blood vessels, and increases blood pressure. Compared with nonsmokers, smokers are at greater risk for heart attack and stroke. Tobacco use also increases the risk of cancers of the mouth, larynx, pharynx, lungs, esophagus, pancreas, breast, cervix, uterus, kidneys, and bladder. The incidence of obstructive lung diseases such as emphysema and chronic bronchitis is significantly higher in people who smoke. Tobacco users also have a higher incidence of gastrointestinal problems such as gastric ulcers and cirrhosis. Careless smoking can cause burns and accidental deaths. Recent studies indicate increased prevalence of cataracts and diminished hearing in smokers. Over time, smokers (especially women) develop premature and more abundant facial wrinkles. Nicotine contributes to male impotence. Smoking during pregnancy increases the risks for spontaneous abortion, preterm birth, low birth weight, and fetal and infant deaths. Secondhand smoke has harmful effects on nonsmokers in the smoker's environment.

Caffeine

Caffeine is a xanthine alkaloid, a bitter crystalline substance found in coffee, tea, chocolate, and cola and other soft drinks. Caffeine is a mild CNS stimulant, cardiac stimulant, vasodilator, and diuretic. It also stimulates gastric acid and suppressed appetite. Caffeine is a part of many personal and social rituals. Individuals "need" their morning coffee, "enjoy" an afternoon cup of tea, and "relax" with hot chocolate after skiing or with a six-pack of cola at a picnic.

Users claim that caffeine increases their energy, helps them stay awake, and stimulates alertness. Users report other highly individual effects. Caffeine tolerance and dependence are common.

Excessive caffeine consumption can cause heart palpitations, tachycardia, cardiac arrhythmias, hypotension, and even circulatory failure. Individuals may experience difficulty breathing, flushing, and diuresis. Other symptoms include headache, light-headedness, dizziness, ringing in ears, and visual flashes of light. Gastrointestinal disturbances include nausea, gastric irritation and pain, and diarrhea. Caffeine intoxication can cause insomnia with periods of inexhaustibility and excessive sensibility. Clients may experience reflex hyperexcitability, muscle twitching, and psychomotor agitation. They may describe a rambling flow of thoughts and speech as well as feelings of nervousness, jitteriness, restlessness, and apprehension.

Adverse effects from caffeine ingestion include acid indigestion and gastric ulcer. Caffeine contributes to increased intraocular pressure with unregulated glaucoma. Caffeine increases plasma glucose and lipid levels. The incidence of angina and myocardial infarction is higher in caffeine users than in nonusers. Caffeine withdrawal is characterized by headache, irritability, tremulousness, restlessness, lethargy, and often an inability to work productively.

Opioids

Opium, which is obtained from the *Papaver somniferum* poppy plant, has been used for centuries as a medicinal and recreational drug. The term *opiate* refers to any drug derived from opium, such as morphine, codeine, and heroin. Morphine and codeine are used therapeutically, whereas heroin is predominantly a substance of abuse. The development of synthetic drugs led to use of the term *opioid* to designate both naturally occurring opiates and synthetic and semisynthetic opiates.

Opioids depress the central nervous system and are used primarily to manage severe pain. Initially, the drug has a calming effect and produces a feeling of euphoria that is followed by drowsiness. Tolerance to opioids develops rapidly, and dependence is high.

Opioid Analgesics

Oxycodone/acetaminophen (Percocet), hydrocodone/acetaminophen (Vicodin), and acetaminophen/codeine (Tylenol with Codeine) are effective but highly addictive pain medications. Other prescribed and abused opioid analgesics include natural alkaloids of morphine and codeine, the semisynthetic analog hydromorphone (Dilaudid), and synthetic compounds of meperidine (Demerol), methadone hydrochloride (Dolophine), and fentanyl (Sublimaze, Duragesic). Opiate agonist-antagonists include pentazocine hydrochloride (Talwin), nalbuphine hydrochloride (Nubain), butophanol (Stadol), dezocine (Dalgan), and buprenorphine (Buprenex). Routes of administration include by mouth, injection (intravenous, intramuscular, subcutaneous, and epidural), rectal suppository, intranasal spray, and transdermal patch. Nalozone (Narcan) is an opiate antagonist used to counteract narcotic-induced respiratory depression.

Heroin

Heroin is a semisynthetic opiate isolated in 1898 in Germany in the search for a non-habit-forming analgesic to replace morphine. Heroin, however, is two to three times as potent as morphine. Heroin was considered nonaddictive when it was first introduced into the United States, but by 1924 Congress prohibited its manufacture. Today, heroin remains a potent and popular street drug. In the Boston suburbs, new users tend to be young adults who inhale rather than inject. Heroin is highly addictive and accounts for many overdose drug deaths. The logistics of heroin trafficking are complex, yet the production and distribution of this drug yield great financial rewards for many.

Users inject, smoke, or inhale heroin and experience an initial feeling of euphoria, a thrill similar to sexual orgasm, then relaxation, detachment, indifference to anxiety, and diminished response to pain. Common signs of use include nausea and vomiting, constricted pupils with watery eyes, dermatitis with "itching all over," and constipation. Many users become preoccupied with obtaining and using heroin. They may lose interest in their hygiene and appearance, food, and sex. Users have difficulty concentrating; memory and judgment are impaired. They often withdraw from friends and isolate themselves. Heroin users may steal, sell drugs, or prostitute themselves to support their habit. Chronic intravenous users often develop abscesses; they are at high risk for HIV, hepatitis, tetanus, and other infections from contaminated needles. Hypoglycemia and malnutrition may develop.

Signs and symptoms of heroin intoxication include initial euphoria, psychomotor agitation or retardation, and impairment in attention, memory, and judgment. Constricted pupils, slurred speech, and drowsiness are common. "Nodding out" is a semistuporous state characterized by head bobbing, bowed head, and drooping eyelids. Feelings of apathy, unrest, restlessness, anxiety, discomfort, unhappiness, dissatisfaction, unpleasantness, and depression follow. Even in hot weather, intravenous drug users often wear long sleeves and other body-covering clothing to hide needle marks and scarred veins. Snorting heroin leads to inflamed nasal mucosa. Heroin overdose can cause major CNS depression, with symptoms of pinpoint pupils, bradycardia, lowered blood pressure, respiratory depression and arrest, pale and cold clammy skin with cyanosis, convulsions, shock, loss of consciousness, coma, and death.

Opioid withdrawal is uncomfortable but rarely fatal. Following cessation or reduction in heavy or prolonged use, individuals experience tachycardia, hypertension, chills or fever, profuse diaphoresis (sweating), gooseflesh, dilated pupils with tearing, runny nose and sneezing, nausea, vomiting, diarrhea, stomach cramps, muscle aches, yawning and insomnia, exaggerated feeling of depression, irritability, restlessness, and jerking motions.

Chronic intravenous use, especially with shared or contaminated needles, contributes to hepatitis, endocarditis, and HIV. Pulmonary emboli, cardiac arrest, and renal failure occur. Heroin use during pregnancy can lead to premature birth, stillbirth, or addicted infants who experience severe withdrawal symptoms.

Hallucinogens

Hallucinogens are natural and synthetic drugs that distort reality, often by producing hallucinations, or false perceptions of reality. These drugs alter sensation, mood, and consciousness. Most experiences are visual, but changes in hearing, touch, smell, and taste can occur, sometimes simultaneously. The effects of hallucinogens vary widely with drug, dose, setting, and the unique sensitivity of the user at the time of use. Users prefer the term *psychedelic* in reference to these drugs.

Lysergic Acid Diethylamide

Lysergic acid diethylamide (LSD), commonly referred to as acid, is one of the most potent mind-altering chemicals known. LSD is classified as a Schedule I controlled substance; it has no medical use and high potential for abuse. LSD is usually taken by mouth. It is ingested from absorbent blotter paper that has been saturated with the chemical and divided into small decorative squares, with each square representing one dose. LSD significantly alters perception, mood, and psychological processes; it can impair motor coordination and skills. During the 1950s and 1960s, LSD experimentation was legally conducted by psychiatrists and others in the health and mental health professions.

The effects of LSD are especially unpredictable; they depend on the amount taken, the surroundings in which the drug is used, and the user's personality, mood, and expectations. LSD does not produce craving in the way that alcohol, cocaine, nicotine, heroin, and amphetamines do. However, users develop tolerance and must take progressively higher doses to achieve the desired state of intoxication.

Physical effects of LSD include dilated pupils, raised body temperature, increased heart rate and blood pressure, sweating, loss of appetite, sleeplessness, dry mouth, and tremors. The sensations and feelings induced by the drug are much more dramatic than the physical effects. The user may feel several different emotions at once or may swing rapidly from one emotion to another. Large doses can produce delusions and visual hallucinations. Senses of time and self change. Sensations may seem to "cross over," giving the user the feeling of "hearing colors" or "seeing sounds." Users may experience anxiety, loss of control, great confusion, suspicion, and panic. Users refer to their experiences with LSD as trips or tripping. An acute adverse reaction is a "bad trip." Some LSD users experience severe, terrifying thoughts and feelings, fear of losing control, fear of insanity and death, and despair. Fatal accidents have occurred during LSD intoxication. Many LSD users experience flashbacks, or recurrences of the drug experience without taking the drug again. In addition to bad trips and flashbacks, LSD users may develop long-lasting psychoses.

Phencyclidine Hydrochloride

Phencyclidine hydrochloride (PCP) was developed in 1959 as an anesthetic. PCP interrupts the functions of the neocortex, the section of the brain that controls the intellect and keeps instincts in check. Therapeutic use of PCP was discontinued in 1965 because of the drug's bizarre and volatile effects; individuals often become agitated, delusional, and irrational following use. Today, PCP is illegally manufactured in clandestine laboratories and sold on the street under such names as angel dust, killer weed, and rocket fuel. PCP is snorted, smoked, or eaten.

Low to moderate doses of PCP produce a slight increase in pulse and respiration rates and a rise in blood pressure. Respirations become shallow; flushing and profuse sweating occur. Muscular coordination decreases and body movement slows down; speech is blocked and incoherent, and senses are dulled. The psychological effects of PCP are similar to those associated with alcohol intoxication. Users report feelings of strength, power, and invulnerability; time seems to slow down. PCP blocks pain receptors, and this numbing effect on the mind often results in anger, rage, and the disappearance of unpleasant memories; violent PCP episodes may result in self-inflicted injuries.

With high doses of PCP, there is a drop in blood pressure, pulse, and respiratory rates. Individuals may experience nausea, vomiting, blurred vision, flicking up and down of eyes, drooling, loss of balance, and dizziness. Illusions, hallucinations, and paranoia may develop. PCP mimics symptoms of schizophrenia, such as delusions, mental turmoil, and a sense of distance and estrangement from one's environment. Large doses of PCP, or use with CNS depressants such as alcohol and benzodiazepines, may produce convulsions and coma as well as heart and lung failure.

Peyote and Mescaline

Peyote is a small cactus that has a head, or "button," that contains mescaline. Peyote is native to northern Mexico and Texas, where Aztecs and Native Americans used the drug to heal the sick and as an aid to their search for divine visions. Today, bona fide members of the Native American Church may use peyote legally.

Mescaline is an alkaloid with hallucinogenic properties that is derived from the heads of the peyote cactus or produced synthetically. It is less potent than LSD but, like LSD, it alters perception and can produce hallucinations.

Marijuana

Marijuana is the most widely used illicit drug in the United States and tends to be the first illegal drug teens use. The term *marijuana* encompasses several varieties of cannabis cultivated for their intoxicating properties, including marijuana, tetrahydrocannabinol (THC), hashish, and hashish oil. Marijuana is usually smoked, as a cigarette or with a wet or dry pipe, or eaten as a solid or liquid preparation. Research shows that THC changes the way sensory information enters and is acted on by the brain—more specifically, the information-processing system of the hippocampus. The activity of nerve fibers is suppressed by THC; learned behaviors also deteriorate. Marijuana alters perceptions, emotions, movement and coordination, hunger, pain, vision, and hearing. Users often believe that marijuana enhances their self-awareness, but controlled studies show just the opposite effect: Marijuana serves as a barrier against self-awareness. Long-term cannabis users may develop tolerance and psychological dependence. Users require more of the drug to get the same effects, and cannabis can become the center of their lives.

The effects of marijuana are highly variable and uncertain, ranging from minimal sensations to hallucinations, from relaxed euphoria to acute feelings of discomfort and panic. The desired effects sought by users mimic mild intoxication from alcohol and include a sense of well-being, a dreamy state of relaxation, vivid sensory perceptions, and euphoria. Undesirable effects may include increased heart rate, bloodshot eyes, dry mouth and throat, and sleepiness. Increased heart rate carries a potential cardiac danger for individuals with preexisting heart disease. When a person shoots cocaine while smoking marijuana, heart rate and blood pressure increase dramatically.

Parents, teachers, and employers are concerned about marijuana because users often experience decreased attention span, impaired or reduced short-term memory and comprehension, distorted sense of time and space, and reduced ability to perform tasks requiring concentration. Marijuana impairs psychomotor coordination, making it difficult for a user, for example, to drive a car or operate machinery safely. Motivation and cognition are altered, making acquisition of new information difficult. Marijuana can produce disorientation, disorganized thought processes, paranoia, and psychosis.

Marijuana damages the lungs and respiratory system because users usually inhale unfiltered smoke deeply and hold it in their lungs as long as possible. Marijuana smoke contains more carcinogens than tobacco smoke, and risk for cancer increases with chronic use. Long-term use by men can cause a decrease in testosterone levels and lowered sperm count. In women, testosterone levels rise and risk of infertility increases. Both men and women may experience diminished or extinguished sexual pleasure.

Inhalants

Volatile substances that are inhaled for psychoactive (mind) effects are called inhalants. People are often unintentionally or accidentally exposed to inhalants at home and in the workplace. Young people, however, abuse inhalants because they are readily available and inexpensive, possibly serving as a cheap, accessible substitute for alcohol. Some inhalants, such as certain glues, gasoline, paint thinner, correction fluid, and felt-tip marker fluid, contain solvents. Other inhalants contain gases (e.g., butane lighters and propane tanks, aerosol cans of whipped cream, spray paint, or hair spray), medical anesthetic bases (e.g., nitrous oxide, or laughing gas), or nitrites (e.g., amyl nitrite and butyl nitrite).

Users sniff, or "huff," inhalants to get an immediate head rush or high. However, most inhalants are depressants with sedative effects; some have psychedelic or hallucinogenic effects. When first inhaled, they usually make the user feel slightly stimulated. With repeated use, the user may feel less inhibited and less in control; finally, the user can lose consciousness. One-time use can cause death. Unlike other inhalants, amyl nitrite is a CNS stimulant; positive experiences for the user include feelings of excitation and exhilaration, auditory or visual hallucinations, and profound vasodilation, which contributes to heightened sexual response.

Signs and symptoms of inhalant use include headache, dizziness, blurred vision, nystagmus, slurred speech, nausea, sneezing, coughing, nosebleed, and loss of appetite. Other effects include heart palpitations, decreased pulse and respiratory rates, a feeling of suffocation, psychomotor retardation, muscle weakness, numbness and tingling of the hands and feet, depressed reflexes, lack of coordination, unsteady gait and tremors, and decreased or loss of sense of smell. Individuals may pass urine or feces involuntarily. Psychological experiences range from euphoria to apathy or lethargy. Visual hallucinations and severe mood swings may occur. Inhalant use can cause unconsciousness, stupor, coma, and death. Deaths associated with inhalant use usually result from asphyxia, suffocation, choking on vomit, careless behavior in a dangerous setting, or sudden sniffing death syndrome cardiac arrest.

Serious, but possibly reversible, effects of inhalant use include weight loss, fatigue, electrolyte imbalance, blood oxygen depletion, irregular heartbeat, abdominal pain, hepatitis, and liver, lung, and kidney damage. Chronic inhalant abusers usually experience multiple psychological and social problems, leading in some instances to violent behavior. Irreversible effects associated with inhalant use include hearing loss, bone marrow damage, peripheral neuropathy (limb spasms), and brain damage. Inhaling highly concentrated amounts of chemicals can induce heart failure and death, especially from abuse of fluorocarbons and butane-type gases. Amyl and butyl nitrites have been associated with Kaposi's sarcoma (KS), the most common cancer reported among AIDS clients. Nitrites may contribute to the development of KS in HIV-infected people.

Anabolic Steroids

Steroids are naturally occurring or synthetic hormones that affect growth and other bodily physiological and sexual functions. Steroids include adrenal, cortical, testicular, and ovarian hormones and their derivatives. Anabolic steroids are of primary concern in the context of drug use and drug problems. Related to male sex hormones, anabolic steroids increase muscle mass and, in women, cause masculinization. Taken in combination with a program of muscle-building exercise and diet, steroids may contribute to an increase in body weight and muscular strength. Steroid misuse is considered abuse of a non-dependence-producing substance; users, however, can develop psychological dependence.

Some athletes misuse anabolic steroids because they believe that by taking them they can increase their skeletal muscle mass, enhance the physical performance of skeletal muscles, increase their body weight, and improve their athletic abilities. Signs of steroid use include quick weight and muscle gains, aggressiveness and combativeness, jaundice, purpura or red spots on the body, swelling of the feet and lower legs, trembling, unexplained darkening of the skin, and persistent unpleasant breath odor. Psychological effects in both sexes include very aggressive behavior (known as "roid rage") and depression.

Steroid users subject themselves to more than 70 possible side effects, ranging in severity from acne to liver cancer. The liver and the cardiovascular and reproductive systems are most seriously affected by steroid use. In males, use can cause withered testicular atrophy, sterility, and impotence. In females, irreversible masculine traits can develop, along with breast reduction and sterility. Some side effects appear quickly, whereas others, such as heart attack, stroke, and fatal hemorrhagic liver disease, may not show up for years.

In 1997, a troubling article in *Sports Illustrated* reported widespread use of performance-enhancing drugs by Olympic athletes despite supposedly rigorous drug testing (see Bamberger, 1997; Bamberger & Yaeger, 1997). In addition, the International Olympic Committee (IOC) tolerates the presence of high levels of testosterone in both male and female athletes. Steroid users range from weight lifters, shot-putters, and bobsledders to swimmers, marathon runners, and gymnasts. Male gymnasts may take steroids to develop strength, whereas some female gymnasts are said to intentionally retard their growth by taking so-called brake drugs.

According to *Sports Illustrated,* some athletes refer to the Olympic Games held in Atlanta in 1996 as the Growth Hormone Games. Human growth hormone (hGH) helps muscles recover rapidly after an intense workout and thereby enables athletes to train harder and more often. Urine tests do not detect hGH. The article reports that the use of steroids and other substances has spread to almost every sport, from major league baseball to college basketball to high school football. Some athletes allegedly use drug gurus to develop "designer steroids," steroids that have been chemically tailored to the athletes' particular needs and that are difficult to identify with urine testing.

In the summer of 1998, five cyclists in the prestigious Tour de France admitted that they had taken the banned substance erythropoetin (EPO). Whereas growth hormone is popular among strength athletes, competitors who rely on endurance, such as long-distance runners, cross-country skiers, and distance swimmers, prefer genetically engineered versions of EPO, a natural hormone that is effective in the treatment of anemia, kidney disease, and other medical disorders. It stimulates the formulation of red blood cells, which carry oxygen to the muscles, thus fostering greater endurance for users. Urine testing does not detect EPO use. Detection of both hGH and EPO requires blood testing, an invasive procedure.

Designer Drugs

A designer drug is an analog of another, legal drug that differs slightly in structure but mimics the psychoactive effects of the legal drug. Designer drugs can be several hundred times stronger than the drugs they are designed to imitate. Designer drugs are produced in clandestine laboratories and are available through the illicit drug market. The most common designer drugs are analogs of fentanyl and meperidine (both synthetic opioids), PCP, and amphetamines and methamphetamine. The street names of designer drugs change frequently.

Fentanyl Analogs

Fentanyl is a synthetic opioid analgesic used in surgical procedures. Fentanyl analogs are 80 to 1,000 times more potent than heroin and 200 times more potent than morphine. Because of the potency and quick onset, even a very small dose of a fentanyl analog can cause sudden death. Injection is the most common route of administration, although smoking and snorting are becoming more popular. Death from respiratory paralysis as the result of fentanyl analog use can be so sudden that the needle may still be present in the dead user's arm. Names of fentanyl analogs include China White, synthetic heroin, Tango, and Cash. Fentanyl analogs have been responsible for many overdose deaths.

Meperidine Analogs

Illicit use of meperidine increases when heroin is scarce. Meperidine analogs (new heroin, synthetic heroin) are inhaled or injected and produce a euphoria similar to that produced by heroin. Adverse effects resemble symptoms seen in Parkinson's disease: uncontrollable tremors, drooling, impaired speech, paralysis, and irreversible brain damage.

Methamphetamine Analogs

Dozens of analogs of amphetamines and methamphetamine are manufactured for their hallucinogenic properties. MDA (3,4-methylenedioxyamphetamine) and MDMA (3.4-methylenedioxymethamphetamine) are of current concern. Both drugs have been shown to be neurotoxic.

It is purported that MDA, the "love drug," produces a heightened need for interpersonal relationships; users report increased need to talk to and be with other people. However, MDA damages the brain's serotonin neurons as well as the brain itself. Effects of MDA mimic amphetamine intoxication: hyperactivity, hyperthermia, tachycardia, hypertension, and seizures.

MDMA is a designer drug with hallucinogenic and amphetamine-like properties. Proponents claim that MDMA, sometimes called Adam, Ecstasy, or X-TC, can make people trust each other, that it breaks down barriers between lovers and family members. Adverse effects are similar to those found with use of amphetamines and cocaine. MDMA increases heart rate and blood pressure;

other physical symptoms include muscle tension, involuntary clenching of teeth, nausea, blurred vision, rapid eye movement, faintness, chills or sweating, and sleep problems. Psychological problems include confusion, severe anxiety, depression, and paranoia—during use and sometimes weeks after ingestion of MDMA.

Other Designer Drugs

Teenagers and young adults who abuse drugs frequently mix and use potions with little concern for adverse effects. In Salem, Massachusetts, three college students almost died after drinking a concoction they had made from a recipe they got off the Internet. They mixed gamma hydroxbutyrate (GHB) with orange juice. They became violently ill, with vomiting, severe shaking, and unconsciousness; they were hospitalized, with one of them in intensive care. The main ingredient in GHB is sodium hydroxide, a Drano-like lye substance. GHB is one of the so-called date-rape drugs; it has caused death.

Researchers continue to study the pharmacodynamic effects of designer drugs as well as the personal and public responses to their use.

Herbs

Nature was our first pharmacy. Animals and primitive humans depended on the use of plants and herbs to maintain health, promote vigor, and cure disease. For thousands of years, herbal medicine, together with acupuncture, acupressure, and moxibustion, has been central to the practice of preventive medicine in China.

In colonial America, the family was the natural locus for care of the sick. Many homes had a "sick room" just off the kitchen for births and nursing the sick. Women kept stocks of remedies on hand, and in the fall they put away medicinal herbs just as they preserved food for winter storage. In addition, lay practitioners used native herbs and folk remedies to minister to the sick; newspapers, almanacs, and books such as *Domestic Medicine* (the second edition of which was published in 1771) guided their practice. The colonists observed that the Indians seemed to be free of the dread diseases that afflicted the European settlers, and many thought this good health was a product of the Indians' special knowledge of medicinal herbs.

Physicians began to practice in America in the mid-18th century. Homeopathy, a school of medicine founded by the German physician Dr. Samuel Hahnemann (1755-1843), flourished in the United States after the Civil War. Homeopathy is based in the beliefs that disease is fundamentally a matter of spirit and that disease can be cured through the administration of certain drugs in minute doses. The American Medical Association fought the growth of homeopathy, and by the early 1900s, schools, practitioners, and adherents of homeopathy had declined. It is interesting to note that in the early 1900s, fully 90% of all medicines were derived from roots, barks, and leaves.

In the 1990s, alternative medicine became big business in the United States, Canada, and other Western countries. Natural food stores now abound, and herbal products occupy as many shelves as vitamins in drug and grocery stores. Mail-order businesses selling herbs and other "natural products" are booming. Herbs are promoted as useful for increasing mental alertness, promoting relaxation, heightening sexual performance, preventing infection, and reducing cold symptoms.

Celestial Seasonings, a company that has been selling herbal teas for many years, now also packages single herbs and herbal blends for use as dietary supplements. The company's line of extracts includes cranberry ("for a healthy urinary tract," according to the label), echinacea ("for the body's defenses"), garlic ("for a healthy heart"), ginkgo ("for mental clarity and memory"), green tea ("for antioxidant protection"), panax ginseng ("for energy and stamina"), saw palmetto ("for a healthy prostate"), and St. John's wort ("for a positive outlook"). The company's line of "advanced formula blends" includes Echinacea Cold Season, GinkgoSharp, Ginseng Energy, Heart Health, Mood Mender, Prostate Health, Sleepytime Extra, Tension Tamer, and Total Antioxidant. Celestial Seasonings and other companies that market herbal supplements are careful to state that their products are not intended to treat, cure, or prevent any disease. These products are not evaluated by the U.S. Food and Drug Administration (FDA).

In 1996, after 16 fatalities, the FDA issued a warning about the dangers of the Chinese herbal stimulant *ma huang* (ephedra). In 1997, Massachusetts asked for a voluntary recall of alcohol-based products containing ginseng following an incident in which an 11-year-old boy suffered chest pains, shortness of breath, and heart palpitations after downing a 99 cent vial of Dr. Chan's High Potency Ginseng. The boy stopped at a local convenience store en route to school and bought the ginseng preparation because "the saleswomen told him it would be like a Power Bar or a cup of coffee." According to the report, the boy had a gym class in school that day and figured "a little energy couldn't hurt."

More complex is the increasing use and possible abuse of erogenic dietary supplements, especially amino acids. Mark McGwire, 1998 home-run hero of America, used creatine and androstenedione as part of his conditioning routine; however, he reportedly stopped using these during the 1999 baseball season. Physicians, other health care professionals, and parents question what kind of message McGwire's use of these supplements sent to youth. Androstenedione use is banned by the National Football League, the National Collegiate Athletic Association, and the IOC, but not by Major League Baseball. Sales of creatine, a popular performance-enhancing substance, soared from $50 million in 1996 to $200 million in 1998. Creatine is derived from the amino acids arginine, glycine, and methionine. It is promoted as useful for improving performance, power, body size, and strength.

An increasing number of health practitioners, including physicians, are using herbal medicine to complement Western pharmacotherapeutics. Many substance abuse clients can become addicted to prescription medications designed to treat anxiety, so practitioners are increasingly recommending the herb kava for that use. Addiction practitioners, however, must be alert to possible excessive use of herbs by individuals who abuse alcohol or other drugs.

Summary

Understanding the pharmacology of drug use plus the complex dimensions and dynamics of substance abuse is essential for addiction practice. Pharmacology includes the pharmaceutics, pharmacokinetics, and pharmacodynamics of drug use. Different drugs have different properties and effects. Alcohol and sedative, hypnotic, and anxiolytic drugs are central nervous depressants. CNS stimulants include cocaine, amphetamines, nicotine, and caffeine. Analgesics such as morphine, codeine, meperidine, oxycodone, and heroin are classified as opioids. LSD, PCP, peyote, and mescaline are hallucinogens. Marijuana (itself a category that includes several varieties of cannabis) is the most widely used illicit drug in the United States. Inhalants, anabolic steroids, and designer drugs are also abused. Americans currently spend an estimated $70 million a year on herbal remedies. Do some individuals abuse herbs or use them to excess? Addiction practitioners must learn to recognize signs and symptoms of substance abuse, especially intoxication and withdrawal. Chronic or heavy use of alcohol and other drugs has adverse medical, psychological, and social effects.

Related Skills Checklist

Practitioner skills related to substance abuse as discussed in this chapter include the ability to do the following:

- Classify substances according to their expected actions.
- Identify the expected actions of CNS depressants, CNS stimulants, and opioids; of hallucinogens, inhalants, and marijuana; and of anabolic steroids, designer drugs, and herbs.
- Recognize signs and symptoms of substance intoxication and withdrawal.

Special Topics for Further Study

Given the addictive properties of nicotine, should it be classified as a controlled substance? Argue the pros and cons regarding decriminalization of marijuana. How risky is AndroGel? Should performance-enhancing substances be controlled or banned? If so, how and by whom? Should the FDA evaluate and regulate herbal supplements?

Addiction Practice 2000

Addiction practice 2000 demands comprehensive community-based substance abuse education, prevention, and early intervention. Effective programs involve the family, church, school, work site, and every small group or social network available. Aggressive leadership is needed to develop policies to reduce access to alcohol, tobacco, and other drugs, especially by youth and other high-risk populations.

References

Bamberger, M. (1997, April 14). Under suspicion. *Sports Illustrated,* pp. 72-85.
Bamberger, M., & Yaeger, D. (1997, April 14). Over the edge. *Sports Illustrated,* pp. 60-70.

Other Sources

Buchan, W. (1982). Domestic medicine. In P. Starr (Ed.), *The social transformation of American medicine.* New York: Basic Books.
Center for Substance Abuse Prevention. (1994). *Inhalants* (DHHS Publication No. SMA 94-2084). Rockville, MD: Author.
Deglin, J. H., & Vallerand, A. H. (1999). *Davis's drug guide* (6th ed.). Philadelphia: F. A. Davis.
Economos, C., & Wein, D. (1998, October). The creatine craze. *MetroSports Magazine,* p. 56.
Epstein, J. F., & Gfroerer, J. C. (1997). *Heroin abuse in the United States* (Working Paper No. RP0919). Rockville, MD: Substance Abuse and Mental Health Services Administration, Office of Applied Studies.
Greenblatt, J. C., & Gfroerer, J. C. (1996). *Methamphetamine abuse in the United States* (Working Paper No. RP0906). Rockville, MD: Substance Abuse and Mental Health Services Administration, Office of Applied Studies.
Kinney, J., & Leaton, G. (1994). *Loosening the grip* (5th ed.). St. Louis: C. V. Mosby.
Kuhn, M. (1998). *Pharmacotherapeutics* (4th ed.). Philadelphia: F. A. Davis.

National Institute on Alcohol Abuse and Alcoholism. (1991). *Alcohol research: Promise for the decade* (NIAA Publication No. ADM 92-1990). Bethesda, MD: Author.

National Institute on Drug Abuse. (1991). *Cocaine/crack the big lie* (RPO 929). Washington, DC: Government Printing Office.

National Institute on Drug Abuse. (1991). *Methamphetamine abuse: Epidemiologic issues and implications* (DHHS Publication No. ADM 91-1836). Rockville, MD: Author.

National Institute on Drug Abuse. (1994). *Inhalant abuse* (NIH Publication No. 94-3818). Rockville, MD: Author.

National Institute on Drug Abuse. (1995). *Epidemiology of inhalant abuse: An international perspective* (NIH Publication No. 95-3712). Rockville, MD: Author.

National Institute on Drug Abuse. (1997). *Pharmacokinetics, metabolism, and pharmaceutics of drugs of abuse* (NIH Publication No. 97-4141). Rockville, MD: Author.

National Institute on Drug Abuse & National Institutes of Health. (1996). *National conference on marijuana use: Prevention, treatment, and research* (NIH Publication No. 96-4106). Rockville, MD: National Institutes of Health.

Solowij, N. (1998). *Cannabis and cognitive function.* New York: Cambridge University Press.

Tye, L. (1997, July 13). Herbal renewal. *Boston Globe,* pp. 18-28.

U.S. Department of Education. (1991). *A parent's guide to prevention: Growing up drug free.* Washington, DC: Author.

4

Other Addictions

Objectives

- Understand that nonchemical addictions resemble substance-related disorders in etiology, expression, and treatment.
- Identify the dimensions and dynamics of pathological gambling.
- Acknowledge the addictive aspects of compulsive shopping.
- Recognize a continuum of sexual addictions.
- Compare and contrast addictive love with healthy love.
- Understand the severity of eating disorders.
- Appreciate the problems associated with other addictive behaviors.

Outline

- **Other Addictions**
- **Pathological Gambling**
  - Gambling
  - Incidence, Prevalence, and Trends
  - The National Gambling Impact Study Commission
  - Populations at Risk
  - Pathological Gambling
- **Compulsive Shopping**
  - The Problem
  - Addictive Aspects
  - Gender Differences

Other Addictions

No slurred speech, no dilated pupils, no dirty urine—in fact, no substance use—yet compulsive gambling, an "invisible" addiction, has been called the "addiction of the nineties" and interest in it continues to grow in the 21st century. By definition, addictions include both chemical and nonchemical addictive disorders. Because nonchemical addictive disorders resemble substance-related disorders in etiology, expression, and treatment, it is useful for addiction practitioners to identify the characteristics and acknowledge the treatment implications of disorders such as pathological gambling, compulsive shopping, sex and love addictions, eating disorders, and other addictive behaviors. In addition, cross-addiction between chemical and nonchemical addictive disorders is common.

- Will R., a 31-year-old single man who abuses cocaine, is concerned about his recurrent, intense, sexually arousing fantasies, sexual urges, and sexual encounters with prostitutes. On a daily basis, Will has been trading coke for sex. His job as a loan officer at a city bank is in jeopardy because of his increasing absenteeism.

- Dawn H., a 39-year-old divorced high school teacher, is alarmed and near panic because her credit card debt exceeds $75,000. She is experiencing severe headaches. She has prescriptions from three different physicians for lorazepam (Atavin), clonazepam (Klonopin), and butalbital/acetaminophen/caffeine (Fioricet). The holiday season is approaching and Dawn knows she will not be able to control her compulsive shopping.

- Pat W., a 46-year-old married woman with three teenage children, works full-time as a registered nurse at a local community hospital. She was recently admitted to the inpatient psychiatric unit with diagnoses of alcohol dependence, bulimia nervosa, and posttraumatic stress disorder. Pat acknowledges that she is involved in an extramarital affair that is physically and sexually abusive.

- Gerry S., a 52-year-old disabled Vietnam veteran, has 8 years clean and sober from what he describes as a 25-year-love affair with alcohol and marijuana. Gerry is worried that his daily lottery habit and weekly sports betting could trigger a relapse with alcohol or other drugs. "I don't like what I am doing and how I am feeling. I'm losing more and more money too. I felt better when I was drinking and using," he states.

Pathological Gambling

Gambling

Gambling has been a human activity throughout recorded history. Drawing lots is mentioned in the Bible. Betting on sports and games of chance is common in many cultures and societies. Most people gamble occasionally for pleasure, not profit, and with no adverse personal or financial problems.

For some people, however, gambling provides action, thrills, and feelings of intense excitement, tension, anticipation, and power. *Action* is an aroused state similar to the high produced by cocaine and other drugs; it makes the adrenalin flow. For example, Erik P., a young married professional, feels a high as he conjures up clever excuses to leave home about 6:30 P.M. to place an illegal sports bet at a designated telephone. He asks his wife, "Lisa, do we need any milk? Does the baby have enough diapers? I'm headed out to mail a letter."

Pathological gambling is characterized by an overwhelming, uncontrollable impulse to gamble. A gambler can become dependent upon action in the same way a person becomes dependent on the effects of alcohol or other drugs. Some gamblers experience phenomena similar to alcoholic memory blackouts, trances, or dissociative states. Gamblers call this being "on tilt." (For further possible indications of a gambling addiction, see Exhibit C in the appendix to this volume.

The 20 questions in the exhibit were developed by Gamblers Anonymous for individuals who are questioning whether they might have a gambling problem.)

Incidence, Prevalence, and Trends

Some form of legalized gambling exists in 48 of the 50 states: bingo, lotteries, horse and dog racing tracks, casinos. Off-track betting parlors, on-line casinos, gambling opportunities in family theme parks, and riverboat and airline casinos have increased legal access to gambling for millions of individuals and families. Illegal wagering takes place as well, in sports betting, numbers rackets, and card games, and by those who are too young to gamble legally in any venue.

Today, millions of Americans participate in some kind of gambling. In 1993, Americans spent some $380 billion on legal forms of gambling, 70 times the amount Americans spent that year to attend movies. It has been estimated that three times the amount spent on legal gambling is wagered illegally each year. Billions of dollars change hands in gambling on such sports events as the Super Bowl and the NCAA's annual basketball tournament (March Madness). The office sports pool is standard operating procedure in many organizations. Gambling industry analysts have projected 78 million adult Internet users in North America by the year 2000, with one out of five of them potential gamblers, despite federal laws against interstate gambling. The analysts estimate that Internet gambling will be a $60 billion business.

Access increases gambling and problem gambling. With the explosive growth of legal gaming, there has been a dramatic increase in gambling and, concomitantly, in the incidence of problem gambling. The number of compulsive gamblers is growing. A 1995 survey reported that the prevalence of pathological gambling in the United States may be as high as 5.4% of the adult population.

The National Gambling Impact Study Commission

With opportunities for Americans to wager having increased exponentially in the preceding decade, the U.S. Congress in 1996 appointed a nine-member panel to conduct a comprehensive fact-finding study of the social, emotional, and economic ramifications of legalized gambling in the United States. The final report was delivered to the president, Congress, state governors, and Native American tribal leaders on June 18, 1999 (see James, 1999).

Not since 1975 had a national gambling survey been conducted. The panel took testimony throughout the country from people with both positive and negative gambling experiences. The commission also contracted for research to examine the impact of legalized gambling expansion on state lotteries and private and Native American tribal casinos, pathological gambling and its effects on families and communities, youth gambling, Internet gambling, gambling and public policy, gambling advertising, and availability of problem gambling treatment. Findings included the following (as reported in "Federal Commission's Report," 1999):

- Lotteries and casinos are now the most popular forms of gambling. In the year preceding the study, more of the adult population played a lottery game and nearly 30% visited a casino. Pari-mutuel revenues have not undergone the rapid growth of lotteries and casinos.

- In 1973, only 7 states had lotteries and only Nevada had casinos; today wagering is legal in 48 states (the exceptions being Utah and Hawaii); 37 states plus the District of Columbia have lotteries; per capita lottery sales increased from $35 in 1973 to $150 in 1997. Casinos are now authorized to operate in 28 states.

- Legal gambling revenues have risen from $10.4 billion in 1982 to more than $50 billion in 1997. Since 1976, gambling expenditures as a percentage of income have increased more than 150%.

- In 1974, 68% of the adult general population had gambled. By 1997, that figure had risen to 86%.

- Roughly 5.5% of adults from the general population—or about 11 million U.S. citizens—have had a gambling problem in their lifetimes.

- One study concluded that within a 50-mile radius of a casino, there is about double the prevalence of problem and pathological gambling that is found in areas more distant from casinos.

- Gambling patterns among women are increasingly resembling those of men.

- There has been an increase in the number of seniors who gamble.

- Adolescents are about twice as likely as adults to develop a gambling problem. It is estimated that there are about 8 million adolescent problem gamblers in the United States.

- Problem gambling costs the nation about $5 billion per year in creditor losses, insurance fraud, bankruptcies, social and health care services, legal fees, and diminished productivity.

- Gambling advertising contributes to compulsive gambling.

- It is estimated that one out of five compulsive gamblers has attempted suicide. The suicide rate for pathological gamblers is higher than that for persons with any other addictive disorder.

Populations at Risk

Currently, one-third of gamblers are women, yet more than 90% of individuals in treatment or in Gamblers Anonymous are men. Like men, women too seek action, but often women gamble to escape personal problems. Gambling serves as an "anesthetic." For some women, gambling provides an opportunity to compete equally with men and to experience feelings of power in a male-dominated world.

Gambling is increasing among adolescents. A review of nine studies of adolescent gambling in North America found that 4.4% to 7.4% of adolescents could be diagnosed as pathological gamblers, and a much larger proportion of adolescents gamble illegally. Gambling is also a serious problem for many elderly people on fixed incomes. It is an increasing problem as well for minority populations in the United States.

People living in poverty and individuals with limited education and skills dream of winning money and envision becoming wealthy through luck. Slot machines, lotteries, and other games offer the illusion of instant rewards with no expenditure of judgment or skill. Although prohibited, gambling is widespread in prison populations.

Several studies have found that approximately 50% of problem gamblers have coexisting alcohol or drug problems. Among alcohol and other drug abusers, estimated problem gambling rates range from 10% to 30%.

Pathological Gambling

Pathological gambling is characterized by a preoccupation with gambling and a need to gamble increasing amounts of money to achieve the desired excitement or high. When compulsive gamblers try to control, cut back, or stop their gambling, they become irritable and restless. Such gamblers lie to family members and others about the extent of their gambling. Many compulsive gamblers become pathological liars. After losing money, individuals gamble more in an attempt to recoup their losses; this is often called "the chase." Compulsive gamblers may commit illegal acts such as forgery, fraud, theft, or embezzlement to support their gambling habit. In 1997, Boston College suspended eight student bookmakers and three football players following an investigation into betting and gambling on campus. In 1998, a Columbia University student was arrested for his alleged role in a $10 million-a-year sports-gambling ring. Pathological gambling can destroy individuals, crush careers, and devastate families.

Pathological gambling usually develops as a progressive process that is characterized by three phases: winning, losing, and desperation. During the *winning* or adventurous phase, gambling is fun, exciting, and enjoyable. The gambler feels self-confident and savors his or her self-image as a big shot. During this phase, the gambler recovers losses through further gambling, borrowing from household accounts or from family and friends. These associated activities add to the excitement of the gambling itself.

During the *losing* phase, or the chase, the gambler's self-esteem is threatened because his or her gambling losses exceed winnings. The gambler borrows more, uses more credit, and bets more to make up for losses. The gambler spends more and more time gambling to repay debts. The gambler's family members and close friends may be hurt by the time and money he or she spends on gambling. The possibility of "winning big" encourages the gambler to stay in the action long after losing more than he or she can afford. In this phase the gambler often isolates from family and friends. Work frequently suffers because the gambler is preoccupied with getting money to gamble.

During the *desperation* phase, the gambler's betting is uncontrollable. The gambler often borrows or steals money to pay off debts but then gambles the money away and only digs a deeper hole for him- or herself. The gambler is now so obsessed with gambling that work is neglected and his or her job may be in jeopardy. The gambler may "borrow" (steal or embezzle) money from an employer with every intention of repaying it after the big win.

Desperation and panic become a reality when the gambler faces the fact that his or her credit resources have dried up. Irrational behavior escalates and the outcomes are devastating; losses are great and indebtedness increases. Physical and emotional symptoms at this stage include gastrointestinal distress, insomnia, hypersensitivity, irritability, and restlessness. Individuals and families are destroyed financially and emotionally. Depression is common; pathological gamblers have the highest rate of suicide among persons with addictive disorders.

One useful source of current information about gambling and related problems is *The WAGER (The Weekly Addiction Gambling Education Report),* published by the Division on Addictions at Harvard Medical School. Information about this publication is available on-line at http://www.wager.org.

Compulsive Shopping

The Problem

According to Dr. B. Kenneth Nelson, director of treatment for pathological gamblers and compulsive shoppers at the Valley Forge Hospital in Pennsylvania, 1-3% of the U.S. population, some 6-10 million people, are compulsive shoppers.

Individuals who shop compulsively may save carefully, then binge spend; they buy in bulk or use coupons whether they need the products or not. Compulsive shoppers are short on money at the end of each month; they max out their credit cards, yet react with surprise when the bills come in. They may file bills in the wastebasket. Some compulsive shoppers try to "buy" friends with gifts they cannot afford.

Many compulsive shoppers describe dysfunctional childhoods. Shopping to excess increases their feelings of self-worth and self-esteem, at least for a short time. Individuals who grew up in abject poverty and never seemed to have enough of anything often shop to excess and hoard. For such people, shopping may ease the pain of loneliness, disappointment, rejection, or loss.

Addictive Aspects

Compulsive shoppers experience a euphoria similar to a drug high or the action that gamblers seek. For example, Diana F., a self-admitted compulsive shopper, stated, "Once I buy something, I feel almost like I just had sex." Some compulsive shoppers describe going into a trancelike state when they enter a store, only to end up at the cash register with a cart full of items they are unaware they grabbed. Such individuals crave the instant gratification that alcohol and drug users experience. Compulsive shoppers deny and rationalize their shopping behavior. The *collector* claims, "I need it." The *underspender* boasts, "It was a bargain." The *hoarder* declares, "It's mine!"

Access increases behavior. Advertising encourages shoppers to buy now and pay later. Sales, special promotions, and the holidays invite shopping; television commercials, home shopping cable television networks, "infomercials," and the Internet entice shoppers. Unsolicited, preapproved credit cards encourage excessive buying: In 1996, outstanding consumer credit in the United States reached $1.18 trillion. Compulsive shoppers resent spending money on necessities; many of them refuse to pay income taxes. Some compulsive shoppers may also exhibit kleptomania.

Gender Differences

More women than men are compulsive shoppers, buying personal items such as makeup, jewelry, clothing, and household items. Ruth B., a 60-year-old assembly-line worker in Detroit, lives alone and has four freezers full of food in her basement. Her closets are full of shoes still in their boxes, and price tags hang from dresses she has never worn. In the United States, an inordinate number of young girls begin shoplifting and develop a passion for possessions at a very early age. Boys, in contrast, steal cars. When men shop compulsively, their purchases tend to be big-ticket items such as stereos, computers, or cars. Such men enjoy "throwing money around" and the image of themselves as "big spenders."

Sexual Addictions

Sex

Sex is a dynamic and creative part of living. It is one aspect of the psychic energy present in and manifested by persons across the life span. Sex is a natural need; it is an integral part of the healthy functioning of the whole person. Physical satisfaction in sexual behavior is intimately related to psychological gratification: the need for security, feelings of personal worth, feelings of empowerment, as well as the assurance of being loved and lovable. A spontaneous and affectionate sex life contributes to the well-being of self and others.

Sexual Addiction

Sexual addiction is manifested in obsessive/compulsive sexual behavior that causes severe stress for the individual and may victimize others. The sexual behaviors of persons with a sexual addiction may violate social standards and result in extreme legal consequences. Sexual addiction is similar to alcohol and other drug dependencies in that the sexual behavior controls the individual and his or her life becomes unmanageable.

Many sexual addicts have been or currently are victims of emotional, physical, or sexual abuse. Sexual addicts usually have few or no nonsexual relationships. Many sexual addicts may equate sexualizing with nurturing. Codependent personality characteristics are common in these individuals. Sexual addicts usually keep "secrets" and may lead "double lives." Concomitant substance abuse is common. Patrick J. Carnes, clinical director of sexual disorders services at the Meadows in Wickenburg, Arizona, reports that most of his patients are corporate executive officers, physicians, attorneys, or priests—that is, they are people with a great deal of power. Carnes (1992) estimates that 6% of the U.S. population is afflicted with sexual addiction. Other experts estimate that more than 20% of the U.S. adult male population suffers to some degree from sexual addiction. Women sex addicts' problems are even less understood than men's (see Morris, 1999).

Obsessions with sexual behaviors and fantasies become the sex-addicted individual's primary coping strategy. Similar to the heroin addict's obsession with getting and using heroin, sexual behavior is the central organizing principle of daily life for the sex addict. Inordinate amounts of time are devoted to sexual experiences: planning and performing them, and then more planning and performing. The amount, extent, and duration of sexual behavior exceed what the person intended. Severe mood shifts accompany sexual acting out. Tolerance develops—that is, the previous level of sexual activity is no longer satisfying and the individual must initiate and pursue new and riskier sexual behavior, possibly behavior that is illicit, immoral, and violent. The individual may desire and try to limit his or her sexual behavior but is unable to stop despite adverse consequences.

Sexual addicts may demonstrate compulsive sexual behavior for a period of years as well as a pattern of alternating excessive control and out-of-control behavior over longer periods of time. Shame and excessive denial characterize coping by sexual addicts. Depression with suicide ideation and history of attempted suicide is common.

Cycles

Carnes, a recognized leader in the diagnosis and treatment of sexual addictions and author of *Out of the Shadows: Understanding Sexual Addiction* (1992), has pioneered the recognition and treatment of sexual addiction. He describes a four-step cycle of sexual addiction that intensifies with each repetition:

1. *Preoccupation:* the trance or mood wherein the person's mind is completely engrossed with thoughts of sex. This mental state creates an obsessive search for sexual stimulation.

2. *Ritualization:* the individual's own special routines that lead up to the sexual behavior. The ritual intensifies the preoccupation, adding arousal and excitement.

3. *Compulsive sexual behavior:* the actual sexual activity, which is the end goal of the preoccupation and ritualization. Sexual addicts are unable to control or stop this behavior.

4. *Despair:* the feeling of utter hopelessness sexual addicts have about their behavior and powerlessness. (Carnes, 1992, p. 9)

The SAFE Formula

Carnes has developed the "SAFE Formula" to help determine when sexual behavior is addictive. According to Carnes (1992, pp. 158-159), sexual behavior is addictive when (a) it is a *secret* (sexual behavior that cannot pass public scrutiny or will create the sense of a double life), (b) it is *abusive* to self or others (sexual behavior that exploits or harms others or degrades oneself), (c) it is used to avoid or is a source of painful *feelings* (sexual behavior that alters moods or results in painful mood shifts), and (d) it is *empty* of a caring, committed relationship. Fundamental to the whole concept of addiction and recovery is the healthy dimension of human relationships. The addict runs a great risk of being sexually active outside of a committed relationship.

Levels of Sexual Addiction

Carnes (1992) identifies three levels of sexual addiction. Level I sexual behaviors are generally tolerated by society yet can be devastating when repeated compulsively; these include masturbation, heterosexual relationships, homosexual behaviors, pornography, cybersex, phone sex, and prostitution. Note that millions of people visit sexually oriented adult Web sites, post messages on sex-related bulletin boards, and engage in sex talk that can be benign, titillating, or exploitative. Level II sexual behaviors are socially intrusive and warrant legal sanctions; someone is victimized by such behaviors. These include exhibitionism, voyeurism, indecent phone calls, and indecent liberties. Level III sexual behaviors represent profound violations of cultural mores and have serious legal consequences: molestation, incest, rape, and violent sex with children.

Consequences

The consequences of sexual addiction include the addict's progressive retreat from the reality of friends, family, and work. Overwhelming denial, shame, and depression dominate the sexual addict's being. Suicide ideation and attempted suicide are frequent. Sexual addicts are at risk for substance-related disorders and many other physical, psychological, and social problems, including sexually transmitted diseases (STDs), unwanted pregnancy, HIV/AIDS, broken relationships, social scorn, lost jobs and financial ruin, and arrest and incarceration.

Consequences for the victims of sexual abuse are legion; they include substance abuse, STDs, and unwanted pregnancy. Sexual intimacy is difficult, and attempted suicide is common. Posttraumatic stress disorder and other mental and physical health problems may plague victims all their lives.

Treatment

Dr. Martin Kafka, a recognized expert in the treatment of sexual addiction, suggests a comprehensive treatment program that includes 12-step programs such as Sex and Love Addicts Anonymous, individual and group psychotherapy, and medications. Cognitive-behavioral therapy has been found to be effective. With many clients, selective serotonin reuptake inhibitors such as fluoxetine (Prozac) and sertraline (Zoloft) lower impulsivity and the high sex drive that gets many addicts into trouble. Depression often coexists with sexual addiction (see Kasdon-Sidell, 1998).

Addictive Love

Healthy Love

Healthy love is a demonstrated concern of one person for another that transcends the self. It is a human capacity for commitment to values and persons over and above immediate self-centered interests. Love is a humanizing virtue. It is central to many religious beliefs and practices. Love is a basic human need. As lover and beloved, a person needs to love, to cherish, and to aid others; all persons need to be loved, cherished, and aided by others.

Addictive Love

In her book *Is It Love or Is It Addiction?* (1997), Brenda Schaeffer contrasts the characteristics of addictive love with those of healthy love (see Table 4.1). Frequently, addictive love coexists with substance-related and other addictive disorders.

Eating Disorders

Eve T. developed bulimia nervosa at age 18. She had dieted and exercised to control her weight for several years. Now she eats huge amounts of food on a regular basis and maintains her normal weight by forcing herself to vomit. She is angry, frightened, and depressed; she isolates herself and feels lonely. She overcomes these negative feelings by satisfying an uncontrollable desire for sweets. Eve eats pounds of candy and an entire cake at one sitting, stopping her eating only when she is exhausted or in severe pain. Overwhelmed with disgust, she then makes herself vomit. Eve kept these eating habits secret until she became so depressed that she attempted suicide. While recuperating in the hospital, she was referred to an eating disorders clinic.

Food is essential for life because it supplies energy and needed nutrients for health and well-being. Eating is usually a self-regulatory activity. Attitudes toward food and eating are strongly influenced by family expectations, ethnic practices, and cultural traditions. Eating, however, can also assume importance and meaning beyond that of nutrition. Eating can become associated with complex pathological biopsychosocial processes.

TABLE 4.1 Comparison of Characteristics of Addictive and Healthy Love

Addictive Love	Healthy Love
Feels all-consuming	Allows for individuality
Cannot define ego boundaries	Experiences and enjoys both oneness with and separation from partner
Has elements of sadomasochism	Brings out best qualities in both partners
Fears letting go	Accepts endings
Fears risk, change, and the unknown	Experiences openness to change and exploration
Allows little individual growth	Invites growth in both partners
Lacks true intimacy	Experiences true intimacy
Plays psychological games	Feels freedom to ask honestly for what is wanted
Gives to get something back	Experiences giving and receiving in the same way
Attempts to change partner	Does not attempt to change or control partner
Needs the other to feel complete	Encourages self-sufficiency of partner
Seeks solutions outside the self	Accepts limitations of self and partner
Demands and expects unconditional love	Does not insist on unconditional love
Refuses commitment (antidependency)	Has the ability to make commitment
Looks only to partner for affirmation and worth	Has high self-esteem and sense of well-being
Fears abandonment upon routine separation	Trusts memory of beloved; enjoys solitude
Re-creates old negative feelings	Expresses feelings spontaneously
Desires yet fears closeness	Welcomes closeness; risks vulnerability
Attempts to "take care" of partner's feelings	Cares, but can remain detached
Plays power games (one-upmanship)	Affirms equality and personal power of self and partner

SOURCE: Adapted from *Is It Love or Is It Addiction?* by Brenda Schaeffer. Copyright 1987, 1997 by Brenda Schaeffer. Used by permission of the Hazelden Foundation, Center City, Minnesota.

Eating disorders in adults and adolescents include compulsive overeating, binge-eating disorders, bulimia nervosa, and anorexia nervosa. Persons with eating disorders manifest many addictive behaviors; eating disorders often co-exist with substance-related and other addictive disorders. Many women with eating disorders reveal histories of sexual abuse.

Each year, millions of people in the United States develop serious and some-times life-threatening eating disorders. Compulsive overeating resulting in obe-sity is the most prevalent in people between the ages of 20 and 50. Approxi-mately 2-3% of young women develop bulimia nervosa; an estimated 1% of adolescent girls develop anorexia nervosa. According to the American Acad-emy of Child and Adolescent Psychiatry, anorexia nervosa and bulimia are on the increase among teenage girls and young women. Data suggest that from 1 in 4 to 1 in 10 college women has an eating disorder. It is estimated that 1 in 10 cases leads to death from starvation, cardiac arrest, or suicide. Eating disorders also occur in younger children and in older women.

Men also have eating disorders. Men may diet, fast, or exercise excessively because they have been teased, criticized, or bullied for being overweight. They diet and exercise to eliminate "flab" and accentuate their "abs," or to make a re-quired weight for a specific sport or class, such as crew or wrestling. Men may diet to be more attractive for their partners, to look less like their fathers, or to re-semble the male models they see in the print and broadcast media. Dieting and fasting may be associated with vegetarianism.

Compulsive Overeating

Obesity is defined as weight that exceeds recommended body weight by 20%, as measured by standard height and weight tables. Obesity may be caused by poor eating habits, compulsive overeating (addictive behavior), genetic factors, or a combination of these. Stress, depression, and a sedentary lifestyle contribute to obesity in many people. Overweight people eat more than their bodies require and expend fewer calories in exercise and activity than they take in. In our soci-ety, the health hazards of being moderately overweight are greatly exaggerated, yet the social stigma of being overweight is significant.

In the October 27, 1999, issue of the *Journal of the American Medical Associ-ation,* which addressed obesity, it was reported that more than half of all Ameri-can adults—about 63% of men and 55% of women age 25 and older—are over-weight. The rate of obesity has increased from 12% to 18% in 7 years, making the United States the fattest nation in the developed world ("Obesity Research," 1999).

Thin is in. In the 1970s, we idolized the "waif look"; in the 1990s, the "emaci-ated heroin-addict look" became chic. Many college campuses participate in a yearly awareness campaign during "Eating Disorders Month" in February, but concerned health professionals agree that most programs to prevent eating disorders begin too late. In a recent survey, 80% of 11-year-old girls interviewed said that they felt overweight and were dieting. In the United States, the diet industry is big business. Recently, many weight loss centers have added physicians to their staffs to prescribe diet drugs as part of weight-loss regimens.

Obesity can be mild, moderate, or severe as related to individual height, weight, and proportion of body fat. People with mild to moderate obesity often report histories of being able to eat without weight gain for many years. At some point, however, they found themselves exercising less, eating more, and sometimes binge eating, and they began to notice a steady rise in body weight and fat. Most people can lose weight safely and stop binge eating if they make the commitment to change their behavior patterns in relation to food and exercise. Many times, they need to resolve related problems, such as acute stress, situational depression, or unresolved grief. People with weight problems should consult their physicians before changing their diets radically.

Body weight of more than 40% over recommended weight poses serious health problems. People who are severely obese usually have been overweight all their lives. Obese people usually eat quickly and without pleasure; they take large bites of food and gulp liquids. They often hoard food, eat at night, and binge.

Medical conditions associated with obesity include high blood pressure, elevated cholesterol levels, and shortness of breath after mild exertion. Many overweight people have accepted their weight, their eating patterns, and associated problems. Other overweight individuals may experience shame and guilt, demonstrate anxiety, or express anger, especially when confronted by others about their eating. They may minimize, deny, or lie about their eating. Distorted body image with negative feelings of low-esteem, anxiety, and depression may lead to isolation and social withdrawal. Because of excess weight and disgust with their body image, obese people often markedly limit their social activities. Many report dieting constantly but to no avail. They try every fad diet and further compromise their medical and psychological problems. Some 95% of diets are unsuccessful.

In the 1980s, clinical investigators discovered a link between eating disorders and serotonin. During clinical trials of fluoxetine (Prozac), weight loss was one side effect. Researchers theorized that when dietary starch is converted to sugar, the sugar stimulates the pancreas to release insulin, and insulin raises brain levels of the amino acid tryptophan (a precursor of serotonin); the serotonin, which regulates mood, produces a sense of well-being. This theory in part explains why people feel good after eating carbohydrates; obese people load up on carbohydrates to elevate mood. Sibutramine (Meridia) is weight-loss drug that acts on brain chemicals to suppress appetite. Orlistat (Xenical), a widely marketed drug, inhibits the absorption of dietary fats. Both medications are being used for weight loss and weight maintenance in conjunction with reduced-calorie diet and exercise.

Binge-Eating Disorder

Binge-eating disorder is characterized by the eating of a larger amount of food than most people would eat in a discrete period of time or under similar circumstances and a sense of lack of control over the eating. During binge-eating episodes, the binge eater may (a) eat much more rapidly than normal, (b) eat until feeling uncomfortably full, (c) eat large amounts of food when not feeling physically hungry, (d) eat alone because of embarrassment about how much he or she is eating, and (e) feel disgust, guilt, or depression afterward.

Binge eating is usually defined as a disorder when it occurs at least twice a week over 6 months. Binge-eating disorder is not associated with the regular use of inappropriate compensatory behaviors, such as purging, fasting, or excessive exercise; it is not part of the course of anorexia nervosa or bulimia nervosa (which is discussed below).

Binge eating usually begins in adolescence or young adulthood, and it is more common in women than in men. Specific triggers, such as stress, anxiety, or depression, may precipitate binge eating, but often individuals report a nonspecific feeling of tension that is relieved by binge eating. Some individuals experience a dissociative state during binge episodes.

Binge eaters may or may not have weight problems. Approximately 15-30% of people in weight-control programs meet the criteria for binge eating. Most individuals who binge eat do not like themselves. They experience self-loathing and express disgust with their body size and shape. Binge eating may interfere with personal relationships, work, and social activities. Chronic binge eating is associated with many somatic concerns and heightened interpersonal sensitivity as well as major depressive disorders, substance-related disorders, and personality disorders.

Bulimia Nervosa

According to the National Institute of Mental Health, 2-3% of young women develop bulimia nervosa, "a destructive pattern of excessive overeating followed by vomiting or other purging behaviors to control their weight." Bulimia nervosa is characterized by recurrent episodes of binge eating followed by inappropriate compensatory purging or nonpurging behaviors to prevent weight gain. Purging includes regular misuse of laxatives, diuretics, enemas, and other medications; nonpurging behaviors include fasting and excessive exercise. Individuals with bulimia can be overweight, underweight, or within normal weight range for their height and body frame. However, they are all obsessed with body shape and weight; they usually have histories of dieting and weight fluctuations. Teenagers with bulimia are often very good at hiding signs of the disorder; they may spend inordinate amounts of time in the bathroom, where running water hides the sound of throwing up. They binge and purge in secret and maintain normal or above-normal body weight successfully for years.

Criteria for a diagnosis of bulimia nervosa include the presence of binge eating and purging/nonpurging behaviors at least twice a week for 3 months, on average. Individuals with this disorder demonstrate extreme fear of gaining even a small amount of weight. They have a distorted body image and see themselves as "fatter" than they are. Other signs and symptoms of bulimia include dry skin and very brittle hair; swollen glands under the jaw from vomiting, which creates "chipmunk cheeks"; and fatigue and cold sweats from rapid changes in sugar levels. Mood swings with feelings of fear, guilt, anger, and depression are common. Binge eating and purging damage the digestive system, and mild starvation causes serious health risks, including laxative dependence, throat damage, dental problems, stomach rupture, hormonal imbalance with irregular menstruation, dehydration with electrolyte imbalance, irregular heart rate, kidney damage, and heart failure.

Anorexia Nervosa

According to the National Institute of Mental Health, approximately 1% of adolescent girls develop anorexia, "a dangerous condition in which they can literally starve themselves to death." An intense fear of gaining weight or becoming fat, even though underweight, characterizes individuals with anorexia nervosa. Persons with this disorder refuse to maintain body weight at or above a minimally normal weight for age and height, demonstrating body weight less than 85% of that expected. They dangerously distort their actual weight or body shape and deny the seriousness of their low body weight. Amenorrhea is common in women with anorexia nervosa. This disorder may be of the *binge-eating/purging* type or the *restricting* type, with no regular binge-eating or purging behaviors.

The typical anorexic is a teenage girl who is bright, capable, and a high-achieving perfectionist. At the same time, she suffers from low self-esteem, irrationally believing that she is fat regardless of how thin she becomes. She desperately needs a feeling of mastery over her life, and she experiences a sense of control only when she says no to the normal food demands of her body. In her relentless pursuit of thinness she starves herself, causing serious damage to her body and possible death.

In addition to fear of gaining any weight and distorted body image, other symptoms of anorexia include dry, cold skin with downy hair (lanugo) on arms, legs, back, face, or chest; insomnia and hyperactivity; extreme, excessive, and rigid exercise routines; and strict rules for eating, such as no liquids, no eating without exercise first, or eating at midnight. Physical and social development may be delayed. (It should be noted that exercise/sports addiction may become a problem in and of itself, with or without a related eating disorder.)

Health risks for individuals with anorexia nervosa are very serious. These include digestive problems, electrolyte imbalance, low protein stores (protein from muscles and organs is used to fuel body needs), heart failure, kidney failure, and suicide.

Other Addictive Behaviors

Addictive behaviors mimic substance abuse or substance dependence criteria. A recent article in *Runner's World* tells the story of David Hobler, who once sipped booze while driving to work the way some commuters drink coffee. After 25 years of heavy drinking, Hobler entered treatment. Although he had run for exercise while drinking, running now grounded his sobriety. Hobler founded Runners in Recovery and now teaches aerobic exercise—especially running—to recovering alcoholics (Brant, 1999). Even fitness, however, can become an obsession; Kaminker (1999) calls this behavior "exercise addiction."

According to Killinger (1997), workaholics are "respectable addicts." Jerome (1999) questions whether or not on-line trading is a form of gambling. And, according to a 1999 story in *Time* magazine, Maressa Hecht Orzack, founder of the Computer Addiction Service at McLean Hospital in Belmont, Massachusetts, is wary of the risk for addictive behavior that the recent Pokémon craze has posed for children (McLaughlin, 1999). Excessive use of credit cards and Internet addiction are discussed below.

"The Plastic"

As noted earlier, consumer credit is currently at an all-time high in the United States, due in large part to excessive use of credit cards. High school seniors report receiving unsolicited, preapproved credit cards. Individuals who hold credit cards are constantly encouraged to upgrade to "gold" or "platinum" privileges. People use their plastic to buy almost any goods and services. Credit card addicts use several cards at one time, obtain cash advances with their cards, and pay only the minimum amounts due each month, thus incurring exorbitant interest charges over time. Compared with the public as a whole, credit card abuse is significantly higher among people with gambling and compulsive shopping problems and among people who abuse alcohol and other drugs. Credit card debt has contributed to the rise in personal bankruptcies in the United States, which went from 341,189 in 1985 to a record 1,350,118 in 1997.

The Internet

In the late 1990s, clinicians began to see clients who had developed "Internet addiction." At the 1999 annual meeting of the American Psychological Association, David Greenfield reported his estimate that 6% of Internet users suffer from some form of addiction to being on-line (see Donn, 1999). Marriages are disrupted by this form of addiction; kids get into trouble and adults spend too much money. Sometimes, Internet addicts commit illegal acts. Research with college students has placed the estimate for Internet addiction in this population at 10% (see Donn, 1999; Yang, 2000). As with other chemical and nonchemical addictive disorders, Internet addicts describe behaviors that meet "abuse" or "dependence" criteria, such as the following:

- Failure to fulfill major role obligations at work, school, or home
- Longer use with less enjoyment
- Restlessness, irritability, and anxiety when not using
- Extended use with unsuccessful attempts to cut down, control, or stop use
- Continued use despite knowledge of physical, psychological, and social problems associated with excessive use

Bob K., a sophomore college student, got a new computer for his birthday and discovered the Internet. He has virtually stopped attending classes and "surfs the Net 'round the clock," barely stopping to eat or shower. He has tried to cut back but acknowledges that he is "hooked." His roommates leave him alone because he has "turned ugly"; his girlfriend has stopped calling. Bob is failing all his classes.

Fortunately, addiction clinicians are responding with treatment for such newly emerging addictive behaviors as Internet addiction. Hilarie Cash and Jay Parker, cofounders of Internet/Computer Addiction Services in Redmond, Washington, are testing the efficacy of three treatment modalities: cognitive-behavioral therapy, a 12-step addiction treatment program, and expressive arts therapy (Yang, 2000). Dr. Kimberly S. Young offers a self-help guide to "online-aholics" in her book *Caught in the Net* (1998). Whenever a substance or behavior meets abuse or dependence criteria, addiction treatment is needed.

Summary

Addiction includes both chemical and nonchemical addictive disorders. Increasingly, addiction practice addresses pathological gambling, compulsive shopping, sex and love addiction, eating disorders, and other addictive behaviors. Nonchemical addictive disorders resemble substance-related disorders in etiology, expression, and response to treatment. Cross-addiction between substance-related disorders and other addictive disorders is common.

Related Skills Checklist

Practitioner skills related to the forms of addiction discussed in this chapter include the ability to do the following:

- Identify the addictive properties of pathological gambling, compulsive shopping, sex and love addictions, eating disorders, and other addictive disorders.

- Utilize addiction concepts to help explain nonchemical addictions.

- Employ addiction treatment concepts whenever appropriate with pathological gambling, compulsive shopping, sex and love addictions, eating disorders, and other addictive behaviors.

Special Topics for Further Study

Why is there such widespread public acceptance of legal and illegal gambling? What is the relationship between aggressive advertising and compulsive shopping? Could early intervention with Level I sexual behaviors prevent progression? What are the relationships among childhood trauma, eating disorders, and substance abuse? What are some new and emerging addictive disorders in the new millennium?

Addiction Practice 2000

Addiction practice 2000 requires practitioners to broaden their practice to include nonchemical addictive disorders such as pathological gambling, compulsive shopping, sex and love addictions, eating disorders, and other addictive behaviors. Clients need primary, secondary, and tertiary prevention programs. Addiction practitioners must educate their colleagues about nonchemical addictions.

References

Brant, J. (1999, November). Recovery time. *Runner's World,* pp. 72-76.

Carnes, P. J. (1992). *Out of the shadows: Understanding sexual addiction* (2nd ed.). Center City, MN: Hazelden.

Donn, J. (1999, August 23). Internet reported addictive to some: Psychologist says 6 percent of users are hooked. *Boston Globe,* p. 3.

Federal commission's report raises awareness of nation's gambling behavior. (1999, Summer). *Compulsive Gambling Newsletter, 11,* 1, 3.

James, K. C. (1999, June 18). *National Gambling Impact Study Commission report.* Photocopy.

Jerome, M. (1999, August 22). On-line trading, or gambling? *Boston Globe,* p. C13.

Kaminker, L. (1999). *Exercise addiction: When fitness becomes an obsession.* Center City, MN: Hazelden.

Kasdon-Sidell, L. (1998, February 19). Sex is not enough. *Boston Globe,* pp. C1, C8.

Killinger, B. (1997). *Workaholics: The respectable addicts.* Buffalo, NY: Firefly.

McLaughlin, L. (1999, November 22). Should children play with monsters? *Time, 154.*

Morris, B. (1999, May 10). Addicted to sex. *Fortune,* pp. 68-80.

Obesity research [Theme issue]. (1999, October 27). *Journal of the American Medical Association, 282.*

Schaeffer, B. (1997). *Is it love or is it addiction?* Center City, MN: Hazelden.

Yang, D. J. (2000, January 17). Craving your next Web fix: Internet addiction is no laughing matter. *U.S. News & World Report,* p. 41.

Young, K. S. (1998). *Caught in the Net: How to recognize the signs of Internet addiction—and a winning strategy for recovery.* New York: John Wiley.

Other Sources

American Psychiatric Association. (1993). Practice guidelines for eating disorders. *American Journal of Psychiatry, 150,* 212-223.

Baszczynski, A., & Silove, D. (1995). Cognitive and behavior therapies for pathological gambling. *Journal of Gambling Studies, 11,* 195-220.

Berman, L., & Siegel, M.-E. (1998). *Behind the 8-ball: A guide for families of gamblers.* San Jose, CA: toExcel.

Brustuen, S., & Gabriel, G. (n.d.). *Pathological gambling and chemical dependency: Similarities and unique characteristics.* Granite Falls, MN: Vanguard.

Coleman, S., & Hull-Mast, N. (1995). *Can't buy me love: Freedom from compulsive spending and money obsessions.* Minneapolis: Fairview.

Custer, R., & Milt, H. (1985). *When luck runs out: Help for compulsive gamblers and their families.* New York: Warner.

Dostoyevsky, F. (1981). *The gambler.* New York: W. W. Norton. (Original work published 1866)

Galaski, T. (Ed.). (1987). *The handbook of pathological gambling.* Springfield, IL: Charles C Thomas.

Heineman, M. (1993). *When someone you love gambles.* Center City, MN: Hazelden.

Jantz, G. L. (1998). *Hidden dangers of the Internet: Using it without abusing it.* Wheaton, IL: H. Shaw.

Katherine, A. (1997). *Anatomy of a food addiction: The brain chemistry of overeating: An effective program to overcome compulsive eating* (3rd ed.). Carlsbad, CA: Gürze.

Kaye, Y. (1991). *Credit, cash and co-dependency.* Dearfield Beach, FL: Health Communications.

Kinoy, B. P. (1999). *Eating disorders: New directions in treatment and recovery.* New York: Columbia University Press.

Lesieur, H. R. (1984). *The chase: Career of the compulsive gambler.* Cambridge, MA: Schenkman.

Lesieur, H. R. (1993). *Understanding compulsive gambling.* Center City, MN: Hazelden.

National Association of Anorexia Nervosa and Associated Disorders. (1996). Anorexia nervosa and bulimia nervosa: When the pursuit of bodily "perfection" becomes a killer. *Postgraduate Medicine, 99,* 161-164, 167-169.

National Council on Problem Gaming. (n.d.) *Psychiatric illnesses suffered by compulsive gamblers; suicide among pathological gamblers; and compulsive gambling and family violence* (Fact sheet). New York: Author.

Pathological gambling. (1996). *Harvard Mental Health Letter, 12,* 1-5.

Schaumburg, H. W. (1997). *False intimacy: Understanding the struggle of sexual addiction.* Colorado Springs: Navpress.

Shaffer, H. J., Stein, S., Gambino, B., & Cummings, T. N. (1989). *Compulsive gambling: Theory, research, and practice.* Lexington, MA: Lexington.

Tannewald, R. (Ed.). (1995). *Casino development.* Boston: Federal Reserve Bank of Boston.

The WAGER: The weekly addiction gambling education report (Vol. 1). (1996). Boston: Harvard Medical School, Division on Addictions.

The WAGER: The weekly addiction gambling education report (Vol. 2). (1997). Boston: Harvard Medical School, Division on Addictions.

The WAGER: The weekly addiction gambling education report (Vol. 3). (1998). Boston: Harvard Medical School, Division on Addictions.

Young, K. S. (1998). *Caught in the Net: How to recognize the signs of Internet addiction—and a winning strategy for recovery.* New York: John Wiley.

5

Addiction Practitioners

Objectives

- Understand that a multidisciplinary group of professionals, paraprofessionals, and volunteers works in the addiction field.
- Recognize that nurses, physicians, counselors, social workers, psychologists, clergy, and educators provide addiction treatment.
- Recognize the roles in addiction practice of other contributing professionals, such as public health officials and college and university faculty.
- Acknowledge the special contribution of individuals in recovery from addiction to addiction practice.
- Become familiar with the professional associations for addiction practitioners.

Outline

- **Addiction Practitioners**
  - Nurses
  - Physicians
  - Counselors
  - Social Workers
  - Psychologists
  - Clergy
  - Educators
- **Other Contributors to Addiction Practice**
  - Health Care Administrators
  - Government Officials

Addiction Practitioners

The professionals, paraprofessionals, and volunteers who work in the addiction field make up a multidisciplinary group. Addiction practitioners need a working knowledge of various disciplines, their similarities and differences, and their respective roles and responsibilities. Addiction treatment is provided by nurses, physicians, counselors, social workers, psychologists, clergy, and educators. Addiction programs are guided and managed by health care administrators, and the policies of such programs are developed and implemented by public health officials. At colleges and universities, many faculty members teach about and conduct research on addiction as well as help to develop addiction policy. In addition, people in recovery often work in addiction treatment. Many volunteers augment the work of professionals in addiction treatment programs; their contribution to the recovery environment is significant.

Addiction practitioners exhibit their expertise and excellence through credentialing, and practitioners need a thorough understanding of this process. In the United States, *licensure* of practitioners is currently a function of individual states, whereas *certification* is typically granted by professional organizations. Professional associations set standards of care to guide addiction practice, such as the influential patient placement criteria developed by the American Society of Addiction Medicine (1991, 1996 [*ASAM PPC-2*]) and the standards of addictions-related nursing practice developed by the American Nurses Association and the National Nurses Society on Addictions (1988). Addiction practitioners subscribe to the codes of ethics advanced by their respective professional associations, such as that developed by the National Association of Alcoholism and Drug Abuse Counselors (1995); see especially *Addiction Counseling Competencies: The Knowledge, Skills, and Attitudes of Professional Practice* (1998), published by the Substance Abuse and Mental Health Services Administration (SAMHSA).

Nurses

Nurses play a major role in the care of substance abuse clients during withdrawal. As key members of treatment teams providing medically managed intensive inpatient services, nurses are prepared and licensed to administer medications. Additionally, they often coordinate care for clients at the residential/ inpatient and partial hospitalization levels of care. In these settings, nurses provide support, education, and counseling to individuals and groups of clients. Nurses also help addiction clients access other necessary health care services. Often nurses serve as client case managers.

Nurses who work in community settings, especially in schools and colleges and in occupational health care, play a critical role in developing and implementing prevention and early intervention programs. Children and employees often seek out school and company nurses for help with problems related to their own alcohol and drug abuse, other addictive disorders, or those of family members. Nurses with advanced practice preparation, most often as nurse practitioners or clinical specialists, provide counseling and medical management to clients in outpatient settings. Nurses are in a unique position to identify coexisting addictive disorders in clients receiving care in clinical settings such as emergency rooms, trauma centers, ambulatory care centers, physicians' offices, medical-surgical hospital units, psychiatric facilities, and home care—wherever nursing is provided.

In the United States, nurses educated in baccalaureate, diploma, or associate degree nursing programs are eligible to write a national examination offered by each state to become registered nurses. Graduates of practical/vocational programs, usually 9-12 months in length, are eligible to write an exam to become licensed practical/vocational nurses. Advanced-practice nurses usually complete a master's degree program. Each state, as well as the American Nurses Association, has guidelines for credentialing nurses prepared for advanced practice. Today, many nurses pursue doctoral degrees in nursing or related areas. The National Nurses Society on Addiction advances addiction nursing practice.

Physicians

Physicians manage withdrawal in substance abuse clients at all levels of care. For example, medical protocols guide the treatment of withdrawal in outpatient services (Level I, *ASAM PPC-2*), and daily physician contact is required for clients who meet criteria for detoxification in a medically managed intensive inpatient setting (Level IV, *ASAM PPC-2*). In addition, clients with serious coexisting medical and/or psychological conditions or complications require physician management. Depending on their needs and the provider services available, these clients may be admitted to inpatient addiction treatment units; medical, surgical, or psychiatric units; or intensive or critical care units.

Physicians review and monitor clients' addiction severity and coexisting problems, treatment plans, progress, and complications. They also review discharge plans for clients meeting the criteria for admission to residential/inpatient services (Level III, *ASAM PPC-2*). Nonmedical staff, including counselors, social workers, and paraprofessionals, provide most treatment for clients who meet the criteria for intensive outpatient/partial hospitalization services (Level II, *ASAM PPC-2*) or outpatient services (Level I, *ASAM PPC-2*). At these levels of care, clients usually complete medical self-reports for review by physicians, who then flag any actual and/or potential problems that require medical assessment or intervention. Treatment staff follow established medical protocols for referral of clients to physicians when needed.

Physicians who specialize in addiction treatment seek credentialing through the American Society of Addiction Medicine or the American Psychiatric Association. The Association for Medical Education and Research in Substance Abuse supports addiction education and research for physicians. In May 1998, the American Medical Association hosted the 11th Alcohol Policy Conference, titled "Common Goals, Common Challenges: Creating Alcohol-Safe Communities Through Alcohol Policies"; at this 4-day forum, individuals from public health, research, medicine, education, government, and community activism came together to support the reduction of alcohol-related problems in the United States.

Counselors

Counselors work with clients and their families throughout the treatment process. Traditionally, counselors in addiction practice have been individuals in recovery from their own addictions who have been employed to support the work of physicians and nurses in inpatient settings. Today, counselors include individuals trained in addiction at a paraprofessional level, but more often they are baccalaureate- and master's-prepared professionals with education, certification, and/or licensure in substance abuse, chemical dependency, and/or addictions.

Counselors provide counseling for individuals, groups, and families at all levels of care. Counselors facilitate education groups, address relapse prevention, and plan aftercare with clients and families. In inpatient settings, counselors are part of multidisciplinary treatment teams. In outpatient settings, counselors may fulfill multiple treatment roles, as counselors, educators, advocates, and case managers. Counselors with preparation and experience in the area of mental health disorders are key members of treatment teams for clients with dual disorders; they may work in inpatient and outpatient psychiatric mental health settings.

Several states license substance abuse/chemical dependency counselors. More often, counselors seek to become certified alcohol and drug abuse counselors (CADACs). To receive such certification, counselors must have extensive knowledge about substance abuse, counseling techniques, and substance abuse ethics; it is also recommended that they learn about HIV/AIDS and counseling multicultural clients. Certified alcohol and drug abuse counselors are expected to demonstrate competence in five performance domains: assessment, counseling, case management, education, and professional responsibilities. A CADAC must document supervised experience in the "12 core functions of the substance abuse counselor" (Herdman, 1994): screening, intake, orientation, assessment, treatment planning, counseling, case management, crisis intervention, client education, referral, reporting, and record keeping. Through a written examination and case presentation, candidates for certification confirm their familiarity with the 46 global criteria identified by the International Certification Reciprocity Consortium. The certification is recognized in most states as well as in Canada and several other countries.

Major professional membership associations for counselors include the American Counseling Association, the American Mental Health Counselors Association, and the National Association of Alcoholism and Drug Abuse Counselors.

Social Workers

Social workers function in multiple roles and in many different addiction treatment and prevention settings. Social workers help clients and their families understand and address addiction problems. Social workers assist clients with myriad economic, housing, occupational, and educational problems. They often interface with community agencies on behalf of clients and their families. Social workers serve as case managers.

Social workers frequently direct and staff outpatient services for addiction clients. Here they provide counseling, education, and support to individuals, groups, and families. Historically, social workers have played a leading role in the development of employee assistance programs (EAPs) and drug-free work sites. They assess and refer individuals and family members in need of active treatment and then facilitate support and reintegration when employees return to work. Social workers develop work-site prevention and intervention programs such as family alcohol and drug awareness and smoking cessation programs.

Social workers have a minimum of a baccalaureate degree in social work. Most social workers are prepared at the master's level and seek licensure as licensed clinical social workers or licensed independent clinical social workers.

Social workers engaged in addiction practice often pursue certification in substance abuse/chemical dependency/addiction. The National Association of Social Workers is the major professional association for social workers.

Psychologists

Psychologists in addiction practice provide counseling for individuals, groups, and families. They may be integral parts of treatment teams, especially for children and teen clients, dual-disorder clients, forensic clients, and older clients. Psychological testing and assessment provide invaluable data for diagnosis, treatment, and planning, especially realistic goal setting and plans for long-term rehabilitation. Psychological testing may include objective and projective assessment of psychopathology, neuropsychological assessment, and testing of cognitive functioning and intellectual capacity. Psychologists working in vocational rehabilitation settings use a variety of testing and assessment tools to help clients explore educational and career opportunities. Psychologists often direct treatment programs.

Psychologists have graduate degrees at the master's or doctoral level; they are licensed by state authorities. In addition, psychologists may demonstrate specialization in substance abuse through a certification process developed by the American Psychological Association.

Clergy

Individuals and families with problems often seek help from clergy. Many priests, ministers, and rabbis are formally prepared as pastoral counselors, and their counseling caseloads include many people with addiction problems. Churches and other houses of worship sponsor many youth and family programs to address addiction in their neighborhoods. As Vivian L. Smith, M.S.W., acting director of the Center for Substance Abuse Prevention, has written:

> Faith and religion play an enormous role in the lives of many individuals. This reality gives leaders of faith communities a unique and wonderful opportunity to reach and help many people in their congregations and neighborhoods. One of the most crucial concerns affecting Americans today, unfortunately, is alcohol, tobacco, and other drug (ATOD) problems. (in Green, 1997, p. 1)

Clergy may be integral members of treatment teams that employ a 12-step approach to treatment or follow the Minnesota treatment model (see Chapter 6). In that capacity, they provide individual and group counseling for clients and families. They may help clients to take the fifth step in a 12-step program, of admitting "to God, to ourselves, and to another human being the exact nature of our wrongs."

The American Association of Pastoral Counselors supports individuals engaged in pastoral counseling. The Health Ministries Association represents people of faith working together for healthier communities. The American Association of Christian Counselors integrates biblical truth with practical counseling principles and helps members to pursue excellence in their counseling practice.

Educators

Classroom educators as well as health educators in community settings play key roles in addiction education. Addiction educators promote prevention, encourage early intervention, and expedite treatment. Decision making about substance use and other risky behaviors is the foundation of many successful prevention programs in schools, with families, and with entire communities. Educators utilize the materials and media available from local prevention centers as well as the many other resources provided by local, state, and federal governments. Educators in addiction practice often become members of the American Public Health Association, which has many special interest groups devoted to the areas of public health education and health promotion; alcohol, tobacco, and other drugs; and mental health. They may also join the Society of Public Health Educators.

Client and family education about addiction is an integral part of all addiction treatment, relapse prevention, and aftercare. Treatment clinicians (nurses, physicians, counselors, social workers, psychologists, and clergy) educate clients and families about addiction. Education is one of the five performance domains that individuals must master in order to receive certification as alcohol and drug abuse counselors. Client education is one of the 12 core functions of the substance abuse counselor.

Other Contributors to Addiction Practice

Health Care Administrators

Health care administrators contribute to addiction practice by providing essential administrative, management, and support services for thousands of public and private addiction treatment providers throughout the United States. Professionals from the Joint Commission on Accreditation of Health Care Organizations and the Commission on Accreditation of Rehabilitation Facilities work with treatment provider staff to achieve and maintain program accreditation. The National Association of Addiction Treatment Providers is a membership organization for providers that advocates for legislation and funding for addiction treatment.

Government Officials

Many federal, state, and local government agencies are charged with responsibility for addiction treatment and prevention. Each state has a designated substance abuse or addiction authority that is responsible for public policy, agency or service licensure, and, in some cases, the funding and operation of public treatment programs. State directors of such agencies belong to the National Association of State Alcohol and Drug Abuse Directors. Each state also has a state prevention contact. SAMHSA publishes the *National Directory of Drug Abuse and Alcoholism Treatment and Prevention Programs,* which lists the locations and describes selected characteristics of all treatment providers and prevention services that are recognized by state substance abuse authorities.

Within the U.S. government, addiction professionals and support staff work in many departments and agencies, including the following:

- The Center for Substance Abuse Prevention

- The Center for Substance Abuse Treatment

- The National Clearinghouse for Alcohol and Drug Information

- The National Institute on Alcohol Abuse and Alcoholism

- The National Institute on Drug Abuse

- The Substance Abuse and Mental Health Services Administration

Higher-Education Faculty

Colleges and universities employ faculty and researchers who are dedicated in part or whole to addiction teaching, research, and policy development. Unfortunately, most students who select health and human service majors are exposed to little addiction theory or practice in their basic preparatory programs. Yet there are many opportunities for faculty and students to teach and learn about addiction, given the prevalence of substance use and other addictive behaviors as well as the coexistence of addiction with varied medical, psychological, and social problems. Once interested in addiction practice, individuals usually pursue specialization and credentialing after they complete their undergraduate degrees and gain some work experience. Many colleges and universities offer continuing education courses and summer institutes in addiction.

Increasingly, basic curricula are including more addiction content and experience, often as part of psychology, sociology, criminology, or related degrees. Cambridge College in Massachusetts offers a master's degree in addiction studies. The University of Maryland offers a master's degree in nursing with specialization in addiction nursing. Doctoral and postdoctoral students study addiction theory, research, and policy in depth at such prestigious institutions of higher education as Brandeis, Brown, Columbia, Rutgers, and Yale Universities, as well as the Universities of New Mexico and Washington, to name but a few.

Researchers

The National Institute on Alcohol Abuse and Alcoholism, the National Institute on Drug Abuse, and other government departments and agencies fund a significant amount of basic and applied research. In addition, many private organizations, such as the Robert Wood Johnson Foundation, designate moneys for addiction research. Established in 1972 as a national philanthropy, today the Robert Wood Johnson Foundation is the largest foundation in the United States devoted to health care (see Robert Wood Johnson Foundation, 1998). It concentrates on awarding grants for research aimed at three goal areas: (a) assuring that all Americans have access to basic health care at reasonable cost, (b) improving the way services are organized and provided to people with chronic health conditions, and (c) promoting health and reducing the personal, social, and economic harms caused by substance abuse—of tobacco, alcohol, and illicit drugs.

In *Health Resources Online: A Guide for Mental Health and Addiction Specialists,* Sheerer, Kimball, Ungerleider, Meyer, and Zevnik (1999) review more than 300 World Wide Web sites of special interest to behavioral health professionals.

Addiction Practitioners in Recovery

People in recovery from addictions often seek employment in the addiction field. Historically, health professionals have avoided working with alcoholics and other drug addicts; however, recovering alcoholics and addicts with "good" recovery, but with little academic preparation, were some of the first addiction counselors. Recovering people spearheaded the development of EAPs in business and industry. Today, the National Association of Alcoholism and Drug Abuse Counselors reports that some 60% of its members are in recovery.

Licensure and accreditation requirements for treatment providers specify the academic preparation, experience, and credentialing required for addiction practice staff. Individuals meet the job description requirement for "experience with addiction" in many ways. Qualified, competent addiction practitioners may or may not be in recovery. Concerning clients' questions about practitioners' recovery status, addictions staff are urged to discuss the matter of self-disclosure with their immediate supervisors. Reviewing agency policy and professional codes of ethics can help practitioners to make appropriate decisions about disclosing their recovery status.

Doyle (1997) identifies many ethical dilemmas faced by recovering practitioners. Self-disclosure may be therapeutic, but it may lead to the client-clinician relationship's becoming more personal than professional. If client and clinician attend the same self-help recovery groups, this could threaten client confidentiality and counselor anonymity. What happens if a practitioner relapses? Should individuals apply for work where they received treatment? Doyle urges addiction practitioners in recovery to examine the relevant regulations and codes of ethics, seek out experienced colleagues for consultation, utilize a wide range of self-help meetings, and self-disclose very judiciously. Such individuals must advocate for additional clarification within their professional codes of ethics to guide their ethical behavior. (For an article about substance abuse among nurses, see Exhibit D in the appendix.)

American Academy of Health Care Providers in the Addictive Disorders

The American Academy of Health Care Providers in the Addictive Disorders was founded in 1989 to establish a core set of standards of competence for addiction treatment professionals throughout the world. The academy is a nonprofit credentialing organization devoted to maintaining quality standards for the provision of treatment in the addictive disorders.

The academy created the certified addiction specialist (CAS) credential, which reflects "the highest and most comprehensive standard in the field today," a standard that is based on contemporary research findings (the academy's code of ethics appears in Exhibit E in the appendix). The academy unites clinicians from a variety of disciplines under a single standard of health care. Its membership includes nurses, doctors, psychologists, psychiatrists, social workers, and counselors who are unified in their commitment to providing the highest quality of health care for individuals suffering from addiction.

The CAS is a comprehensive credential with specialty areas covering alcoholism, other drug addiction, eating disorders, compulsive gambling, and sex addiction. The academy maintains an international registry of health care providers in the addictive disorders.

Summary

A multidisciplinary group of health professionals, paraprofessionals, and volunteers works in the addiction field. Nurses, physicians, counselors, social workers, psychologists, educators, and clergy provide addiction treatment and prevention services. Health care administrators guide and manage addiction programs, and public health officials develop and implement program policy. Addiction treatment providers demonstrate safety and quality through accreditation. Practitioners are licensed and/or certified. Professional associations set standards to govern programs and develop codes of ethics to guide practitioners in practice. Faculty at colleges and universities contribute to addiction practice through teaching, research, and policy development. Public and private foundation money supports the work of scientists who advance addiction research. People in recovery often work in the addiction field. (For a list of some of the organizations and associations involved in addiction practice and research, see Exhibit F in the appendix.)

Related Skills Checklist

Practitioner skills related to the discussion of addiction practitioners in this chapter include the ability to do the following:

- Obtain appropriate license or certificate credential to work in the addiction field.
- Uphold standards of professional responsibility and accountability.
- Support professional organizations and associations.

Special Topics for Further Study

What are the minimum requirements for entry into practice as an addiction clinician? Discuss the rationale for national licensure of health and human service professionals. Review the public policy initiatives of various agencies, associations, and foundations to advance addiction treatment and prevention.

Addiction Practice 2000

Addiction practice 2000 requires practitioners to expand and extend their knowledge and skills. Addiction practitioners must strive to meet the highest criteria of professional responsibility and public accountability. Practitioners must increase excellence in and advance addiction practice through basic and continuing education. Provider accreditation and practitioner licensure and certification will raise practice standards. Addiction practice needs to reach out to an array of multidisciplinary and culturally and ethnically diverse practitioners, scholars, and other professionals to attract them to work in the addiction field. How can addiction practice integrate people in recovery into addiction prevention and treatment programs in a planned, purposeful way? Broad-based collaboration is required to develop local, national, and global policies concerning alcohol, drugs, and other addictions.

References

American Nurses' Association and National Nurses Society on Addictions. (1988). *Standards of addictions nursing practice with selected diagnoses and criteria.* Kansas City, MO: American Nurses' Association.

American Society of Addiction Medicine. (1991). *Patient placement criteria for the treatment of psychoactive substance use disorders.* Washington, DC: Author.

American Society of Addiction Medicine. (1996). *Patient placement criteria for the treatment of substance-related disorders* (2nd ed.). Chevy Chase, MD: Author.

Doyle, K. (1997). Substance abuse counselors in recovery: Implications for the ethical issue of dual relationship. *Journal of Counseling and Development, 75,* 428-432.

Green, J. (Ed.). (1997). *Faith communities* (NCADI Publication No. 98-05043). Rockville, MD: Center for Substance Abuse Prevention.

Herdman, J. W. (1994). *The twelve core functions of the substance abuse counselor.* Holmes Beach, FL: Learning Publications.

National Association of Alcoholism and Drug Abuse Counselors. (1995). *Ethical standards of alcoholism and drug abuse counselors.* Arlington, VA: Author.

Robert Wood Johnson Foundation. (1998). *Substance policy research program 1997.* Princeton, NJ: Author.

Sheerer, L., Kimball, C., Ungerleider, S., Meyer, G., & Zevnik, B. L. P. (1999). *Health resources online: A guide for mental health and addiction specialists* (2nd ed.). Eugene, OR: Integrated.

Substance Abuse and Mental Health Services Administration. (1998). *Addiction counseling competencies: The knowledge, skills, and attitudes of professional practice* (DHHS Publication No. SMA 98-3171). Rockville, MD: Author.

Other Sources

Angres, D. H., & Talbott, G. D. (1998). *Healing the healer: The addicted physician.* Madison, CT: Psychosocial Press.

Bissell, L., & Royce, J. E. (1994). *Ethics for addiction professionals* (2nd ed.). Center City, MN: Hazelden.

Bluestone, B. (1986). *The impaired nurse.* Center City, MN: Hazelden.

Board of Registration in Nursing. (1995). *Substance abuse rehabilitation: Program participant handbook.* Boston: Commonwealth of Massachusetts.

Center for Substance Abuse Prevention. (1992). *ATOD resource guide: Foundations* (MS447). Rockville, MD: Author.

Center for Substance Abuse Prevention. (1995). *Healthcare providers* (DHHS Publication No. SMA 95-3035). Rockville, MD: Author.

Coombs, R. H. (1997). *Drug-impaired professionals.* Cambridge, MA: Harvard University Press.

Freeman, E. M. (1992). *The addiction process: Effective social work approaches.* New York: Longman.

Miller, W. R., & Brown, S. A. (1997). Why psychologists should treat alcohol and drug problems. *American Psychologist, 52,* 1269-1279.

Naegle, M. A. (1992). Impaired practice by health professionals. In M. A. Naegle (Ed.), *Substance abuse education in nursing* (Vol. 2, pp. 117-219). New York: National League for Nursing Press.

National Institute on Drug Abuse. (1993). *Impact of prescription drug diversion control systems on medical practice and patient care* (NIH Publication No. 93-3507). Rockville, MD: Author.

Substance Abuse and Mental Health Services Administration. (1996). *National directory of drug abuse and alcoholism treatment and prevention programs: 1995 survey* (DHHS Publication No. SMA 96-3108). Rockville, MD: Author.

Talbott, G. D., & Gallegos, K. V. (1990, September). Intervention with health professionals. *Addiction and Recovery.*

Part II

Addiction
Treatment

6

Treatment Methodology

Objectives

- Grasp the concept of methodology.
- Recognize that a treatment methodology is the explicit, purposeful, organized way in which clinicians and clients conduct treatment.
- Understand that clinicians employ a variety of approaches to addiction treatment.
- Compare and contrast different treatment methodologies.
- Identify client and clinician roles in various treatment modalities.

Outline

- **Treatment Methodology**
  - Methodology
  - Treatment Approaches
  - Client and Clinician Roles
- **Natural Recovery**
  - Approach
  - Clients
  - Clinicians
- **Twelve-Step Recovery**
  - Approach
  - Clients
  - Clinicians
- **The Minnesota Model**
  - Approach

- Clients
- Clinicians
■ **Psychodynamic Approaches to Treatment**
  - Approach
  - Clients
    Dual Disorders
    Denial and Mechanisms of Defense
  - Clinicians
■ **Cognitive-Behavioral Therapies**
  - Approach
  - Clients
  - Clinicians
■ **Motivational Enhancement Therapy**
  - Approach
  - Clients
  - Clinicians
■ **Stages-of-Change Model**
  - Approach
  - Clients
  - Clinicians
■ **Problem-Oriented Treatment**
  - Approach
  - Clients
  - Clinicians
■ **Solution-Focused Treatment**
  - Approach
  - Clients
  - Clinicians
■ **Group Therapy**
  - Approach
    Psychoeducation Groups
    Mutual Self-Help Groups
    Psychotherapy
  - Clients
  - Clinicians
■ **Family as Treatment**
  - Approach
  - Clients
  - Clinicians
■ **Community as Treatment**
  - Approach

Treatment Methodology

Methodology

The explicit, purposeful, and organized ways in which clinicians and clients conduct treatment are referred to as *treatment methodologies.* Such methodologies take into account the scientific principles and practical techniques that clinicians use with clients. The term *methodology* comes from the Greek word *methodos,* which means "way," such as a way followed, the pursuit of a path. Classical definitions of method are particularly relevant for contemporary addiction practice. Method means a transition, a movement, and one step after another. Method means also to forge ahead. Progress and unity characterize the passage or movement. Continuity is critical for progressive transition.

Treatment Approaches

Individual addiction practitioners usually embrace particular theories or models of addiction; that is, they have particular theoretical orientations. In addition, clinicians employ a variety of approaches to addiction treatment. Descriptions of several traditional and emerging approaches to addiction treatment follow. As the Project MATCH Research Group (1993) has noted: "No single treatment approach is effective for all persons with alcohol problems. A more promising strategy involves assignment of patients to alternative treatments based on specific needs and characteristics of patients" (p. 1130). Project MATCH, supported by the National Institute on Alcohol Abuse and Alcoholism, tried out three approaches to treatment with clients: 12-step facilitation, cognitive-behavioral coping skills therapy, and motivational enhancement therapy.

Client and Clinician Roles

Client factors, resources for treatment, agency mission and philosophy, and clinician expertise determine approach to treatment. Currently, clinicians are specifying, trying, and evaluating a variety of treatment approaches. For each approach described below, I include discussion of the roles of clients and clinicians.

Natural Recovery

Approach

Historically, and prior to modern addiction treatment, many people with addictive disorders recovered on their own. In the 1970s, Sobell and Sobell (see, e.g., 1975, 1978) studied the resolution of alcohol addiction problems without treatment. They found that some respondents demonstrated abstinent recovery. Other respondents reported nonabstinent recovery, but with significantly fewer alcohol-related consequences. Sobell and Sobell (1993) identify *self-change* as the predominant avenue to recovery.

Although natural recovery is a process of self-change, not all individuals who recover on their own progress through all the stages of change identified by Prochaska and his colleagues, described later in this chapter. Often people augment natural recovery and self-change with support from mutual self-help groups and use of over-the-counter (OTC) medications.

Clients

Even today, the majority of people with addictive disorders *do not seek treatment,* yet they arrest their problems and recover from the consequences of their addictions. Since 1935, millions of people have used Alcoholics Anonymous (A.A.) to help them stop drinking and maintain abstinence. Some of the "old-timers" pride themselves on doing it "the old-fashioned way: no treatment!" Following the U.S. surgeon general's warning in 1969 that smoking may be hazardous to health, most adults who stopped smoking stopped on their own. Today, many individuals use OTC nicotine gum or the nicotine patch to "kick the smoking habit on their own."

Clinicians

Millions of people continue to recover from the ravages of addiction on their own and without formal treatment. As advocates for recovery, addiction practitioners acknowledge and applaud natural recovery. They actively seek out opportunities to educate individuals, families, and the community about natural recovery and self-change.

In addition, many addiction practitioners are involved with prevention programs. Addiction education, especially with populations at risk, can help individuals and families to develop healthy, addiction-free lifestyles. Specific addiction prevention strategies emphasize knowledge, values, and personal decision making. Public policy and prevention programs promote drug-free schools and drug-free workplaces.

Twelve-Step Recovery

Approach

Twelve-step recovery programs maintain that addiction is a chronic, progressive disease. Abstinence is the treatment goal for individuals who abuse alcohol and drugs as well as for problem gamblers. Recovery is possible through active participation in the fellowship, steps, and traditions of the relevant 12-step program, such as Alcoholics Anonymous, Narcotics Anonymous, Gamblers Anonymous, Overeaters Anonymous, or Sex and Love Addicts Anonymous. Many of these organizations have parallel groups for families and friends of addicts. Al-Anon Family Group, which includes Alateen, has been in existence for almost 50 years as a community resource providing support to those affected by someone else's drinking. Today, there are more than 30,000 Al-Anon and Alateen groups meeting in 112 countries.

Alcoholics Anonymous, recognized as a prototype for similar mutual self-help support groups, began in 1935 in Akron, Ohio. Bill Wilson (Bill W.) and Robert Holbrook Smith, M.D. (Dr. Bob), two professional men with serious drinking problems, met and told each other their stories. Through their mutual support, they both achieved and maintained sobriety. Other A.A. groups followed, in New York, Philadelphia, and Washington. The "Twelve Steps" were written in 1938, and *Alcoholics Anonymous*—fondly called the Big Book—was published in 1939, with a second edition in 1955, a third edition in 1976, and a soft-cover edition in 1986; a pocket edition is also available. A 1941 *Saturday Evening Post* article about Alcoholics Anonymous by Jack Alexander greatly accelerated expansion and recognition of the movement. The monthly magazine *A.A. Grapevine* was launched in 1944. *The Twelve Traditions of A.A.* were formulated and published in 1946. Physicians, psychiatrists, and public health professionals have recognized and embraced A.A. The book *Twelve Steps and Twelve Traditions,* often referred to as the 12 and 12, was published in 1953 (see A.A. World Services, 1953/1989).

The symbol of Alcoholics Anonymous is a circle enclosing a triangle. The circle represents the whole world of A.A., and the triangle stands for the three legacies of recovery, unity, and service. These three legacies chronicle the growth and development of the fellowship. *Recovery* tells the story of the people and influences that began A.A. *Unity* describes the traditions that hold A.A. together. Carrying the message of recovery is the third legacy of *service.* Such service is considered necessary for personal recovery as well as for the existence and growth of A.A. itself.

Over the years, A.A. meetings themselves have changed, in part to reflect the expanding and changing membership. There are open and closed meetings, speaker and discussion meetings, Big Book and Twelve Step meetings, men's meetings, women's meetings, meetings for young people, gay meetings, no-smoking meetings, meetings accessible to people with disabilities, and meetings with interpretation for deaf members. Today many individuals "have to attend A.A." and get meeting cards signed to verify their attendance. Courts routinely order A.A. attendance as a condition of parole or probation, social service agencies mandate A.A. for alcoholic mothers who want to keep their children, and rehabilitation programs require attendance at A.A. meetings as part of treatment.

In 1995, A.A. turned 60 years old. At that time, an article in the *New Yorker* described the organization as being at a crossroads (Delbanco & Delbanco, 1995). Although its size and reach show no sign of waning, the membership and meetings have changed. Some A.A. members worry that A.A. is becoming more of a social club than a recovery fellowship. In 1996, according to a membership survey taken that year, there were more than 96,000 A.A. groups throughout the world. The average age of an A.A. member was 44 years, and average length of sobriety of members was more than 6 years. Some 33% of members were women. Of the members surveyed, 60% said that before coming to A.A., they received some type of treatment, which often included referral to A.A.; 62% reported that receiving treatment was an important part of their recovery (see A.A. World Services, 1997).

Alcoholics Anonymous does have its critics, however. Some claim that A.A. is a religious program, and that it encourages powerlessness because, for A.A. members, an individual's sobriety depends upon other people or a higher power. It has also been asserted that A.A. follows a male model of recovery.

Clients

The role of the client in 12-step recovery is best expressed in the Preamble to *Alcoholics Anonymous:*

> ALCOHOLICS ANONYMOUS is a fellowship of men and women who share their experience, strength and hope with each other that they may solve their common problem and help others to recover from alcoholism.
>
> ■ The only requirement for membership is a desire to stop drinking. There are no dues or fees for A.A. membership; we are self supporting through our own contributions.

- A.A. is not allied with any sect, denomination, politics, organization or institution; does not wish to engage in any controversy, neither endorses nor opposes any causes.

- Our primary purpose is to stay sober and help other alcoholics to achieve sobriety. (Reprinted with permission from *A.A. Grapevine.*)

(See also "How It Works" and the Twelve Steps, which are reproduced in Exhibit G in the appendix.)

Clinicians

Participation in 12-step groups may be an integral part of formal treatment and aftercare. Addiction clinicians educate clients about 12-step recovery and facilitate client involvement in relevant 12-step groups. Education includes an overview of 12-step recovery; a presentation of recovery goals and priorities; an introduction to the 12 steps; an explanation of the key concepts, traditions, and slogans of 12-step groups; and clarification of the role of a sponsor.

Addiction clinicians encourage attendance at community 12-step meetings and suggest that clients become actively involved with a home group, such as by setting up the hall or making coffee. Clinicians recommend progressive involvement in step meetings, discussion meetings, or A.A. retreats.

Note that an addiction clinician need not be in recovery to employ a 12-step approach in treatment. Clinicians' self-disclosure of their own recovery status is determined by clinical and professional guidelines.

The Minnesota Model

Approach

The Hazelden Foundation in Center City, Minnesota, began with the idea of creating a humane therapeutic community for alcoholics and addicts. What started in 1949 as a guest house for alcoholic men is recognized today as a world leader in addiction treatment, education, and publishing. Several core perspectives ground what has come to be known as the Minnesota model:

- Treat alcoholics and addicts with dignity and respect.

- Treat alcoholism as a primary illness, not a symptom of another condition.

- Treat alcoholism as a chronic illness—one that calls for coping, not curing.

- Treat alcoholics and addicts as whole persons.

- Remember that this illness affects people in many dimensions—physical, psychological, social, and spiritual.

- Offer a full continuum of care, ranging from diagnosis and detoxification to aftercare and family services.

- Treat alcoholics and addicts with the talents of people from many disciplines—physicians, psychologists, counselors, clergy, recovering people themselves, and more.

- Offer treatment based on the Twelve Steps of Alcoholics Anonymous, which call for lifelong abstinence. Include other compatible approaches as needed.

- Allow addicts to learn from their peers in recovery. It's sometimes said that treatment begins after the staff goes home, when one alcoholic talks to another over a cup of coffee. (Toft, 1995; see also Spicer, 1993)

Critics of the Minnesota model charge that it is inflexible, that its one-size-fits-all approach forces people into A.A., and that it works best with inpatients. Yet, at Hazelden, treatment is based on individualized plans. The model is not strictly A.A., but a blend of many perspectives, borrowing the best of many disciplines. Today, with the challenges of managed care, addiction clinicians are attempting to use the Minnesota model at a variety of outpatient levels of care. When a Hazelden-type program was compared with a psychotherapy approach a year after treatment, it was found that patients treated according to the Hazelden approach were seven times more likely to have remained abstinent.

Proponents of the Minnesota model acknowledge that addictive disorders are complex diseases; a single type of treatment probably cannot help every alcoholic or addict. Yet they strongly believe that the premises of the Minnesota model will endure for decades because they are humane, holistic, and flexible.

First, treat chemically dependent people with dignity. Second, treat them as whole persons—body, mind, spirit. As long as people suffer the consequences of addiction, these ideas will never go out of date. (Toft, 1995, p. 16)

Hazelden Educational Materials, a division of the Hazelden Foundation, distributes an extensive line of recovery literature, cassettes, videotapes, and other products for clinicians and clients. Hazelden also offers training for addiction professionals.

Clients

Clients referred to a Minnesota model program experience treatment with dignity and respect. Clients and their families learn about addiction, sobriety, relapse, and recovery. Clients address biopsychosocial and spiritual aspects of their addictions. During treatment, clients work with a variety of treatment professionals as well as people in recovery. Involvement in A.A. is an integral part of treatment; this involvement may include beginning the 12 steps.

Clinicians

Addiction clinicians who utilize the Minnesota model recognize addictive disorders as chronic, progressive illnesses that can be managed. They believe that addiction affects the whole person: physical, psychological, social, and spiritual dimensions. Treatment involves a continuum of care and is based on the 12 steps of Alcoholics Anonymous; other compatible approaches are included as needed.

Clinicians employing the Minnesota model function as members of multidisciplinary teams that include individuals who are in recovery. Above all, these clinicians treat addiction clients with *dignity* and *respect*. Hazelden offers a wide variety of individualized training options, ranging from 1 week to 6 months, designed to meet the learning needs of a variety of addiction clinicians.

Psychodynamic Approaches to Treatment

Approach

Given the dramatic shift in the contemporary treatment of mental disorders away from extensive psychotherapy, readers may question the relevance of a discussion of psychodynamic approaches to addiction treatment. Early psychoanalytic studies of addiction sought specific, deep-seated causes of addiction. Psychodynamic theory examined the role of the ego in the development of addiction and the distorted and extreme use of denial by clients. Psychiatrists were some of the first clinicians to recognize and treat clients with dual disorders. Today's addiction clinicians use many psychodynamic concepts to understand and treat addiction. The contributions of psychoanalytically trained psychiatrists, especially those deeply involved in social and community applications of dynamic concepts, provided strong support for Alcoholics Anonymous and its Twelve Steps and Twelve Traditions.

Clients

Dual Disorders

Many clients use alcohol, other drugs, or addictive behaviors to manage their discomfort associated with Axis I *DSM-IV* (American Psychiatric Association, 1994) diagnoses of mood disorders, anxiety disorders, impulse-control disorders, obsessive-compulsive disorders, or posttraumatic stress disorder. Individuals with Axis II *DSM-IV* personality disorders or mental retardation often abuse substances. The substance or behavior relieves psychological or physical distress and pain; it provides pleasure or reward, usually with instant gratification.

Psychopathology may antedate and contribute to the development of addiction, or it may follow and complicate addiction. Clients with primary diagnoses of addictive disorders often demonstrate depression, anxiety, impulsivity, self-centeredness, self-destructiveness, irresponsibility, poor judgment, regression, irritability, and labile mood; they employ a defense system based on denial, rationalization, projection, and minimization. Failure of clinicians to address concomitant psychopathology, irrespective of its onset, significantly increase risk of relapse. (For more on dual disorders, see Chapter 19.)

Denial and Mechanisms of Defense

The ego employs defense mechanisms to regulate instincts, maintain ego integrity, and protect itself from internal and external threats. When defense mechanisms decrease anxiety or pain, they are adaptive. When they threaten, harm, or even destroy the ego, they are destructive.

Client denial distinguishes addiction. Clients doubt and disbelieve that they have addiction problems and thereby justify their continued drinking, substance use, gambling, or shopping. Clients refuse to admit to or accept even the most obvious harmful effects of addiction. Denial is the way clients maintain self-esteem in the face of the destructive consequences of addiction. Denial may serve clients well in the short term, but clinicians have recognized the devastating effects of long-term denial on addiction clients. Denial lowers client acceptance of addiction and treatment and increases client resistance to treatment. Denial thwarts recovery. When denial dominates, hope is diminished. Chronic denial contributes to despair. Rationalization, minimization, and projection are other primary defense mechanisms used by addiction clients.

Many of the slogans clients use to support their recovery have a strong psychodynamic base. For example:

- HALT: Don't get too hungry, angry, lonely, or tired.

- HOW: Honesty, open-mindedness, and willingness.

- KISS: Keep it simple, stupid!

Clinicians

Clinicians taking a psychodynamic approach use the concept of the id to help clients understand their addictions. The id operates according to the pleasure principle. Current concepts about the etiology of addiction strongly support the presence of a reward center in the brain. Brain reward explains why individuals self-administer drugs again and again. The effects are pleasant. Alcohol and other drugs, as well as addictive behaviors such as gambling and shopping, increase pleasure and/or reduce pain.

Clinicians use the concept of the ego to confront clients with the reality of their addiction problems and the necessity of self-responsibility for change. The ego is governed by the reality principle. Self-governance is the actual or potential ability to be in charge of oneself. As a condition of self-pathology, addiction damages formulation and development of self, including identity, body image, self-esteem, and expected roles. Addiction is dangerous in that it erodes an individual's capacity for self-care and self-preservation. Clients have difficulty regulating their affect, their feelings, and their subjective sense of well-being.

The concept of the superego helps clinicians to understand and address the overwhelming sense of guilt and shame experienced by many clients. Clients often demonstrate the absence or diminished concept of the "ego ideal," with the prevailing beliefs that "I do such stupid things," "I am a bad person," or "I always settle for less."

A psychodynamic approach offers strong support for clinicians who incorporate A.A. into their clients' treatment regimens (see, e.g., *Alcoholism: A Merry-Go-Round Named Denial*; Kellerman, 1969). The first of A.A.'s Twelve Steps can help clients break the cycle of denial: "We admitted we were powerless over alcohol—that our lives had become unmanageable."

Cognitive-Behavioral Therapies

Approach

Addiction clinicians employ cognitive-behavioral approaches to help clients master the skills they need to achieve their treatment goals. Cognitive-behavioral methodology reflects learning theory, social learning theory, behavior therapy, and cognitive-behavioral therapy. Albert Ellis pioneered the development of rational-emotive therapy (RET) and the A-B-C model of thinking and feeling, as illustrated here (see Ellis & Grieger, 1977):

$$A \to B \to C$$

Events $\to$ Thoughts $\to$ Feelings/Behavior

Cognitive therapy, as developed by Aaron Beck, employs cognitive and behavioral techniques in an active, structured, and usually time-limited approach to treatment (see Beck, Wright, Newman, & Liese, 1993). Specific cognitive-behavioral strategies include thought stopping, thought replacement, cognitive restructuring, self-talk, problem solving, behavior reduction, behavior enhancement, behavior rehearsal, role playing, role reversal, and modeling.

> As the individual undergoes a process of deconditioning, cognitive restructuring, and skills acquisition, he or she can begin to accept greater responsibility for changing the behavior. This is the essence of the self-control or self-management approach: one can learn how to escape from the clutches of the vicious cycle of addiction, regardless of how the habit pattern was originally acquired. (Marlatt & Gordon, 1985, p. 12)

Clients

Stop! Think! Act! Clients assume primary responsibility for learning coping skills to arrest addictive behavior and create long-lasting behavioral change, characterized by heightened cognitive awareness and responsible problem solving. Clients learn and practice the skills they need to achieve their treatment goals. They develop skills for coping with high-risk situations, both those caused by external stressors and those stemming from internal cognitions and emotions. Clients identify their urges and practice refusal skills. They develop skills for handling emergency situations. Clients master coping skills to avoid those people, places, and things that may trigger relapse and to choose those people, places, and things that support recovery. Treatment may include training in communication and interpersonal skills; in stress management and relaxation skills; in anger management and skills for coping with other negative moods, thoughts, and behaviors; and in ways to increase social support skills and positive moods, thoughts, and behaviors.

Clinicians

Clinicians who take a cognitive-behavioral approach function as active teachers and role models, much like "player coaches"—active participants who direct treatment through demonstration, practice, and constructive feedback. These clinicians are experienced in behavioral principles and in interpersonal and self-management skills. They encourage clients to bring events from their daily lives into treatment and use these experiences as frames of reference for problem-solving exercises, role playing, and homework practice assignments. Clinicians help clients replace harmful behaviors with healthy behaviors. They monitor clients' progress in acquiring and applying new skills and help clients to manage difficulties as they arise.

Motivational Enhancement Therapy

Approach

Based on the principles of motivational psychology, motivational enhancement therapy (MET) aims to produce prompt, internally motivated client change. Research has demonstrated that MET usually requires fewer clinician-client sessions than some alternative approaches. Miller and Rollnick (1992) list five basic motivational principles that underlie the MET approach:

1. Express empathy.

2. Deploy discrepancy.

3. Avoid argumentation.

4. Roll with resistance.

5. Support self-efficacy.

Elements of MET are evident in natural recovery and the stages-of- change model. The contemplation and determination stages of change are critical.

Clients

Clients in motivational enhancement therapy first consider how much of a problem their addictions pose for them and how their addictions affect them, positively and negatively. Next, clients contemplate the possibility and the costs and benefits of changing their problem behaviors. They consider whether they will be able to make changes and the impacts those changes will have on their lives. In the determination stage, clients develop a firm resolve to take action. To specify their action plans, clients may use a "change plan worksheet" on which they complete sentences such the following:

1. The changes I want to make are:

2. The most important reasons that I want to make these changes are:

3. The steps I plan to take in changing are:

4. The ways other people can help me are:

5. I will know that my plan is working if:

6. Some things that could interfere with my plan are:

Clinicians

Clinicians using the MET approach evoke statements of problem perception and need for change from their clients. Clinicians emphasize their clients' ability to change (self-efficacy).

In Phase 1, "building motivation for change," the clinician elicits self-motivational statements, listens with empathy, questions, and presents personal feedback. The clinician affirms the client, handles resistance, reframes, and summarizes. During Phase 2, "strengthening commitment to change," the clinician recognizes change readiness, discusses a plan with the client, and communicates free choice as well as the consequences of action and inaction. The clinician offers information and advice, emphasizes treatment goals, and deals with resistance. Toward the end of the commitment process, the clinician recapitulates client information from Phase 1 and asks the client for a commitment to change. Involving the client's spouse or significant other can enhance motivation. In Phase 3, "follow-through strategies," the clinician reviews progress, renews motivation, and continues commitment. The clinician listens with empathy, questions, presents personal feedback, affirms the client, handles resistance, reframes, and summarizes.

Stages-of-Change Model

Approach

According to James Prochaska and his colleagues, an individual moves through a series of five stages of change as he or she arrests an addiction and recovers. Each stage requires the accomplishment of particular tasks, and the individual must use certain processes to achieve change. The stages-of-change model systematically and explicitly incorporates principles of motivational psychology and behavior change to produce internally motivated, immediate change. An individual may need to go through several cycles of the stages of change to initiate and sustain change. In the 1980s, clinicians using this model employed five stages of change: (a) precontemplation, (b) contemplation, (c) decision making, (d) action, and (e) maintenance (Prochaska & DiClemente, 1983). Prochaska, now director of the Cancer Prevention Research Center at the University of Rhode Island and coauthor of the book *Changing for Good* (Prochaska, Norcross, & DiClemente, 1995), now employs six stages of change: (a) precontemplation, (b) contemplation, (c) preparation, (d) action, (e) maintenance, and (f) termination.

Clients

Initially, clients do not consider any change relative to their addictions (*precontemplation*). Clients are not ready to change, although thinking about change may be subconscious. The positive aspects of addiction still outweigh the negative effects. Clients' denial of their addictions and their negative consequences is high. Clients underestimate the benefits and overestimate the costs of changing. Their thoughts and feelings reinforce reasons *not* to change.

Clients next contemplate whether or not they have an addiction problem; they consider the feasibility of change and review the costs and benefits of change versus no change (*contemplation*). Clients consider whether or not they will be able to change and how that change will affect their lives. Contemplation is a process of critical psychoeducation. Clients learn about their problems and the possibility and desirability of change. They talk about change with friends, family, people in recovery, and addiction clinicians. Clients acknowledge that there are immediate and personal benefits to change.

Clients then decide to take action and change (*determination*). Clients develop a firm resolve to act, to actually change ("I'm going to quit smoking on my birthday with the patch"). Their resolve is influenced by past successes and/or failures with change.

Once clients begin to modify the addictive problem, they enter the *action* stage. Typically, conscious action continues for 3 to 6 months. Clients use their own inner resources to change as well as support from their helping relationship environment. (Bill J. buys the nicotine patch; he is pleased with the support his wife and two children give him.)

After successfully negotiating the action stage, clients move on to *maintenance,* or sustained change. (Bill has not smoked for 3 months. He works out at the gym after work and says, "I never felt better in my life. Maybe I'll live long enough to see my kids graduate from college.")

Clinicians

Clinicians using the stages-of-change model motivate clients to change and to strengthen their commitment to change. Clinicians assume that the responsibility and capability for change lie within the client. First, clinicians help clients consider how much of a problem their addictions cause them. How are their addictions affecting them, both positively and negatively? Second, clinicians help clients contemplate and assess the possibility and feasibility of changing the problem behavior. Clinicians assess clients' perceptions of their problems and their abilities to change, or self-efficacy.

Clinicians employ motivational principles to help clients change. The stages-of-change approach de-emphasizes client helplessness and powerlessness over the addiction. Clinicians do not prescribe or attempt to teach clients specific coping skills. Clinicians motivate clients to mobilize their own resources to effect change. Clinicians elicit ideas from clients about how they might change. Clinicians foster motivation for change, strengthen commitment to change, and monitor and encourage actions that will lead clients to initiate and persevere with change. Clinicians monitor and encourage progress throughout the stages of change with structured feedback.

Problem-Oriented Treatment

Approach

In a problem-oriented treatment approach, treatment is organized by the client's problems. Following assessment and diagnosis, client and clinicians develop a problem list. This comprehensive database is the foundation for identifying client problems and developing a problem-oriented treatment plan. Ideally, a multidisciplinary team of addiction clinicians contributes to a single problem list and a common treatment plan.

Client and clinicians prioritize problems, often ranking them according to their urgency. For example, severe alcohol withdrawal may be assigned a high priority because client and clinician conclude that it requires immediate intervention. Spiritual distress related to loss of home, family, and job because of problem gambling may be assigned a medium priority and addressed during weekly counseling. A weight gain of 5 pounds following smoking cessation may be assigned low priority and can be discussed at a Smokers Anonymous meeting.

For each problem, client and clinicians formulate treatment *goals* and specify *expected outcomes*. These goals and expected outcomes direct treatment planning, determine interventions, and guide evaluation. They are stated in behaviorally measurable terms, and each contains a time element.

A goal is a broad, client-centered statement that reflects health and well-being. Short-term goals are expected to be achieved in brief periods of time, usually less than a week for inpatient treatment and within 3 months for outpatient treatment. Long-term goals are expected to be achieved over longer periods of time, usually over weeks or months.

An expected outcome is a very specifically stated step-by-step objective that leads to attainment of the goal and resolution of the problem. An outcome is a measurable change in client status in response to treatment interventions. Outcomes are the desired changes in client condition.

Staff document the date a problem is identified, the team members assigned to address the problem, and the date the problem is resolved. High-priority problems are addressed immediately during the current treatment episode (short-term problems). Other problems may be addressed in continuing care (long-term problems). Some problems may be monitored; others may be noted. Depending on the capabilities of the clinicians and treatment facility, consultation or referral may be required to address certain problems. New problems are added to the problem list as they are identified.

Clinicians who employ a problem-oriented approach to treatment often use the "SOAP method" of documentation. SOAP is an acronym for *subjective* data (what the client says), *objective* data (what clinicians observe and measure), *assessment* (decisions based on the data), and *plan* (blueprint for action).

Clients

Clients enter treatment "with problems." Clients provide clinicians with comprehensive data for assessment and diagnosis. Clients help clinicians prioritize problems, formulate goals and outcomes, and select interventions. Client outcome data are critical for the evaluation of treatment. How did the client respond to treatment? What changes did the client experience or report relative to addiction severity?

Clinicians

Clinicians using problem-oriented treatment collaborate with clients and clients' families to collect all relevant data about client problems. Comprehensive data provide the basis for a determination of addiction severity and formulation of a diagnosis. Clinicians use addiction severity and diagnosis to plan treatment, including placing the client in the most appropriate level of care. Clinicians develop treatment plans using a problem-focused format. Broad goals and specific outcomes relate to problems. Clinicians specify the interventions that will help clients reach outcomes, achieve goals, and ultimately resolve their addiction problems.

Solution-Focused Treatment

Approach

In response to the increasing costs of health care and the growth of the managed care industry, health care practitioners have developed brief therapy approaches to treatment. In this area, the work of Insoo Kim Berg on solution-focused brief therapy (SFBT; Berg & Miller, 1992; Berg & Reuss, 1998) and that of Bill

O'Hanlon on brief solution-oriented therapy (O'Hanlon & Bertolino, 1998) is particularly important.

SFBT shifts from a problem-solving approach to solution building. It builds upon the tradition of social constructivism and the brief therapy framework developed by the Mental Research Institute of Palo Alto, California. The phenomenon of *exception* is critical to client and clinicians in this approach. Has the client had periods of abstinence from substance use or the addictive behavior? If so, how long have these been: 3 days, 1 week, or a period of years? These exceptions to addiction are considered resources and the beginning of a solution. Clinicians and client investigate this abstinence in depth: how, what, when, where, with whom? Clinicians validate and value clients' exceptions to addiction. Exceptions can be random or deliberate. For deliberate exceptions, clients can describe the conscious, step-by-step way they stayed away from a drink, drug, or addictive behavior. Random exceptions are also periods of abstinence, but clients are unable to explain what they did to bring this about.

Clinicians then help clients utilize their existing resources (their mastery and past achievement of exceptions) to develop solution-building activities to solve the presenting problems. Clinicians ask "miracle questions" to help clients create a picture, an image, or a vision of solutions rather than try to help clients understand how and why they developed the addictive disorder.

Clients are asked to scale their motivation and confidence to solve their addiction problems. At second and subsequent treatment sessions, clinicians track behavioral change by asking clients, "What's better, what's the same, what's worse?" Clients and clinicians decide, often through scaling, when to terminate treatment.

Clinicians build a constructive, confident client-clinician relationship. Solution-focused treatment emphasizes client collaboration in formulating treatment goals. Solution-focused treatment is easiest when clients want help. Even "codependent" clients and clients who are mandated to treatment are likely to help solve their problems when they perceive that clinicians recognize their strengths and motivate them to solve their addiction problems.

Solution-focused treatment can be used with groups. It is simple, positive, and humanistic as well as efficient, effective, and attractive to insurers, clinicians, and clients. Its usefulness has been demonstrated with a diverse population of clients, from inner-city, homeless walk-in substance abusers to high-tech engineers visiting an employee assistance counselor.

Clients

Clients describe exceptions to their addiction problems. For example, Bob P. reports: "I attended five A.A. meetings a week; I joined a group; I got a sponsor.

My wife and I attended couples counseling for about 2 months" (a deliberate exception). Joe W. recalls: "Over school vacation, we went to Disney World. I didn't want to drink in front of the kids; it wasn't that easy to get my drugs. We were so busy and had so much fun, I guess I really didn't need to drink or use" (a random exception).

Clients respond to scaling questions. Mary S. states with confidence: "I'm about an 8 out of 10. I would do most anything to stop smoking" (motivation scaling). "Yes, on a scale of 1 to 10. I am at about a 7 and moving higher when it comes to stopping smoking and feeling comfortable about being a former smoker" (confidence scaling).

Clinicians

Clinicians assess exceptions to the problem: "You told me you did not smoke or drink during your first pregnancy. That was wonderful! Tell me just how you did that." Clinicians ask miracle questions: "Imagine a miracle: You wake up one morning with no craving to smoke. You get up, shower, dress, eat breakfast, and head out to work. Will you tell me more about this situation, this solution?" Clinicians prompt scaling: "Mary, how confident are you, on a scale of 1 to 10 where 10 stands for the most confidence you can have, that you can abstain from having that first cigarette in the morning?" (termination scaling).

Clinicians expect that clients are solving their problems. Clinicians ask: "What is better?" Clinicians reinforce client mastery of problems and motivate them to continue working toward solutions. If a client reports that nothing has changed, clinicians and client closely reexamine the goal and the client's effort. Most likely, they discover that the client has initiated small changes. Together they plan how to continue the changes toward the solution. When a client reports, "My problems are worse," clinicians and client chronicle the events and details of the problem that the client perceives as "worse." With this additional information, they may revise the initial assessment and initiate the solution-focused process anew.

Group Therapy

Group therapy is a primary treatment modality with addiction clients and their families, especially psychoeducation, mutual self-help, and psychotherapy groups. Groups can effect change in clients' thoughts, feelings, and actions. Group therapy is a cost-effective, clinically sound treatment modality for client and clinician.

Approach

A group is a cluster of individuals with something in common, such as the Patterson family, Mrs. Lester's third-grade class, the Green Bay Packers football team, or the Riverside Gospel Choir. From a sociological perspective, society is made up of groups. From a psychological perspective, groups can be viewed as reflective of society, as microcosms of the world.

Psychoeducation Groups

Within a psychoeducation group, clients can learn about addiction, relapse, recovery, and myriad specific treatment topics; practice sobriety skills such as refusal skills, assertiveness, self-esteem exercises, and self-management; develop trust and control, acceptance, and affection; and acquire decision-making, problem-solving, and anger management strategies. Groups have ground rules that usually include respect, responsibility, accountability, and loyalty. Group process invites participation, encourages communication, and fosters socialization.

Mutual Self-Help Groups

Groups such as Alcoholics Anonymous, Narcotics Anonymous, Gamblers Anonymous, and Smart Recovery can help many clients achieve and maintain abstinence, prevent relapse, and develop an addiction-free lifestyle. Many treatment approaches refer clients to mutual self-help groups to continue their recovery. Such groups are integral parts of the 12-step approach and the Minnesota model.

A mutual self-help group is a group of people facing a common problem who meet together to share their experience, strength, and hope. Individuals who accept their addiction, commit to recovery, have stable biopsychosocial systems, and *accept personal responsibility* for their treatment and recovery do well in mutual self-help groups. Mutual self-groups began in 1935 with an encounter between Bill W. and Dr. Bob, who first met to help each other stay sober and eventually founded Alcoholics Anonymous. No professional staff is required for most self-help groups.

The only requirement for admission to a self-help group is an individual desire to stop (arrest) the addictive process: drinking, using, gambling, smoking, or whatever. Recovering people create the therapeutic milieu and provide mutual support. Meetings are conducted according to established traditions or guidelines and follow a variety of formats—there are discussion meetings, open meetings, closed meetings, meetings for men or women only, and meetings for young people only. In 12-step groups, recovering peers recognize one another's continuing abstinence milestones: 30 days, 60 days, 90 days, 6 months, 9 months, and anniversaries. Recovering peers sponsor newcomers and may "12-

step" others who fail to stay abstinent and facilitate their admission into treatment.

There are many different kinds of mutual self-help groups. The following take the 12-step approach:

- Alcoholics Anonymous
- Narcotics Anonymous
- Cocaine Anonymous
- Gamblers Anonymous
- Debtors Anonymous
- Overeaters Anonymous
- Sex and Love Addicts Anonymous

Some self-help groups are based in religious principles, whereas others are secular in nature. The following are some currently active secular support groups:

- Rational Recovery
- Smart Recovery
- Women for Sobriety
- Secular Organization for Sobriety
- Moderation Management

Some of the groups based in religion are as follows:

- SAVE (Mormon)
- Christians in Recovery
- Alcoholics Victorious (Christian)
- Calix Society (Catholic)
- JACS (Jewish)

Psychotherapy

Historically, group psychotherapy has employed a psychodynamic approach. Today, addiction clinicians employ a variety of group approaches, and many base their approaches on the seminal work of Irwin D. Yalom in *interactional group therapy*. Yalom (1995) describes the therapeutic factors in group therapy as follows:

1. Instillation of hope

2. Universality

3. Imparting of information

4. Altruism

5. The corrective recapitulation of the primary family group

6. Development of socializing techniques

7. Imitative behavior

8. Interpersonal learning

9. Group cohesiveness

10. Catharsis

11. Existential factors

Interactional group therapy emphasizes the here and now; it is equally effective with inpatient and outpatient groups. Other kinds of group psychotherapy include analytic group psychotherapy, psychodrama, transactional analysis, supportive therapy, cognitive therapy, behavior therapy, and short-term dynamic psychotherapy. An effective group therapist needs education in small group dynamics and group therapy theory, clinical practice with groups, and expert supervision.

Clients

Clients can begin to change in a safe, secure, supportive environment within groups. Groups can facilitate changes in client thoughts, feelings, and actions. In psychoeducation groups, clients can acquire basic knowledge about addiction. They can learn and practice recovery skills. In mutual self-help groups, clients share their experiences, strength, and hope. Mutual self-help groups help many clients achieve early treatment goals. Continuing participation in mutual self-help groups helps clients maintain long-term recovery. Group therapy affords addiction clients the opportunity to address the many related personal, interpersonal, and social issues that characterize their addictions and often complicate recovery.

Clinicians

Clinicians conduct groups at all levels of care, including inpatient facilities, outpatient settings, and in the community. Groups may be facilitated by professional staff, volunteers, or peers. The clinician's role varies with the type of group and may be that of educator, facilitator, or therapist. Client treatment needs determine the kind and number of groups. The kind of group reflects its membership, size, meeting place, and times.

Family as Treatment

Approach

Many addiction professionals view the family as instrumental in the development, perpetuation, and treatment of addiction. Traditional treatment emphasizes intervention with the client as individual. The family may be consulted during the treatment process but rarely is central to treatment. A systems theory of addiction supports family-focused treatment. Systems theory suggests that the family contributes to the development of addiction in a family member and that the family is essential to treatment and recovery of the client.

Family as treatment is reflected in provider treatment philosophy and clinician preparation; for example, family nurse practitioners, marriage and family counselors, and staff social workers often implement family-focused treatment.

Clients

Families often initiate treatment with addiction clinicians through planned interventions with clients. With the expert guidance of addiction clinicians, the family confronts the client about the addiction. Many times, employers and other people affected by the client's addiction participate in this intervention. Together, family members, friends, and employer express their care and concern for the client. They then spell out very clearly the adverse effects of the client's addiction and the need for treatment *now*. Family members and colleagues agree on serious sanctions if the client refuses treatment—for example, a restraining order to prohibit the client from returning home, suspension from work, or a court order for involuntary treatment.

Family as treatment actively involves the family throughout the treatment process: assessment, diagnosis, treatment planning, intervention, and evaluation. The family may support or thwart continuing care in the community.

Clinicians

Addiction clinicians involve the family to varying degrees throughout the treatment process. Family history is one of seven problem areas assessed by the

Addiction Severity Index (ASI). The recovery environment is one of the six assessment dimensions of *ASAM PPC-2* (American Society of Addiction Medicine, 1996). Families are involved when clinicians work with children, adolescents, and elderly clients. Depending on the philosophy of the treatment providers and the preparation of the clinician, the entire family may be considered the client.

Community as Treatment

Approach

Increasingly, clients live at home or in the community during initial treatment, continuing care, remission, and recovery. Halfway houses provide residential inpatient treatment for clients. Recovering individuals may live in sober houses. Therapeutic communities (TCs) represent best the concept of community as treatment. Therapeutic communities are long-term, drug-free residential programs. They first developed in the 1960s and 1970s to help inner-city drug users with social problems. Many staff members of the early TCs were recovering addicts themselves.

Therapeutic community programs are based on the belief that clients have social deficits and require social treatment. Recovery is a developmental process that integrates explicit social, psychological, and developmental goals. The TC itself is the method or intervention. The purposeful use of the community is the primary method for facilitating growth and change in individuals. There is an

> emphasis on structure and hierarchy within the program, a need to isolate the individual from competing influences during treatment, a need for a prolonged period of treatment that is phased and intensive, and clear norms regarding personal responsibility and behavior. Learning, accepting, and internalizing these norms is accomplished through a highly structured treatment process that requires active participation by the client in a context of confrontation (to address denial, false beliefs, and defense mechanisms), mutual self-help, and affirmation of program expectations. (National Institute on Drug Abuse, 1994, p. 3)

De Leon (1994) asserts that recovery is a developmental process that can be understood as a passage through states of incremental learning: motivation, self-help, mutual self-help, and social learning. Community is the primary method for facilitating social and psychological change in individuals. Specific features of the community-as-method model include use of participant roles, membership feedback, and membership as role models; use of collective formats for guiding individual change; used of shared norms and values; use of structure and systems; and use of open communication and relationships.

Clients

Today, many TC clients still present with social deficits; they have neither developed nor demonstrated socially productive, conventional lifestyles. For these individuals, *habilitation* is the overall TC treatment goal. Other clients come from advantaged backgrounds, and their drug abuse is perceived as more directly expressive of psychopathology, personality disturbance, or existential malaise. For these clients, rehabilitation is the TC treatment goal, with a return to a lifestyle previously lived, known, and perhaps rejected. Currently, TCs offer programs for men, women, adolescents, women and children, and individuals with HIV/AIDS, as well as programs in prisons.

Clients demonstrate progress toward goal achievement through internalization of the change process as characterized by compliance, conformity, commitment, integration, and identity change. Both objective and subjective data demonstrate goal achievement or failure as well as client self-perceptions and experiences.

Clinicians

Change in the whole person is the goal of a therapeutic community:

1. *Socialization:* evolution of the individual as a prosocial member of society as evidenced by changes in social deviance, habilitation, and lifestyle

2. *Developmental change:* personal growth as reflected by maturity and responsibility, self-regulation, social management, and consistency in meeting obligations to self and others

3. *Psychological change:* personal growth in cognitive skills, such as awareness, judgment, insight, reality, and decision making; and in emotional skills, including communication and management of feeling states

Clinicians actively involve clients in the following series of program stages and phases, which reflect the developmental process required to effect change in clients:

- *Stage 1: Induction:* assessment and orientation (1-60 days)

- *Stage 2: Primary treatment:* social and psychological change

  Phase 1 (2-4 months): junior resident

  Phase 2 (5-8 months): intermediate resident

  Phase 3 (9-13 months): senior resident

- *Stage 3: Reentry:* separation from the TC to "live-out"
  Early phase: 13-18 months
  Late phase: 18-24 months

Summary

A treatment methodology is the explicit, purposeful, organized way in which clinicians and clients conduct treatment. Approaches to treatment include 12-step recovery, the Minnesota model, psychodynamic approaches, cognitive therapies, motivational enhancement therapy, the stages-of-change model, problem-oriented treatment, and solution-focused treatment. Group therapy is a primary treatment modality with addiction clients and their families, especially psychoeducation, mutual-self-help, and psychotherapy groups. Family as treatment and community as treatment represent two further approaches. Many people with addiction problems stop their substance use or addictive behavior on their own, without formal treatment. Addiction clinicians support this natural recovery.

Related Skills Checklist

Practitioner skills related to the treatment methodologies discussed in this chapter include the ability to do the following:

- Utilize three or more different treatment methods.
- Match treatment methodology to client variables.
- Conduct psychoeducation groups with clients.
- Refer clients to mutual self-help groups as appropriate.
- Facilitate group psychotherapy.
- Determine resources for family as treatment.
- Refer clients to therapeutic communities when indicated.

Special Topics for Further Study

Review clinical studies of treatment matching and treatment outcome studies. How do the following client variables determine selection of treatment methodology: addiction severity, age, ethnocultural characteristics, gender, sexual orientation? How does patient placement—level of care—influence treatment methodology? Compare and contrast treatment approaches with addiction clients in a medically managed intensive detoxification unit, in a mental health outpatient clinic, and in a therapeutic community in a prison.

Addiction Practice 2000

Addiction practice 2000 urges clinicians to (a) try a variety of approaches to treatment, (b) demonstrate the efficacy of specific treatment methods, and (c) show the relationship between treatment intervention and client outcome. Research is needed to investigate treatment inputs and stages. Inputs include staffing, clients, and the organization. Treatment stages include assessment, planning, core treatment, support services, and aftercare (Price, 1997).

References

Alcoholics Anonymous World Services. (1976). *Alcoholics Anonymous* (3rd ed.). New York: Author.

Alcoholics Anonymous World Services. (1989). *Twelve steps and twelve traditions.* New York: Author. (Original work published 1953)

Alcoholics Anonymous World Services. (1997). *Alcoholics Anonymous 1996 membership survey.* New York: Author.

American Psychiatric Association. (1994). *Diagnostic and statistical manual of mental disorders* (4th ed.). Washington, DC: Author.

American Society of Addiction Medicine. (1996). *Patient placement criteria for the treatment of substance-related disorders* (2nd ed.). Chevy Chase, MD: Author.

Beck, A. T., Wright, F. D., Newman, C. F., & Liese, B. S. (1993). *Cognitive therapy of substance abuse.* New York: Guilford.

Berg, I. K., & Miller, S. D. (1992). *Working with a problem drinker: A solution-focused approach.* New York: W. W. Norton.

Berg, I. K., & Reuss, N. H. (1998). *Solutions step by step: A substance abuse treatment manual.* New York: W. W. Norton.

Delbanco, A., & Delbanco, T. (1995, March 20). A.A. at the crossroads. *New Yorker,* 50-53, 59-63.

De Leon, G. (1994). The therapeutic community: Toward a general theory and model. In National Institute on Drug Abuse (Ed.), *Therapeutic community: Advances in research and application* (NIH Publication No. 94-3633) (pp. 16-53). Rockville, MD: National Institute on Drug Abuse.

Ellis, A., & Grieger, R. (Eds.). (1977). *Handbook of rational-emotive therapy.* New York: Springer.

Kellerman, J. L. (1969). *Alcoholism: A merry-go-round named denial.* New York: Al-Anon Family Group Headquarters.

Marlatt, G. A., & Gordon, J. R. (Eds.). (1985). *Relapse prevention: Maintenance strategies in the treatment of addictive behaviors.* New York: Guilford.

Miller, W. R., & Rollnick, S. (1992). *Motivational interviewing: Preparing people to change addictive behavior.* New York: Guilford.

National Institute on Drug Abuse. (Ed.). (1994). *Therapeutic community: Advances in research and application* (NIH Publication No. 94-3633). Rockville, MD: Author.

O'Hanlon, B., & Bertolino, B. (1998). *Even from a broken web: Brief, respectful solution-oriented therapy for sexual abuse and trauma.* New York: John Wiley.

Price, R. H. (1997). What we know and what we actually do: Best practices and their prevalence in substance-abuse treatment. In J. A. Egertson, D. M. Fox, & A. I. Leshner (Eds.), *Treating drug abusers effectively* (pp. 125-155). Malden, MA: Blackwell.

Prochaska, J. O., & DiClemente, C. C. (1983). Transtheoretical therapy: Toward a more integrative model of change. *Psychotherapy: Theory, Research, and Practice, 20,* 161-173.

Prochaska, J. O., Norcross, J. C., & DiClemente, C. C. (1995). *Changing for good.* New York: Simon & Schuster.

Project MATCH Research Group. (1993). Project MATCH: Rationale and methods for a multisite clinical trial matching patients to alcoholism treatment. *Alcohol: Clinical and Experimental Research, 17,* 1130-1145.

Sobell, M. B., & Sobell, L. C. (1975). Outpatient alcoholics give valid self-reports. *Journal of Nervous and Mental Disease, 17,* 32-42.

Sobell, M. B., & Sobell, L. C. (1978). *Behavioral treatment of alcohol problems.* New York: Plenum.

Sobell, M. B., & Sobell, L. C. (1993). *Problem drinkers: Guided self-change treatment.* New York: Guilford.

Spicer, J. (1993). *The Minnesota model: The evolution of the multidisciplinary approach to addiction recovery.* Center City, MN: Hazelden.

Toft, D. (1995, January). The Minnesota model—humane, holistic, flexible. *Hazelden News,* pp. 1-2, 16.

Yalom, I. D. (1995). *The theory and practice of group psychotherapy* (4th ed.). New York: Basic Books.

Other Sources

Alcoholics Anonymous World Services. (1975). *Alcoholics Anonymous comes of age: A brief history of A.A.* New York: Author.

Alcoholics Anonymous World Services. (1984). *This is A.A.: An introduction to the A.A. recovery program.* New York: Author.

Bean, M. H., & Zinberg, N. E. (Eds.). (1981). *Dynamic approaches to the understanding and treatment of alcoholism.* New York: Free Press.

Berg, R. C., & Landreth, G. L. (1998). *Group counseling: concepts and procedures* (3rd ed.). Philadelphia: Taylor & Francis.

Ciaramicoli, A. P. (1997). *Treatment of alcoholism and addiction: A holistic approach.* Northvale, NJ: Jason Aronson.

Dorsman, J. (1998, July/August). A survey of different approaches to treatment. *Counselor, 16,* 27-31.

Flores, P. J. (1997). *Group psychotherapy with addicted populations: An integration of twelve-step and psychodynamic theory* (2nd ed.). New York: Haworth.

Fox, V. (1998). *Addiction, change and choice.* Tucson, AZ: SeeSharp.

Galanter, M. (1993). *Network therapy for alcohol and drug abuse.* New York: Guilford.

Hester, R., & Miller, W. (Eds.). (1995). *Handbook of alcoholism treatment approaches: Effective alternatives* (2nd ed.). Boston: Allyn & Bacon.

Johnson Institute-QVS. (1995). *Recovery is a family affair.* Minneapolis: Author.

Jordan, M. R. (1999). *Treating addiction as a human process.* Northvale, NJ: Jason Aronson.

Kadden, R. (1995). *Cognitive-behavioral coping skills manual: A clinical research guide for therapists treating individuals with alcohol abuse and dependence* (Project MATCH Monograph Series, Vol. 3; NIH Publication No. 94-3724). Rockville, MD: National Institutes of Health.

Lewis, S. A. (Ed.). (1994). *Addictions: Concepts and strategies for treatment.* Gaithersburg, MD: Aspen.

Louie, K. (1993). Patterns of addiction in the family. In M. A. Naegle (Ed.), *Substance abuse education in nursing* (Vol. 3, pp. 45-86). New York: National League for Nursing Press.

Margolis, R. D., & Zweben, J. (1997). *Treating patients with alcohol and other drug problems: An integrated approach.* Washington, DC: American Psychological Association.

Miller, S. D., Hubble, M. A., & Duncan, B. L. (Eds.). (1996). *Handbook of solution-focused brief therapy.* San Francisco: Jossey-Bass.

Miller, W. R. (1995). *Motivational enhancement therapy manual: A clinical research guide for therapists treating individuals with alcohol abuse and dependence* (Project MATCH Monograph Series, Vol. 2; NIH Publication No. 94-3723). Rockville, MD: National Institutes of Health.

National Institute on Drug Abuse. (1993). *Behavioral treatments for drug abuse and dependence* (NIH Publication No. 93-3684). Rockville, MD: Author.

Nowinski, J., Baker, S., & Caroll, K. (1995). *Twelve-step facilitation manual: A clinical research guide for therapists treating individuals with alcohol abuse and dependence* (Project MATCH Monograph Series, Vol. 1; NIH Publication No. 94-3722). Rockville, MD: National Institutes of Health.

Stanton, M. D., & Todd, T. C. (1999). *The family therapy of drug abuse and addiction* (2nd ed.). New York: Guilford.

Trimpey, J. (1996). *Rational recovery: The new cure for substance addiction.* New York: Pocket Books.

Trimpey, J. (1996). *The small book: A revolutionary approach to overcoming drug and alcohol dependence.* New York: Dell.

Tucker, J. A., Donovan, D. M., & Marlatt, G. A. (1999). *Changing addictive behavior: Bridging clinical and public health strategies.* New York: Guilford.

Wegscheider-Crus, S. (1989). *Another chance: Hope and health for the alcoholic family.* Palo Alto, CA: Science & Behavior Books.

7

Treatment Goals

Objectives

- Collaborate with clients to set treatment goals.
- Acknowledge that goals reflect desired client change.
- Specify short-term, immediate goals, such as safe withdrawal, abstinence, harm reduction, or moderate drinking.
- Identify intermediate goals, such as relapse prevention and remission.
- Recognize recovery as a comprehensive, long-term client goal.

Outline

- **Treatment Goals**
- **Short-Term, Immediate Goals**
  - Safe Withdrawal
  - Abstinence
  - Harm Reduction
  - Moderate Drinking
- **Intermediate Goals**
  - Relapse Prevention
  - Remission
- **Recovery: A Long-Term Goal**
- **Summary**
- **Related Skills Checklist**
- **Special Topics for Further Study**
- **Addiction Practice 2000**

Treatment Goals

Treatment works! With effective treatment, clients change. Treatment goals describe desired client changes related to substance use, consequences of substance use, other addictive disorders, and coexisting medical, psychological, and social problems. Goals are broad statements that delineate expected client behavioral change as well as changes in thoughts and feelings: changes in the cognitive, affective, and psychomotor domains. Client and clinicians collaborate to develop treatment goals. Goals identify client needs, problems, and limitations related to addiction severity. Goals also reflect client strengths, abilities, and preferences related to recovery potential. Goals take into account client age, ethnocultural background, gender, and sexual orientation. Treatment goals address coexisting medical, psychological, and social problems. Treatment goals reflect state-of-the art addiction theory and treatment methodology. In addition, they may reflect program philosophy; for example, abstinence would be a client goal in a drug-free therapeutic community.

Short-Term, Immediate Goals

Short-term, immediate goals relate directly to client substance use or addictive behavior. Safe withdrawal, abstinence, harm reduction, and moderate drinking are all examples of short-term, immediate client goals.

Safe Withdrawal

Safe withdrawal is an immediate treatment goal. Clients experience withdrawal when they stop or reduce heavy or prolonged substance use. Withdrawal may be uncomfortable or even fatal. Withdrawal signs and symptoms are substance specific. For example, clients who stop drinking may experience nausea and vomiting, tremors, sweating, anxiety, and agitation; tactile, auditory, or visual disturbances; and headaches and disorientation. Narcotic withdrawal causes mild to severe discomfort. First, individuals experience craving and restlessness; slight aching of muscles, joints, and bones; mild lower back pain; tension and insomnia; dilated pupils; lethargy; sweating; hot and cold flashes; and runny nose. Next, they often go through moderate aching of muscles, joints, and bones; moderate lower back pain; and increased pulse and moderate increase in blood pressure. Finally, they experience anorexia, nausea, or stomach cramps; yawning, tearing, and gooseflesh; and diarrhea, vomiting, pulse above 100, tremors, increased respiratory rate and depth, low-grade temperature, and doubling over with stomach cramps, with kicking movement.

Clinicians assess clients to determine withdrawal risk. Dimension 1 of *ASAM PPC-2* addresses intoxication and/or withdrawal potential (American Society of Addiction Medicine, 1996). Assessment data document client needs. Using the assessment data, clinicians and client plan treatment to assure a safe, comfortable withdrawal. Treatment intensity, including level of care, varies with addiction severity. Ned L. reports drinking daily for 8 years; he receives income from Social Security Disability Insurance for major depression. Ned had a seizure and fell and cut his head open; his sister called 911. Ned received a score of 28 on the Clinical Institute Withdrawal Assessment of Alcohol Scale (CIWA-Ar) and required medically managed intensive inpatient detoxification. Stan P. describes snorting cocaine off and on for 3 years; he also binge drinks. Stan "detoxed" safely and comfortably in a clinically managed partial hospitalization program.

Abstinence

Abstinence has been the traditional treatment goal for most clients with substance use disorders and addictive behaviors such as pathological gambling. Abstinence means that clients refrain completely, totally, 100% from using psychoactive and addictive substances, both licit and illicit. Abstinent problem gamblers avoid any and all wagering, including "mind bets."

Abstinence is the treatment goal of choice for programs and clinicians that embrace a 12-step approach to treatment and recovery. Alcoholics Anonymous and other mutual self-help groups that build upon the A.A. model require abstinence as the primary treatment goal. Programs based on the Minnesota model also emphasize abstinence-based treatment. Treatment providers usually make their positions on abstinence clear in their mission statements, statements of philosophy, and program goals. This information is readily available for client and clinician use. Abstinence is the treatment goal for any program designated as "drug-free."

Abstinence is the treatment goal for inmates in correctional facilities and individuals on parole or probation, and for residents of halfway houses and therapeutic communities, as well as in rehabilitation programs for physicians, dentists, pharmacists, and nurses. The occupational fields of construction and transportation, as well as all others involving heavy equipment, require drug-free work sites. Cooperation with preemployment drug screening, random urine testing, and urine testing for probable cause is a condition of employment for increasing numbers of employees.

Harm Reduction

The concept of harm reduction builds upon a general model of drug treatment developed in Great Britain and the Netherlands to reduce the risk of transmission of HIV/AIDS. A harm-reduction model views substance use, as well as other addictive behaviors, as a continuum of behaviors from excess to moderation to abstinence. Excess is associated with increased risks to health and well-being; risks decrease with abstinence. The harm-reduction model holds that any step away from excess toward abstinence is positive. The goal of harm reduction is to help clients move away from excessive use and excessive behaviors and in this way reduce the harmful consequences of their addictions, such as accidental deaths from drunk driving, abuse and violence, suicide and homicide, unwanted pregnancies and HIV/AIDS, and many other medical, psychological, and social problems associated with excess.

In the United States, where people strongly embrace abstinence as a treatment goal, treatment providers, clinicians, and the general public have been reluctant to consider harm reduction as an appropriate treatment goal for addictive disorders. Harm-reduction programs such as needle exchange programs for injection drugs users and methadone maintenance treatment for heroin users are controversial. Although study after study has demonstrated that needle exchange programs do not increase injection drug use and do greatly reduce the incidence of HIV, in 1998 the Clinton administration and the U.S. House of Representatives refused to fund needle exchange programs. Even so, such programs have expanded in terms of the numbers of syringes exchanged, the geographic distribution of programs, and the range of services offered (Paone, Clark, Qiuhu, Purchase, & Des Jarlais, 1999). Methadone maintenance eliminates the need for the use of illicit drugs and the criminal lifestyle often associated with illicit drug use. Opioid maintenance therapy (methadone maintenance) may be an intermediate treatment goal, with abstinence as the ultimate goal. Some clients may be maintained on methadone indefinitely. A methadone maintenance program, however, is only as good as the comprehensive rehabilitation program that supports it.

The rationale behind the harm-reducing "designated driver" campaign was questioned when the idea was first introduced. People asked, "Does this mean that four people can get smashed if the fifth friend doesn't drink and drives?" Yes. A harm-reduction model for health education in schools remains controversial. Many parents, religious leaders, and educators accept only "Just say no," the abstinence approach to substance use and sex education. Despite data indicating that increasing numbers of adolescents are having sex, opposition is strong to sex education for schoolchildren that includes information on condom use to prevent sexually transmitted diseases, including HIV/AIDS, let alone un-

wanted pregnancy. In contrast, in the 1990s there seemed to be widespread acceptance of the harm-reducing use of nicotine replacement therapy (in the form
of nicotine patch or nicotine gum) by people trying to give up smoking.

When clients are highly resistant to abstinence-based treatment, or are inappropriate candidates for such treatment, harm reduction may be the next best
goal. Such clients include chronic intravenous heroin users; individuals who relapse repeatedly; teens, college students, and other young adults; and possibly
the 40 million problem drinkers in the United States who do not meet diagnostic
criteria for dependence. Treatment providers are beginning to identify harm reduction as the most realistic and appropriate treatment goal for certain clients.
For example, the High Risk Drinker Project at the University of Washington is
an effective campus-based program aimed at reducing alcohol-related problems
based on the principles of harm reduction.

Drug distributors and dealers understand the concept of harm reduction well.
Many suburban adults who cringe at the idea of ever sticking needles in their
arms are readily snorting heroin. When excessive alcohol consumption started
to drop in this country, companies developed and promoted wine coolers,
seltzers, and bottled water to maintain a young adult market.

Ethan Nadelmann (1998) has presented a convincing case for harm reduction
in an article in *Foreign Affairs*; he concludes his argument by stating:

> The lessons from Europe and Australia are compelling. Drug control policies
> should focus on reducing drug-related crime, disease, and death, not the number of
> casual drug users. Stopping the spread of HIV by and among drug users by making
> sterile syringes and methadone readily available must be a first priority. American
> politicians need to explore, not ignore or automatically condemn, promising pol-
> icy options such as cannabis decriminalization, heroin prescription, and the inte-
> gration of harm-reduction principles into community policing strategies. Central
> governments must back, or at least not hinder, the efforts of municipal officials and
> citizens to devise pragmatic approaches to local drug problems. Like citizens in
> Europe, the American public has supported such innovations when they are ade-
> quately explained and allowed to prove themselves. As the evidence comes in,
> what works is increasingly apparent. All that remains is mustering the political
> courage. (p. 126)[1]

Moderate Drinking

According to an article published in *U.S. News & World Report* in 1997, at that
time there were estimated to be 40 million problem drinkers in the United States.
Although alcohol consumption has fallen by 15% since 1980, between 44% and
51% of Americans drink regularly. Some 32 million Americans binge drink at

least once a month. Yet the majority of problem drinkers do not meet *DSM-IV* criteria for alcohol dependence (American Psychiatric Association, 1994). Abstinence may not be the best treatment goal for these drinkers. The article's author suggests controlled drinking as a goal for "problem drinkers," that is, individuals who drink but who are not physiologically dependent on alcohol. The author acknowledges, however, that it is difficult to draw a clear line between problem drinking and alcohol dependency (Shute, 1997).

The National Institute on Alcohol Abuse and Alcoholism (NIAAA) acknowledges that moderate drinking means different things to different people; "moderate drinking" is often confused with "social drinking." The U.S. Department of Agriculture and Department of Health and Human Services define moderate drinking as no more than one drink a day for most women, and no more than two drinks a day for most men. A standard drink is generally considered to be 12 ounces of beer, 5 ounces of wine, or 1.5 ounces of 80-proof distilled spirits (all of these drinks contain roughly the same amount of absolute alcohol). These guidelines exclude pregnant women, people who plan to drive or operate heavy equipment, people taking certain medications (including some over-the-counter drugs), recovering alcoholics, persons under the age of 21, and elderly persons. Alcohol is contraindicated for people with certain medical conditions.

Moderate drinking has both risks and benefits. The NIAAA acknowledges that moderate drinking may have psychological benefits. After "a drink or two" some people report reduced tension, stress, and anxiety; alcohol promotes relaxation and increases self-confidence and conviviality ("I feel warm and good all over"). In the elderly, moderate drinking can stimulate appetite, promote regular bowel function, and improve mood. The most convincing medical case for moderate drinking has been made by recent research that found it has certain cardiovascular benefits. The University of Michigan Health System and Medical School has developed Drink Wise, a program patterned after the moderate drinking approach developed at the Addiction Research Foundation in Toronto. Drink Wise offers "health choices for people who drink." The program is designed for individuals with mild to moderate alcohol problems, not for people who are severely dependent upon alcohol. Moderation Management is a self-help and Internet discussion group based on the Office for Substance Abuse Prevention's 1992 book *Moderate Drinking.*

Moderate drinking, however, increases risks for motor vehicle accidents, interactions with medications, stroke, cancer, and birth defects. Abstinent individuals with a diagnosis of alcohol dependence should not drink "moderately" in an attempt to protect themselves against coronary artery disease. Drinking moderately is difficult for individuals with a diagnosis of alcohol dependence. Recovering alcoholics, as well as individuals from families with histories of alcoholism, risk relapse and progression from moderate to heavy drinking.

Intermediate Goals

Relapse Prevention

With the 1985 publication of the now-classic book *Relapse Prevention: Maintenance Strategies in the Treatment of Addictive Behaviors,* edited by Marlatt and Gordon, clinicians began to understand the concept of relapse and to incorporate relapse prevention into client treatment. For many addiction clinicians, relapse prevention is almost synonymous with the lifelong work of Terence T. Gorski.

According to Gorski and other experts in the field, relapse is a process that begins long before a person uses alcohol or drugs or places a wager. Clients and clinicians can recognize the warning signs of a potential relapse, which are known collectively as BUDDING (building up to drink or drug). Clients may relapse by drinking, using, or returning to addictive behavior. Sometimes clients become very dysfunctional without actually using substances or engaging in addictive behavior. A person who exhibits this behavior is often called a "dry drunk."

Gorski and Miller (1986) have identified early warning signs of relapse that clinicians and clients use extensively. They have further suggested that post-acute withdrawal syndrome (PAWS) follows actual withdrawal and characterizes early recovery. Symptoms of PAWS include inability to think clearly, memory problems, emotional overreactions or numbness, sleep disturbances, physical coordination problems, and stress sensitivity.

Gorski's *Relapse Prevention Counseling Workbook* (1995) is designed to help clinicians and clients identify, analyze, and manage high-risk situations that can trigger relapse: irrational thoughts, unmanageable feelings, self-destructive urges, and self-defeating behaviors. In the workbook, Gorski includes a list of relapse warning signs for use by clinicians with their clients (pp. 6-17):

1. *Internal change* as evidenced by increased stress, change in thinking, change in feeling, and change in behavior

2. *Denial* as evidenced by worrying about myself or denying that I'm worried

3. *Avoidance and defensiveness* as evidenced by believing I'll never relapse, focusing on others instead of myself, getting defensive, getting compulsive, acting impulsively, and getting lonely

4. *Crisis building* as evidenced by seeing only a small part of the problem, getting depressed, poor planning, and plans that begin to fail

5. *Immobilization* as evidenced by daydreaming and wishful thinking, feeling that nothing can be solved, and an immature wish to be happy

6. *Confusion and overreaction* as evidenced by difficulty in thinking clearly, difficulty in managing feelings and emotions, difficulty in remembering things, periods

of confusion, difficulty in managing stress, irritation with friends, and becoming easily angered

7. *Depression* as evidenced by irregular eating habits, lack of desire to take action, difficulty sleeping restfully, loss of daily structure, and periods of deep depression

8. *Loss of control* as evidenced by hiding my problems, feeling powerless and helpless, refusing help, breaking my recovery program, going against my values, complete loss of self-confidence, unreasonable resentment, and overwhelming loneliness, frustration, anger, and tension

9. *Thinking about relapse* as evidenced by thinking relapse will help me feel better, getting dissatisfied with recovery, getting obsessed with relapse, and convincing myself to relapse

10. *Relapse* as evidenced by starting the relapse, attempting to control, feeling disappointed, loss of control, as well as life and health problems

Gorski believes that planned relapse prevention is appropriate for people in early recovery and for all clients at high risk for relapse. The program is compatible with brief strategic group therapy methods. Gorski and his colleagues have written extensively about relapse prevention; currently, Gorski directs the National Relapse Prevention Certification School.

Remission

By definition, remission is a lessening of severity of symptoms or a period during which symptoms subside. Individuals with leukemia, arthritis, and addictive disorders experience remission. *DSM-IV* applies the specifier *remission* to diagnoses when none of the criteria for substance dependence or substance abuse have been present for at least a month. Further specification is based on the interval of time that has elapsed since the end of dependence, plus continuing evidence of the signs and symptoms (the criteria) for dependence or abuse:

- *Early full remission:* The client demonstrates no signs or symptoms of dependence or abuse for at least 1 month, but less than 12 months.

- *Early partial remission:* One or more criteria for dependence or abuse have been met (but not full criteria for dependence) for at least 1 month, but less than 12 months.

- *Sustained full remission:* No signs or symptoms of dependence of abuse have been met for 12 months or longer.

- *Sustained partial remission:* One or more criteria for dependence or abuse have been met (but not full criteria for dependence) for 12 months or longer.

Remission is a useful concept for clinicians and clients when abstinence is the treatment goal. Lack of remission, especially inability to abstain for a month, motivates clinicians and clients to develop rigorous relapse prevention plans. Clinicians can adapt and still use the concept of remission when harm reduction or moderate drinking is a treatment goal.

Recovery: A Long-Term Goal

Recovery is optimal client health, well-being, and functioning. Definitions of recovery vary with theories and models of addiction as well as broad treatment goals. Recovery is highly individual. First, there is agreement among clinicians and clients that recovery includes sustained management of the addictive disorder as evidenced by client abstinence, harm reduction, moderate drinking, relapse prevention, or remission. Second, recovery includes increased biopsychosocial and spiritual well-being as perceived and demonstrated by the client. Third, recovery reflects improved client functioning in psychological, social, and occupational spheres. High-quality recovery enhances interpersonal and family relationships and fosters social and community competence. Recovery is often described as a process rather than an end point: Recovery is a journey, not a destination. Many people describe themselves as "recovering," but not "recovered." For some, recovery is synonymous with the concept of sobriety.

What does recovery look like? Bill D., age 42, has been alcohol- and drug-free for 5 years. His gastrointestinal distress has resolved. He took antidepressant medications for 2 years, but today takes only a daily multivitamin and aspirin. Bill and his wife, Nancy, separated briefly during his early recovery. They sought couples counseling, and several sessions included their two children. They now describe their marriage and family as "the best ever!" Throughout his drinking and drug use, Bill remained employed, although his job was in jeopardy several times. Last year, his company promoted him to regional sales manager. Bill attends two A.A. meetings a week and is active in a men's fellowship group at his community church. Most of all, Bill describes an "inner peace that transcends understanding." Bill is in recovery.

Gorski (1989) has proposed a developmental model of recovery that comprises six progressive stages: transition, stabilization, early recovery, middle recovery, late recovery, and maintenance (see Table 7.1). Most clinicians recognize early, middle, and late recovery. Although it is difficult to designate specific time intervals for each stage of recovery, clinicians usually consider early recovery to be the first 2 years of sustained full remission. Middle recovery covers the period of years 2 to 5, and later recovery describes progress beyond 5 years. In a study of male alcohol abuse over a 30-year period, Vaillant (1996) found that when individuals maintained abstinence for 5 years, relapse was rare.

TABLE 7.1 The Development Model of Recovery: The Relapse/Recovery Grid

I. Transition	II. Stabilization	III. Early Recovery	IV. Middle Recovery	V. Late Recovery	VI. Maintenance
1. Develop motivating problems	1. Recognition of the need for help	1. Full conscious recognition of addictive disease	1. Resolving the demoralization crisis	1. Recognizing the effects of childhood problems on sobriety	1. Maintain a recovery program
2. Failure of normal problem solving	2. Recovery from immediate after-effects	2. Full acceptance and integration of the addiction	2. Repairing addiction-caused social damage	2. Learning about family-of-origin issues	2. Effective day-to-day coping
3. Failure of controlled use strategies	3. Interrupting pathological preoccupation	3. Learning non-chemical coping skills	3. Establishing a self-regulated recovery program	3. Conscious examination of childhood	3. Continued growth and development
4. Acceptance of need for abstinence	4. Learning non-chemical stress management methods	4. Short-term social stabilization	4. Establishing lifestyle balance	4. Application to adult living	4. Effective coping with life transitions
	5. Developing hope and motivation	5. Developing a sobriety-centered value system	5. Management of change	5. Change in lifestyle	

SOURCE: Gorski (1989), Copyright T. T. Gorski, 1987 (revised May 1987). Reprinted by permission.

143

Summary

Client and clinicians collaborate to set treatment goals that reflect desired client change. Short-term, immediate goals include safe withdrawal, abstinence, harm reduction, and moderate drinking. Relapse prevention and remission are intermediate client goals. Recovery is a comprehensive, long-term client goal.

Related Skills Checklist

Practitioner skills related to treatment goals include the ability to do the following:

- Set short-term treatment goals with clients, including safe withdrawal, abstinence, and harm reduction.
- Develop intermediate treatment goals with clients, emphasizing relapse prevention and remission.
- Identify long-term recovery goals with clients.

Special Topics for Further Study

Investigate the theory and research that support harm reduction as a treatment goal of choice for some clients. Why is harm reduction such a controversial treatment goal? Examine the longitudinal research of George Vaillant (1996), especially his observation that relapse is rare after 5 years of continuous abstinence.

Addiction Practice 2000

Addiction practice 2000 encourages clinicians to increase their competence in developing challenging, yet realistic, treatment goals with clients. Practitioners should encourage clients to strive for nontraditional outcomes and goals to promote client well-being and optimal functioning. Clinicians must also assess relapse potential and intervene aggressively when necessary. Simpson (1997) identifies three phases of treatment—induction, intervention, and transition to aftercare—and suggests that clinicians identify treatment goals for each phase. Induction includes admission, assessment, and treatment planning. Intervention consists of engagement, therapeutic compliance, and the recovery process. Transition to aftercare involves family and friends, work and leisure, and support networks.

Note

1. This excerpt is reprinted by permission of *Foreign Affairs,* vol. 7, no. 1, 1998. Copyright 1998 by the Council on Foreign Relations, Inc.

References

American Psychiatric Association. (1994). *Diagnostic and statistical manual of mental disorders* (4th ed.). Washington, DC: Author.

American Society of Addiction Medicine. (1996). *Patient placement criteria for the treatment of substance-related disorders* (2nd ed.). Chevy Chase, MD: Author.

Do women benefit from light drinking? (1995, June). *Harvard Heart Letter,* pp. 1-2.

Gorski, T. T. (1989). *Passages through recovery: An action plan for preventing relapse.* Center City, MN: Hazelden.

Gorski, T. T. (1995). *Relapse prevention counseling workbook: Managing high-risk situations.* Independence, MO: Herald House/Independence.

Gorski, T. T., & Miller, M. (1986). *Staying sober: A guide for relapse prevention.* Independence, MO: Herald House/Independence.

Marlatt, G. A., & Gordon, J. R. (Eds.). (1985). *Relapse prevention: Maintenance strategies in the treatment of addictive behaviors.* New York: Guilford.

Nadelmann, E. A. (1998). Commonsense drug policy. *Foreign Affairs, 77,* 111-126.

Office for Substance Abuse Prevention. (1992). *Moderate drinking: Alcohol alert* (NIAAA Publication No. 16, PH315). Rockville, MD: Author.

Paone, D., Clark, J., Qiuhu, S., Purchase, D., & Des Jarlais, D. C. (1999). Syringe exchange in the United States, 1996: A national profile. *American Journal of Public Health, 89,* 43-46.

Shute, N. (1997, September 6). The drinking dilemma. *U.S. News & World Report,* pp. 54-55, 57-58, 60-62, 64-65.

Simpson, D. W. (1997). Effectiveness of drug-abuse treatment: A review of research from field settings. In J. A. Egertson, D. M. Fox, & A. I. Leshner (Eds.), *Treating drug abusers effectively* (pp. 41-73). Malden, MA: Blackwell.

Vaillant, G. E. (1996). A long-term follow-up of male alcohol abuse. *Archives of General Psychiatry, 53,* 243-249.

Other Sources

Ashley, M. J., Ferrence, R., Room, R., Rankin, J., & Single, E. (1994). Moderate drinking and health: Report of an international symposium. *Canadian Medical Association Journal, 151,* 1-16.

Gorski, T. T. (1995). *The phases and warning signs of relapse.* Independence, MO: Herald House/Independence.

Marlatt, G. A. (1998). *Harm reduction: Pragmatic strategies for managing high-risk behaviors.* New York: Guilford.

National Institute on Drug Abuse. (1994). *Outreach/risk reduction strategies for chang-ing HIV-related risk behaviors among injection drug users* (NIH Publication No. 94-3726). Rockville, MD: Author.

Payte, J. T. (1997). Methadone maintenance treatment: The first thirty years. *Journal of Psychoactive Drugs, 29,* 149-153.

Sanchez-Craig, M., Wilkinson, A., & Davila, R. (1995). Empirically based guidelines for moderate drinking: 1-year results from three studies with problem drinkers. *American Journal of Public Health, 85,* 823-828.

Solberg, R. J. (1993). *The dry drunk syndrome.* Center City, MN: Hazelden.

Washton, A. M. (1990). *Maintaining recovery: Enjoying life without cocaine.* Center City, MN: Hazelden.

Washton, A. M. (1990). *Staying off cocaine: Cravings, other drugs and slips.* Center City, MN: Hazelden.

Zweben, J. E. (1991). Counseling issues in methadone maintenance treatment. *Journal of Psychoactive Drugs, 23,* 177-190.

8

Addiction Severity and Treatment Intensity

Objectives

- Grasp the concepts of addiction severity and treatment intensity.
- Understand the relationship between addiction severity and treatment intensity.
- Appreciate the treatment background that gave rise to patient placement criteria.
- Employ standardized tools to determine addiction severity.
- Employ assessment criteria to place clients in appropriate levels of care.
- Recognize congruence between client assessment and placement.

Outline

- **Addiction Severity and Treatment Intensity**
- **Treatment Background**
  - The 1950s
  - The 1960s
  - The 1970s
  - The 1980s
  - The 1990s
  - ASAM PPC-2

- ■ **Addiction Severity**
  - – DSM-IV
  - – The Addiction Severity Index
  - – ASAM PPC-2 Assessment Dimensions
- ■ **Treatment Intensity**
  - – ASAM PPC-2 Levels of Care
  - – Early Intervention
  - – Detoxification
  - – Opioid Maintenance Therapy
- ■ **Client Assessment and Placement**
- ■ **Summary**
- ■ **Related Skills Checklist**
- ■ **Special Topics for Further Study**
- ■ **Addiction Practice 2000**

Addiction Severity and Treatment Intensity

The term *addiction severity* refers to the seriousness of a client's symptoms and the degree of impairment related to the addiction per se as well as coexisting medical, psychological, and social problems. Broadly speaking, a client's condition may be stable, serious, or critical. Client stress may be minimal, mild, moderate, or severe. Client functioning can range from superior to the client's presenting a danger to self and others. Addiction severity determines treatment intensity.

Treatment intensity includes the number, types, and frequency of interventions and services; it is often associated with level of care. Treatment intensity reflects addiction severity in that the higher the addiction severity, the greater the treatment intensity. Clinicians use addiction severity data to place clients in levels of care appropriate to their needs, to plan treatment, and to specify interventions and services.

Treatment Background

The 1950s

Specific treatment for addictive disorders as we know it today developed in the 1950s. Alcoholics received care in freestanding residential programs staffed primarily by nonprofessionals who were themselves in recovery and who embraced 12-step programs. Clients were usually in the late stages of their disease. A few facilities offered medical treatment or psychiatric care. There was no third-party reimbursement for treatment. Alcoholics who could not afford inpatient treatment utilized outpatient services. Convicted drug addicts were treated in prison; more affluent addicts received treatment in discreet private inpatient facilities.

In the 1950s, the pharmaceutical industry in the United States introduced tranquilizers, antidepressants, diet pills, and many other new psychoactive drugs. These "miracle" drugs were marketed aggressively, and physicians wrote millions of prescriptions, especially for women.

The 1960s

Synanon was founded in 1958 and became a model for other therapeutic communities (TCs) that developed in the 1960s and 1970s, such as Daytop Village, Phoenix House, Gateway Houses Foundation, and Odyssey House. These TCs were 6- to 24-month, drug-free residential programs staffed primarily by recovering drug addicts. The typical client was a minority male from the inner city; he had a limited education, a poor job history, and an extensive history of criminal activity. Staff worked with clients to help them kick the drug habit and develop the personal and social skills necessary to support a drug-free lifestyle back in the community. Drug-free outpatient programs as well as outpatient methadone maintenance programs were also available to drug addicts.

With the 1960 publication of Jellinek's *The Disease Concept of Alcoholism,* public and professional acceptance of alcoholism as a disease increased. During the next decade, many new alcoholism treatment facilities opened and prospered. Treatment for alcoholics included detoxification plus the classic 28-day (fixed-length-of-stay) inpatient rehabilitation program, with its emphasis on individual and group education and counseling.

The 1970s

The 1970s saw a significant increase in the number of people receiving treatment for alcoholism. Public education about alcoholism as a disease increased. Prominent public figures disclosed their own alcoholism, and this helped reduce the stigma associated with the "disease." Employee assistance programs in business and industry identified employees with alcohol problems and referred them for treatment.

In 1974, the National Institute on Alcohol Abuse and Alcoholism, and subsequently the National Institute on Drug Abuse, advocated for accreditation of alcohol and drug abuse treatment programs, credentialing of counselors, and insurance reimbursement for services. Third-party reimbursement for treatment developed, primarily for inpatient treatment, usually for fixed-length-of-stay programs. A one-size-fits-all philosophy permeated the treatment field. Outpatient programs for alcoholics continued, but with little growth, in part due to lack of licensure regulations and reimbursement mechanisms. Drug treatment continued in TCs, drug-free outpatient programs, and outpatient methadone maintenance programs.

The 1980s

In the early 1980s, addiction professionals observed that the client profile was changing. Clients represented a spectrum of addiction severity, from very early to late-stage disease. Clients presented for treatment with *both* alcohol and other drug problems—for instance, women with prescription drug addiction plus alcoholism. The 1980s witnessed widespread use of illicit drugs, especially heroin and cocaine. A significant number of clients suffered from coexisting psychiatric disorders, both *DSM-III* Axis I and Axis II diagnoses (American Psychiatric Association, 1980). Hepatitis and sexually transmitted diseases, including HIV/AIDS, were increasing in clients seeking treatment for drug addiction. More women, youth, and minorities needed treatment, including pregnant addicts and homeless people.

During the 1980s, the number of alcohol-only and drug-only treatment programs declined, and most treatment providers began to offer substance abuse treatment. Some substance abuse providers began to treat dual-addiction clients. More psychiatric facilities undertook treatment of clients' "psychoactive substance problems." Addiction professionals started to use *DSM-III* as a diagnostic tool. In 1980, Dr. A. Thomas McClellan and his colleagues at the Philadelphia Veterans Administration Center developed the Addiction Severity Index (ASI) for use by clinical researchers in evaluating treatment for clients in six different substance abuse treatment programs. Clinicians began to use severity criteria to plan, monitor, and evaluate treatment.

Yet treatment was still characterized by a limited range of interventions and services, usually offered in inpatient fixed-length-of-stay programs. Addiction professionals expressed frustration with the treatment provider system and their inability to provide individualized, quality care. Diagnostic-related groups (DRGs) were introduced as part of the Social Security Amendments of 1983. Each DRG was assigned an average length of stay, and facilities received payment based on flat rates, regardless of actual costs. Private insurance companies developed similar reimbursement programs. Treatment providers were motivated to streamline services and shorten length of treatment.

The 1990s

In the 1990s, escalating health care and insurance costs prompted both private and public insurance payers to question the clinical and fiscal efficacy of a predominantly inpatient, fixed-length-of-stay treatment model. Too often, the same treatment was offered for individuals with different addiction problems. For example, both Sam T., a 45-year-old homeless man with a 25-year drinking history, and Catherine J., a 29-year-old schoolteacher with a history of episodic drinking and one arrest for operating under the influence, would receive a 5-day detoxification program followed by a 28-day inpatient rehabilitation.

Sometimes, different treatments were prescribed for individuals with similar problems, as in this scenario: Three college students worked construction during the summer. All three snorted cocaine daily when working and drank heavily on weekends. During a wild Fourth of July party, the three were arrested for assault and battery. Tom H. received inpatient treatment for 4 weeks, Dick L. saw an outpatient counselor once a week for 8 weeks, and Harry A. attended some Alcoholics Anonymous (A.A.) and Narcotics Anonymous (N.A.) meetings. Their treatment outcomes were similar—all returned to college in the fall "clean and with good intentions to control their drug use."

Insurance companies and other payers noticed the similar outcomes from different treatments and questioned treatment providers, especially challenging providers to justify expensive inpatient treatment versus less costly outpatient treatment. With the rapid growth of managed care and these insurance challenges, treatment providers scrambled to survive and moved to shift treatment for substance abuse from inpatient to outpatient settings. Addiction researchers were quick to point out that rarely, if ever, had addiction severity guided patient placement. This dilemma became the focus for identification of patient placement standards for admission, continued stay, and discharge criteria as first set forth in *The Cleveland Admission, Discharge, and Transfer Criteria* (Hoffmann, Halikas, & Mee-Lee, 1987) and *Admission, Continued Stay and Discharge Criteria for Adult Alcoholism and Drug Dependence Treatment Services* (Weedman, 1987) developed by the National Association of Addiction Treatment Providers (NAATP).

Subsequently, and building upon these two guides, the NAATP and the American Society of Addiction Medicine (ASAM) formed work groups to develop adult and adolescent patient placement criteria, which were then published in *Patient Placement Criteria for the Treatment of Psychoactive Substance Use Disorders* (ASAM, 1991). Six dimensions of addiction severity guided placement of adults and adolescents in four levels of care. These criteria were expanded and/or refined in the subsequent 1996 ASAM publication *Patient Placement Criteria for the Treatment of Substance-Related Disorders,* second edition, which is known as *ASAM PPC-2.*

ASAM PPC-2

ASAM PPC-2 identifies six primary problem areas or assessment dimensions. Assessment of severity in each dimension directs treatment intensity. Four major levels of care for treatment of adults and adolescents are identified and described. The criteria reflect characteristics of clients who require each level of care. *ASAM PPC-2* distinguishes among levels according to clients' needs for (a) direct medical management; (b) structure, safety, and security; and (c) treatment intensity.

Addiction Severity

As noted above, *addiction severity* refers to the seriousness of the client's addiction, including degree of impairment. Clients acknowledge different degrees of addiction severity in their own statements. "I can take it or leave it." "I can stop any time." "Thank God, I didn't lose my job or my family." "I'm sick and tired of being sick and tired." "I've hit bottom!" "I said I never would work the streets or shoot up. Never say never!" The fourth edition of the *Diagnostic and Statistical Manual of Mental Disorders* (*DSM-IV;* American Psychiatric Association, 1994), the ASI, and *ASAM PPC-2* are standardized tools that addiction clinicians use to determine addiction severity.

DSM-IV

DSM-IV divides substance use disorders into *abuse* and *dependence;* clinicians specify *with physiological dependence* if the client manifests tolerance or withdrawal and *without physiological dependence* if there is no evidence of tolerance or withdrawal. Four course specifiers describe remission. In addition, clinicians document whether clients are receiving *agonist therapy,* such as methadone maintenance treatment, or are living *in a controlled environment,* such as prison. Clinicians may also designate diagnoses of intoxication, withdrawal, or other specific substance-induced disorders.

The Addiction Severity Index

The ASI is a structured clinical interview that can be used to assess client substance abuse, screen for related problems, and rate the severity of the addiction and related problems. Both client and clinicians contribute to the database and severity rating. Clinicians use the ASI to guide treatment planning, monitoring, and outcome evaluation.

The ASI, which is administered by a trained clinician during a 50-minute interview, has high validity and reliability with diverse populations of substance abusers. It is the most widely used addiction assessment tool in the field and has been translated into many languages. The ASI is not a diagnostic tool per se; rather, it is primarily a clinical tool for assessing client needs and developing individualized treatment plans. It also offers client and clinicians an objective way to measure treatment progress and outcome. The ASI covers seven problem areas:

- Medical status
- Employment and support status
- Drug/alcohol use
- Legal status
- Family history
- Social relationships
- Psychiatric status

Clients are asked to discuss the problems they have experienced within the past 30 days and over their lifetimes. In this way, clinicians identify both urgent and chronic problems. Clients are also asked to rate how severe each problem has been within the past 30 days and how important it is for them to seek treatment for the problem at this time. (Note that the client does not provide any family history ratings.) Clinicians also assess the severity of each problem, using the following scale:

0-1 = no real problem, treatment not indicated

2-3 = slight problem, treatment probably not necessary

4-5 = moderate problem, some treatment indicated

6-7 = considerable problem, treatment necessary

8-9 = extreme problem, treatment absolutely necessary

Client and clinician ratings are calculated together to determine the severity rating, and a single number indicates the final severity rating for each problem area.

Eddie M. is a 51-year-old homeless male with a history of chronic alcohol dependence. Eddie drinks daily and uses cocaine whenever he has money to buy a line. Eddie lost track of his family years ago. He has been unemployed for 15 years; he receives Social Security Disability Insurance payments for what he describes as "stress from Nam." Eddie is sometimes barred from shelters because

TABLE 8.1 Example of an ASI Addiction Severity Profile

Problems	Addiction Severity								
	1	2	3	4	5	6	7	8	9
Medical				4					
Employment/support					5				
Alcohol							7		
Drug					5				
Legal		2							
Family/social									9
Psychiatric								8	

he has been involved in fights. His severity profile on the ASI might look like the one shown in Table 8.1.

ASAM PPC-2 Assessment Dimensions

The following six *ASAM PPC-2* assessment dimensions guide admission, continued service, and discharge. Clinicians ask the questions shown to collect data on each dimension.

■ *Dimension 1. Acute Intoxication and/or Withdrawal:* What risk is associated with the patient's current level of acute intoxication? Is there serious risk of severe withdrawal symptoms or seizures based on the patient's withdrawal history, amount, frequency, and recent discontinuation or significant reduction of alcohol or other drug use? Are there current signs of withdrawal? Does the patient have supports to assist in ambulatory detoxification if medically safe?

■ *Dimension 2. Biomedical Conditions and Complications:* Are there recurrent physical illnesses, other than withdrawal, that need to be addressed or that may complicate treatment? Are there chronic conditions that affect treatment?

■ *Dimension 3. Emotional/Behavioral Conditions and Complications:* Are there current psychiatric illnesses or psychological, behavioral, or emotional problems that need to be addressed or which complicate treatment? Are there chronic conditions that affect treatment? Do any emotional/behavioral problems appear to be an expected part of addiction illness or do they appear to be separate? Even if connected to addiction, are they severe enough to warrant specific mental health treatment?

■ *Dimension 4. Treatment Acceptance/Resistance:* Does the patient feel coerced into treatment or actively object to receiving treatment? How ready is the patient to change? If willing to accept treatment, how strongly does the patient disagree with others' perceptions that s/he has an addiction problem? Is the patient compliant to avoid a negative consequence, or internally distressed in a self-motivated way about his or her alcohol/other drug use problem?

- *Dimension 5. Relapse Potential:* Is the patient in immediate danger of continued severe distress and drinking/drugging behavior? Does the patient have any recognition and understanding of, and skills for how to cope with his or her addiction problems and prevent relapse or continued use? What severity of problems and further distress will potentially continue or reappear, if the patient is not successfully engaged into treatment at this time? How aware is the patient of relapse trigger, way to cope with cravings to use and skills to control impulses to use?

- *Dimension 6. Recovery Environment:* Are there any dangerous family, significant others, living or school/working situations threatening treatment engagement and success? Does the patient have supportive friendship, financial or educational/vocational resources to improve the likelihood of successful treatment? Are there legal, vocational, social service agency or criminal justice mandates that may enhance motivation for engagement into treatment? (ASAM, 1996, pp. 2-3; reprinted by permission)

ASAM PPC-2 criteria describe each treatment level and typical length of service. The descriptions include examples of the services and settings; requirements for support systems and staff; therapies offered; standards for assessment, treatment plan, and review; and documentation. Diagnostic criteria are specified for admission, continued service, and discharge for each level of care. Client data for each of the six addiction severity dimensions guide placement for admission, continued service, and discharge for each level of care.

Treatment Intensity

Treatment intensity includes the number, types, and frequency of interventions and services; treatment intensity is often associated with level of care. Medical and psychiatric treatment intensity reflects the severity of the problem. For example: Paul M. had a severe upper respiratory infection and received 10 million units of penicillin G potassium infused over 24 hours. Frank S. had a moderate respiratory infection and received 200,000 units of penicillin G (125 mg tablet) by mouth every 6 hours for 10 days. Evelyn G. attempted suicide and remained actively suicidal following admission; she was placed in a seclusion room on a locked inpatient psychiatric unit. Pauline C. visits her psychiatrist once a month for monitoring of the medication she takes for her depression; she attends group therapy on a weekly basis to address psychosocial and environmental problems and improve her overall functioning. As in such cases, addiction treatment intensity varies with addiction severity.

ASAM PPC-2 Levels of Care

The levels of care described in *ASAM PPC-2* share elements of treatment with variations that respond to client addiction severity and reflect treatment intensity. For instance, an acute-care hospital offers the medical, psychological, psychiatric, laboratory, and toxicology support systems required for Level IV care, "medically managed intensive inpatient services." An interdisciplinary team of physicians, nurses, counselors, a psychologist, and social workers provide treatment 24 hours a day for clients admitted to Level IV acute care. At Level II (intensive outpatient/partial hospitalization services), consultations, referrals, or affiliations would be used for these same services; staff may include counselors and social workers. The number, types, and frequency of therapies vary with levels of care. Assessment, treatment planning, review of treatment plan, and documentation are required for each level of care.

For both clinical and financial reasons, the preferred level of care is the least intensive level that can accomplish treatment objectives while providing safety and security for clients. Although each level and gradations are discrete, they represent a continuum of treatment. In *ASAM PPC-2,* 12-step mutual self-help groups do not constitute a treatment level; rather, they are recognized as crucial elements of *all* levels of care. *ASAM PPC-2* recognizes four major levels of care:

- *Level I:* outpatient services

- *Level II:* intensive outpatient/partial hospitalization services

- *Level III:* residential/inpatient services

- *Level IV:* medically managed intensive inpatient services

The 1996 criteria specify gradations of intensity within the levels of care ranging from .1 to .9 (e.g., Level II has gradations from II.1 to II.9). They also describe general placement criteria for Level 0.5 (early intervention) as well as criteria for intoxication, withdrawal, and opioid maintenance therapy (OMT). Some descriptions of various levels of care, along with examples, appear in Table 8.2.

AdCare Hospital of Worcester, Massachusetts, a recognized leader in addiction treatment, offers a continuum of care that includes the following:

- Observation, evaluation, and stabilization
  23-hour observation beds
  Urgent evaluation
- Outpatient continuum of care
  Outpatient detoxification services

TABLE 8.2 *ASAM PPC-2* Levels of Care, With Examples

Level	*Examples*
Level 0.5: early intervention	psychoeducation group
Opioid maintenance therapy	methadone and LAAM
Level I: outpatient services	office practice, behavioral health clinic, primary care clinic
Level II.1: intensive outpatient services	evening treatment program
Level II.2: partial hospitalization	day treatment program
Level III.1: clinically managed low-intensity residential services	halfway house
Level III.3: clinically managed medium-intensity residential services	extended-care facility
Level III.5: clinically managed medium/high-intensity residential services	therapeutic community
Level III.7: medically monitored intensive inpatient services	inpatient treatment center
Level IV: medically managed intensive inpatient services	acute-care general hospital, acute psychiatric hospital or unit, chemical dependency specialty hospital care facility

    Day and evening treatment

    Adolescent after-school program

    Outpatient counseling and comprehensive evaluation

    Supervised sober living

■ Inpatient management

    Inpatient detoxification

    Acute inpatient treatment

■ Discharge planning and aftercare

■ Anesthesia-assisted detoxification

Admission, transfer, and discharge criteria guide effective utilization of a continuum of care by clinicians for clients.

Early Intervention

ASAM PPC-2 includes a level of care not found in ASAM's original criteria: early intervention (Level 0.5). Early intervention addresses problems or risk factors related to substance use and helps individuals recognize the harmful consequences of substance abuse. Early intervention strategies include school-based prevention programs and programs concerning driving under the influence of alcohol and other drugs. Staff assess clients for substance-related disorders and refer them appropriately. Interventions involve individual, group, or family education and counseling. Documentation reflects assessment, referral, attendance, and any significant data or events.

The case of Erik R. provides an example of early intervention. At age 16, Erik has been smoking pot off and on for the past 2 years. He drinks at parties with friends but does not like getting drunk. He has no medical or mental health problems. His parents are concerned about his declining grades, "new friends," and mood changes. Erik is willing to attend a weekly outpatient psychoeducation group for teens called Teen Talk.

Detoxification

Clinicians recognize the life-threatening potential of substance intoxication for clients and others. Clinicians recognize substance withdrawal and differentiate among varying degrees of severity. Detoxification services are often provided separately from other addiction treatment. *ASAM PPC-2* describes criteria for detoxification at all four levels of care. Addiction severity determines the appropriate level for detoxification.

Substance-specific tools such as the Clinical Institute Withdrawal Assessment of Alcohol Scale (CIWA-Ar) can be used to determine withdrawal severity. The CIWA-Ar measures 15 symptoms in 3 to 5 minutes. A score of less than 20 on the CIWA-Ar indicates minimal to mild withdrawal, a score of 20-25 indicates moderate withdrawal, and a score of greater than 25 indicates severe withdrawal (impending DTs). If a client's score is less than 10 after two 8-hour reviews, monitoring can stop. If scores are above 20, the client should be assessed hourly until symptoms subside.

Another helpful tool for assessing withdrawal severity is the narcotic withdrawal scale developed by Fultz and Senay (1975). This scale breaks withdrawal down into four grades:

- *Grade 1:* lacrimation, rhinorrhea, diaphoresis, yawning, restlessness, and insomnia

- *Grade 2:* dilated pupils, piloerection, muscle twitching, myalgia, arthralgia, and abdominal pain

- *Grade 3:* tachycardia, hypertension, tachypnea, fever, anorexia, nausea, and extreme restlessness

- *Grade 4:* diarrhea, vomiting, dehydration, hyperglycemia, hypotension, and curled-up position

(The CIWA-Ar and another useful tool, the Clinical Institute Withdrawal from Narcotics Scale [CINA], appear in Exhibits H and I in the appendix.)

Opioid Maintenance Therapy

OMT is the daily therapeutic use of opioid compounds such as methadone and levo-alpha-acetylmethadol (LAAM) plus psychosocial treatment to manage the client's addiction. These compounds occupy the opiate receptors in the brain. With an adequate level of dose, there is no craving or euphoria and the client maintains a steady state of drug tolerance. A multidisciplinary team of physicians, nurses, counselors, and social workers implements the program. Treatment goals include change in client lifestyle, such as modification of thoughts, attitudes, and behaviors that undermine recovery, and client learning of psychosocial skills to support recovery and develop a drug-free lifestyle. Therapies include medication, monitored urine testing, counseling, case management, and psychoeducation. Because so many OMT clients are intravenous drug users, health education about tuberculosis and HIV and other sexually transmitted diseases is critical. The length of OMT service varies with the severity of client opioid dependence, treatment goals, and response to treatment.

Assessment for admission to OMT is based on the following data, which are organized according to the six *ASAM PPC-2* dimensions:

1. Client meets diagnostic criteria for opioid dependence as defined by *DSM-IV* with a history of continuous or episodic addiction for at least a year prior to admission to the program.

2. Biomedical conditions can be monitored or managed on an outpatient basis.

3. Emotional/behavioral problems can be monitored or managed (often with medication) on an outpatient basis.

4. Client requires pharmacotherapy and psychosocial interventions to achieve treatment goals.

5. Client is at high risk of relapse to opiate use without OMT, close monitoring, and structured support.

6. A supportive psychosocial environment, especially family and/or significant others, improves the likelihood of treatment success.

Clients in OMT are usually placed in an ambulatory facility, such as a free-standing clinic or mobile unit, or receive service within a community mental health center, community health center, or hospital.

Client Assessment and Placement

The following vignettes demonstrate client assessment and placement using *ASAM PPC-2* and illustrate the relationship between addiction severity and treatment intensity.

> *Ray M.: admission to Level I.2 outpatient treatment.* Client meets *DSM-IV* criteria for opioid dependence (304.00). Client "self-detoxed" and has not used for 30 days. He has no pressing biomedical or emotional problems. He acknowledges craving and wants help staying clean. He is confident he can maintain abstinence as an outpatient. Ray attends five A.A./N.A. meetings a week; he has a home group and sponsor. He works as a construction manager. His wife is a nurse and works part-time. They have two children, ages 4 years and 7 months. Ray's mother baby-sits when they both work; she is understanding and supportive. Ray meets *ASAM PPC-2* criteria for admission to Level I.2 outpatient treatment.

> *Barbara F.: discharge from Level II.1 intensive outpatient treatment.* Client met *DSM-IV* criteria for alcohol dependence with physiological dependence (303.90) and cocaine dependence with physiological dependence (304.20). Following a 3-day inpatient detoxification, Barbara completed a 4-week intensive evening program: 9 hours per week, 3 evenings a week. She states she is still tired but sleeping fairly well; there is evidence of agitation, and anxiety is minimal. There are no urgent biomedical or emotional problems to manage. This was her third detox in the past year, but her first intensive outpatient treatment; previously, she returned home planning to attend meetings but never followed through. She admitted reluctantly that she would probably drink and use again without some structured treatment. Her husband stated he "was tired of promises," yet attended three of the four family nights. Barbara used vacation time from work for inpatient detoxification. She stated, "Unless I clean up my act, I will lose my job." She has attended five different recovery groups in the community, joined a women's substance abuse recovery group, and obtained a sponsor. She plans to see an outpatient counselor weekly for at least 4 weeks. She has said, "I feel different this time. A.A. is attitude and activity for me. I'm going to make it—one day at a time." Barbara meets *ASAM PPC-2* criteria for discharge from Level II.1 intensive outpatient treatment.

> *Rosa M.: continued service in Level III.3 clinically managed medium-intensity residential treatment.* Client meets *DSM-IV* criteria for opioid dependence (304.00) and alcohol dependence (303.90). Rosa has been incarcerated for 15 months; she is abstinent with no withdrawal problems. Rosa has non-insulin-dependent diabetes mellitus and takes chlorpropamide (Diabinese) 250 mg two times a day. She takes her own medication and monitors her blood glucose levels daily by meter. Rosa ex-

perienced a single episode of depression when she was incarcerated and her three children were placed in foster care. Her depression has subsided; her children visit her once a month. She is addressing long-standing issues associated with post-traumatic stress disorder. Rosa is highly motivated to manage her addiction "this time!" She has a history of relapse and recidivism. Rosa has few, if any, clean and sober supports in the community. She received her general equivalency diploma while incarcerated and has begun working with a state rehabilitation counselor for vocational training. Rosa meets *ASAM PPC-2* criteria for continued service at Level III.3 clinically managed medium-intensity residential treatment.

Joe M.: admission to Level IV medically managed intensive inpatient treatment. Client meets *DSM-IV* criteria for alcohol withdrawal with perceptual disturbances (291.8) and has a CIWA-Ar score of 30. Biomedical conditions and crmplications include cardiomyopathy, chronic obstructive pulmonary disease, cirrhosis, esophageal varices, and alcoholic pancreatitis. Joe, a Vietnam veteran, has a history of seizures during withdrawal. He was a mechanic but has not worked for 17 years. He receives disability payments and lives alone in subsidized housing. Joe meets *ASAM PPC-2* criteria for admission to Level IV medically managed intensive inpatient treatment for detoxification in an acute-care general hospital.

Summary

Addiction severity is the seriousness of a client's symptoms and degree of impairment. To determine addiction severity, clinicians use standardized tools such as *DSM-IV,* the ASI, *ASAM PPC-2,* and the CIWA-Ar. Clinicians use addiction severity data to place clients in levels of care appropriate to their needs, to plan treatment, and to specify the number, types, and frequency of interventions and services. The higher the addiction severity, the greater the treatment intensity.

Related Skills Checklist

Practitioner skills related to addiction severity and treatment intensity include the ability to do the following:

- Employ standardized tools such as *DSM-IV,* the ASI, and *ASAM PPC-2* to ascertain addiction severity.
- Use addiction severity to determine treatment intensity.
- Specify number, types, and frequency of interventions and services.
- Place client in the level of care appropriate for the addiction severity and exemplary of the proper treatment intensity.

Special Topics for Further Study

To what extent do public and private insurers use the concept of addiction severity to authorize level of care and treatment intensity?

Addiction Practice 2000

Addiction practice 2000 expects clinicians to operationalize the concepts of addiction severity and treatment intensity and incorporate them into treatment process with all clients and families. Clinicians must adapt the concepts for use with diverse clients and utilize them fully with complex clients who have coexisting medical, psychological, and social problems. Clinicians must develop strategies to enhance treatment acceptance and counteract treatment resistance directly with active intervention. Clinicians must advocate for open access to treatment in both public and private sectors, especially increased treatment options for populations at risk and for clients with coexisting medical, psychological, and social problems.

References

American Psychiatric Association. (1980). *Diagnostic and statistical manual of mental disorders* (3rd ed.). Washington, DC: Author.

American Psychiatric Association. (1994). *Diagnostic and statistical manual of mental disorders* (4th ed.). Washington, DC: Author.

American Society of Addiction Medicine. (1991). *Patient placement criteria for the treatment of psychoactive substance use disorders.* Washington, DC: Author.

American Society of Addiction Medicine. (1996). *Patient placement criteria for the treatment of substance-related disorders* (2nd ed.). Chevy Chase, MD: Author.

Fultz, J. M., & Senay, E. C. (1975). Guidelines for the management of hospitalized narcotic addicts. *Annals of Internal Medicine, 82,* 815-818.

Hoffmann, N. G., Halikas, J. A., & Mee-Lee, D. (1987). *The Cleveland admission, discharge, and transfer criteria: Model for chemical dependency treatment program.* Cleveland: Northern Ohio Chemical Dependency Treatment Directors Association.

Jellinek, E. M. (1960). *The disease concept of alcoholism.* New Haven, CT: College & University Press.

Weedman, R. D. (1987). *Admission, continued stay and discharge criteria for adult alcoholism and drug dependence treatment services.* Irvine, CA: National Association of Addiction Treatment Providers.

Other Sources

Center for Substance Abuse Treatment. (1995). *Intensive outpatient treatment for alcohol and other drug abuse* (DHHS Publication No. SMA 94-2077). Rockville, MD: Author.

Center for Substance Abuse Treatment. (1995). *The role and current status of patient placement criteria in the treatment of substance use disorders* (DHHS Publication No. SMA 95-3021). Rockville, MD: Author.

D'Arcangelo, J. S. (1992). Addictions: Nursing diagnosis and treatment. In M. A. Naegle (Ed.), *Substance abuse education in nursing* (Vol. 2, pp. 221-253). New York: National League for Nursing Press.

Galanter, M., & Kleber, H. D. (Eds.). (1999). *The American Psychiatric Press textbook of substance abuse treatment* (2nd ed.). Washington, DC: American Psychiatric Press.

Miller, N. S. (1997). *Principles and practice of addictions in psychiatry.* Philadelphia: W. B. Saunders.

Miller, N. S., Gold, M. S., & Smith, D. E, Jr. (1997). *Manual of therapeutics for addictions.* New York: Wiley-Liss.

National Institute on Drug Abuse. (1995). *Assessing client needs using the ASI: A handbook for program administrators* (NIH Publication No. 95-3619). Rockville, MD: Author.

National Institute on Drug Abuse. (1995). *Diagnosis and severity of drug abuse and drug dependence* (NIH Publication No. 95-3884). Rockville, MD: Author.

National Institutes of Health, Consensus Development Conference on Effective Medical Treatment. (1997). *Effective medical treatment of opiate addiction: NIH consensus statement* (NIH Pub. No. 99-05193). Bethesda, MD: Author.

Rasmussen, S. (Ed.). (1990). *Addiction treatment standards for adults.* Norfolk, MA: NORCAP Center.

Schuckit, M. A. (1999). *Drug and alcohol abuse: A clinical guide to diagnosis and treatment* (5th ed.). New York: Plenum.

Stine, S. M., & Kosten, T. R. (1997). *New treatments for opiate dependence.* New York: Guilford.

Strain, E. C., & Stitzer, M. L. (1999). *Methadone treatment for opioid dependence.* Baltimore: Johns Hopkins University Press.

Part III

Treatment Process

9

Assessment

Objectives

- Identify the database required to assess addictive disorders.
- Recognize objective and subjective evidence of substance use.
- Note psychosocial indicators of substance use.
- Understand the purpose of screening.
- Utilize standardized screening tools.
- Understand the components of a comprehensive assessment.
- Demonstrate familiarity with standardized assessment tools such as the Addiction Severity Index.
- Organize assessment to reflect ASAM PPC-2 dimensions.

Outline

- **Assessment of Addictive Disorders**
- **Indicators of Substance Use**
  - Objective Data
  - Subjective Data
  - Psychosocial Indicators
- **Screening**
  - Purpose
  - Standardized Tools
- **Comprehensive Assessment**
  - History and Physical Examination
  - Mental Status Examination

Assessment of Addictive Disorders

Assessment is a collaborative process between client and clinicians in which data are collected about the client's substance use or other addictive behavior, the client him- or herself, and the client's environment. Using the database created during assessment, clinicians and client make decisions about treatment. Usually a team of clinicians conducts the assessment: nurse, physician, counselor, social worker, and psychologist.

Assessment begins with screening, which is followed by a comprehensive assessment that includes a health history and physical examination, substance use/addiction assessment, mental status examination, psychosocial assessment, family assessment, toxicology testing, and any needed specialized testing. The client and the client's family provide primary information. Collateral information may be obtained from the client's employer or school as well as from health and human service agencies, the criminal justice system, and other relevant individuals or agencies.

Clinicians use standardized screening tools and assessment instruments, especially if the data are being collected for research purposes. Increasingly, clinicians organize assessment data to reflect the dimensions of addiction identified by the American Society of Addiction Medicine's (1996) patient placement criteria, or *ASAM PPC-2.*

Indicators of Substance Use

Clinicians need to recognize the general biopsychosocial indicators of substance use. Clinicians observe objective data. The client provides subjective data. Psychosocial indicators of substance use reflect psychosocial or environmental stress as well as impaired psychological, social, and occupational functioning.

Clinicians who must assess diverse clients, such as children and adolescents, the elderly, individuals of varying ethnocultural backgrounds, pregnant addicts, and gay/lesbian individuals, need special skills and sensitivity. Collaboration between clinicians and specialists is in order when clients present with coexisting medical, psychological, and social problems. (The specific criteria for diagnoses of substance abuse, substance dependence, intoxication, withdrawal, and other addictive disorders are discussed in Chapter 10.)

Objective Data

What are the signs and symptoms of substance use that family, friends, and clinicians observe? In general, individuals who abuse substances neglect their health and personal care; they may present as malnourished, with an unkempt appearance, and appear older than their stated age. The biological manifestations of substance use include the following:

- *Gastrointestinal signs* of substance use include nausea, vomiting, constipation or diarrhea, pain, and weight loss. Halitosis, gingivitis, and dental caries are common. Hepatitis and cirrhosis characterize chronic use. Ascites (an accumulation of fluid in the abdominal cavity) is often seen with chronic liver disease. Individuals who inhale their drugs may present with irritations of the nasal mucosa and bleeding or even destruction of the nasal septum.

- *Skin manifestations* of substance use include sweating, flushing, and dehydration. Skin may appear pale, or it may be reddened, especially the palms of the hands. Skin may feel clammy or dry. Acne, spider nevi, and jaundice are common; reddened eyes, together with the loss of eyelashes and eyebrows, may occur. Substance abusers often burn their skin. Intravenous drug users may exhibit needle marks and scarring of the veins. Contact dermatitis, skin infections, cellulitis, and abscesses are common. Bruising (ecchymosis) is obvious.

- *Genitourinary signs* of substance use may include decreased urine production. Substance abusers experience more episodes of sexually transmitted diseases than do nonusers.

- *Neuromuscular indicators* of substance abuse are typically slurred speech, tremors, lack of coordination, poor muscle tone, extremity weakness, hyperactive reflexes, seizures, and coma. Other neurological manifestations include dilated or pinpoint pupils, elevated temperature (hyperthermia), and loss of the senses of smell and taste.

- *Cardiovascular signs* of substance abuse often include chest pain, palpitations, and various cardiac dysrhythmias; changes in pulse and blood pressure are significant. Intravenous drug users may develop enlarged lymph nodes and sepsis. Individuals may be HIV-positive or diagnosed with AIDS.

- *Respiratory signs* associated with substance use include alcohol on the breath; rapid, deep, or depressed respirations; shortness of breath; crackles and wheezes; inflamed throat; and a chronic, productive cough.

- *Trauma* from assaults, fights, or accidents while drinking or using is often a sign of substance use. A history of trauma, especially after age 18, is common. Adult substance abusers, especially elderly individuals, experience many falls, with resulting fractures or dislocations of bones or joints.

Subjective Data

Individuals who use substances experience extremes in thoughts, feelings, and behaviors. Clients report feeling stimulated or depressed. They experience giddiness, euphoria, and grandiosity as well as feelings ranging from anxiety to panic and from fear to paranoia. Substance users report overwhelming feelings of grief, hopelessness, powerlessness, and spiritual distress.

Substance abusers complain of sleep disturbances: wakefulness and insomnia as well as sleepiness, drowsiness, and sedation. Clients complain of headaches, dizziness, and fatigue. Loss of appetite, dysphagia (difficulty swallowing), and anorexia are frequent complaints. Clients describe heightened sexual desire with sexual promiscuity (usually associated with early substance use), then loss of libido with sexual dysfunction (usually associated with continued substance use). Men may have difficulty obtaining or maintaining an erection, experience a delayed orgasm, or fail to reach orgasm.

Psychosocial Indicators

Substance abusers experience recurrent or persistent interpersonal problems; being dependent persons, they are at risk for victimization. Social isolation occurs, with estrangement from friends and family. Quality of family life deteriorates: families become highly dysfunctional, and family conflicts and violence increase. Friends and family members express anger and resentment with overwhelming feelings of helplessness and hopelessness. Marital stress with separation and divorce are common. Social supports diminish.

Substance users usually have academic problems in school or drop out. They demonstrate poor job performance and make frequent job changes. Their work histories are characterized by lateness, absenteeism, and work-related accidents. Reliability, responsibility, and accountability are compromised. Financial problems are common, including those related to loss of job, inability to work, and money spent buying alcohol or other drugs. Leisure activities are non-existent or reflect an alcohol- or drug-related lifestyle.

Children of substance abusers often demonstrate problems with trust, lack of self-esteem, and poor academic performance. These children are often parentified; that is, they assume the caretaker role for parents or young siblings. Children of substance abusers may be neglected or abused emotionally, physically, or sexually.

Lack of work or income, and the resulting loss of health insurance, leads to the substance abuser's inadequate care for self and family. Substance abusers are at high risk for arrest, incarceration, and litigation, as well as for becoming victims of crime. Substance abusers settle for less and less in terms of housing; they move often and frequently become homeless.

Screening

Purpose

The screening process involves a simple, brief initial assessment designed to identify the presence or absence of a substance use problem or other addictive disorder. Screens flag an actual or potential problem and suggest the need for comprehensive assessment. Screens help clinicians determine whether or not a client is at imminent risk to harm self or others. Screens may also provide data to certify eligibility for treatment.

A screen is easy to administer and interpret; screening is often conducted by generalists or paraprofessionals. Screening for substance abuse and other addictive disorders is easily included with any general health assessment or health promotion program. Screening lends itself to use with individuals, groups, or entire community programs. Many health care providers sponsor national public education and screening programs for alcoholism, eating disorders, depression, and anxiety.

Standardized Tools

Following are brief descriptions of some of the tests used to screen for substance use:

- *AUDIT (Alcohol Use Disorder Identification Test):* A 10-item, multinational test for adults; the cutoff score is 8 points or more, with a range of 0-40. AUDIT gathers information on use and problem history in the past year; it does not detect past alcohol use problems. (A copy of AUDIT appears in Exhibit J in the appendix.)

- *CAGE:* A screen widely used with adults to assess four areas related to lifetime alcohol use: Have you ever felt the need to *cut* down on your drinking? Have you ever felt *annoyed* by someone criticizing your drinking? Have you ever felt *guilty* about your drinking? Have you ever felt the need for an *eye-opener*? Cutoff score is 2 or more positive responses. This screen is short and easy for treatment clinicians to remember. It addresses lifetime but does not measure levels of consumption or episodes of heavy drinking. It is less sensitive with women than with men.

- *T-ACE:* A modification of CAGE that is more useful with women. A *tolerance* question is substituted for the "guilt" question in CAGE: How many drinks does it take to make you high? How many drinks can you hold (women)?

- *TWEAK:* Useful with women; 5 items, with cutoff score of 3 or more positive responses. *Tolerance:* How many drinks does it take to make you high? How many drinks can you hold? *Worried:* Have friends or family worried or complained about your drinking? *Eye-opener:* Do you sometimes take a drink in the morning to wake up? *Amnesia:* Have friends or family ever told you things you said or did while you were drinking that you cannot remember? *K* (for *cut*): Do you sometimes feel the need to cut down on your drinking?

- *MAST (Michigan Alcoholism Screening Test):* A 25-item instrument to screen adults; cutoff score is 5 points or more (items are weighted). MAST assesses lifetime alcohol problems but does not contain quantity-frequency questions.

- *SMAST (Short MAST):* A 13-item screen for use with adults; cutoff score is 2 points or more (items are weighted). SMAST is useful in primary care settings (the B-MAST contains 10 questions).

- *SAAST (Self-Administered Alcoholism Screening Test):* A 35-item instrument to screen adults; cutoff score is 10 points or more. This screening tool focuses on detection of dependence.

- *POSIT (Problem-Oriented Screening Instrument for use with Teenagers):* Used with adolescents to assess 10 problem areas, including a 14-item subscale measuring alcohol and other drug use and abuse. Cutoff is 1 or more positive responses.

In addition to the tools listed above, the Health Screening Questionnaire (HSQ), Health Screening Survey (HSS), Life-Style Risk Assessment, and Life Style Test combine alcohol questions with items on other health issues.

When screening determines that a client is at risk of hurting self or someone else, the client needs immediate crisis intervention. He or she requires monitoring, further evaluation, and intensive treatment in a secure, inpatient setting until symptoms stabilize.

Questions about insurance, private or public, are often asked as part of a screen to certify client eligibility for further assessment and subsequent treatment. Practitioners should not schedule a client for a comprehensive assessment or refer the client for other services without a plan for payment. Addiction staff need to be knowledgeable about insurance benefits and referral sources.

Comprehensive Assessment

During a comprehensive assessment, extensive, in-depth data are collected about the client's substance use or other addictive behavior, the client him- or herself, and the client's environment. Clinicians and client use the assessment findings to formulate diagnoses and place the client in the appropriate level of care. Assessment data help clinicians and clients to develop treatment plans and select interventions. Continuing assessment is used to monitor treatment; assessment grounds and guides quality improvement. Clinicians use assessment data to evaluate treatment outcomes.

A comprehensive assessment of substance use and other addictive disorders includes a health history and physical examination, assessment of substance use and/or the addictive disorder, family assessment, toxicology testing, and any necessary specialized testing.

History and Physical Examination

A physician, nurse practitioner, or other qualified health professional obtains a health history from the client and performs a physical examination. The level of care or setting determines just when the taking of the history and the physical exam take place: immediately upon admission to an acute inpatient setting for detoxification or within 2 weeks of admission for outpatient services.

The information recorded in the client's history includes identifying data, referral source, source of history, source's reliability, chief complaint(s), and present illness. Past history includes general state of health, childhood illnesses, adult illnesses, psychiatric illnesses, accidents and injuries, operations, hospitalizations, and pregnancies. Information is obtained about current health status and current medications (including nonprescription drugs, street drugs, vitamin/mineral supplements, herbs, and home remedies) as well as any allergies. The history also includes information on substance use (tobacco, alcohol, drugs, and related substances), diet, sleep patterns, exercise and leisure activities, environmental hazards, and use of safety measures. Are immunizations current? Has the client had appropriate screening tests, such as tuberculin test, Pap smear, or mammogram? The family history includes information about family mortality and morbidity as well as psychosocial data about the client's home situation, significant others, daily life, important experiences, religious beliefs, and outlook on life.

The physical examination begins with a general survey, vital signs, and height and weight. This is followed by a head-to-toe assessment of the skin, the head and neck, the thorax and lungs, and the cardiovascular system. The exam proceeds to the breasts and axillae, the abdomen; it includes the male genitalia and prostate, the female genitalia, and the anus and rectum. The exam also assesses the peripheral vascular system, musculoskeletal system, and the nervous system.

Common laboratory tests and diagnostic procedures that are part of the physical examination include urinalysis, complete blood count, differential white blood count, and blood chemistry profile. An electrocardiogram, chest X ray, liver enzyme levels, and other specialized tests may be ordered when indicated. (For an example of the notes from a client's history and physical examination, see Exhibit K in the appendix.)

Mental Status Examination

Clinicians use a mental status examination (MSE) to assess a client's immediate risk of harm to self or others, to corroborate diagnoses, and to help plan realistic treatment. The purpose of the MSE is to identify the client's *present* mental status, including risk for suicide or homicide. The sections of the MSE may vary slightly from one assessment form to another, but they usually include the following basic categories:

- Appearance and behavior

  Appearance: hygiene, dress, grooming; appropriateness; facial expressions, body and limb movement; mannerisms

  Behavior: cooperative, frank, open; fearful, hostile, reticent; level of anxiety; congruence with situation

- Speech and language

  Quantity: incessant, "flight of ideas," scant, mute

  Quality: circumstantial, perseveration, incongruent, irrelevance, incoherence; jargon, jumbles, slang; stammers, stutters, lisps

- Mood or affect

  Mood: sad, depressed, happy, elated, euphoric; angry, hostile, suspicious, fearful; calm, anxious, near panic; appropriate to thought content? expected level of intensity?

  Affect: blunted, flattened

- Thoughts and perceptions

  Hallucinations: auditory, visual, olfactory, tactile

  Delusions: paranoid, grandiose, depressive, somatic

  Illusions: any false perception of stimuli

  Ideas of reference: all behavior of others refers to self

  Obsessions: with or without compulsion; level of distress

  Suicidal: ideation, urges, plans

  Homicidal: ideation, urges, plans

- Sensorium functions

  Orientation: person, time, place

  Memory and learning: recent, remote

  Attention and concentration: level of arousal; ability to concentrate

  Information and intelligence: general knowledge and reasoning

- Insight and judgment

  Insight: awareness of problem and need for help

  Judgment: level of judgment; any deterioration

Substance Use/Addiction Assessment

Clinicians and client assess substance use and/or addictive behavior per se, including an inventory of lifetime use and current use. Clinicians often find it helpful to use a grid to record data about substance use: types of substances, amounts used, routes, and frequency. Information about use or behavior during the past 30 days and lifetime use or behavior is valuable. In addition, data are collected about patterns of use or behaviors, the highest dose ever used or behavioral excesses, and the last time and amount used. Clinicians use this information to determine intoxication state and withdrawal potential and to formulate a diagnosis of substance abuse or substance dependence. The data help clinicians to diagnose other addictive disorders.

Psychosocial Assessment

Psychosocial and environmental problems affect diagnosis, treatment, and prognosis for clients with substance-related diagnoses and other addictive disorders. According to *DSM-IV,* a psychosocial or environmental problem may be a negative life event, an environmental difficulty or deficiency, a familial or other interpersonal stress, an inadequacy of social support or personal resources, or other problem relating to the context in which a person's difficulties have developed (American Psychiatric Association, 1994, p. 41). When positive stressors contribute to a problem, they should be noted—for instance, the stress of marriage. Addictive disorders contribute to the development of many psychosocial problems.

Usually clinicians note psychosocial problems present during the year preceding the current assessment. Sometimes, however, chronic psychosocial problems contribute to current pathology, such as many years of domestic abuse or multiple arrests and repeated incarcerations.

DSM-IV categories for assessment of psychosocial problems include the following:

- Problems with primary support group
- Problems related to the social environment
- Educational problems
- Occupational problems
- Housing problems
- Economic problems
- Problems with access to health care services
- Problems related to interaction with the legal system
- Other psychosocial and environmental problems

Information about the client's leisure and recreation is also important. Often, substance use or the addictive behavior becomes an end in itself. Clients need to learn how to relax and have fun without alcohol, other drugs, or behavioral excesses. Assessment explores the client's spirituality to identify problems with overwhelming guilt and toxic shame that could block recovery. Assessment can identify spiritual resources and religious practices the client can use to support recovery. Unless such information is noted elsewhere, the psychosocial assessment also includes pertinent ethnocultural data on the client to help clinicians and client plan effective treatment.

Family Assessment and the Genogram

Biological theories as well as family systems theory support a transgenerational basis for substance abuse/dependence: Both genetic factors and dysfunctional family interaction contribute to addiction. A great deal of information about the family may be collected in the psychosocial assessment, including data on ethnocultural characteristics, religious practices, and family roles. Families with histories of alcohol/drug abuse as well as families in which there are active substance abusers experience many associated medical, psychological, and social problems; these might include HIV/AIDS, major psychiatric disorders, child neglect and abuse, or compromised socioeconomic conditions. On the other hand, addiction practitioners recognize that strong family values, expectations, and practices can help children and teens resist alcohol and drug use.

Family assessment data need to answer the question, How supportive is the client's recovery/living environment? A family that is full of toxic shame and chronic codependence, with highly dysfunctional patterns of communication, can impede, or even sabotage, client recovery. A family in which the members support treatment by learning about addiction and recovery, resisting temptations to enable the client, and taking care of themselves through counseling or support groups such as Al-Anon strengthens client recovery.

A genogram is a tool for understanding family functioning. Like a family tree, it reflects information about family members over several generations: genders, births, birth order, deaths (and data about deaths), marriages and divorces, and health problems. A genogram can be very simple or rather complex. It represents an especially valuable diagnostic and treatment tool when both the client and the client's family participate in formulating the picture. (For examples of some genogram forms, see Exhibit L in the appendix.)

Toxicology Testing

Clinicians employ toxicology screening to confirm a diagnosis, guide intervention, and monitor treatment. In many workplaces, drug and alcohol testing is conducted as a preemployment requirement, on a random basis, and/or for probable cause. A simple breath analysis or urinalysis with the Roche OnTrak TesTcup for amphetamines, cocaine, THC, and morphine gives clinicians immediate (within 1 minute) evidence of alcohol or other drug use by clients.

Urine Testing

The most common laboratory test used to ascertain the presence or absence of alcohol or other drugs is performed on urine. Drug concentrations remain elevated for some time in the urine, so urine testing can detect substances that may not be detected in blood testing. Drug metabolites are excreted for a longer time period through urine. In addition, urine specimens are easily obtained; collection does not involve an invasive procedure and is fairly economical. Clinicians need to be thoroughly familiar with agency policies and procedures for collecting witnessed urine samples and with chain-of-custody documentation.

Common urine tests screen for the following substances:

- Amphetamines
- Alcohol
- Barbiturates
- Benzodiazepines
- Cocaine (in any form)
- Opioids
- Stimulants
- Marijuana (THC)
- Phencyclidine (PCP)
- Lysergic acid diethylamide (LSD)
- Analgesics
- Sedatives
- Major tranquilizers
- Sympathomimetics

Many of these drugs are not detectable in blood serum. However, most drugs detectable in blood serum are detectable in urine. Because minor tranquilizers are almost completely metabolized, they are not likely to be detected in urine unless an overdose is taken.

Testing of Blood, Breath, and Gastric Contents

Blood is the preferred medium for ethyl alcohol testing because alcohol concentration (level) is more elevated and more reliable in a blood sample than in a urine sample. A blood test measures the actual amount of alcohol or other drugs in the blood at the time of the test. A breath test is currently the most common method of testing for alcohol. A breath test is easy to administer, noninvasive, and less costly than a blood test. The results tell if the individual is under the influence of alcohol at the time the breath sample is taken (alcohol stays in the body for a relatively short period of time). Breathalyzer is the trade name of the apparatus used to analyze the alcohol content of expired air, most often to determine whether a person is legally intoxicated. Clinicians sometimes use breath samples to monitor abstinence in outpatient/community programs.

Gastric contents may also be analyzed to determine the presence of drugs, especially in cases of overdose. Sweat, saliva, and other bodily fluids may be analyzed for drug content.

Hair Testing

Hair testing for drugs of abuse is being used increasingly by courts, clinicians, and parents who want to monitor their children. In contrast to urinalysis, which detects only recent drug use, hair analysis has a wide window of detection that depends only on the length of available hair. For example, in workplace testing, hair analysis typically covers the past 3 months if 3.9 cm of hair can be obtained. Washing and chemical treatments such as permanents and dyeing do not remove the drug content from hair. Hair analysis greatly reduces the likelihood of false positive test results. In 1996, the U.S. Food and Drug Administration approved the sale of "do-it-yourself" hair-testing kits, which are marketed primarily to parents.

Specialized Testing

Client history and condition determine the need for specialized testing. Medical consultations identify coexisting problems that complicate management of substance-related and other addictive disorders. Psychological testing may confirm concomitant psychiatric disorders. Neurological assessment frequently identifies cognitive impairment. These findings greatly influence diagnosis, prognosis, and treatment planning.

Standardized Assessment Instruments

Over the past 20 years, clinicians and researchers have developed and standardized many assessment instruments designed to assist with diagnosis, treatment planning, and outcome evaluation. In contrast to screening tools, assessment instruments need to be administered by trained clinicians. They are usually more complex and take longer to administer than simple, short screens.

The Addiction Severity Index

As discussed in Chapter 8, the Addiction Severity Index (ASI) was developed in 1980 by Dr. A. Thomas McClellan and his colleagues at the Philadelphia Veterans Administration Center. The ASI helps clinicians identify client needs, develop individualized treatment plans, monitor treatment progress, and assess client outcomes. Use of standardized assessment tools such as the ASI increases the efficacy of assessment, diagnosis, and treatment; fosters communication among addiction treatment providers, payers, and public policy and accrediting agencies; and contributes to the database for clinical research.

ASAM PPC-2 Dimensions of Addiction

Clinicians often use the six *ASAM PPC-2* dimensions of addiction to organize screening information and the comprehensive assessment data they have obtained:

1. Acute intoxication/withdrawal potential

2. Biomedical conditions and complications

3. Emotional/behavioral conditions and complications

4. Treatment acceptance/resistance

5. Relapse potential/continued use potential

6. Recovery living environment

(For an example of an admission intake/assessment that incorporates these dimensions, see Exhibit M in the appendix.)

Summary

Assessment is the collaborative process between client and clinicians during which data are collected about the client's substance use or addictive behavior, the client him- or herself, and the client's environment. These data include objective and subjective evidence about the addictive disorder. Assessment begins with screening, which is followed by comprehensive assessment. A screen is a simple, brief initial appraisal to identify the presence or absence of an addiction problem. A comprehensive assessment includes a history and physical examination, mental status exam, substance use assessment, assessment of other addictive disorders, psychosocial assessment, family assessment, toxicology testing, and specialized testing. Addiction clinicians utilize standardized assessment instruments such as the ASI, and assessment data are organized to reflect *ASAM PPC-2* dimensions.

Related Skills Checklist

Practitioner skills related to client assessment include the ability to do the following:

- Screen clients for substance use and other addictive disorders.
- Employ standardized tools whenever possible to assess clients.
- Conduct a mental status exam.
- Assess clients' substance use and other addictions.
- Interview clients to obtain a psychosocial history.
- Construct a genogram.
- Obtain a breath sample.
- Collect a chain-of-custody urine sample.
- Refer clients for specialized testing when appropriate.
- Utilize data from other disciplines to complete a comprehensive client assessment.
- Organize assessment data to reflect the six *ASAM PPC-2* dimensions.

Special Topics for Further Study

Determine the availability of computerized tools to assist with assessment. Are the tools valid and reliable? Are they client- and clinician-friendly?

Addiction Practice 2000

Addiction practice 2000 encourages clinicians to enhance their assessment competence by using standardized tools to screen and assess clients for addictive disorders. Clinicians should increase assessment reliability and validity by using standardized screening and assessment tools.

References

American Psychiatric Association. (1994). *Diagnostic and statistical manual of mental disorders* (4th ed.). Washington, DC: Author.
American Society of Addiction Medicine. (1996). *Patient placement criteria for the treatment of substance-related disorders* (2nd ed.). Chevy Chase, MD: Author.

Other Sources

Bates, B. (1999). *A guide to physical examination and history taking* (7th ed.). Philadelphia: J. B. Lippincott.

Center for Substance Abuse Prevention. (1996). *Urine specimen collection handbook for federal workplace drug testing programs* (DHHS Publication No. SMA 96-3114). Rockville, MD: Author.

Chernecky, C. C., & Berger, B. J. (1997). *Laboratory tests and diagnostic procedures* (2nd ed.). Philadelphia: W. B. Saunders.

Cone, E. J., Welch, M. J., & Babecki, M. B. (1995). *Hair testing for drugs of abuse: International research on standards and technology* (NIH Publication No. 95-3727). Rockville, MD: National Institutes of Health.

Donovan, D. M., & Marlatt, G. A. (Eds.). (1988). *Assessment of addictive behavior.* New York: Guilford.

Fischbach, F. T. (1996). *A manual of laboratory and diagnostic tests* (5th ed.). Philadelphia: J. B. Lippincott.

Fultz, J. M., & Senay, E. C. (1975). Guidelines for the management of hospitalized narcotic addicts. *Annals of Internal Medicine, 82,* 815-818.

Giuffra, M. J. (1993). Nursing strategies with alcohol and drug problems in the family. In M. A. Naegle (Ed.), *Substance abuse education in nursing* (Vol. 3, pp. 87-137). New York: National League for Nursing Press.

Lisanti, P. (1991). Assessment of the adult client for drug and alcohol use. In M. A. Naegle (Ed.), *Substance abuse education in nursing* (Vol. 1, pp. 151-247). New York: National League for Nursing Press.

Lopez, F. (1994). *Confidentiality of patient records for alcohol and other drug treatment* (DHHS Publication No. SMA 95-3018). Rockville, MD: U.S. Department of Health and Human Services.

Mieczkowski, T. (1999). *Drug testing technology.* Boca Raton, FL: CRC.

National Institute on Drug Abuse. (1995). *Assessing client needs using the ASI: Training facilitator's manual* (NIH Publication No. 95-3621). Rockville, MD: Author.

National Institute on Drug Abuse. (1995). *Introducing the ASI to program staff* (NIH Publication No. 95-3617). Rockville, MD: Author.

10

Diagnosis

Objectives

- Utilize assessment data to diagnose addictive disorders.
- Recognize the wide acceptance of DSM-IV by addiction clinicians.
- Appreciate the value of a multiaxial diagnostic system.
- Utilize DSM-IV axes to organize, analyze, and interpret assessment data.
- Employ DSM-IV criteria to formulate diagnoses of substance-related disorders and other addictive disorders.
- Develop diagnoses that reflect addiction severity and guide treatment intensity.
- Understand that reliable diagnosis is a prerequisite of treatment planning.

Outline

- **Diagnosis**
- **DSM-IV**
  - Axis I
  - Axis II
  - Axis III
  - Axis IV
  - Axis V
- **Substance-Related Disorders**
  - Substance Use Disorders
  - Substance-Induced Disorders
- **Other Addictive Disorders**
- **Selected Diagnostic Codes**

Diagnosis

Diagnosis is a collaborative process between client and clinicians. Together, they validate, cluster, and interpret assessment data to determine or name the client's problem or formulate a diagnosis. A reliable diagnosis reflects addiction severity and guides treatment intensity. Diagnosis is a standard requirement for planning treatment and predicting prognosis.

DSM-IV

To diagnose addictive disorders, clinicians require information from multiple domains. There is wide acceptance among clinicians of the fourth edition of the *Diagnostic and Statistical Manual of Mental Disorders,* or *DSM-IV* (American Psychiatric Association, 1994), as a system for organizing and communicating clinical information about addictive disorders. *DSM-IV* details a multiaxial diagnostic system that is congruent with the public health agent-host-environment model of addiction. Each axis represents a distinct domain of assessment information that contributes to the comprehensive database that clinicians need to develop a diagnosis:

- *Axis I:* clinical disorders; other conditions that may be a focus of clinical attention

- *Axis II:* personality disorders; mental retardation

- *Axis III:* general medical conditions

- *Axis IV:* psychosocial and environmental problems

- *Axis V:* global assessment of functioning

Axis I

Clinicians use Axis I to record the principal disorder or condition (except for personality disorders and mental retardation). If a client has more than one Axis I disorder, the primary diagnosis or reason for treatment is listed first. Clinicians record code V71.09 if there is no diagnosis or condition on Axis I and code 799.9 if the diagnosis is deferred.

Axis II

Personality disorders and mental retardation are reported on Axis II. As in Axis I, if data do not support an Axis II diagnosis, clinicians record V71.09. Similarly, if an Axis II diagnosis is deferred or pending, clinicians enter the code 799.9.

Axis III

General medical conditions are reported on Axis III. If there are no Axis III conditions, clinicians record "deferred."

Axis IV

Axis IV reports psychosocial and environmental problems that may influence treatment and prognosis. *DSM-IV* groups these problems into the following categories:

- Problems with primary support group
- Problems related to the social environment
- Educational problems
- Occupational problems
- Housing problems
- Economic problems
- Problems with access to health care services
- Problems related to interaction with the legal system/crime
- Other psychosocial and environmental problems

In addition to delineating psychosocial and environmental problems, many clinicians rate the overall severity of the problems as mild, moderate, severe, extreme, or catastrophic—a useful holdover from *DSM-III-R* (the third, revised edition of *DSM*; American Psychiatric Association, 1987).

Axis V

Axis V is a judgment of the client's overall level of functioning that is made using the Global Assessment of Functioning (GAF) Scale. This scale is used to assess psychological, social, and occupational functioning on a mental health-illness continuum (excluding functional impairments due to physical or environmental limitations), as follows:

100 = superior functioning

90 = absent or minimal symptoms; good functioning

80 = transient, expectable symptoms; slight functional impairment

70 = mild symptoms; some difficulty functioning

60 = moderate symptoms; moderate difficulty functioning

50 = serious symptoms; serious functional impairment

40 = some impairment in reality testing or communication; major functional impairment

30 = delusions or hallucinations; serious functional impairment

20 = some danger of hurting self or others; self-care deficit; gross impairment in communication

10 = persistent danger of hurting self or others; serious suicidal act; chronic self-care deficit

Level of functioning is also an important determinant of appropriate patient placement for treatment. For Axis V, the numerical rating and the time period reflected in the rating are reported using the GAF Scale. For example:

GAF = 50 (current)

GAF = 75 (highest past year)

GAF = 100 (at discharge)

Substance-Related Disorders

Common substance-related disorders diagnosed by addiction clinicians include substance dependence, substance abuse, substance intoxication, and substance withdrawal. Substance dependence and substance abuse are substance use disorders. Substance intoxication, substance withdrawal, and a host of other conditions are substance-induced disorders.

Substance Use Disorders

Table 10.1 displays the *DSM-IV* criteria for the diagnosis of substance dependence. Six course specifiers are used with substance dependence diagnoses. Four remission specifiers are applied if the client meets no criteria for dependence of abuse for at least 1 month: *early partial remission, partial remission, early full remission,* and *sustained full remission.* The specifier *on agonist therapy* applies to clients being treated for dependence using prescribed agonist/antagonist medication such as methadone maintenance treatment. The specifier *in a controlled environment* is used when the client is in an environment where access to substances is restricted, such as a substance-free hospital, a prison, or a therapeutic community.

Table 10.2 shows the *DSM-IV* criteria for diagnosis of substance abuse.

Substance-Induced Disorders

Clinicians frequently diagnose clients with substance intoxication or substance withdrawal. Tables 10.3 and 10.4 display the *DSM-IV* criteria for diagnosis of substance intoxication and substance withdrawal, respectively. Other substance-induced disorders include delirium, dementia, amnestic disorder, psychotic disorder, mood disorders, anxiety disorders, sleep disorders, and sexual dysfunctions.

Other Addictive Disorders

Clinicians use *DSM-IV* criteria to diagnosis other addictive disorders, including pathological gambling, eating disorders, and sexual addictions. The diagnostic categories *300.3 obsessive-compulsive disorder* and *312.30 impulse-control disorders not otherwise specified* may help clinicians classify addictive conditions such as compulsive shopping, credit card abuse, and Internet addiction. Tables 10.5, 10.6, and 10.7 show the *DSM-IV* criteria for diagnosis of pathological gambling, anorexia nervosa, and bulimia nervosa, respectively.

Selected Diagnostic Codes

Addiction clinicians are familiar with the following *DSM-IV* diagnostic codes.

(text continues on page 191)

TABLE 10.1 *DSM-IV* Diagnostic Criteria for Substance Dependence

A maladaptive pattern of substance use, leading to clinically significant impairment or distress, as manifested by three (or more) of the following, occurring at any time in the same 12-month period:

1. tolerance, as defined by either of the following:

   a. a need for markedly increased amounts of the substance to achieve intoxication or desired effect

   b. markedly diminished effect with continued use of the same amount of the substance

2. withdrawal, as manifested by either of the following:

   a. the characteristic withdrawal syndrome, for the substance (refer to Criteria A and B of the criteria sets for withdrawal from the specified substances)

   b. the same (or a closely related) substance is taken to relieve or avoid withdrawal symptoms

3. the substance is often taken in larger amounts or over a longer period than was intended

4. there is a persistent desire or unsuccessful efforts to cut down or control substance use

5. a great deal of time is spent in activities necessary to obtain the substance (e.g., visiting multiple doctors or driving long distances), use the substance (e.g., chain-smoking), or recover from its effects

6. important social, occupational, or recreational activities are given up or reduced because of substance use

7. the substance use is continued despite knowledge of having a persistent or recurrent physical or psychological problem that is likely to have been caused or exacerbated by the substance (e.g., current cocaine use despite recognition of cocaine induced depression, or continued drinking despite recognition that an ulcer was made worse by alcohol consumption)

Specify if:

With Physiological Dependence: evidence of tolerance or withdrawal (i.e., either Item 1 or 2 is present).

Without Physiological Dependence: no evidence of tolerance or withdrawal (i.e., neither Item 1 nor 2 is present).

SOURCE: Reprinted with permission from the *Diagnostic and Statistical Manual of Mental Disorders,* Fourth Edition. Copyright 1994 American Psychiatric Association.

TABLE 10.2 *DSM-IV* Diagnostic Criteria for Substance Abuse

A. A maladaptive pattern of substance use leading to clinically significant impairment or distress, as manifested by one (or more) of the following, occurring within a 12-month period:

   1. recurrent substance use resulting in a failure to fulfill major role obligations at work, school, or home (e.g., repeated absences or poor work performance related to substance use; substance related absences, suspensions, or expulsions from school; neglect of children or household)

   2. recurrent substance use in situations in which it is physically hazardous (e.g., driving an automobile or operating a machine when impaired by substance use)

   3. recurrent substance-related legal problems (e.g., arrests for substance-related disorderly conduct)

   4. continued substance use despite having persistent or recurrent social or interpersonal problems caused or exacerbated by the effects of the substance (e.g., arguments with spouse about consequences of intoxication, physical fights)

B. The symptoms have never met the criteria for Substance Dependence for this class of substance.

SOURCE: Reprinted with permission from the *Diagnostic and Statistical Manual of Mental Disorders,* Fourth Edition. Copyright 1994 American Psychiatric Association.

TABLE 10.3 *DSM-IV* Diagnostic Criteria for Substance Intoxication

A. The development of a reversible substance-specific syndrome due to recent ingestion of (or exposure to) a substance. **Note:** Different substances may produce similar or identical syndromes.

B. Clinically significant maladaptive behavioral or psychological changes that are due to the effect of the substance on the central nervous system (e.g., belligerence, mood lability, cognitive impairment, impaired judgment, impaired social or occupational functioning) and develop during or shortly after use of the substance.

C. The symptoms are not due to a general medical condition and are not better accounted for by another mental disorder.

SOURCE: Reprinted with permission from the *Diagnostic and Statistical Manual of Mental Disorders,* Fourth Edition. Copyright 1994 American Psychiatric Association.

TABLE 10.4 *DSM-IV* Diagnostic Criteria for Substance Withdrawal

A. The development of a substance-specific syndrome due to the cessation of (or reduction in) substance use that has been heavy and prolonged.

B. The substance-specific syndrome causes clinically significant distress or impairment in social, occupational, or other important areas of functioning.

C. The symptoms are not due to a general medical condition and are not better accounted for by another mental disorder.

SOURCE: Reprinted with permission from the *Diagnostic and Statistical Manual of Mental Disorders,* Fourth Edition. Copyright 1994 American Psychiatric Association.

TABLE 10.5 *DSM-IV* Diagnostic Criteria for Pathological Gambling

A. Persistent and recurrent maladaptive gambling behavior as indicated by five (or more) of the following:

    1. is preoccupied with gambling (e.g., preoccupied with reliving past gambling experiences, handicapping or planning the next venture, or thinking of ways to get money with which to gamble

    2. needs to gamble with increasing amounts of money in order to achieve the desired excitement

    3. has repeated unsuccessful efforts to control, cut back, or stop gambling

    4. is restless or irritable when attempting to cut down or stop gambling

    5. gambles as a way of escaping from problems or of relieving a dysphoric mood (e.g., feelings or helplessness, guilt, anxiety, depression)

    6. after losing money gambling, often returns another day to get even ("chasing" one's losses)

    7. lies to family members, therapist, or others to conceal the extent of involvement with gambling

    8. has committed illegal acts such as forgery, fraud, theft, or embezzlement to finance gambling

    9. has jeopardized or lost a significant relationship, job, or educational or career opportunity because of gambling

    10. relies on others to provide money to relieve a desperate financial situation caused by gambling

B. The gambling behavior is not better accounted for by a Manic Episode.

SOURCE: Reprinted with permission from the *Diagnostic and Statistical Manual of Mental Disorders,* Fourth Edition. Copyright 1994 American Psychiatric Association.

TABLE 10.6 *DSM-IV* Diagnostic Criteria for Anorexia Nervosa

A. Refusal to maintain body weight at or above a minimally normal weight for age and height (e.g., weight loss leading to maintenance of body weight less than 85% of that expected; or failure to make expected weight gain during period of growth, leading to body weight less than 85% of that expected).

B. Intense fear of gaining weight or becoming fat, even though underweight.

C. Disturbance in the way in which one's body weight or shape is experienced, undue influence of body weight or shape on self-evaluation, or denial of the seriousness of the current low body weight.

D. In postmenarcheal females, amenorrhea, i.e., the absence of at least three consecutive menstrual cycles. (A woman is considered to have amenorrhea if her periods occur only following hormone, e.g., estrogen, administration.)

Specify type:

Restricting Type: during the current epsiode of Anorexia Nervosa, the person has not regularly engaged in binge-eating or purging behavior (i.e., self-induced vomiting or the misuse of laxatives, diruetics, enemas).

Binge-Eating/Purging Type: during the current episode of Anorexia Nervosa, the person has regularly engaged in binge-eating or purging behavior (i.e., self-induced vomiting or the misuse of laxatives, diuretics, or enemas).

SOURCE: Reprinted with permission from the *Diagnostic and Statistical Manual of Mental Disorders,* Fourth Edition. Copyright 1994 American Psychiatric Association.

Substance-Related Disorders

- Alcohol-related disorders
    - 303.90 Alcohol dependence
    - 305.00 Alcohol use
    - 303.00 Alcohol intoxication
    - 291.8   Alcohol withdrawal
- Amphetamine (or amphetamine-like)-related disorders
    - 304.40 Amphetamine dependence
    - 305.70 Amphetamine use
    - 292.89 Amphetamine intoxication
    - 292.0   Amphetamine withdrawal

TABLE 10.7 *DSM-IV* Diagnostic Criteria for Bulimia Nervosa

A. Recurrent episodes of binge eating. An episode of binge eating is characterized by both of the following:

    1. eating, in a discrete period of time (e.g., within any 2-hour period), an amount of food that is definitely larger than most people would eat during a similar period of time and under similar circumstances

    2. a sense of lack of control over eating during the episode (e.g., a feeling that one cannot stop eating or control what or how much one is eating).

B. Recurrent inappropriate compensatory behavior in order to prevent weight gain, such as self-induced vomiting; misuse of laxatives, diuretics, enemas, or other medications; fasting; or excessive exercise.

C. The binge eating and inappropriate compensatory behaviors both occur on average, at least twice a week for 3 months.

D. Self-evaluation is unduly influenced by body shape and weight.

E. The disturbance does not occur exclusively during episodes of Anorexia Nervosa.

Specific Type:

Purging Type: during the current episode of Bulimia Nervosa, the person has regularly engaged in self-induced vomiting or the misuse of laxatives, diuretics, or enemas.

Nonpurging Type: during the current episode of Bulimia Nervosa, the person has used other inappropriate compensatory behaviors, such as fasting or excessive exercise, but has not regularly engaged in self-induced vomiting or the misuse of laxatives, diruetics, or enemas.

SOURCE: Reprinted with permission from the *Diagnostic and Statistical Manual of Mental Disorders,* Fourth Edition. Copyright 1994 American Psychiatric Association.

    ■ Caffeine-related disorders

       305.90 Caffeine intoxication

       292.89 Caffeine-induced anxiety disorder

       292.89 Caffeine-induced sleep disorder

    ■ Cannabis-related disorders

       304.30 Cannabis dependence

       305.20 Cannabis abuse

       292.89 Cannabis intoxication (specify if with perceptual disturbances)

    ■ Cocaine-related disorders

       304.10 Cocaine dependence

       305.60 Cocaine abuse

292.89 Cocaine intoxication (specify if with perceptual disturbances)

292.0 Cocaine withdrawal

- Hallucinogen-related disorders

    304.50 Hallucinogen dependence

    305.30 Hallucinogen abuse

    292.89 Hallucinogen intoxication

    292.89 Hallucinogen persisting perception disorder (flashbacks)

- Inhalant-related disorders

    304.60 Inhalant dependence

    305.90 Inhalant abuse

    292.89 Inhalant intoxication

- Nicotine-related disorders

    305.10 Nicotine dependence

    292.0 Nicotine withdrawal

- Opioid-related disorders

    304.00 Opioid dependence

    305.50 Opioid abuse

    292.89 Opioid intoxication (specify if with perceptual disturbances)

    292.0 Opioid withdrawal

- Phencyclidine (or phencyclidine-like)-related disorders

    304.90 Phencyclidine dependence

    305.90 Phencyclidine abuse

    292.89 Phencyclidine intoxication

- Sedative-, hypnotic-, or anxiolytic-related disorders

    304.10 Sedative, hypnotic, or anxiolytic dependence

    305.40 Sedative, hypnotic, or anxiolytic abuse

    292.40 Sedative, hypnotic, or anxiolytic intoxication

    292.0 Sedative, hypnotic, or anxiolytic withdrawal (specify if with perceptual disturbances)

- Polysubstance-related disorder

    304.80 Polysubstance dependence

- Other (or unknown) substance-related disorders

    304.90 Other (or unknown) substance dependence

    305.90 Other (or unknown) substance abuse

292.89 Other (or unknown) substance intoxication (specify if with other perceptual disturbances)

292.0 Other (or unknown) substance withdrawal

(See *DSM-IV* for a detailed list and descriptions of the many substance-induced disorders not included above.)

Other Addictive Disorders

- Impulse-control disorders not elsewhere classified

    312.31 Pathological gambling

    312.30 Impulse-control disorder not otherwise specified (useful for compulsive shopping)

- Eating disorders

    307.1 Anorexia nervosa
    Restricting type
    Binge-eating/purging type

    307.51 Bulimia nervosa
    Purging type
    Nonpurging type

    307.50 Eating disorders not otherwise specified

- Obsessive-compulsive disorder

    300.3 Obsessive-compulsive disorder

- Sexual and gender identity disorders (selected diagnoses)

    302.3 Exhibitionism

    303.91 Fetishism

    302.89 Frotteurism

    302.2 Pedophilia

    302.83 Sexual masochism

    302.94 Sexual sadism

    302.3 Transvestic fetishism

    302.82 Voyeurism

    302.9 Paraphilia not otherwise specified

    V61.21 Sexual abuse of child (perpetrator)
    Specify 995.5 child (victim)

    V61.1 Sexual abuse of adult (perpetrator)
    Specify 995.81 adult (victim)

    302.9 Sexual disorder not otherwise specified

- Relational problems
  V61.1   Partner relational problem
  V62.81 Relational problem not otherwise specified

Summary

Diagnosis is the collaborative process by which client and clinicians validate, cluster, and interpret assessment data to determine or name the client's problems. There is wide acceptance among clinicians of *DSM-IV* as a system for organizing and communicating clinical information about addictive disorders. Each *DSM-IV* axis represents a distinct domain of assessment information that contributes to the comprehensive database clinicians use to formulate a diagnosis. Addiction clinicians need to be able to use *DSM-IV* with confidence. Diagnosis reflects addiction severity and guides treatment intensity. Reliable diagnosis is a prerequisite of effective treatment planning.

Related Skills Checklist

Practitioner skills related to the diagnosis of addiction disorders include the ability to do the following:

- Employ diagnostic criteria from *DSM-IV* to diagnose substance dependence, substance abuse, substance intoxication, and substance withdrawal.

- Utilize *DSM-IV* diagnoses for pathological gambling and eating disorders.

- Apply *DSM-IV* diagnostic criteria codes for relational problems, paraphilias, and sexual abuse to sex and love addictions.

- Use the *DSM-IV* diagnoses for obsessive-compulsive disorder and impulse control disorder as appropriate for compulsive shopping and other addictive behaviors.

Special Topics for Further Study

Develop a diagnostic client profile for the past 3, 6, 9, or 12 months for your practice or agency. Using a simple frequency count, what were the Axis I and Axis II diagnoses? What were the most common Axis III medical problems? What kinds of psychosocial and environmental stressors were identified? What was the mean GAF? What was the GAF range? Does the profile reveal any patterns or trends? Is the client profile changing? What are the treatment implications of the client profile?

Addiction Practice 2000

Addiction practice 2000 expects clinicians to utilize *DSM-IV* fully and with confidence to diagnose substance-related disorders and other addictive disorders.

Reference

American Psychiatric Association. (1987). *Diagnostic and statistical manual of mental disorders* (3rd ed., rev.). Washington, DC: Author.
American Psychiatric Association. (1994). *Diagnostic and statistical manual of mental disorders* (4th ed.). Washington, DC: Author.

Other Sources

Chernecky, C. C., & Berger, B. J. (1997). *Laboratory tests and diagnostic procedures* (2nd ed.). Philadelphia: W. B. Saunders.
Fischbach, F. T. (1996). *A manual of laboratory and diagnostic tests* (5th ed.). Philadelphia: J. B. Lippincott.
National Institute on Drug Abuse. (1995). *Diagnosis and severity of drug abuse and drug dependence* (NIH Publication No. 95-3884). Rockville, MD: Author.
Schuckit, M. A. (1999). *Drug and alcohol abuse: A clinical guide to diagnosis and treatment* (5th ed.). New York: Plenum.
Woody, G., Schuckit, M. A., Weinribe, R., & Us, E. (1993). A review of substance use disorders section of the *DSM-IV. Psychiatric Clinics of North America, 16,* 21-32.

11

Treatment Planning

Objectives

- Acknowledge the value of treatment planning.
- Understand the treatment planning process.
- Recognize the factors that influence treatment plans.
- Identify client problems or needs, strengths, limitations, and preferences, as well as provider resources.
- Address clients' needs as related to addiction severity, client diversity, and coexisting medical, psychological, and social problems.
- Utilize the ASAM PPC-2 dimensions to develop a problem list and establish goals.
- Establish short-term, intermediate, and long-term treatment goals.
- Develop objectives and specify outcomes.
- Select interventions and designate services.
- Determine level of care and intervention dose.
- Plan treatment monitoring and evaluation.

Outline

- **Purpose of Treatment Planning**
- **The Treatment Planning Process**
- **Treatment Plans**
- **Assessment Elements**
  - Problems and Needs
  - Client Strengths, Limitations, and Preferences
  - Provider Resources

- – Addiction Severity, Client Diversity, and Coexisting
    Problems
  – ASAM PPC-2 Dimensions
- ■ **Goals**
  – Short-Term Goals
  – Intermediate Goals
  – Long-Term Goals
- ■ **Objectives and Outcomes**
- ■ **Interventions**
- ■ **Treatment Intensity**
  – Level of Care
  – Dose
- ■ **Monitoring and Evaluation**
- ■ **Summary**
- ■ **Related Skills Checklist**
- ■ **Special Topics for Further Study**
- ■ **Addiction Practice 2000**

Purpose of Treatment Planning

Client and clinicians collaborate to develop a treatment plan. The treatment plan is an individualized, written description of the client's planned treatment. Treatment plans reflect addiction severity and treatment intensity. Each plan builds upon the comprehensive assessment of the client and the client's *DSM-IV* diagnosis (American Psychiatric Association, 1994). Treatment plans identify clients' problems or needs, strengths, limitations, and preferences; they also take into account provider resources. Client and clinicians establish treatment goals, then specify objectives or expected outcomes. The treatment plan identifies the interventions and services necessary to achieve treatment goals. Placing the client in the appropriate level of care and selecting the correct intervention "dose" are critical parts of treatment planning.

The Treatment Planning Process

Treatment planning is a collaborative process between client and clinicians. The client's family also participates in the treatment planning process whenever possible. The formulation of a treatment plan includes the following:

- ■ Identification of client problems or needs

- An inventory of client strengths, limitations, and preferences
- Determination of provider resources
- Establishment of treatment goals
- Development of treatment objectives and/or specification of outcomes
- Selection of interventions and services
- Placement of the client in an appropriate level of care
- Planning for the evaluation of treatment

After treatment planning is complete, the plan must be implemented, and the client's responses to treatment and progress must be monitored. The treatment plan is then modified as needed. Together, clinicians and client evaluate the goal achievements of the client on an ongoing basis and coordinate continuing care.

In regard to treatment planning, *ASAM PPC-2* (American Society of Addiction Medicine, 1996) employs the concept of client *problems* and the development of a problem list, whereas the Joint Commission on Accreditation of Healthcare Organizations (JCAHO, 1996, 1999), in its *Comprehensive Accreditation Manual for Behavioral Health Care,* uses the word *need.* Increasingly, treatment planning language also includes the concepts of *expected outcomes* and *outcome criteria.*

Delivering care and services effectively and efficiently requires planning. The treatment-planning process is designed to identify and incorporate each individual's unique needs, expectations, and characteristics into an individualized and appropriate plan. The nature of the individual's needs and condition, as determined through assessment, is a primary consideration during the planning process. (JCAHO, 1996, p. 210)

Treatment Plans

The treatment plans established in a given organization reflect that organization's mission and philosophy as well as accreditation standards. A sound treatment plan builds upon a dominant theory or model of addiction and a particular treatment methodology; current addiction research and policy influence treatment planning.

Providers' policies, procedures, and protocols determine treatment plan formats, and such formats vary with treatment settings and levels of care. Treatment plan language often reflects regional practice and agency preference. Treatment plans may use handwritten notes, preprinted forms, standards of practice, decision algorithms, critical pathways, care maps, and/or computerized records. Whatever the format, the treatment plan is worded in a manner that is understood clearly by the client; it is often signed by both client and clinicians. Clinicians document any inability or unwillingness on the part of clients to participate in the treatment planning process. Note that therapy often begins with a preliminary treatment plan, based on initial screening data.

Assessment Elements

Problems and Needs

Using assessment data and the client's *DSM-IV* diagnosis, client and clinicians identify client problems or needs. A *problem* represents a state of stress, most often distress. A *need* is a requirement or essential condition for life, health, and well-being. Treatment problems and needs reflect addiction severity, client characteristics, and the recovery environment. Problems and needs are signs and symptoms of the addictive process; the distress, pain, and suffering associated with the addiction; and the damaging, often devastating, destructive consequences of addictive disorders for the client as well as the client's family and community. Life-threatening client problems and needs are addressed immediately. Client and clinicians prioritize other problems and needs, which are expressed as simple, direct statements. Clinicians note the client's and the client's family members' perceptions of the client's problems and needs. Clinicians justify why any identified problems and needs are not addressed.

Client Strengths, Limitations, and Preferences

Client and clinicians inventory the client's strengths, limitations, and preferences. Strengths are assets such as talents and skills, accomplishments, and achievements, as well as family and community resources that support treatment and recovery. Limitations are liabilities—client factors that confound, constrain, or complicate treatment and recovery. Sometimes family members thwart or even sabotage client recovery. Community conditions, such as lack of transportation and lack of health insurance, can restrict access to treatment or obstruct recovery. What factors facilitate treatment? What are the blocks or barriers to treatment?

The client's preferences are taken into account in the choices made in treatment planning, especially concerning interventions and possibly level of care. For example, Amos L. works days as a supervisor in a local manufacturing plant. He prefers to be treated for his heroin dependence in an outpatient detoxification program rather than through inpatient admission. Mary P. tells the clinician that she has difficulty reading. Are any of the education materials available on tape?

Provider Resources

Clinicians assess provider resources to determine whether or not the organization and clinicians can meet the client's treatment needs. If not, clinicians expedite referral of the client in an efficient, effective manner. For inpatient treatment, clinicians factor into the treatment plan the projected average length of stay for the diagnostic-related group into which the client falls.

Addiction Severity, Client Diversity, and Coexisting Problems

Clinicians who use the Addiction Severity Index may identify client problems and needs related to medical status, employment/support status, drug/alcohol use, legal status, family/social relationships, and psychiatric status. Addiction treatment also addresses spiritual problems and needs. Treatment planning must be especially sensitive and responsive to the needs of diverse clients, especially regarding issues related to age, ethnocultural characteristics, gender, and sexual orientation. Clinicians and client also identify and address coexisting medical, psychological, and social problems. (For more on these topics, see the chapters in Parts IV and V of this volume.)

ASAM PPC-2 Dimensions

It may be useful for clinicians to develop client problem lists that reflect the *ASAM PPC-2* dimensions. For example:

1. Severe withdrawal risk from alcohol

2. Type 2 diabetes mellitus; noncompliant with treatment regimen

3. History of suicide attempts × 3

4. Resistance high; no evidence of motivation to change

5. Unable to control use despite dangerous consequences

6. Erratic use of support network; limited recovery skills

Goals

Based upon identified client problems or needs, strengths, resources, and limitations, client and clinicians establish goals. Goals are client-centered, measurable, time-limited objectives. Sound goals are realistic and feasible for client and clinicians to achieve. Goals are linked directly and logically to client needs or problems and are stated in a clear, concise, coherent way. They describe what the client must achieve in treatment to solve a problem or meet a need. Goal achievement reflects client change and demonstrates that a problem has been resolved or that a need has been met. (See also the discussion of treatment goals in Chapter 7.)

Short-Term Goals

Short-term goals address acute addiction needs or problems and are achieved in a brief period of time, usually less than a week for inpatient treatment and within 3 months for outpatient treatment. As noted in Chapter 7, safe withdrawal, abstinence, harm reduction, and moderate drinking may be short-term treatment goals. For example, a client might state short-term goals such as the following:

Jay C. will
1. experience a safe and comfortable detoxification.
2. encounter few medical complications.
3. experience few emotional/behavioral complications.
4. increase treatment acceptance; decrease treatment resistance.
5. initiate a relapse prevention plan.
6. utilize a supportive recovery environment.

Intermediate Goals

Intermediate goals follow the achievement of short-term goals. Relapse prevention and remission are appropriate intermediate goals. For example:

Alan M. will
1. sustain full remission.
2. exhibit improvement in medical functioning.
3. experience improvement in emotional/behavioral functioning.
4. accept responsibility for management of his addictive disorder.
5. address relapse triggers with strategies and skills.
6. strengthen his supportive recovery environment.

Long-Term Goals

Long-term goals address chronic addiction needs or problems, sustain remission, and promote recovery. For example:

Gladys W. will

1. fulfill all requirements of federal probation for continuous abstinence for 3 years.
2. maintain optimal medical health.
3. demonstrate optimal psychological well-being.
4. develop a substance-free lifestyle.
5. update her relapse prevention plan as necessary.
6. reunite with her three children, who are currently in foster care.

Objectives and Outcomes

Goals require client outcome statements to provide evidence of goal achievement. An expected outcome is a very specific, time-limited, step-by-step behavioral objective that leads to goal achievement. An outcome is a measurable change in client status in response to treatment interventions. Outcome statements are short, simple, and explicit. Outcomes provide the evidence for goal achievement. The following example illustrates the treatment planning process, using assessment data to identify a problem, establish a goal, and specify client outcomes.

Date: 6/1/99

Assessment data: Client is disoriented, holding head; shaking, sweating, hyperventilating; vomited × 2; lacks coordination; swears and strikes out at staff; history of seizures with one previous episode of delirium tremens; CIWA-Ar is 25.

Problem: Risk for injury related to acute alcohol withdrawal.

Goal: Client will experience a safe and comfortable detoxification as evidenced by the ability to:

Outcomes:

Remain injury free stat.

Display no seizure activity by 6/1.

Experience no medical complications by 6/1.

Sleep at least 6 hours a night by 6/2.

Consume 1,500 ml fluids and 2,400-calorie high-carbohydrate diet daily by 6/2.

Exhibit orientation × 3 by 6/3.

Demonstrate appropriate behavior by 6/3.

Interventions

Interventions are actions and services the client and clinicians use to achieve treatment goals. Clinicians express interventions as behavioral strategies and skills. Interventions reflect client strengths, limitations, and preferences; agency mission and philosophy, provider resources, and treatment methodology; and clinician competencies and expertise. Interventions include all services needed to support treatment, such as consultation, transportation, and child care. (Intervention with individuals, groups, families, and the community is examined in Chapter 12.)

Treatment Intensity

Addiction severity determines treatment intensity. The higher the addiction severity, the greater the treatment intensity. Level of care and "dose" of intervention are key indicators of treatment intensity.

Level of Care

As noted in Chapter 8, the *ASAM PPC-2* criteria recognize four major levels of care: Level I, outpatient services; Level II, intensive outpatient/partial hospitalization services; Level III, residential/inpatient services; and Level IV, medically managed intensive inpatient services.

Dose

Dose includes the number, types, and frequency of interventions and services (see the discussion of treatment intensity in Chapter 8). Following are some examples of dose for addiction:

- Jim T. attends intensive evening treatment 3 hours per evening, 4 nights a week, for 4 weeks.

- Sharon B. provides random urines weekly as part of her 2-year supervised probation.

- Ted P. has his alcohol withdrawal status assessed every 30 minutes by the nurse until his CIWA-Ar score is less than 20.

- Bill N. qualified for the Substance Abuse Rehabilitation Program while incarcerated. His participation in the following treatment requirements is mandatory:

  Group treatment: concept, skills, process groups, 3 per day × 5 days per week for 12 weeks

Homework: as required by treatment staff for 12 weeks

Institutional support groups (Alcoholics Anonymous, Narcotics Anonymous, Smart Recovery): 3 per week for 12 weeks

Couples/family counseling: optional, 1 per week for 12 weeks

Family support and education: optional, 10:00 A.M.-12:00 noon every Saturday for 12 weeks

Random urine testing, monthly and for probable cause for 12 weeks

Monitoring and Evaluation

To ensure quality of treatment, treatment plans incorporate professional standards of care. Client and clinicians utilize outcome criteria to monitor client response to treatment and progress. This ongoing evaluation guides modification of the treatment plan as necessary. Evaluation indicators determine goal achievement, readiness for discharge, and continuing care. (For a more thorough discussion of process and outcome evaluation, see Chapter 13.)

Summary

Client and clinicians collaborate to develop an individualized, written treatment plan. The plan builds upon the comprehensive assessment and diagnosis of the client. Treatment plans identify client problems or needs, strengths, and limitations as well as provider resources. Clients' needs relate to addiction severity, client diversity, and coexisting medical, psychological, and social problems. Client and clinicians establish and prioritize goals, specify objectives or expected outcomes, select interventions, and designate services. The treatment plan reflects level of care and intervention dose. The plan specifies the way client and clinicians will monitor and evaluate treatment.

Related Skills Checklist

Practitioner skills related to treatment planning include the ability to do the following:

- Use comprehensive client assessment data and *DSM-IV* diagnosis to develop the treatment plan.
- Collaborate with client to plan treatment.
- Involve the client's family in treatment planning.

- Inventory client strengths, limitations, and preferences.

- Consider provider resources when planning treatment.

- Identify and prioritize problems or needs with the client.

- Formulate treatment goals, objectives or outcomes, and interventions or actions that are acceptable to both clinicians and client.

- Set goals that reflect client needs or problems.

- Identify outcomes (the steps) necessary to achieve goals.

- Select interventions that emphasize behavioral strategies and skills.

- Use addiction severity to determine treatment intensity.

- Select level of care and intervention dose to reflect treatment intensity.

- Develop a plan to monitor and evaluate client treatment.

Special Topics for Further Study

Review the requirements of the Joint Commission on Accreditation of Healthcare Organizations and the Commission on Accreditation of Rehabilitation Facilities for treatment plans. Investigate the feasibility and acceptability of using standardized treatment plans from books or electronic media as guides for individual client treatment plans.

Addiction Practice 2000

Addiction practice 2000 suggests that clinicians standardize the treatment planning process to improve client treatment outcomes and increase clinician effectiveness and efficiency.

References

American Psychiatric Association. (1994). *Diagnostic and statistical manual of mental disorders* (4th ed.). Washington, DC: Author.
American Society of Addiction Medicine. (1996). *Patient placement criteria for the treatment of substance-related disorders* (2nd ed.). Chevy Chase, MD: Author.
Commission on Accreditation of Rehabilitation Facilities. (1999). *Standards manual and interpretive guide for behavioral health.* Tucson, AZ: Author.

Joint Commission on Accreditation of Healthcare Organizations. (1996). *1997-98 comprehensive accreditation manual for behavioral health care.* Oakbrook Terrace, IL: Author.

Joint Commission on Accreditation of Healthcare Organizations. (1999). *1999-2000 comprehensive accreditation manual for behavioral health care.* Oakbrook Terrace, IL: Author.

Other Sources

Center for Substance Abuse Treatment. (1994). *Confidentiality of patient records for alcohol and other drug treatment* (DHHS Publication No. SMA 95-2010). Rockville, MD: Author.

Center for Substance Abuse Treatment. (1997). *Diagnostic source book on drug abuse research and treatment* (NIH Publication No. 96-3508). Rockville, MD: Author.

Daley, D. C., & Zuckoff, A. (1999). *Improving treatment compliance: Counseling and systems strategies for substance abuse and dual disorders.* Center City, MN: Hazelden.

National Institute on Drug Abuse. (1997). *Beyond the therapeutic alliance: Keeping the drug-dependent individual in treatment* (NIH Publication No. 97-4142). Rockville, MD: Author.

Perkinson, R. R., & Jongsma, A. E., Jr. (1998). *The chemical dependence treatment planner.* New York: John Wiley.

12

Intervention

Objectives

- Collaborate with clients to choose and carry out interventions.
- Select interventions for individual clients, including medical management, nursing, counseling, mutual self-help groups, and family support.
- Employ pharmacological intervention, spiritual care, social services, and psychological services as indicated.
- Intervene with groups of clients, client families, and the community.

Outline

- **Intervention**
- **Individual as Client**
  - Medical Management
  - Nursing
  - Counseling
  - Family Support
  - Community Care
    - Aftercare
    - Halfway Houses
    - Sober Housing
    - Therapeutic Communities
  - Pharmacological Intervention
  - Social Services
  - Spiritual Care

Intervention

Interventions are the actions that client and clinicians take to reach treatment outcomes, achieve goals, and ultimately resolve client problems and meet client needs. Interventions reflect actions in all three learning domains: cognitive, affective, and psychomotor. Interventions help clients develop new insights, attitudes, and behaviors. As noted previously, the treatment plan, and especially the interventions, reflect the organization's mission and philosophy, dominant theory or model of addiction, and treatment methodology.

Clinicians determine addiction severity by gathering assessment data, particularly information about acute intoxication and/or withdrawal potential and biomedical and emotional/behavioral conditions and complications (Dimensions 1, 2, and 3 *ASAM PPC-2;* American Society of Addiction Medicine, 1996), or by using the Addiction Severity Index. Assessment of client treatment acceptance/resistance, relapse potential, and recovery environment (Dimensions 4, 5, and 6 *ASAM PPC-2*) is critical to help client and clinicians select and execute interventions. Clients participate actively in choosing and carrying out interventions.

The focus of an intervention may be the client as an individual, a group, the client's family, or the community. Interventions include medical management, nursing, counseling, mutual self-help groups, family involvement, and community care. Individual treatment plans may include pharmacological intervention, social services, spiritual care, and psychological services.

Treatment intensity includes level of care: outpatient services, intensive outpatient or partial hospitalization services, residential or inpatient services, or medically managed intensive inpatient services. Clients who are intoxicated or experiencing withdrawal require highly individualized treatment plans and interventions. Interventions are specialized for clients receiving opioid maintenance therapy and methadone treatment. Certain client characteristics, such as age, culture, gender, and sexual orientation, demand treatment matching. Many agencies and health professionals collaborate to provide effective treatment for addiction clients with coexisting medical, psychological, and social problems.

Individual as Client

Medical Management

Physicians write orders to assure a safe, comfortable withdrawal, develop protocols for opioid maintenance therapy and methadone treatment, and coordinate pharmacological intervention. They also manage biomedical conditions and complications, treat concomitant psychiatric problems, and supervise client treatment in residential/inpatient settings. Physicians may provide client education and counseling. For very complex clients, clinicians may seek additional medical consultation or expedited referral. Physicians also direct anesthesia-assisted detoxification.

Nursing

Nurses provide 24-hour skilled observation, care, and coordination when clients receive medically managed intensive inpatient services. Nurses monitor client responses to withdrawal protocols and treatment in general, and usually administer the medications clients receive for opioid maintenance therapy and methadone treatment. Nurses care for clients with biomedical and psychiatric conditions and complications; they also help clients meet their needs for nutrition and health promotion. In residential/inpatient treatment settings, nurses manage the health care needs of clients. Nurses provide addiction education and counseling, especially HIV/AIDS education. Nurses play a lead role with clients in ambulatory and home detoxification programs.

Counseling

Clinicians from many professions provide counseling for clients: counselors per se, nurses, social workers, clergy, psychologists, and psychiatrists. Professional counseling reflects a dominant theory or model of addiction and follows a particular treatment methodology: for instance, many counselors view addiction as a biopsychosocial process that responds well to brief cognitive-behavioral intervention.

Counselors provide support, education, and psychotherapy for clients in all levels of care. Inpatient clients receive daily counseling and education. Counselors help clients in residential and outpatient settings learn about addiction. They address client acceptance or resistance to treatment and work with clients to develop the strategies and skills they need to achieve abstinence or reduce harm. Counselors help clients identify relapse triggers, find ways to cope with cravings, and develop skills to control impulses to use. With their clients, counselors develop realistic relapse prevention plans. They address blocks or barriers to recovery in clients' environments, such as problems with family, employment, or housing; financial, legal, or leisure concerns; spiritual distress; and other psychosocial problems. Counselors recognize cross-addiction. They help clients prepare for participation in mutual self-help groups and continuing care in the community. Counselors may also provide HIV/AIDS education and counseling. They often determine client needs for consultation and initiate referral for special services.

Family Support

It is difficult for individual clients who lack family involvement to engage in treatment and achieve recovery goals. Relapse is significantly higher for individuals who return to homes and families that threaten, undermine, or sabotage their recovery. Whether or not one embraces a systems theory of addiction, family involvement in treatment improves individual client outcomes. Ideally, the family supports the client and is involved in assessment, treatment, and recovery. With family involvement, the client can address trust issues earlier and confront overwhelming feelings of guilt and shame that can trigger relapse. Family members learn how to decrease *enabling*—that is, their own attitudes and behaviors that encourage the client to perpetuate his or her addiction. The role of the family in treatment is especially important today because the great majority of clients receive treatment while living at home or in the community.

Community Care

Increasingly, clients are living at home or in the community during initial treatment, continuing care, remission, and recovery. Levels of treatment taking place in the community include initial treatment, opioid maintenance therapy, residential programs, and aftercare.

Aftercare

During aftercare, the recovery environment (Dimension 6 *ASAM PPC-2*) is critical to the prevention of relapse. Clients return to the community, often to the same neighborhoods where they bought and used drugs. The community also offers around-the-clock support for recovering men, women, and youth "who want it." Aftercare plans identify a host of community contacts, including mutual self-help groups, sponsors, and sober housing, as well as referrals to community agencies for assistance with training, employment, chronic health problems, and other long-term problems or needs that were identified during treatment.

Halfway Houses

Many clients live for 6 months or longer in halfway houses that offer structured, sober living and treatment environments in the community. Interventions emphasize group counseling and peer support. Treatment helps residents prevent relapse and begin to develop addiction-free lifestyles. Rehabilitation goals include the improvement of communication skills, development of healthy interpersonal relationships, and resocialization in the community, with work being an important expectation of most halfway house programs. Halfway houses often serve particular populations exclusively, such as men, women, adolescents, or pregnant addicts.

Sober Housing

Some individuals may not be ready to live independently in the community following "graduation" from a halfway house. Some treatment programs have developed transition or three-quarter houses, which offer semistructured, sober living environments with a shifting of responsibility for recovery from the program to the individual. In some communities, organizations such as the Salvation Army operate sober houses.

Therapeutic Communities

Therapeutic communities offer long-term, intensive residential treatment for clients. In a therapeutic community, the community itself is the intervention. Clients have social deficits and require social treatment. Recovery is a *habilitation* process that integrates explicit psychological, developmental, and social goals. Clinicians facilitate personal growth and social change in clients through the purposeful use of the community.

Pharmacological Intervention

Pharmacological intervention with addiction clients includes symptomatic treatment, agonist substitution, and antagonist treatment. In *symptomatic treatment,* medications are used to treat the symptoms associated with substance use. These medications usually have the opposite effects of the abused drugs. For instance, antianxiety medications may be used with clients who have stopped taking cocaine or amphetamines (CNS stimulants) to manage their high anxiety. A client with a diagnosis of alcohol dependence in early sustained remission takes an antidepressant medication to manage symptoms of a major depression. Clinicians are testing the efficacy of selective serotonin reuptake inhibitors such as fluoxetine (Prozac) and fluvoxamine (Luvox) for use with a wide variety of addictive disorders. Buspirone (BuSpar) is a nonaddictive antianxiety medication that inhibits the action of serotonin (5-HT). Extensive research continues to discover and develop medications to counter craving.

Agonist substitution is the use of medications having pharmacological actions similar to the abused substances. Folklore suggests that a person bitten by a dog use the "hair of the dog" as a remedy. Alcoholics well know that the "morning-after" drink calms the shakes of a hangover. With the evolution of formal treatment for alcoholism, physicians began using sedative-hypnotic medications such as chlordiazepoxide (Librium), clorazepate (Tranxene), diazepam (Valium), and oxazepam (Serax) to assure safe and comfortable withdrawal and prevent delirium tremens, seizures, and death. Agonist medications are used to manage withdrawals from other CNS depressants.

Opioid maintenance therapy, the use of medications such as methadone and levo-alpha-acetylmethadol (LAAM), is a well-known example of agonist substitution. Methadone and LAAM occupy the same opiate receptors in the brain as heroin, meperidine (Demerol), and oxycodone (Percocet). Agonist substitute medications provide a continuous, balanced steady state; clients experience neither euphoria nor the usual intoxication or withdrawal symptoms that accompany opioid abuse. Physiological craving is extinguished.

Antagonist treatment uses medications that block the pharmacological effects of the abused drugs. Naltrexone (Trexan, ReVia) actually competes with narcotics to occupy the narcotic receptor site. Should clients use heroin or other opiates on top of the naltrexone, they experience no additional effect. Research studies have demonstrated the efficacy of naltrexone in reducing alcohol-dependent behavior.

Nalzone (Narcan), an antidote for opioid abuse, blocks the effects of opioids and reverses CNS depression and respiratory depression due to opioid overdose without producing any agonist (opioid-like) effects. Disulfiram (Antabuse), an alcohol deterrent, inhibits or blocks the oxidation of alcohol at the acetaldehyde stage of metabolism. Clients take Antabuse to deter their drinking. It is especially useful when a client makes a contract with a family member or significant other not to drink and takes the medication in that person's presence. Drinking on top of Antabuse produces very uncomfortable, even severe, effects. Accumulation of acetaldehyde produces a disulfiram-alcohol reaction as evidenced by flushing, throbbing headache, nausea, vomiting, sweating, thirst, confusion, dyspnea with hyperventilation, and chest pain with palpitations and tachycardia. When the reaction is severe, an individual can experience cardiovascular collapse, myocardial infarction, congestive heart failure, convulsions, and death. Clients taking Antabuse need extensive education about its use, side effects, and adverse reactions; those receiving such treatment should carry Antabuse identification cards.

Social Services

Many clients have psychosocial and environmental problems related to their addictions that require social service intervention. Data from Axis IV *DSM-IV* (American Psychiatric Association, 1994) help clinicians to identify problems such as unemployment, inadequate housing, financial difficulties, scarce health care services, lack of transportation, inadequate health insurance, legal problems, and other social problems that confound recovery and place clients at high risk for relapse. A Global Assessment of Functioning (GAF) Scale score of 50 (Axis V *DSM-IV*) identifies serious symptoms or impairment in social functioning: judgment, thinking, or mood; work, family, or school. A current GAF of 30 or below reflects an inability to function in almost all activities of daily living.

Spiritual Care

Treatment facilities, clinicians, and support groups that embrace a 12-step approach to treatment acknowledge the usefulness of belief in a *higher power* to help addicts stop using, prevent relapse, and develop a drug-free lifestyle. Clergy are often the first professionals sought out by individuals and families for help with addiction problems. Treatment facilities such as Hazelden utilize clergy as part of their multidisciplinary treatment teams. When such referral is indicated, addiction clinicians may refer clients to clergy to help them resolve issues of guilt and shame. Clients in recovery who "do the steps" often use clergy to help them take their Fifth Step. Yet some people with addiction problems shun A.A. and other 12-step groups because they find them "too religious." A.A. members, for their part, describe the fellowship as "spiritual."

A 1997 poll commissioned by the Pew Research Center reported that 71% of respondents said they never doubted the existence of God. In 1987, the figure in response to the same item was 60%. Some 61% of Americans believe that miracles come from the power of God. *Touched by an Angel* ranks among television's highest-rated shows, and books on angels, miracles, and spirituality line bookstore shelves. A survey of HMO executives conducted by Yankelovich Partners for the John Templeton Foundation found that 94% of the respondents believed that prayer, meditation, and other spiritual practices enhance healing and medical treatment. However, few HMO health plans and institutions reflect this belief. Some 89% of the HMO executives answered no to the question, "Do the rules and policies of your health plan take into account scientific and research findings regarding the relationship between spirituality and well-being?"

Psychological Services

Clients with addictive disorders may require specialized psychological assessment and testing in order for clinicians to assess any coexisting emotional/behavioral conditions and complications (Dimension 2 *ASAM PPC-2*) as well as true dual disorders. A psychological assessment often helps the treatment team and client identify recovery potential, accept limitations, plan realistic treatment, and select appropriate interventions. Psychologists are more apt to provide services to addiction clients in psychiatric/mental health treatment facilities, at schools and colleges, and within the criminal justice system than in other settings. Psychologists provide diagnostic and treatment services for clients with dual disorders as well as children and teens, forensic clients, and the elderly.

Alternative Therapies

Surveys indicate that one in two Americans uses alternative medicine, often to complement "traditional" therapies. Millions of people pay billions of dollars out of pocket for alternative treatments. Many alternative therapies emphasize a mind-body connection. An increasing number of addiction treatment providers and clinicians integrate alternative therapies into their treatment regimens. In 1997, more than 1,000 health care professionals attended a 3-day course titled "Spirituality and Healing in Medicine," which was hosted by Dr. Herbert Benson, president of the Mind/Body Medical Institute at Beth Israel Deaconess Medical Center and associate professor at Harvard Medical School. Benson is well-known for his development of the "relaxation response."

Common alternative therapies include hypnosis, acupuncture, herbal medicine, reflexology, craniosacral therapy, and aromatherapy, to name but a few. Public and private insurance is beginning to pay for select alternative therapies. Many alternative therapies are extremely cost-effective—for example, use of the herb St. John's wort versus prescription antidepressant medications. One treatment with "thought field therapy," developed by Dr. Roger J. Callahan, may correct or relieve a disturbing condition.

Group Intervention

Psychoeducation Groups

The following list details the extensive use of psychoeducation groups by the AdCare Recovery Services Substance Abuse Treatment Program for inmate clients at MCI-Longwood Treatment Center, a minimum-security coeducational prison that is part of the Massachusetts Department of Corrections. The treatment program is accredited by the Commission on Accreditation of Rehabilitation Facilities. (The following information appears by permission of AdCare Recovery Services.)

- Orientation (O) phase: 1 week
    - 101. What Is Treatment and How Do I Participate?
    - 102. Self-Report/Timeline
    - 103. Etiology: Am I Chemically Dependent?
    - 104. Treatment Definitions/Introduction to Self-Help
    - 105. Treatment Schedule, Test, Surveys
- Initial (I) phase: 4 weeks
    - 201. Physical Aspects of Addiction and the Brain
    - 202. Disease Concept: Use, Abuse, Addiction, and Progression
    - 203. Spiritual and Emotional Aspects of Addiction
    - 204. History of Substance Abuse/Classification
    - 205. HIV and Addiction
    - 206. Denial
    - 207. PAWS (Post-Acute Withdrawal Syndrome)
    - 208. Family and Substance Abuse
    - 209. A.A. Step 1
    - 210. A.A. Step 2
    - 211. Relapse Dynamics: Mental, Emotional, Social
    - 212. What Is A.A.? History of A.A.
    - 213. A.A. Step 3
    - 214. Concepts and Components of Community Resources
    - 215. Guilt and Shame
    - 216. Overview of the 12 Steps
- Application (A) phase: 5 weeks
    - 301. Relapse Prevention: Triggers, Urges, and Cravings

302. Relapse Prevention and Relationships
303. Relapse Prevention and Emotions I
304. Relapse Prevention and Emotions II
305. Relapse Prevention and Spirituality/Values
306. Relapse Prevention and Work
307. Criminal Thinking
308. Critical Thinking/Alternative Choices
309. Attitude/Goal Setting
310. Stress Management
311. Meditation/Relaxation
312. Communication
313. Parenting
314. Defense Mechanisms
315. Family Systems I
316. Family Systems II
317. Social Skills: Inmate, Worker, Recovering Person, Friend
318. Aftercare Group
319. Recreation/Leisure Skills
320. Grief and Addiction

■ Transitional (T) phase: 2 weeks
401. Going Home: What to Expect
402. Am I an Ex-Con, Drunk, Addict, or What?
403. Final Aftercare Review
404. Self-Help and Sponsorship
405. Me as a Facilitator/Helper
406. Living Sober
407. New Roles/Responsibilities
408. Managing Early Recovery Conflicts

■ Specialty Groups
Anger Management
Domestic Violence
Motor Vehicular Homicide
Addiction Topics
Relapse Prevention
Living Sober

Artistic Expression
Writers Group
A.A. Open Discussion
A.A. 12 Steps
Step Meetings 1, 2
A.A. Big Book
Spirituality
Bible Study
Power Talks
Cultural Issues

- Additional Specialty Groups for Women
Eating Disorders
Gender Differences and Criminality
Values Clarification
Our Bodies Ourselves
Positive Feelings

In addition to these many psychoeducation groups, inmate clients participate in two process groups each week facilitated by the same staff member. Inmate clients may request and receive individual counseling, usually from the staff member who facilitates their process group. Inmates may also request and receive couples counseling by the family therapist. Family members and significant others are invited to weekly family education groups.

Group Psychotherapy

Interactional group psychotherapy, as developed by Yalom (1995), is effective with clients. Group psychotherapy is a primary intervention with clients in residential settings, clients receiving intensive outpatient or partial hospitalization services, and outpatient clients. Many clients with dual disorders benefit from group psychotherapy.

Mutual Self-Help Groups

Mutual self-help groups have supported recovery for more than 60 years; these include 12-step groups such as Alcoholics Anonymous and Overeaters Anonymous, secular support groups such as Rational Recovery and Women for Sobriety, and religious groups such as Christians in Recovery. Clients at all levels of care can participate in mutual self-help groups. Self-help groups support clients in their attempts to meet short-term, intermediate, and long-term treatment goals.

Family as Client

The family may be the client of record. Interventions with the family include psychoeducation in the family as system as well as the dysfunctional dynamics that contribute to the development and perpetuation of addiction. Family members and clinicians collaborate to assess and diagnose the family's needs, problems, strengths, and competencies. Treatment goals guide intervention. Clinicians may refer families to mutual self-help groups such as Al-Anon, Nar-Anon, Gam-Anon, and Tough Love. Clinicians may provide marital and family psychotherapy.

Community as Client

Prevention programs target the community as client: schools, work sites, and neighborhoods. Education is the primary intervention. Addiction clinicians may participate in critical-incident debriefing when a community experiences an alcohol/drug-related catastrophe. For example, when alcohol, other drugs, and excessive speed contributed to a head-on car crash in which eight teens were killed on prom night, addiction clinicians met with students, parents, and teachers at the teenagers' school.

Summary

Interventions are the actions that client and clinicians take to reach outcomes, achieve treatment goals, meet client needs, and ultimately resolve client problems. Interventions with individual clients often include medical management, nursing, counseling, mutual self-help groups, family support, and community care. As appropriate, individual clients may require pharmacological intervention, spiritual care, social services, and psychological services. Use of alternative therapies is increasing. Many interventions with addiction clients utilize groups for education, support, and therapy, Psychoeducation groups are widely used across all levels of care. Mutual self-help groups support recovery. Interactional group psychotherapy, as developed by Yalom, is effective with clients at both inpatient and outpatient levels of care. The family may be the client of record. Prevention programs target the community as client. Addiction clinicians may participate in critical-incident debriefing when a community experiences an alcohol/drug-related catastrophe.

Related Skills Checklist

Practitioner skills related to intervention include the ability to do the following:

- Select interventions to help clients reach outcomes, achieve goals, resolve problems, and meet needs identified in the treatment plan.

- Utilize interventions in the cognitive, affective, and psychomotor domains.

- Initiate and/or support a variety of interventions with individual clients, including medical management, nursing, counseling, mutual self-help groups, family support, community care, pharmacological intervention, spiritual care, and psychological services.

- Facilitate group intervention including psychoeducation groups, group psychotherapy, and referral to mutual self-help groups.

- Intervene with families as client, including psychoeducation, psychotherapy, and referral to family mutual self-help groups.

- Provide prevention education and critical-incident debriefing to the community as client.

Special Topics for Further Study

Review clinical research studies to identify the "active ingredients" in treatment. Develop pilot studies to demonstrate intervention efficacy. What is the smallest intervention "dose" that will produce the desired outcome?

Addiction Practice 2000

Addiction practice 2000 asks clinicians to identify the "active ingredients" in intervention. Clinicians strive to demonstrate intervention efficacy. Clinicians test an array of interventions with individuals, groups, families, and the community.

References

American Psychiatric Association. (1994). *Diagnostic and statistical manual of mental disorders* (4th ed.). Washington, DC: Author.
American Society of Addiction Medicine. (1996). *Patient placement criteria for the treatment of substance-related disorders* (2nd ed.). Chevy Chase, MD: Author.

Yalom, I. D. (1995). *The theory and practice of group psychotherapy* (4th ed.). New York: Basic Books.

Other Sources

American Society of Addiction Medicine. (1994). *Principles of addiction medicine.* Chevy Chase, MD: Author.

Brown, S., & Lewis, V. (1999). *The alcoholic family in recovery.* New York: Guilford.

Brum, A. G. (1994). *Transformation and recovery: A guide for the design and development of acupuncture-based chemical dependency treatment programs.* Santa Barbara, CA: Stillpoint.

Burke, M. T., & Miranti, J. G. (1995). *Counseling: The spiritual dimension.* Alexandria, VA: American Counseling Association.

Deglin, J. H., & Vallerand, A. H. (1999). *Davis's drug guide* (6th ed.). Philadelphia: F. A. Davis.

Caplan, G., & Killilea, M. (Eds.). (1976). *Support systems and mutual help.* New York: Grune & Stratton.

Center for Substance Abuse Prevention. (1993). *Intervention* (DHHS Publication No. ADM 92-1983). Rockville, MD: Author.

Center for Substance Abuse Treatment. (1995). *Detoxification from alcohol and other drugs* (DHHS Publication No. SMA 95-3046). Rockville, MD: Author.

Center for Substance Abuse Treatment. (1995). *Matching treatment to patient needs in opioid substitution therapy* (DHHS Publication No. SMA 95-3049). Rockville, MD: Author.

Center for Substance Abuse Treatment. (1997). *50 strategies for substance abuse treatment* (DHHS Publication No. SMA 96-8029). Rockville, MD: Author.

Compton, M. (1992). Nursing care in acute intoxication. In M. A. Naegle (Ed.), *Substance abuse education in nursing* (Vol. 2, pp. 347-408). New York: National League for Nursing Press.

Compton, M. (1992). Nursing care in withdrawal. In M. A. Naegle (Ed.), *Substance abuse education in nursing* (Vol. 2, pp. 409-462). New York: National League for Nursing Press.

De Leon, G. (1994). The therapeutic community: Toward a general theory and model. In National Institute on Drug Abuse (Ed.), *Therapeutic community: Advances in research and application* (NIH Publication No. 94-3633) (pp. 16-53). Rockville, MD: National Institute on Drug Abuse.

Green, J. (Ed.). (1997). *Faith communities* (NCADI Publication No. 98-05043). Rockville, MD: Center for Substance Abuse Prevention.

Kaufman, E. (1994). *Psychotherapy of addicted persons.* New York: Guilford.

Kelly, E. W., Jr. (1995). *Spirituality and religion in counseling and psychotherapy: Diversity in theory and practice.* Alexandria, VA: American Counseling Association.

Kuhn, M. (1998). *Pharmacotherapeutics* (4th ed.). Philadelphia: F. A. Davis.

Lawson, G., Lawson, A., & Rivers, P. C. (1996). *Essentials of chemical dependency counseling* (2nd ed.). Gaithersburg, MD: Aspen.

Morgan, O. J. (1999). *Addiction and spirituality: A multidisciplinary approach*. St. Louis: Chalice.

National Institute on Drug Abuse. (1993). *Medications development: Drug discovery, databases, and computer-aided drug design* (NIH Publication 93-3638). Rockville, MD: Author.

National Institute on Drug Abuse. (1994). *Psychotherapy and counseling in the treatment of abuse* (NIH Publication No. 94-3716). Rockville, MD: Author.

National Institute on Drug Abuse. (Ed.). (1994). *Therapeutic community: Advances in research and application* (NIH Publication No. 94-3633). Rockville, MD: Author.

National Institute on Drug Abuse. (1995). *Integrating behavioral therapies with medications in the treatment of drug dependence* (NIH Publication No. 95-3899). Rockville, MD: Author.

Nowinski, J. (1999). *Family recovery and substance abuse: A twelve-step guide for treatment*. Thousand Oaks, CA: Sage.

O'Malley, S. S., Jaffe, A. J., Change, G., Shottenfeld, R. S., Meyer, R. E., & Rounsaville, B. (1992). Naltrexone and coping skills therapy for alcohol dependence: A controlled study. *Archives of General Psychiatry, 49,* 881-887.

Perkinson, R. R. (1997). *Chemical dependency counseling*. Thousand Oaks, CA: Sage.

Schneider, J. P., & Schneider, B. (1989). *Rebuilding trust: For couples committed to recovery*. Center City, MN: Hazelden.

Steinglass, P., Wolin, S., Bennett, L., & Reiss, D. (1987). *The alcoholic family*. New York: Basic Books.

Sutherland, L. L. (1998). *Facilitating spiritual growth in psychotherapy: A recovery model based upon the twelve steps of Alcoholics Anonymous*. Unpublished master's thesis, Cambridge College.

Swanson, J., & Cooper, A. (1994). *Coping with emotional and physical high-risk factors*. Center City, MN: Hazelden.

Swanson, J., & Cooper, A. (1994). *Coping with personal and social high-risk factors*. Center City, MN: Hazelden.

Trotzer, J. P. (1999). *The counselor and the group: Integrating theory, training, and practice* (3rd ed.). Philadelphia: Taylor & Francis.

Vannicelli, M. (1992). *Removing the roadblocks: Group psychotherapy with substance abusers and family members*. New York: Guilford.

Volpicelli, J. R., Alterman, A. I., Hayashida, M., & O'Brien, C. P. (1992). Naltrexone in the treatment of alcohol dependence. *Archives of General Psychiatry, 49,* 876-880.

Wakefield, P. J., Williams, R. E., Yost, E. B., & Patterson, K. M. (1996). *Couple therapy for alcoholism*. New York: Guilford.

Washton, A. M. (1996). *Psychotherapy and substance abuse*. New York: Guilford.

White, R. K., & Wright, D. G. (1998). *Addiction intervention: Strategies to motivate treatment-seeking behavior*. New York: Haworth.

Wolf, M. S. (1993). Group modalities in the care of clients with drug and alcohol problems. In M. A. Naegle (Ed.), *Substance abuse education in nursing* (Vol. 3, pp. 1-44). New York: National League for Nursing Press.

13

Evaluation

Objectives

- Understand the origins and development of program evaluation.
- Grasp the basic elements of addiction practice evaluation.
- Demonstrate competence in client evaluation.
- Participate in program evaluation.
- Understand the concept and process of quality improvement.
- Be familiar with the concepts of continuous quality improvement and total quality management.
- Participate in the quality improvement plan.

Outline

- **Evaluation**
- **Origins and Development**
  - The Great Society Programs
  - Suchman's Criteria
  - Evaluation Concepts
- **Addiction Practice Evaluation**
- **Client Evaluation**
  - Treatment Outcomes
  - Treatment Improvement
- **Program Evaluation**
  - Program Outcomes
  - Program Improvement

- **Continuous Quality Improvement and Total Quality Improvement**
  - The Quality Improvement Plan
- **Summary**
- **Related Skills Checklist**
- **Special Topics for Further Study**
- **Addiction Practice 2000**

Evaluation

Program evaluation is the systematic application of social science knowledge and methodology to health and human service programs to help practitioners appraise outcomes and guide improvements. More specifically, addiction clinicians and clients ask these questions: (a) Did the client achieve treatment goals? (b) How can we improve treatment? In addition, addiction practitioners evaluate the program itself and ask, (a) Were the program goals achieved? and (b) How can we improve the treatment program?

Origins and Development

The Great Society Programs

With the proliferation of human service programs after World War II, government and concerned citizens began to demand systematic, data-based evaluation of these programs. Evaluation was needed to document the merits of successful programs and to help policy makers decide whether funding should be continued. In 1963, Campbell and Stanley first published the classic monograph *Experimental and Quasi-Experimental Designs for Research*. Evaluators utilized a predominantly empirical-analytic approach, with rigorous reliance on measurement.

Suchman's Criteria

In 1967, when he was professor of sociology and public health practice at the University of Pittsburgh, Edward Suchman proposed five categories of criteria according to which the success or failure of a program may be evaluated: effort, performance, adequacy of performance, efficiency, and process. These criteria are as useful today as they were 30 years ago.

1. *Effort* is the quantity and quality of program activity. What did you do? How well did you do it? Effort is program input or energy regardless of output.

2. *Performance* refers to the results or effects of the effort. Did the client achieve treatment goals? What changed? Clear goal statements and specific outcomes are required if performance is to be evaluated.

3. *Adequacy of performance* describes the degree to which effective performance is sufficient to total need. What is the impact of the program?

4. *Efficiency* is concerned with costs: in money, time, personnel, and public convenience. Efficiency is the ratio between effort and performance—in essence, output divided by input. What is the capacity of the program to achieve the desired results in proportion to the effort expended? Is there a better way to attain the same results?

5. *Process* refers to how and why a program works or does not work. Process evaluation is especially useful if the objective is to modify or change a program, to improve a program so that it will work.

Evaluation Concepts

In 1967, Scriven introduced the concepts of formative and summative program evaluation. In 1969, Donabedian added the ideas of structure, process, and outcome. During the 1970s and 1980s, evaluators began to use ethnography and qualitative methodology to study programs. Theory-based evaluation developed during the late 1980s and 1990s as a powerful movement in program evaluation (see Fitz-Gibbon & Morris, 1996; Weiss, 1997). The concept of empowerment evaluation was advanced in the mid-1990s in a volume edited by Fetterman, Kaftarian, and Wandersman (1995). Empowerment evaluation builds on action research, community psychology, and action anthropology. It is an open, democratic group process that involves the people affected by the evaluation. For example, in addiction practice, clinicians and client evaluate client treatment together. Treatment providers, licensing agencies, accrediting associations, and funding sources collaborate to evaluate treatment programs. A demand for outcome-based evaluation surfaced in the 1990s (Schalock, 1995).

Addiction Practice Evaluation

Building on a model of basic types of evaluation developed by Chen (1996), addiction practitioners can conceptualize evaluation as shown in Table 13.1.

TABLE 13.1 Addiction Practice Evaluation

	Improve Process	*Assess Outcome*
Client	Improve client treatment	Appraise client treatment outcome
Program	Improve treatment program	Appraise treatment program outcome

Client Evaluation

Client evaluation has two important goals: to appraise client treatment outcomes and to improve client treatment.

Treatment Outcomes

Clinicians and client evaluate treatment outcomes. An outcome goal is met when there is an expected observable, reportable, measurable, or describable change in client status. Meeting expected outcomes leads to goal achievement. Client evaluation asks the following questions: Did the client meet expected outcomes? Did the client achieve treatment goals? As noted in Chapter 11, an *expected outcome* is a very specific, time-limited, step-by-step behavioral objective that leads to goal achievement. *Goals* are broad, measurable statements that reflect desired client change or problem resolution. Goal achievement is evidence of client change and demonstrates that a need has been met or a problem resolved. (For an example of a follow-up questionnaire for clients regarding treatment outcomes, see Exhibit N in the appendix.)

Treatment Improvement

When a client is unable to meet an expected outcome, and in turn fails to achieve a stated goal, clinicians and client inventory the possible reasons for the difficulty.

- Were the interventions useful?
- Were the outcomes specific enough?
- Were the goals realistic?
- Did the treatment plan identify client strengths?
- Is the client's family participating in treatment?

- Did addiction severity determine treatment intensity?

- Are the diagnoses correct?

- Are more assessment data required?

These are but a few of the questions the clinicians and client might ask and answer. They then must modify the treatment plan to improve treatment.

Program Evaluation

Addiction clinicians, especially program administrators and staff, evaluate treatment programs. Program evaluation has two important goals: to appraise treatment program outcomes and to improve the treatment program.

Program Outcomes

Program goals guide outcome-based program evaluation. In addition, licensing rules and regulations, as well as accreditation standards, dictate program evaluation. Federal, state, county, and city authorities control licensing through rules and regulations. Addiction treatment providers must adhere to the accreditation standards, policies, and procedures developed by the Joint Commission on Accreditation of Healthcare Organizations (JCAHO, 1999) and the Commission on Accreditation of Rehabilitation Facilities (CARF, 1999). JCAHO is moving toward accrediting health care providers based on how well they care for patients—that is, based on their performance. Accreditation will be a data-driven process, more continuous than periodic. Health care organizations will gather and submit data about clinical indicators that reflect outcomes or results of care. Programs with special funding from government agencies or private foundations must follow agency/foundation-specific guidelines for program evaluation. A sound evaluation plan enhances the likelihood that a program proposal will be funded.

Performance evaluation begins with an analysis of treatment outcomes and treatment improvement data from clients. Planned, periodic client satisfaction surveys give treatment providers valuable information to review and use to improve the treatment. Treatment providers use client satisfaction evidence to market their services.

Program efficiency is an important outcome indicator. As described by Suchman (1967), efficiency is the ratio of effort to performance—that is, output divided by input. A cost-benefit analysis demonstrates the economic efficiency of a program expressed as the relationship between costs and outcomes. Benefits include the expected outcomes, expressed in both monetary and nonmonetary values. Benefits include both direct and indirect effects. Costs include direct and indirect expenses as well as the nonmonetary costs of conducting the program. Cost-effectiveness analysis examines alternative ways to achieve the same program goals. For example, in the 1970s, insurers questioned the cost-effectiveness of inpatient versus outpatient substance abuse treatment.

Impact is a public health term that refers to the effects of a program related to total needs. What is the influence of the program? Outreach efforts and prevention initiatives try to show the impacts of their programs. For example, Tom R. facilitates a weekly drug rap group for teens who are court-ordered to counseling as a condition of their probation. During the past year, 35 students at Riverside High School participated in the program; 2 of the 35 students violated probation, and 34 of the 35 remained in school. This is an effective program, but what is its impact? There are some 1,200 students at Riverside, many of whom have alcohol and other drug problems. Evaluation of the program's impact must be tempered by a realistic assessment of resources. Suppose Tom could conduct only one group per week—did he target the right group? Within that group of high-risk students, the impact was significant. (For an example of a program outcome service satisfaction survey, see Exhibit O in the appendix.)

Program Improvement

Treatment providers use information about program outcome—performance, efficiency, and impact—to improve treatment and prevention programs. In addition, practitioners evaluate program quality. *Quality* refers to the characteristics, properties, and attributes of a program that demonstrate excellence. A high-quality program meets or exceeds client expectations and needs. A quality improvement (QI) program is essential for program evaluation and, more specifically, for program improvement. Treatment provider goals for excellence and for meeting licensing rules and regulations, accreditation standards and criteria, and special program requirements guide development of an agency's QI program.

Continuous Quality Improvement and Total Quality Management

Treatment providers who monitor and evaluate quality on a continuous basis are often said to be practicing continuous quality improvement (CQI) or total quality management (TQM). CQI and TQM are team-based management strategies that emphasize improvement of the processes an organization uses to manufacture products or deliver services. CQI was developed in the 1950s by American consultants to Japanese manufacturing organizations. CQI and TQM became very visible in the United States in the 1980s. TQM integrates quality and management methods, practices, concepts, and beliefs into the culture of an organization to bring about continuous improvement. CQI assumes that productivity will increase if an organization focuses on improving the quality of its production processes and meeting client requirements. According to Mark and Pines (1995), CQI encompasses the following elements:

1. a focus on internal and external client needs;

2. training in, and continual practice of, systems analysis and improvement techniques on the organization's processes by all staff members;

3. the use of a team approach to research, analyze, and implement quality improvements;

4. monitoring of process performance to aid in and validate quality improvements; which should result in

5. implementation of quality improvements that help products and/or services meet customer requirements. (p. 132)

The Quality Improvement Plan

Addiction treatment providers often develop quality improvement plans. A QI plan shows clearly the responsibility and accountability for the QI program. The plan delineates the scope of activity for each QI team or unit. Each QI team identifies critical aspects of treatment. The team then identifies quality indicators to monitor and evaluate treatment outcomes. Thresholds for evaluation let staff describe quality in quantitative ways. The QI team collects and analyzes data and uses the data to appraise outcomes. When the data show that a quality indicator falls below an acceptable standard, the QI team develops an action plan to correct the problem. Communication among the many QI teams supports the agency's total quality improvement program.

Summary

Clients, clinicians, and treatment providers evaluate client treatment and treatment programs. Evaluation concepts, licensing rules and regulations, accreditation standards and criteria, and special program requirements guide evaluation. Clients and clinicians monitor and evaluate client treatment. Treatment evaluation has two primary goals: to appraise client treatment outcomes and to improve client treatment. Clinicians and administrators evaluate the treatment program. Program evaluation also has two major goals: to appraise the treatment program and to make improvements in it. *Quality* refers to the characteristics, properties, and attributes of a program that demonstrate excellence. Continuous quality improvement and total quality management involve the continuous monitoring and evaluation of treatment programs to improve both processes and outcomes. Addiction clinicians participate in developing the quality improvement plan.

Related Skills Checklist

Practitioner skills related to treatment and program evaluation include the ability to do the following:

- Specify outcome indicators for client treatment.
- Identify the evidence needed to indicate achievement of treatment goals by the client.
- Select indicators to monitor and evaluate each step of the treatment process: assessment, diagnosis, treatment planning, intervention, and evaluation itself.
- Specify outcome indicators for the treatment program.
- Identify the evidence needed to indicate achievement of program goals.
- Select indicators to monitor and evaluate treatment program process, including needs assessment, planning, operations, and evaluation.
- Participate in development of quality improvement plans.

Special Topics for Further Study

Investigate various theories and models of evaluation. Familiarize yourself with licensing requirements and accreditation standards. How can evaluation theories, licensing requirements, and accreditation standards help clinicians to evaluate and improve client treatment? How can these theories, requirements, and standards help clinicians to evaluate and improve the treatment program?

Addiction Practice 2000

Addiction practice 2000 demands program evaluation to demonstrate the efficacy of addiction treatment. Practitioners must employ rigorous evaluation methodology to monitor and evaluate treatment programs, such as performance-based contracting for addiction services. Treatment providers must use both cost-benefit analysis and cost-effectiveness analysis to evaluate addiction treatment. What is the impact of managed care on treatment access and outcomes? Sound evaluation plans for early intervention and prevention programs are required. Evaluation findings must be disseminated widely, especially to policy makers.

References

Campbell, D. T., & Stanley, J. C. (1963). *Experimental and quasi-experimental designs for research.* Chicago: Rand McNally.

Chen, H.-T. (1996). A comprehensive typology for program evaluation. *Evaluation Practice, 17,* 121-130.

Commission on Accreditation of Rehabilitation Facilities. (1999). *Standards manual and interpretive guide for behavioral health.* Tucson, AZ: Author.

Donabedian, A. (1969). *A guide to medical care administration: Vol. 2. Medical care appraisal.* New York: American Public Health Association.

Fetterman, D. M., Kaftarian, S. J., & Wandersman, A. (Eds.). (1995). *Empowerment evaluation: Knowledge and tools for self-assessment and accountability.* Thousand Oaks, CA: Sage.

Fitz-Gibbon, C. T., & Morris, L. L. (1996). Theory-based evaluation. *Evaluation Practice, 17,* 177-184.

Joint Commission on Accreditation of Healthcare Organizations. (1999). *1999-2000 comprehensive accreditation manual for behavioral health care.* Oakbrook Terrace, IL: Author.

Mark, M. M., & Pines, E. (1995). Implications of continuous quality improvement for program evaluation and evaluators. *Evaluation Practice, 16,* 131-139.

Schalock, R. L. (1995). *Outcome-based evaluation.* New York: Plenum.

Scriven, M. (1967). The methodology of evaluation. In R. E. Stake (Ed.), *Perspectives on curriculum evaluation* (pp. 39-83). Chicago: Rand McNally.

Suchman, E. A. (1967). *Evaluative research.* New York: Russell Sage Foundation.

Weiss, C. H. (1997). Theory-based evaluation: Past, present, and future. *New Directions for Evaluation.* (No. 76, Winter), 41-55.

Other Sources

Center for Substance Abuse Prevention. (1994). *Signs of effectiveness II. Preventing alcohol, tobacco, and other drug use: A risk/factor resiliency-based approach* (DHHS Publication No. SMA 94-2098). Rockville, MD: Author.

Center for Substance Abuse Treatment. (1995). *Developing state outcomes monitoring systems for alcohol and other drug treatment* (DHHS Publication No. SMA 95-3031). Rockville, MD: Author.

Center for Substance Abuse Treatment. (1995). *Forecasting the cost of chemical depend-ency treatment under managed care* (DHHS Publication No. SMA 95-3045). Rock-ville, MD: Author.

Chelimsky, E., & Shadish, W. R. (1998). *Evaluation for the 21st century.* Thousand Oaks, CA: Sage.

Joint Commission on Accreditation of Healthcare Organizations. (1991). *Transitions: From QI to CQI.* Oakbrook Terrace, IL: Author.

Kosecoff, J., & Fink, A. (1982). *Evaluation basics.* Beverly Hills, CA: Sage.

Miller, N. S. (1995). *Treatment of addictions: Applications of outcome research for clini-cal management.* New York: Haworth.

Newcomer, K. E. (Ed.). (1997, Fall). Using performance measurement to improve public and nonprofit programs [Special issue]. *New Directions for Evaluation, 75.*

Office for Substance Abuse Prevention. (1992). *Treatment outcome research: Alcohol alert* (NIAAA Publication No. 17, PH322). Rockville, MD: Author.

Stinchfield, R., & Winter, K. (1994). *Treatment effectiveness of six state-supported com-pulsive gambling treatment programs in Minnesota.* St. Paul: Minnesota Department of Human Services.

U.S. Department of Health and Human Services. (1995). *Effectiveness of substance abuse treatment* (DHHS Publication No. SMA 95-3067). Rockville, MD: Author.

Weiss, C. H. (1998). *Evaluation* (2nd ed.). Upper Saddle River, NJ: Prentice Hall.

Wholey, J. J. (1996). Formative and summative evaluation: Related issues in perfor-mance measurement. *Evaluation Practice, 17,* 145-149.

Part IV

Client Diversity and Treatment Matching

14

Addiction Across
the Life Span

Objectives

- Grasp the significance of addiction across the life span.
- Recognize the problem of perinatal addiction.
- Acknowledge the effects of parental addiction on infants and children.
- Identify the risks associated with adolescent addiction.
- Consider the impact addiction has on the developmental tasks of young adults.
- Recognize the heavy toll addiction takes on middle-aged adults.
- Identify patterns and problems of drinking and use of other drugs in older adults.
- Appreciate the problem of addiction to over-the-counter and prescription drugs in older adults.
- Review the implications for treatment across the life span.

Outline

- **Addiction Across the Life span**
- **Perinatal Addiction**
  - Alcohol and Other CNS Depressants
  - Cocaine and Other CNS Stimulants
  - Opioids
  - Hallucinogens

Addiction Across the Life Span

Addiction has impacts on human development across the life span and in several ways. Biological development may be impaired. Developmental tasks may be delayed, deficient, or missed altogether. The polarities of Erikson's psychosocial crises help explain the impacts of addiction on each developmental stage. People with addictive disorders often fail to master the psychosocial crises associated with developmental life stages. When this happens, these individuals demonstrate a host of psychosocial problems and are left vulnerable and susceptible to unhealthy, even pathological development. On the other hand, positive resolution of each life stage crisis empowers individuals to move forward to meet the challenges of the next developmental stage in a healthy, adaptive way.

Client needs and problems, as well as treatment implications, differ between individuals who have used drugs extensively across the life span and persons who use primarily during one developmental stage. For example, Bill P., age 42, began drinking and smoking pot in his early teens. He tried cocaine in his late teens, and for the past 12 years he has been an intravenous heroin user; he continues to drink and smoke pot. Frank M., age 44, began drinking heavily about a year ago; he says, "I lost my job of 15 years because the plant closed. I still can't accept it." He is currently estranged from his wife of 22 years; their two late-teenaged children are in college. Frank has been snorting heroin daily for the past 6 months.

Perinatal Addiction

Alcohol and other drug use by a pregnant woman can affect the developing fetus and the newborn, and in some cases can have long-term, lifelong deleterious effects on the child. The U.S. Food and Drug Administration has identified the actual and potential harms of certain prescription medications for the developing fetus.

Alcohol and Other CNS Depressants

Alcohol is by far the most lethal drug commonly used by pregnant women. Fetal effects include possible abnormalities in growth and development and the possibility of fetal alcohol syndrome (FAS) or fetal alcohol effects (FAE). Neonatal/infant effects include FAE and FAS. Major characteristics include retarded growth and central nervous system abnormalities, including developmental and mental retardation, as well as structural abnormalities with characteristic facial, skeletal, and organ defects. Alcohol use during pregnancy can cause CNS depression and withdrawal in the newborn, with irritability, restlessness, agitation, and increased risk of neonatal mortality. Long-term effects for the child of alcohol use during pregnancy include mental retardation, developmental delay, and low IQ.

Sedative-hypnotic drugs used by a pregnant woman tend to accumulate in the fetus at greater levels than in the mother. Fetal depression, abnormal heart rhythm, or even death can occur. There is increased risk for cleft lip or palate. Drugs and metabolites may remain in newborns for days or weeks longer than in mothers. These newborns may display lethargy, poor muscle tone, suck difficulties, and even CNS depression; withdrawal may occur. The long-term effects of sedative-hypnotic drugs during pregnancy are not known.

Cocaine and Other CNS Stimulants

Fetal effects from using cocaine or crack cocaine during pregnancy include growth retardation, hypertension and distress, increased risk for intrauterine stroke, and possible genitourinary abnormalities. Newborn/infant effects include intoxication and/or withdrawal characterized by irritability/agitation, increased neuromuscular tone, tremors and jitters, increased respiratory rate, risk for seizures, and inconsolability. Drug excretion is slower in the newborn. Neonates and infants exhibit abnormal sleep and breathing patterns. Long-term effects include the possibility of developmental delays and deficits in attention and learning. Use of amphetamines and other stimulants during pregnancy can cause possible growth retardation and hypoxia in the fetus. Neonatal/infant effects include possible withdrawal or intoxication and low birth weight. Long-term effects are not known.

A woman who smokes or uses other forms of tobacco during pregnancy threatens the fetus with reduced oxygen supply, impaired fetal growth, and increased risk for fetal distress and fetal demise, as well as increases her risk for spontaneous abortion and premature labor. Infants born to mothers who smoked during pregnancy may exhibit growth retardation and smaller head circumference. They are at risk for congenital palate and heart defects. They may demonstrate abnormal nursing. Long-term effects on the child of the mother's smoking during pregnancy are being studied.

Opioids

Pregnant women who abuse heroin or other opioids increase the likelihood of intrauterine growth retardation during fetal development. The risk of HIV infection is also high, especially if the woman is an intravenous drug user. Neonates/infants born to mothers who abused opioids during pregnancy may exhibit addiction and neonatal narcotic withdrawal syndrome as evidenced by hyperactivity, irritability/agitation, and a high-pitched cry; these infants are at risk for increased neuromuscular tone, tremors, and seizure. They exhibit poor feeding behavior, breathing difficulties, and abnormal sleep patterns. Infants may be born HIV-positive and at risk for AIDS. Children of mothers who used opioids during pregnancy may demonstrate long-term neurobehavioral deficits.

Hallucinogens

Use of hallucinogenic drugs during pregnancy can cause damage to CNS development in the fetus. Neonates/infants may experience intoxication and/or withdrawal. Serious neurological and behavioral defects are evidenced by intense irritability and inconsolability, abnormal state control, abnormal muscle tone, tremors, inability to coordinate simple motor tasks, and sensory input problems. Microcephaly may be present. Long-term effects include developmental delays, abnormalities in attention span and organizational abilities, and possible learning problems.

Marijuana

Fetal effects of marijuana use during pregnancy include reduced fetal weight gain, shorter gestation, and possible congenital anomalies. Neonatal/infant effects include possible neurological abnormalities resulting from CNS immaturity characterized by abnormal responses to light and visual stimuli, tremulousness, and a high-pitched cry. The long-term effects on the child of marijuana use during pregnancy are not known.

Other Drugs

Fetal effects from the use of inhalants, anabolic steroids, designer drugs, and herbs during pregnancy are highly specific for drug and host. The long-term effects for the children of mothers' use of these substances during pregnancy are unknown.

Infants

Infants cared for by parents and other adults with active addictions usually lack mutuality with their caregivers and consequently fail to develop healthy social attachments. These infants may experience delays in maturation of sensory, perceptual, and motor functions. Sensorimotor intelligence and primitive causality are deficient. Emotional development is thwarted. Basic mistrust rather than trust characterizes psychosocial development.

Treatment for infants affected by addiction emphasizes safety and nurturance. Clinicians work directly with parents to help them arrest their addictions and develop sufficient parenting skills that they can care for their infants. When addicted parents show no willingness to participate in treatment or fail to respond to treatment in a timely way, their infants are at risk. If infants of parents with addictions fail to thrive, or when neglect or abuse is evident, clinicians may expedite removal of the infants from their parents.

Children

Children growing up in families and homes where parents, other adults, or siblings abuse alcohol or other drugs are at great risk for neglect and abuse. Neglect may be physical or emotional. The children's basic needs for food, clothing, shelter, and safety may go unmet. These children often lack attention, nurturing, and love. Domestic violence is common in the home. Children who witness abuse and violence or endure physical, emotional, or sexual abuse themselves may experience emotional trauma with structural brain changes evident on CAT scans. Children with brain changes demonstrate different cognitive ways of learning compared to children with no brain trauma.

In toddlers who are affected by parental addiction, fine motor development may be delayed. Fantasy and play are limited; language development lags. These toddlers demonstrate little self-control. Shame and doubt dominate their psychosocial development, whereas healthy toddlers manifest autonomy.

Young children from drug-dependent families are often confused in terms of sex role identification. They have little concept of self and demonstrate extremely low self-esteem. Sadly, such children have been known to draw "track marks" on their arms to imitate their parents. Early moral development is lacking for these children, and they are incapable of group play. Guilt characterizes their psychosocial development, and initiative is wanting.

School-age children living with addiction demonstrate multiple emotional, behavioral, and learning problems. They may display major deficiencies in the concrete operations expected in the classroom. They have difficulty being and making friends; team play is hard for them, skill learning is limited, and self-evaluation is distorted. Children of alcoholics/addicts (COAs) experience feelings of inferiority, whereas healthy psychosocial development is characterized by industry. The COA movement has identified the long-term harmful effects of growing up in families and homes where there is active substance abuse.

Clinicians attempt to help parents arrest their addictions and care for their children in a safe, responsible way. Neglect and abuse are reasons to remove children from parents on a temporary or permanent basis. Whether children remain with the parents or not, intensive counseling and remedial work are required to repair the developmental damage the children have experienced because of parental addiction. Multidisciplinary teams of human service professionals coordinate treatment for children of alcoholics/addicts; these teams may include social workers, nurses, counselors, psychologists, special-needs teachers, and lawyers. The costs of parental addiction for children and the community are staggering.

According to a recent study commissioned by the Robert Wood Johnson Foundation and conducted by Harvard School of Public Health, drug abuse is perceived as the biggest problem facing American children today. AIDS and drugs, in fact, were the top health problems named by the 1,500 adults surveyed. School-age children, especially children at risk because of parental substance use, often begin using alcohol, cigarettes, marijuana, and inhalants themselves. Use of these "gateway drugs" may lead to further substance abuse and dependence. Users may progress to more illicit substances and more dangerous patterns of use. Personal and social competency are strong protective factors for children at risk for drug use.

Adolescents

Substance Use/Addictive Behaviors

With the increasingly early onset of puberty, adolescent development now begins about age 10 and extends until 20 years of age. Physiological, psychological, and social developmental variables contribute to increased risk for drug dependencies during adolescence. Increasing numbers of young adolescents, ages 12 to 15, are experimenting with a wide variety of drugs, usually unaware of the actions of the substances they ingest. An increasing number of girls are drinking and using drugs. Middle school children have overdosed on muscle relaxants, antipsychotic medications, animal tranquilizers, and morning glory seeds. For some time, teenagers have constituted a target population for tobacco companies. The recently retired Joe Camel character was intended to appeal directly to this teen market. The tobacco companies know well that when individuals begin smoking in adolescence, their addiction to nicotine is likely to continue into adult life. Currently, a significant number of adolescent boys are using smokeless tobacco in the classroom. Bidis—thin, brown, unfiltered Indian cigarettes in sweet flavors such as cherry and vanilla—are a new teen smoking fad. Anabolic steroid use often begins in adolescence. Although it is illegal for teenagers to wager in any state-sanctioned form of gambling, teen gambling is increasing. Eating disorders usually begin in early adolescence.

Adolescent substance abuse is often part of a cluster of problem behaviors that includes truancy, shoplifting, and other petty crimes. More serious problems often associated with substance abuse include running away, violent crime, and suicide. Motor vehicle accidents resulting in teen deaths usually involve alcohol or other drug abuse. The Youth Risk Behavior Surveillance System of the Centers for Disease Control monitors six categories of priority health risk behaviors among youth and young adults: behaviors that contribute to unintentional and intentional injuries; tobacco use; alcohol and other drug use; sexual behaviors that contribute to unintended pregnancy and sexually transmitted diseases (STDs), including HIV infection; unhealthy dietary behaviors; and physical inactivity. Data are reported by race/ethnicity, gender, and grades 9-12. The substance use category reflects current and lifetime use, frequency, and amount (see Grunbaum et al., 1999; Kann et al., 1998).

Harmful Effects

People who take up drinking before age 15 are more than four times as likely to become alcoholics as those who do not begin drinking so young. Alcohol and other drug abuse can delay physical maturation and emotional development in early adolescence. Formal operations are greatly impaired. Membership in peer groups defines early adolescence; one can appreciate the importance of the peer group in defining group identity. Unfortunately, group identity is often achieved and expressed through "smoking, drinking, and using" and a host of antisocial behaviors associated with gang membership.

Teenagers who were neglected or abused as children and have subsequently developed emotional problems often "self-medicate" their pain with alcohol or other drugs. Substance abuse by adolescents is often a precursor of unprotected sex, which can lead to STDs, including HIV, and unplanned pregnancies.

It is difficult for young people to accomplish the normal developmental tasks of late adolescence—autonomy in relation to parents, sex role identity, internalized morality, career choice—when they have begun regular abuse of alcohol and other drugs as children or young teens. Chronologically, these boys and girls leave adolescence and move into their 20s. However, their psychosocial development is "on hold," or at best characterized by identity confusion. It is hard for an adolescent to develop a healthy sense of individual identity while he or she is abusing alcohol or other drugs.

Assessment

Because so many adolescents live in families where both parents work or in single-parent households, classroom teachers are often the first adults to recognize problem behavior in adolescents. School adjustment counselors and special-needs teachers work with many teens who have substance abuse problems. Students using alcohol or other drugs exhibit changes in affect and mood, cognitive/perceptual capacities, physical functions, and physiological processes. Changes in affect, mood, cognition, and perception are most obvious in the classroom; students with physical and physiological changes often visit the school nurse's office. Students who need help may be identified through school student assistance programs (see Center for Substance Abuse Treatment, 1993; see also Chapters 3 and 4 in this volume).

Academic problems often signal substance use in adolescents. Students who report never receiving good grades are also four times as likely as other students to report using illicit drugs. Students with known learning disorders, physical disabilities, and medical problems are at greater risk of using tobacco, alcohol, and other drugs. Substance use is higher in students who have repeated a grade, need educational intervention, or are in special-needs classes. Substance use is higher in students who have problems with academics, attendance, discipline, motivation, and attitude. Students with major conduct problems (e.g., students who are aggressive, destructive, and deceitful, and who violate major rules) use more alcohol and other drugs than do others. Students who have marketable skills or trades or plans to complete high school, work after high school, or attend college are less likely to smoke, drink, or use drugs.

Mental health indicators often cue teachers and counselors that students may be using drugs. Is the student alert? Are there observable speech problems? Is there anything unusual about the student's appearance? Is the student having any observable difficulties or making any unusual body movements? Is the student's mood or affect unusual? Is the student's activity level unusual? Does the student demonstrate insight? Does the student demonstrate good judgment? Is the student oriented to person, place, and time? Is there evidence of hallucinations or delusions? Does the student have unusual fears? Does the student have difficulty thinking and expressing thoughts? Does the student exercise appropriate impulse control? Is the student depressed? Is there evidence of any bizarre behavior?

Treatment

An adolescent who has experienced a life-threatening overdose may need detoxification or acute medical care. Inpatient psychiatric stabilization is required when an adolescent has attempted suicide or is a suicide risk. In such a case, it is imperative that a thorough history of the individual's substance abuse be taken and an assessment made for coexisting dual disorders. Harm reduction may be an appropriate treatment goal for some adolescents who meet *DSM-IV* diagnostic criteria for substance abuse (American Psychiatric Association, 1994). Abstinence is the suggested treatment goal for teens who meet *DSM-IV* diagnostic criteria for dependence. Family involvement is critical. Addiction clinicians frequently work closely with youth service agencies, the courts, and schools to plan and coordinate treatment. Cognitive-behavioral therapies, in which teens learn decision-making skills, are especially effective. Peer support groups at schools and in the community are critical. Clinicians determine the need for individual, group, or family education, support, and counseling on a case-by-case basis. Medications should be used judiciously with adolescents. Various organizations, such as Students Against Destructive Decisions (formerly known as Students Against Driving Drunk, or SADD), help to promote recreational activities for teenagers that do not include alcohol. Health education emphasizes psychological well-being and safe sexual behavior. Long-term treatment in therapeutic communities benefits many teens.

Unfortunately, students caught using drugs are often punished with suspension rather than helped with treatment. Increasing numbers of older teens are being incarcerated for crimes associated with their alcohol or other drug use.

Young Adults

Decisions about work, marriage, and childbearing challenge young adults. Intimacy characterizes healthy psychosocial development, in contrast to isolation. Between the ages of 20 and 40, adults develop their own individual lifestyles. Substance abuse and addictions such as problem gambling, eating disorders, compulsive shopping, and sex and love addictions have serious impacts on healthy development for young adults.

Alcohol and other drugs dominate and dictate the lifestyles of addicted young adults. Possibly addictive activities such as gambling, sex and love, shopping, and eating can evolve into obsessions. A young adult who does not have a sense of individual identity has great difficulty developing and maintaining satisfactory interpersonal relationships. Dysfunctional relationships characterize most addictive disorders. Addiction contributes to the high divorce rate in the United States, where currently 40% of marriages end in divorce. Other friendships and partnerships are fraught with difficulties if one or both parties are addicted. Young adults with addictions are more likely to batter their partners, neglect or abuse their children, engage in unsafe sex, and commit crime. Addiction causes many young adults to abort their college careers; underemployment and unemployment result. Clinicians working with young adults with addictions commonly observe men and women who are chronologically in their young 30s but have the emotional, social, and moral development of egocentric young adolescents. Rarely, if ever, do these young people demonstrate the tendencies toward adult maturity described by White (1966):

- Stabilizing of ego identity
- Freeing of personal relationships
- Deepening of interests
- Humanizing of values
- Expansion of caring

Relapse prevention is a critical treatment goal for young adults. Clinicians intervene aggressively with young adults to prevent relapse, which in turn prevents the development of medical and social problems associated with chronic addiction. Treatment for young adults frequently deals with dual disorders. Young adults in the criminal justice system confront both their addictions and criminality. Addiction, battering, and childhood trauma often coexist in substance-abusing young adults. Failure of clinicians to recognize and respond to these complex client needs can trigger relapse, invite revictimization, and activate posttraumatic stress disorders.

Initial treatment confronts addiction, and then client and clinicians address the client's destructive and dysfunctional relationships. Extensive treatment facilitates healing from unresolved childhood trauma. Continuing care with most young adults mandates a plan for "developmental catch-up." A new personal identity grounded in an addiction-free lifestyle is a recovery goal for many young adults with addictive disorders.

Middle-Aged Adults

Healthy middle-aged adults invest their time and energy in family, career, and community. Generativity, as opposed to stagnation, characterizes healthy psychosocial development. Substance abuse and other addictive disorders exact a heavy toll on individuals during middle adulthood: job and career loss, financial and legal problems, divorce, alienation from children, and an increasing number of physical and mental health problems. The treatment needs of middle-aged adults are discussed throughout this text.

Older Adults

Late adulthood includes people from approximately age 60 to over 100 years of age. There are marked developmental differences between "younger older people" and the "very frail elderly" (those over 85 years of age). Addiction greatly diminishes quality of life for older people and contributes directly to early mortality. Elderly people with substance abuse problems have significantly more coexisting medical conditions, dual disorders, and serious social problems than do other elders. In addition, there are many societal biases against older people, and especially against older people with addictive problems.

Alcohol and Other Drugs

An estimated 17% of Americans over age 60—almost 6 million people—are dependent on alcohol or prescription drugs, and often both together. A recent University of California study found that among individuals over 65 years old, 27% of men and 9% of women reported having three or more drinks on days that they drank; this is considered to be an unsafe drinking level (Knox, 1999). A comprehensive study by the University of California at Los Angeles, based on a survey of 3,448 people 65 and older, found that more than 7% of elderly Americans are heavy drinkers. About 4% of older individuals are regular binge drinkers; half of the survey respondents said that they consume five or more alcoholic beverages every time they drink (Tye, 1999).

It may be useful to divide alcohol abuse in older adults into two developmental stages. *Early-onset, chronic drinkers* use alcohol heavily throughout their lives. Many chronic drinkers die by middle age, although some survive beyond age 60. Early-onset, chronic drinkers demonstrate more behavioral problems and are more resistant to treatment than are *late-onset, situational drinkers,* who usually begin drinking after age 40 in response to situational stresses, such as changes due to aging, chronic illness, retirement, lowered income, deaths of loved ones. Drinking helps some older people cope with loss and loneliness and offers temporary escape from their problems. Late-onset, situational drinkers exhibit fewer characterological problems and are more accepting of treatment than are chronic drinkers.

Illicit drugs are not used extensively by older persons. Currently, opioids are the most frequently used kind of illicit drug in this age group; there are increasing numbers of clients over age 60 in methadone programs. Caffeine is used daily by a majority of older people, and many older people still smoke, although a significant number have stopped for health reasons, primarily cardiovascular disease, cancer, and chronic obstructive pulmonary disease.

Medications

Older adults abuse over-the-counter (OTC) medications more than do persons in any other age group. Commonly abused OTC medications include analgesics, antidiarrheals/laxatives, vitamins/minerals, antacids, cough/cold formulas, emetics/antiemetics, hemorrhoidal, and ophthalmic/otic preparations. Many of these drugs contain significant amounts of alcohol, sodium, and sugar. Seniors are also a targeted market for herbal products.

Older people use three times as many prescription drugs as all other age groups combined. Often, their multiple chronic health problems result in many prescriptions. In response to concerns about decreased sleep needs, older adults often receive antianxiety medications and sedative-hypnotic drugs. The increased incidence of medical problems and physical pain in old age contributes to misuse of opioid analgesics. Alcohol abuse must be considered in elderly clients being evaluated for depression, anxiety disorders, sleep disorders, cognitive impairment, and acute psychosis.

Older adults who are taking multiple medications are at increased risk for confusion, self-medication efforts, adverse reactions, and drug interactions. Noncompliance in taking medications as prescribed is common. Medication regimens may be complex and difficult to understand, and client education is often limited. Older people frequently stop taking their medications when they experience unpleasant side effects or when they are symptom-free. In addition, older people rarely discard medications; their kitchen cabinets often reveal stores of OTC medications as well as discontinued and out-of-date prescription drugs. Alcohol use with medications is especially dangerous for older adults.

Assessment

Clinicians need to screen elderly clients carefully for substance abuse when they present with depression, anxiety, cognitive impairment, functional impairment in activities of daily living, self-neglect, social withdrawal and isolation, falls and trauma, and incontinence or diarrhea. Older adults who abuse alcohol are likely to have more cognitive impairment, weakness, and significantly more withdrawal symptoms with a longer duration than young alcoholics. Relatively small amounts of alcohol or other drugs can cause serious problems in older adults due to physiological changes associated with aging and chronic illness. The MAST-G, the geriatric version of the Michigan Alcohol Screening Test, is a useful tool to screen for alcohol problems in the elderly (*Alcoholism,* 1993).

Treatment

Few addiction providers or paraprofessionals specialize in addiction services for the elderly. Historically, most chronic alcoholics were housed in public psychiatric hospitals; addicts died young or were incarcerated. The great majority of older adults with substance use problems are seen by medical, psychiatric, and home-care providers. Usually the addictive disorder is considered secondary, and treatment may be limited. Some states offer long-term residential programs for older clients with chronic substance use disorders. An increasing number of clients receive care in inpatient geropsychiatric units, in psychiatric day treatment programs, and through psychiatric home services. Staff are becoming more sensitive and skilled at working with older adults who use alcohol and other drugs.

Summary

Addiction affects individuals across the life span. Failure to thrive is common in infants cared for by adults with active addictions. Children growing up with addicted parents or other caregivers are at increased risk for neglect and abuse. Alcohol and other drug abuse can delay physical maturation and emotional development in early adolescence. Substance abuse is usually part of a cluster of problem behaviors for teens that includes truancy, shoplifting and other petty crimes, academic failure, unprotected sex resulting in STDs and unplanned pregnancies, running away, violent crime, and suicide. Youth who abuse alcohol or other drugs rarely accomplish the expected developmental tasks of late adolescence, especially establishing autonomy in relation to parents, sex role identity, internalized morality, and career choice. Substance abuse and addictions such as problem gambling, eating disorders, compulsive shopping, and sex and love addictions dominate the lifestyles of many young adults. Addiction contributes to dysfunctional, destructive relationships and thwarted careers. Substance abuse, as well as other addictive disorders, exacts a heavy toll on middle-aged adults, including job and career loss, financial and legal problems, divorce, and alienation from children. Clinicians encounter two kinds of alcohol abusers among older adults: early-onset, chronic drinkers who demonstrate more problems and are more resistant to treatment and late-onset, situational drinkers with fewer related problems who are more amenable to treatment. OTC and prescription drugs pose special abuse problems for older adults.

Related Skills Checklist

Practitioner skills related to addiction across the life span include the ability to do the following:

- Advocate for treatment for pregnant addicts.
- Report suspected child neglect or abuse.
- Educate parents and teachers about the prevalence of teen addiction.
- Screen adolescents for substance abuse and related problems.
- Promote psychosocial development with young adult clients.
- Confront middle-aged clients about actual or potential losses associated with their addictions.
- Develop a tertiary prevention program of remotivation, retraining, rehabilitation, and restoration with older clients.

Special Topics for Further Study

Investigate the medical, social, legal, and ethical issues associated with perinatal addiction. When does parental substance abuse constitute child neglect or abuse? Review state laws for reporting child neglect and abuse. What mental health observations indicate possible substance use by schoolchildren? What academic problems increase risk for substance use by teenagers? Develop an eight-session psychoeducation group for young adults in early recovery. Review the efficacy of motivational enhancement therapy, a stages-of-change model, and solution-focused treatment approach with middle-aged adult clients. How does chronic illness in older adults increase their risk of substance abuse?

Addiction Practice 2000

Addiction practice 2000 challenges practitioners to identify behaviors and lifestyles that increase risk for addictive disorders. What factors protect against addiction and enhance resilience? Clinicians must endeavor to develop age-appropriate treatments. Addiction practitioners must advocate for early intervention and prevention initiatives with populations at risk, such as children, teens, young adults, and the elderly. Services for youth must be individualized, comprehensive, family based, community based, and integrated (Henggeler, 1997).

References

Alcoholism (1993). New test designed to screen older patients. *Geriatrics, 48,* 14.

American Psychiatric Association. (1994). *Diagnostic and statistical manual of mental disorders* (4th ed.). Washington, DC: Author.

Center for Substance Abuse Treatment. (1993). *Screening and assessment of alcohol- and other drug-abusing adolescents* (DHHS Publication No. SMA 93-2009). Rockville, MD: Author.

Grunbaum, J. A., Kann, L., Kinchen, S. A., Ross, J. G., Gowda, V. R., Collins, J. L., & Kolbe, L. J. (1999, October 29). Youth risk behavior surveillance: National alternative high school youth risk behavior survey, United States, 1998. *Morbidity and Mortality Weekly Report, 48,* 1-44.

Henggeler, S. W. (1997). The development of effective drug-abuse services for youth. In J. A. Egertson, D. M. Fox, & A. I. Leshner (Eds.), *Treating drug abusers effectively* (pp. 253-279). Malden, MA: Blackwell.

Kann, L., Kinchen, S. A., Williams, B. I., Ross, J. G., Lowry, R., Hill, C. V., Greenbaum, J. A., Blumson, P. S., Collins, J. L., Kolbe, L. J., & state and local YRBSS coordinators. (1998, August 14). Youth risk behavior surveillance: United States, 1997. *Morbidity and Mortality Weekly Report, 47,* 1-89.

Knox, R. A. (1999, July 19). Alcohol use and elders a rising, dangerous mix. *Boston Globe,* pp. C1-C3.

Tye, L. R. A. (1999, April 6). Report cites rate, risks of binge drinking among the elderly. *Boston Globe,* p. A17.

White, R. W. (1966). *Lives in progress* (2nd ed.). New York: Holt, Rinehart & Winston.

Other Sources

Biggers, J. (1998). *Transgenerational addiction.* New York: Rosen.

Black, C. (1991). *It will never happen to me.* New York: Ballantine.

Bukstein, O. G. (1995). *Adolescent substance abuse: Assessment, prevention, and treatment.* New York: John Wiley.

Center for Substance Abuse Prevention. (1992). *Older Americans* (DHHS Publication No. ADM 92-1901). Rockville, MD: Author.

Center for Substance Abuse Prevention. (1993). *Children of alcoholics* (DHHS Publication No. SMA 93-2023). Rockville, MD: Author.

Center for Substance Abuse Prevention. (1995). *Secondary school students* (Publication No. MS423). Rockville, MD: National Clearinghouse for Alcohol and Drug Information.

Center for Substance Abuse Treatment. (1993). *Guidelines for the treatment of alcohol- and other drug-abusing adolescents* (DHHS Publication No. SMA 93-2010). Rockville, MD: Author.

Colvin, R. (1995). *Prescription drug abuse, the hidden epidemic: A guide to coping and understanding.* Omaha, NE: Addicus.

Deitch, I., & Howell, C. W. (Eds.). (1997). *Counseling the aging and their families.* Alexandria, VA: American Counseling Association.

Graham, K. M. (1994). *Addictions treatment for older adults: An innovative client-centered approach.* New York: Haworth.

Guidelines for school health programs to prevent tobacco use and addiction. (1994, February 25). *Morbidity and Mortality Weekly Report, 43,* 1-18.

Gurnock, A. M. (1997). *Older adults' misuse of alcohol, medicines, and other drugs: Research and practice issues.* New York: Springer.

Heuer, M. (1995). *Teen addiction.* New York: Ballantine.

Manelli, G. O. (1995). *Children and addiction.* Westport, CT: Praeger.

Mathwig, G., & D'Arcangelo, J. S. (1992). Drug misuse and dependence in the elderly. In M. A. Naegle (Ed.), *Substance abuse education in nursing* (Vol. 2, pp. 463-530). New York: National League for Nursing Press.

National Institute on Drug Abuse. (1994). *Adolescent drug abuse; Analyses of treatment research* (NIH Publication No. 94-3712). Rockville, MD: Author.

National Institute on Drug Abuse. (1994). *Assessing drug abuse among adolescents and adults: Standardized instruments* (NIH Publication No. 94-3757). Rockville, MD: Author.

National Institute on Drug Abuse. (1994). *Using your medicines wisely: A guide for the elderly* (DHHS Publication No. ADM 90-705). Rockville, MD: Author.

Newman, B. M., & Newman, P. R. (1999). *Development through life* (7th ed.). Pacific Grove, CA: Brooks/Cole.

Nowinski, J. (1990). *Substance abuse in adolescents and young adults: A guide to treatment.* New York: W. W. Norton.

Office for Substance Abuse Prevention. (1992). *Breaking new ground for youth at risk: Program summaries* (DHHS Publication No. ADM 92-1658). Rockville, MD: Author.

Office of Smoking and Health. (1994). *Preventing tobacco use among young people: A report of the surgeon general.* Atlanta, GA: U.S. Department of Health and Human Services.

Pagliaro, A. M., & Pagliaro, L. A. (1996). *Substance use among children and adolescents: Its nature, extent, and effects from conception to adulthood.* New York: John Wiley.

Schinke, S. P., Botvin, G. J., & Orlandi, M. A. (1991). *Substance abuse in children and adolescents.* Newbury Park, CA: Sage.

Sher, K. J. (1997). Psychological characteristics of children of alcoholics. *Alcohol Health and Research World, 21,* 247-254.

Sommers-Flanagan, J., & Sommers-Flanagan, R. (1997). *Tough kids, cool counseling: User-friendly approaches with challenging youth.* Alexandria, VA: American Counseling Association.

Todd, T. C., & Selekman, M. D. (1991). *Family therapy approaches with adolescent substance abusers.* Boston: Allyn & Bacon.

Vannicelli, M. (1989). *Group psychotherapy with adult children of alcoholics.* New York: Guilford.

Wechsler, H., Davenport, A., Dowdall, G. W., Moeykens, B., & Castillo, S. (1994). Health and behavioral consequences of binge drinking in college: A national survey of students at 140 campuses. *Journal of the American Medical Association, 272,* 1672-1677.

Wechsler, H., Dowdall, G. W., Davenport, A., & Castillo, S. (1995). Correlates of college student binge drinking. *American Journal of Public Health, 85,* 921-926.

Wechsler, H., Moeykens, B., Davenport, A., Castillo, S., & Jansen, J. (1995). The adverse impact of heavy episodic drinkers on other college students. *Journal of Studies on Alcohol, 56,* 628-634.

Wiley, J. (1995). *Power recovery: The twelve steps for a new generation.* New York: Paulist Press.

Winters, P. A. (1997). *Teen addiction: Current controversies.* San Diego, CA: Greenhaven.

15

Multiculturalism
and Addiction

Objectives

- Appreciate the multiculturalism of the United States.
- Acknowledge the influence culture and ethnicity have on health beliefs and practices.
- Recognize common ethnocultural characteristics of European Americans, African Americans, Latino Americans, Asian Americans, and Native Americans.
- Identify patterns of addictive disorders in these heterogeneous populations.
- Develop treatment initiatives for clients with diverse ethnocultural characteristics.

Outline

- **Multiculturalism**
  - Culture and Ethnicity
  - Demographic Data
  - Socioeconomic Data
    - Employment
    - Income and Poverty
- **European Americans**
  - Ethnocultural Characteristics
  - Addiction
  - Treatment Initiatives
- **African Americans**
  - Ethnocultural Characteristics

Multiculturalism

Culture and Ethnicity

With the exception of Native Americans, the United States is a country of immigrants; people from many different cultures and countries represent hundreds of different ethnic groups. Culture includes values, beliefs, attitudes, norms, traditions, customs, and practices that a group of people pass from generation to generation. Ethnicity is a sense of identification, affiliation, or classification associated with a group's common social and cultural heritage. Ethnicity includes race as well as symbols, language, and dialect; religious faith and practices; folklore, literature, music, and food; migratory status, settlement, and employment patterns; and political interests.

Individuals' cultures and ethnicities influence their health beliefs and practices. Addiction clinicians need to know whether their clients consider drinking, smoking, gambling, using drugs, and excessive sex to be problems and, if so, whether they are likely to seek or avoid professional help. Clinicians need to know clients' immigration status: Is the client a new immigrant? Is the client a legal or illegal immigrant? Does the client have foreign-born parents? Is the client descended from an immigrant family? Considerations in the treatment of an immigrant client include the client's age at the time of immigration; the client's country of origin; the client's political, economic, and educational background; and the client's native language and religion.

Larry D. Purnell and Betty J. Paulanka (1998) have advanced a model for cultural competence that provides clinicians with a comprehensive, systematic, and concise framework for learning about clients' cultures. They suggest that the assessment of the ethnocultural attributes of an individual, family, or group should encompass the following domains:

1. Overview, inhabited localities, and topography

2. Communication

3. Family roles and organization

4. Workforce issues

5. Biocultural ecology

6. High-risk health behaviors

7. Nutrition

8. Pregnancy and childbearing practices

9. Death rituals

10. Spirituality

11. Health care practices

12. Health care practitioners

DSM-IV (American Psychiatric Association, 1994) recommends that the clinician provide a narrative summary for each of the following categories:

- Cultural identity of the individual

- Cultural explanations of the individual's illness

- Cultural factors related to psychosocial environment and levels of functioning

- Cultural elements of the relationship between the individual and the clinician

- Overall cultural assessment for diagnosis and care

Scholars and clinicians agree that treatment and prevention services for individuals and families from diverse ethnocultural backgrounds are doomed to fail-

TABLE 15.1 U.S. Population Estimates by Race, Hispanic Origin, and Mean Age, September 1999

Race and Origin	Number	%	Mean Age
All races	273,401,000	100.0	36.4
White	225,045,000	82.3	37.3
Black	34,995,000	12.8	32.1
Hispanic origin (of any race)	31,572,000	11.5	28.9
Asian and Pacific Islander	10,959,000	4.0	32.7
American Indian, Eskimo, Aleut	2,403,000	0.9	30.5

SOURCE: Data from U.S. Bureau of the Census Web site (http://www.censuscd.com).

ure if they do not recognize and build upon the ethnocultural integrity of the groups being served. Addiction clinicians are challenged to respond to particular ethnocultural paradigms with effective programs and services.

Demographic Data

As of September 1999, the U.S. population was estimated to be about 273,401,000 (see Table 15.1). The White population includes Americans of German, Irish, and English ancestry as well as people with origins in Scandinavia, the Mediterranean, and eastern Europe. From the 1980s on, the greatest population increases have been among Americans of Latino and Asian origins.

The demographic profile of the United States is changing. What was once a country of predominantly White settlers of European ancestry is projected to be, by about 2065, a nation in which the average citizen will be a person of color. Table 15.2 shows the proportions of the U.S. population represented by different racial/ethnic groups in 1990 and 1999.

Socioeconomic Data

In addition to ethnocultural characteristics per se, socioeconomic factors confound the treatment of addiction in various cultural and ethnic/racial groups. (In Chapter 20, I discuss the impacts of social problems such as limited education, unemployment, poverty, unsafe neighborhoods, and crime on the development and treatment of addictions.)

TABLE 15.2 Proportions of the U.S. Population of Various Groups, 1990 and 1999

Race and Origin	July 1990	September 1999
All races	100.0	100.0
White	83.9	82.3
Black	12.3	12.8
Hispanic origin (of any race)	9.0	11.5
Asian and Pacific Islander	3.0	4.0
American Indian, Eskimo, Aleut	0.8	0.9

SOURCE: Data from U.S. Bureau of the Census Web site (http://www.censuscd.com).

Employment

The U.S. Bureau of Labor Statistics projects a growth of 16 million people in the labor force during the period 1994-2005. The numbers of Latino and Asian Americans in the labor force will continue to increase much faster than the numbers of White non-Latinos, due primarily to immigration. However, White non-Latinos will still account for the vast majority of workers in 2005. The numbers of Blacks in the labor force will grow slightly faster than the labor force as a whole. Women will continue to enter the labor force at a much faster rate than men, increasing to 48%. This rapid rate of increase of women and minority group members parallels a long-term decline in virtually all age groups of men. Increasing numbers of American men report that they are unable to work or to find work. Changes in the U.S. economy have left many men with limited education and training ill prepared for the demands of the kinds of jobs that have been created during the past two decades.

Income and Poverty

The median household income in the United States in 1997 was $44,568. In rank order, Asian and Pacific Islander households had the highest median household income, then White households, Latino households, and Black households; Native American households had the lowest median family income. It should be noted that income is directly related to college education, and a larger percentage of Asian Americans have college degrees than any other racial/ethnic group.

Although 12% of all U.S. families had incomes of $100,000 or more, 13.3% were below the federal government's official poverty line—$16,400 for a family

TABLE 15.3 Persons Below the Poverty Level, Various Years, 1991-1997

Year	Number	%	Income Cutoff ($)
1997	35,600,000	13.3	16,400
1995	35,400,000	13.8	15,569
1993	39,300,000	15.1	14,763
1991	35,700,000	14.2	13,924

SOURCE: Data from *The New York Times World Almanac and Book of Facts* (1999, p. 385).

of four. Yet the numbers and percentages of persons below poverty level remained fairly constant during the 1990s (see Table 15.3).

In 1994, the poverty rate for all persons under 18 years was 21.8%. Half of the nation's poor in 1994 were either under 18 years of age or 65 and over. In 1994, the poverty rate was 11.7% for Whites, 30.6% for Blacks, 30.7% for persons of Latino origin, and 14.6% for Asians and Pacific Islanders. Even though the poverty rate for Whites was lower than that for other racial and ethnic groups, the majority of poor persons in 1994 were White (67%). Blacks showed a decrease in poverty between 1993 and 1994 in both the poverty rate and the number living below poverty. Whereas the poverty rate for Whites decreased, with no significant change in the numbers of poor, persons of Latino origin showed an increase in the number living in poverty, but not the rate. The poverty rate for Asian and Pacific Islander Americans did not change significantly between 1993 and 1994. Some 22% of all Native Americans lived on reservations and trust lands, with 53% of them living below the poverty level. (The data in the above paragraphs are gleaned from publications of the U.S. Bureau of the Census and Bureau of Labor Statistics as reported in *Information Please Almanac,* 1997, pp. 49-82.)

European Americans

Ethnocultural Characteristics

Adventure and exploration, fame and fortune, and religious and political freedom are but a few of the reasons people from Europe have come to the United States, considered the "land of opportunity." European immigrants have sought better lives for themselves and their families. The largest waves of European immigration have involved groups from Germany, Ireland, England, and France. In

1999, European Americans made up 82.3% of the U.S. population, a very heterogeneous group from 30 different countries in northern, southern, eastern, and western Europe. When compared with other American ethnic groups, European Americans have the oldest median age and reflect the smallest projected growth in population. Ethnicity is strong within some European American communities and is reflected in family values and traditions, customs and practices, education, employment, and politics. European Americans represent more than 200 different, predominantly Christian, religious denominations.

On the whole, European Americans value freedom and respect individual rights. The European founding fathers established a democratic form of government that reflects these values and beliefs. A strong work ethic and a belief in the usefulness of education characterize many European Americans. Rugged individualism, together with a pioneering spirit, distinguished the movement west and the development of the country. European Americans tend to believe in personal responsibility and accountability, although they established more and more laws in attempts to keep order as the nation grew. An abundance of natural resources allowed early European Americans to respond to the Industrial Revolution, and the United States quickly become a world leader in trade and industry. Immigration from Europe continued and cities grew rapidly. In the 20th century, science and technology became dominant cultural values among European Americans, and the work, education, and lifestyles of this group reflected these themes. The beliefs and practices noted above influence attitudes toward addiction and treatment for many European Americans.

Addiction

Alcohol use was common in colonial America, but contemporary beliefs and practices among European Americans vary from abstinence to excess. Ethnocultural characteristics, especially religious beliefs and practices, influence addictive behavior. In groups where smoking, drinking, and gambling are considered wrong, sinful, or even evil, overall prevalence rates are lower than in the general population. When someone from such an "abstinent group" develops a substance-related problem or other addictive disorder, treatment can be difficult. Overwhelmed by guilt and consumed with shame, these individuals may avoid treatment or even attempt suicide. According to their beliefs, punishment rather than forgiveness is required.

On the other hand, Christian counseling, together with support from faith communities, strengthens much formal addiction treatment. Christian missions and agencies such as Catholic Charities and the Salvation Army provide many treatment and social services for alcoholics and addicts.

Treatment Initiatives

Addiction treatment as we know it today was developed primarily by European American practitioners, but there is no single theory of addiction or one treatment methodology that is best for European American clients. As I have noted in Chapters 2 and 6, there are many different theories and models of addiction and easily a dozen prevailing treatment methodologies. Effective treatment and prevention for European Americans with addictive disorders requires the same ethnocultural assessment and treatment sensitivity that clinicians must employ with people from other cultural and ethnic groups.

African Americans

Ethnocultural Characteristics

As of 1999, African Americans made up 12.8% of the U.S. population, according to the U.S. Bureau of the Census—some 35 million people. Between 1619 and 1860, Black people were brought to North America as slaves. Today, Black people immigrate to American from African countries, the West Indies, the Dominican Republic, Haiti, and Jamaica. Gordon (1994), a recognized scholar in the area of multiculturalism as it affects substance abuse services, identifies five cultural subgroups of African Americans, distinguished by education and socioeconomic levels, national origin, age, religion, rural versus urban residence, skin color, and degree of acculturation.

Addiction

Blacks are more likely than Whites to be intravenous drug users. Marijuana remains the number one drug of choice among Black teens and young adults who use illicit substances. Black adult substance abusers tend to use heroin, cocaine, and marijuana. Blacks drink less than Whites, but often more heavily. Black youth smoke less than do White youth, a fact that has prompted tobacco companies to target this market, but with little success. The tobacco industry has been accused of trying to market menthol cigarettes to Blacks; in Philadelphia, a civil rights lawsuit was brought concerning this issue. Problem gambling is increasing in the Black community.

Among African American women, alcohol is the most commonly abused substance. Black women are more likely to use opioids and crack cocaine than are White women, but are less likely to abuse prescription drugs. A small but significant number of Black women shop compulsively.

Alcohol and other drug abuse has emerged as the leading personal and public health problem facing the African American community. Substance abuse contributes directly to excess deaths from cancer, hypertension, cirrhosis of the liver, stroke, chronic obstructive pulmonary disease, and malnutrition. For example, cirrhosis rates are six times higher for young Black women than for White women. The risk of fetal alcohol syndrome is seven times higher for African American infants than for Caucasian infants.

Substance abuse causes family stress and dysfunction. It erodes family life and cultural traditions that have served as natural preventive and protective factors for children and youth. Alcohol and other drug abuse is a major factor in the increase in family violence. The rising rate of violent deaths among young Blacks greatly depletes the future resources of the African American community. African Americans experience more occupational, economic, housing, and legal problems than other ethnic groups—all of which contribute to higher substance use. The social problems of African Americans include high rates of underemployment and unemployment, with lower per capita earnings and more poverty than found in other groups. Compared with other ethnic groups, greater percentages of Blacks live in public housing and in unsafe neighborhoods. A disproportionate number of Black American men and women are incarcerated: Blacks comprise 12.8% of the total U.S. population yet make up 48% of the male and almost 40% of the female inmate population.

Racism and economic exploitation are special risk factors that place African Americans at high risk for substance abuse. Alcohol and other drugs are readily available in many Black neighborhoods. The media, popular culture, and advertising campaigns promote drinking, smoking, and lifestyles associated with excess.

Treatment Initiatives

Client Characteristics

Hilliard (1976) has described African American cultural patterns, behaviors, and learning style, noting that African Americans tend to see the whole rather than its parts, prefer inferential reasoning, and tend to approximate space, numbers, and time. In general, African Americans believe that people are more important than things. They have a keen sense of justice and demonstrate altruism and concern for their fellow human beings. According to Hilliard, African Americans tend to prefer novelty, freedom, and personal distinctiveness. They are proficient in nonverbal communication. Black children tend to absorb information best through a relational, interactive learning style, whereas European American children tend to have a rational, analytic learning style. In addition to awareness of these general characteristics, effective addiction treatment and prevention initiatives for African Americans take into account the roles of the traditional Black family, the Black church, and an Afrocentric value system.

The Black Family and the Black Church

The traditional Black family system affirms life and promotes healthy growth and development of children and youth. Extended families are common and, to some extent, the community is family to Black children and youth. Healthy families reduce the incidence of self-destructive addictive behaviors. Structure and loving discipline characterize traditional Black families. Children learn to respect authority, often in the form of a strong, involved mother. The family expects personal accountability and community responsibility.

The church is the most powerful social force in the African American community. Deep spirituality supported Black people in their struggles to survive the pain and suffering of slavery, and over the years, strong convictions of a better life have sustained African Americans and helped them transcend the injustices of discrimination and racism. Today, the church is a place where Black leaders and elders preach and teach social action, where communities unite to boycott tobacco products aimed at Black youth, develop mentor programs to promote completion of high school, and organize mothers' crime watch groups to reduce gang violence in housing projects.

Music defines the Black church and sustains the Black soul through travail and triumph. Spontaneity, improvisation, and member participation distinguish the use of music during church services. Negro spirituals recount the duress of slavery and dreams of emancipation. Gospel music calls the congregation to sing, shout, clap, and dance. Music stirs up out-of-body and out-of-mind experiences; members may become filled with the spirit and speak in tongues. Choirs sing hymns that describe the joys of a personal relationship with Jesus.

Today, a significant number of Black Americans embrace Islam and follow the teachings of Muhammad. Their efforts to empower African American males, strengthen the family, and reduce addiction, violence, and crime are noteworthy.

Afrocentrism

Afrocentrism has roots in the cultural values and practices of Africans as well as people of African descent who reside in the United States and the Caribbean. In the past two decades, the liberating works of Molefi K. Asante (1980, 1987, 1990) have affirmed and advanced the Afrocentric paradigm. The concept of Afrocentrism involves the intellectual and philosophical foundations upon which African people create their own scientific criteria for authenticating African reality. It includes African people's self-conscious act of creating African history, utilizing the African experience as the core paradigm for higher-level human functioning and liberty, and the continuing quest for an indigenous African-centered historical and cultural anchor. Afrocentrism reaffirms the right of African people to exist as a people, contribute to the forward-flowing process of human civilization and culture, and share with and shape the world in response to their energy and spirit (see Goddard, 1993).

An African-centered approach to substance abuse treatment and prevention reflects cultural precepts, ideas, and beliefs of African and African American people. Critical cultural canons include the following:

- *Consubstantiation* assumes that all things in the universe have the same essence.

- *Interdependence* assumes that everything in the universe is connected.

- *Egalitarianism* assumes that the correct relationship between people is one of harmony and balance.

- *Collectivism* assumes that individual effort is a reflection and/or instrument of communal or collective survival/advancement.

- *Transformation* assumes that everything has the potential to function continually at a higher level.

- *Cooperation* assumes that the optimal way of functioning is with mutual respect and encouragement.

- *Humaneness* assumes that all behavior is governed by a sense of vitalism and goodness.

- *Synergism* assumes that the performance outcome of cooperative effort is greater than the sum total of individual effort. (Goddard, 1993, chap. 12, p. 119)

In addition to cultural precepts, this model includes objectives, intent, content, process or method, and outcomes.

An African-centered model of treatment or prevention requires the acquisition of a core set of knowledge, attitudes, beliefs, and behaviors. These outcomes serve as indicators of successful completion of particular program expectations. Note that an African-centered model does not utilize a values clarification process; rather, it promulgates a core set of values. For example, models may employ *Maat,* a system of ethics based on the seven cardinal virtues of truth, justice, righteousness, propriety, balance, harmony, and order. Maulana Karenga has developed a value system embracing unity, self-determination, collective work and responsibility, cooperative economics, purpose, creativity, and faith (see Goddard, chap. 12, p. 125).

Latino Americans

Ethnocultural Characteristics

Latino Americans constitute the fastest-growing and youngest ethnocultural group in the United States. From 1980 to 1990, their numbers increased 53%, compared to an increase of 0.9% for the rest of the population. By 1999, people of Hispanic origin made up 11.5% of the total U.S. population, 31.5 million people. Projections indicate that Latinos will become the largest ethnic minority in the United States by 2050 or earlier. (The term *Hispanic,* which is often used, particularly by the U.S. Bureau of the Census, to refer to this population, accurately describes only people from countries colonized by Spain, including Mexico, Central America, parts of South America, and the Caribbean. Hispanic people adopted the Spanish language, Catholic faith, and many Spanish customs. The term *Latino* is currently preferred over *Hispanic* because it is more inclusive and emphasizes cultural history.)

More than half of the total U.S. Latino population lives in Texas and California; these individuals are mostly of Mexican descent. Puerto Ricans make up the largest Latino population in New York, and Florida is home to much of the Cuban American population. Family, central to Latino American culture, is the principal institution that preserves and transmits Latino culture. Parent-child communication, family cohesion, and loving discipline characterize the Latino family.

Addiction

Factors that contribute to substance abuse by Latino Americans include acculturation and intergenerational stress and conflict. Socioeconomic stress related to limited education, unemployment or underemployment, and poverty contributes to the abuse of alcohol and other drugs, especially among teens and young adults. In Latino youth, substance abuse rarely occurs in isolation; truancy, delinquency, and teen pregnancy are common coexisting problems. Marketers of alcohol, cigarettes, and junk foods often target Latino communities.

Socioeconomic class is an important determinant of drinking and other drug use for Latino Americans. Studies show that for Mexican Americans, the choice of substance, as well as the frequency, route, and setting, varies among the upper class, urban middle class, working class, farmers and ranchers, and farmworkers. Latino women usually do not drink as much as do Latino men; however, drinking by young Latino women is increasing. It has been found that the longer Puerto Rican immigrants live in New York City, the greater their alcohol and drug use.

Intravenous drug use and HIV/AIDS are disproportionately high in Latino Americans. Unprotected sex, related in part to expected role behaviors of Latino men and women, accounts in part for the HIV/AIDS rate as well as the higher-than-average rate of teen pregnancy. Latino women have a high rate of diabetes during pregnancy, which is complicated by alcohol abuse. These factors contribute to infant morbidity and developmental disabilities.

Treatment Initiatives

Effective addiction treatment and prevention with Latino Americans recognizes and respects the values, beliefs, and behaviors of this ethnocultural group. In general, Latino cultures include the belief that people are governed by nature. Latinos tend to orient to the present; they tend to be more emotional than rational, often superstitious and fatalistic. Latino Americans embrace a collective and traditional worldview, in contrast to the more individual and liberal orientation of European Americans. Latinos cooperate rather than compete to achieve goals and success.

Among Latino Americans, the family plays a key role in the origin, prevention, and treatment of alcohol and other drug problems. A strong, traditional family mediates and moderates stress for youth and other family members. Common language and religion increase family and community cohesiveness and contribute to a strong sense of group and individual identity. Extended families, large networks of friends, and many ethnic social clubs offer prevention and recovery networks to support youth and young adults.

Specific treatment initiatives with Latino Americans focus on the family. Building on the philosophy of empowerment and the methods developed by Paulo Freire and the pioneering work of psychiatrist Salvador Minuchin, scholars and clinicians have developed programs to preserve and strengthen the family. Szapocznik and colleagues have developed structural family therapy, an approach used widely throughout the United States and Puerto Rico (see Szapocznik, 1995). Structural family therapy is a family empowerment and family preservation approach, in that families are given the skills to interact in new, successful ways to bring about the outcomes they desire, such as the prevention and elimination of problem behaviors, including substance abuse. Structural family therapy does not take the problem *person* out of the family; instead, it encourages taking the *problem* out of the family. Clinicians and family members identify the interactions that are not working for the family and then orchestrate the opportunities for the family to act in new ways to achieve desired outcomes. The Center for Substance Abuse Prevention's publication *A Hispanic/Latino*

Family Approach to Substance Abuse Prevention (1995) describes many effective family-based, family-oriented, and community-based initiatives.

Asian and Pacific Islander Americans

Ethnocultural Characteristics

The designation *Asian and Pacific Islander Americans* refers to a diverse population of more than 60 groups, each with a distinct culture, language, and ethnic identity. Asians make up one of the fastest-growing minority groups in the United States; the Asian American population doubled from 1970 to 1980. In 1999, 4% of the U.S. population was of Asian and Pacific Islander origins, nearly 11 million people.

The first wave of Chinese immigration to the United States took place in the 1840s, followed by the Japanese beginning in 1890. Filipinos came after the Spanish-American War, Korean immigration increased markedly after the Korean War, and with the fall of Saigon and the withdrawal of the United States from Vietnam in 1975, Southeast Asians from Cambodia, Thailand, Laos, and Vietnam fled to the United States. Many immigrants have come also from India, Pakistan, Sri Lanka (Ceylon), Indonesia, and the Pacific islands of Samoa, Toga, and Guam.

Addiction

Asian Americans drink less and have fewer alcohol-related problems than any other ethnic group in the United States. However, drinking and other drug use differs greatly among ethnic groups. The flushing response, a physiological reaction to alcohol, is common among some Asian American groups and may inhibit drinking in those groups. When such individuals drink, they experience facial flushing accompanied by headaches, dizziness, rapid heart rate, itching, and other symptoms of discomfort.

As Asians assimilate into U.S. society, they begin to use alcohol and other drugs at rates similar to other Americans. For example, many Asian American youth start drinking in college. The prevalence of alcohol and drug use among Asian American women is relatively low but varies with acculturation status. Gambling is common within Asian American groups.

Factors that increase risks for substance abuse problems among Asian Americans include acculturation, which brings with it intercultural and intergenerational conflict and stress. Traditional gender roles are often challenged. New immigrants also may experience prejudice and discrimination in work and housing. Asians in general place a high value on success, and fear of failure can lead to ineffective coping with alcohol and other drugs.

Asian Americans tend to handle problems within the family or the community. They may deny many psychosocial problems, including substance abuse. When depression and anxiety develop, they often go untreated, accounting in part for an increasing suicide rate among Asian American youth and young adults. The family and individual "lose face" if anyone's behavior shames the family. Substance abuse, depression, and anxiety may be considered shameful for the family. It has often been difficult for immigrant Asian men to find employment in the United States. Consequently, Asian women must enter the workforce and so are no longer able to fulfill the traditional roles of subservient wives and nurturing mothers. Asian American youth experience greater independence, freedom, and choice than was available to their immigrant parents. They may try alcohol and other drugs; they may organize gangs. They challenge family traditions and disobey rules; in essence, they rebel against their parents and reject their family and cultural traditions. Parents, in turn, may cope with their own feelings of rejection, failure, isolation, loneliness, anxiety, and depression by abusing alcohol or other drugs.

Smoking is widespread in Asian countries and especially among Asian men. An estimated 650,000 Chinese die each year due to smoking-related causes. The United States is in second place, with 400,000 smoking-related deaths per year. One-third of the 300 million Chinese men now under 30 are expected to die from the effects of smoking cigarettes. According to the U.S. surgeon general, an estimated 43% of Asian American men smoke, compared with 27% of White men. When Boston passed a ban on smoking in restaurants, the residents of that city's Chinatown protested strongly. In a newspaper article about these events, Tigerson Young, a health educator for South Cove Community Health Center, was quoted as saying: "In Asian culture, cigarette smoking is more than a habit, it's a social and cultural event. It is something you do as a friend. You give them a cigarette as a token of a friendship, and if you accept that cigarette it means acceptance of a friendship" (Robertson, 1998, p. B1).

Treatment Initiatives

Clinicians can utilize the individual ethnocultural characteristics of Asian Americans to help them with addiction problems. Eastern religions emphasize harmonious living, respect of parents, moderation in behavior, adherence to specific roles, a hierarchy of relationships, and mutual interdependence. Eastern virtues include respect for life, self-discipline, self-control, emotional restraint, patience, modesty, friendliness, selflessness, compassion, obligation, and shame.

The traditional Asian family is cohesive and is structured with a male head-of-household authority. The family provides stability, interpersonal intimacy, and social support for members.

Morrissey (1997) has written about the challenges of counseling Asian Americans:

> Intelligent, hardworking, enterprising, disciplined—these are all traits that many Americans attribute to Asian Americans. No other minority population is viewed more favorably than the nearly 8 million Asian and Pacific Islander Americans who make up the fastest growing ethnic population in the United States. But this "model minority" status has obscured the psychological and social needs of Asian Americans to the point that some people are now calling this population the "invisible minority." (p. 1)

On the whole, Asian Americans do not readily seek mental health services. According to Daya Sandhu, Asian Americans may prefer the "silent misery" of psychological suffering to openly seeking psychological help, which is considered a "shame or failure in life." Kwong-Leim Karl Kwan has identified several reasons Asian Americans underutilize mental health services: (a) counseling is not common in their home countries; (b) counseling and psychotherapy are considered to be for people who are "crazy"; (c) to "save face," people with troubles seek help only from family members and close friends; (d) traditional once-a-week counseling in an office is not conducive to the cultural needs of Asian Americans; and (e) there is a lack of mental health professionals who can speak Asian American clients' languages and can empathize with their cultural experiences. It should be noted that Asian Americans in general readily utilize academic and vocational counseling (see Morrissey, 1997, pp. 20-21).

Treatment initiatives for Asian Americans engage the client and the client's family. Asian Americans are likely to find interventions that threaten family integrity, question parental authority, or promote autonomy and independence of children and teens to be suspect. Clinicians must collect as much cultural data as possible from the client and his or her family. Asian American clients are not comfortable with clinicians' delving deep into their personal lives. Together, clinicians and client set goals and select interventions. Solution-focused therapy appears especially effective. It emphasizes problem solving rather than a pathological model in which the client is seen as "sick." Interventions that are directive, involve homework, and provide structure work well. The presence of bilingual, bicultural clinicians may be necessary to expedite treatment. Asian American youth who speak English and are more acculturated than their parents may benefit from prevention and early intervention programs in schools and in the community.

Native Americans

Ethnocultural Characteristics

In 1999, 2.5 million American Indians, Eskimos, and Aleuts lived in the United States, constituting 0.9% of the total population. Of this group, 39% were under 20 years old; by contrast, people under 20 make up only 29% of the general population. Some 8% of Native Americans were 60 years old or older in 1999— about half the proportion (17%) of that age group in the nation as a whole. There are more than 500 federally recognized Native American tribes in the United States, including some 226 village groups in Alaska. More than half of the Native American population lives in Oklahoma, California, Arizona, New Mexico, Washington, and Alaska.

The proportion of Native American families headed by women is considerably larger than the proportion in the population as a whole. Educational attainment of Native Americans is increasing, but it is still lower than the national average. Fewer Native Americans are high school graduates, when compared with the overall population. Some two-thirds of Native Americans are in the labor force, working primarily in service occupations; in farming, forestry, and fishing; and as factory workers and laborers. Native Americans are underrepresented in managerial and professional occupations and in technical, sales, and administrative support positions.

Addiction

Substance abuse is a major health and social problem for Native Americans. Alcoholism is considered an epidemic within this population. Native Americans may have a genetic susceptibility to alcoholism; however, direct psychosocial factors contribute to alcohol-related morbidity and mortality. Of the 10 leading causes of death for Native Americans, 4 are alcohol related. The death rate from cirrhosis is five times higher among Native Americans than in the general population. Suicide rates for Native Americans are twice the national average and are strongly linked to substance abuse. Accidental fatalities, 75% of which are estimated to be alcohol related, are three times as high as in other ethnic groups and account for one-fourth of Native American deaths.

Among Native Americans, marijuana is the next most widely used drug after alcohol. Surveys also show very high prevalence rates for inhalants and smokeless tobacco. Native American youth use alcohol and drugs earlier than the general population; substance abuse, academic failure, and delinquent behavior are also quite common in this population. Most crimes committed by Native Americans are drug or alcohol related.

Female Native Americans drink and use drugs at the same rates as males in this ethnic group. Fetal alcohol syndrome is 33 times higher in Native Americans than in Whites. Alcohol-related mortality rates are significantly higher for Native American women than they are for women in other groups. Alcoholism is the fifth most frequent cause of death among Native American women. Increases in cases of child neglect and abuse among Native Americans are associated with increased substance abuse by young parents. Since the 1990s, more Native American women have presented for treatment with a triad of problems: alcoholism, violence, and depression.

Although the recent proliferation of Indian-owned casinos offers a panacea to some of the problems of poverty and addiction for many Indians, problem gambling by Native Americans is higher than in the general population.

Treatment Initiatives

Treatment initiatives with Native American clients integrate traditional Western recovery programs with Native American ethnocultural concepts and tribal practices. According to Thomason (1991), Native Americans believe that health is a harmonious relationship with nature. Disease, disability, and distress reflect disharmony. Nature is whole, truly a biopsychosocial phenomenon. Healing focuses on the complex whole; everything is interconnected. An individual's health problems are deeply rooted in the community; treatment must take place in a recovery environment that includes family, friends, and neighbors. Diagnosis and treatment come from the healer. This approach is quite different from traditional addiction treatment, which emphasizes client-clinician collaboration and client responsibility for recovery. Native American clients tend to expect immediate results and often fail to return for help after an initial visit (see Thomason, 1991).

Peyote, a small cactus that is native to northern Mexico and Texas, contains the hallucinogen mescaline. The Aztecs considered peyote divine. During the 19th century, its use spread among Native Americans, who used it in their religious rites to help them search for divine visions and to heal the sick. This practice evolved into a religion that incorporates elements of Christianity, currently known as the Native American Church. Use of peyote as a sacrament by a bona fide member of this church is permitted by law.

Summary

Culture and ethnicity influence health beliefs and practices. Addiction often manifests in different ways in European Americans, African Americans, Latino

Americans, Asian Americans, and Native Americans. Addiction clinicians need to identify treatment initiatives for clients with diverse ethnocultural characteristics.

Related Skills Checklist

Practitioner skills related to the varied cultural backgrounds of addiction clients include the ability to do the following:

- Consider client ethnocultural characteristics when interpreting standardized assessment data.
- Use Purnell and Paulanka's model for cultural competence, or a similar tool, to collect culturally relevant data.
- Follow the *DSM-IV* outline for cultural formulation.
- Develop treatment goals and outcomes that reflect clients' special ethnocultural needs or problems.
- Select interventions that reflect clients' ethnocultural strengths and preferences.
- Identify treatment outcome indicators that reflect client expectations.
- Evaluate goal achievement in light of client values, beliefs, and practices.

Special Topics for Further Study

Identify indigenous patterns of alcohol and other drug use in several diverse ethnocultural groups. When does the group consider substance use a problem? How is this problem addressed? How is it prevented? Investigate the prevalence of gambling in different ethnocultural groups. Explore the meanings of food in different cultures.

Addiction Practice 2000

Addiction practice 2000 demands advocacy by practitioners for theory, research, public policy, and addiction programs that will increase treatment and prevention effectiveness with clients from varied cultural backgrounds.

References

American Psychiatric Association. (1994). *Diagnostic and statistical manual of mental disorders* (4th ed.). Washington, DC: Author.

Asante, M. K. (1980). *Afrocentricity: The theory of social change.* Buffalo, NY: Amulefi.

Asante, M. K. (1987). *The Afrocentric idea.* Philadelphia: Temple University Press.

Asante, M. K. (1990). *Kemet, Afrocentricity and knowledge.* Trenton, NJ: Africa World Press.

Center for Substance Abuse Prevention. (Ed.). (1995). *A Hispanic/Latino family approach to substance abuse prevention* (DHHS Publication No. SMA 95-3034). Rockville, MD: Author.

Goddard, L. L. (Ed.). (1993). *An African-centered model of prevention for African-American youth at high risk* (DHHS Publication No. SMA 93-2015). Rockville, MD: Center for Substance Abuse Prevention.

Gordon, J. U. (1994). African American perspective. In J. U. Gordon (Ed.), *Managing multiculturalism in substance abuse services* (pp. 45-71). Thousand Oaks, CA: Sage.

Hilliard, A. (1976). *Alternatives to IQ testing: An approach to the identification of gifted minority students.* Final report to the California State Department of Education, Sacramento.

Information please almanac. (1997). Boston: Houghton Mifflin.

Morrissey, M. (1997, October). The invisible minority: Counseling Asian Americans. *Counseling Today,* pp. 1, 20-22.

The New York Times world almanac and book of facts. (1999). Mahwah, NJ: Primedia.

Purnell, L. D., & Paulanka, B. J. (1998). *Transcultural health care: A culturally competent approach.* Philadelphia: F. A. Davis.

Robertson, T. (1998, October 6). Ifs, ands, butts at Chinatown eateries. *Boston Globe,* pp. B1, B8.

Szapocznik, J. (1995). Structural family therapy. In Center for Substance Abuse Prevention (Ed.), *A Hispanic/Latino family approach to substance abuse prevention* (DHHS Publication No. SMA 95-3034). Rockville, MD: Center for Substance Abuse Prevention.

Thomason, T. C. (1991). Counseling Native Americans: An introduction for non-Native American counselors. *Journal of Counseling and Development, 69,* 321-327.

Other Sources

Center for Substance Abuse Prevention. (1995). *The challenge of participatory research: Preventing alcohol-related problems in ethnic communities* (DHHS Publication No. SMA 95-3042). Rockville, MD: Author.

Gardenswartz, L., & Rowe, A. (1998). *Managing diversity in health care.* San Francisco: Jossey-Bass.

Gordon, J. U. (Ed.). (1994). *Managing multiculturalism in substance abuse services.* Thousand Oaks, CA: Sage.

Hayes, L. L. (1997, August). The unique counseling needs of Latino clients. *Counseling Today,* pp. 1, 10.

Hayton, R. (1994). European American perspectives. In J. U. Gordon (Ed.), *Managing multiculturalism in substance abuse services* (pp. 99-116). Thousands Oaks, CA: Sage.

James, W. H., & Johnson, S. L. (1996). *Doin' drugs: Patterns of African American addiction.* Austin: University of Texas Press.

Johnson, O. J. (1997). *Breaking the chains of cocaine: Black male addiction and recovery.* Chicago: African American Images.

Kar, S. B. (Ed.). (1999). *Substance abuse prevention: A multicultural perspective.* Amityville, NY: Baywood.

Lee, C. C. (1997). *Multicultural issues in counseling: New approaches to diversity* (2nd ed.). Alexandria, VA: American Counseling Association.

Lee, W. M. L. (1999). *Introduction to multicultural counseling.* Philadelphia: Taylor & Francis.

National Institute on Alcohol Abuse and Alcoholism. (1994). *Alcohol and minorities: Alcohol alert* (NIAAA Publication No. 23, PH347). Rockville, MD: Author.

Office for Substance Abuse Prevention. (1990). *Asian and Pacific Islander Americans* (DHHS Publication No. ADM 90-1734). Rockville, MD: Author.

Office for Substance Abuse Prevention. (1991). *American Indians and Native Alaskans* (DHHS Publication No. ADM 91-1802). Rockville, MD: Author.

Pedersen, P. (1994). *A handbook for developing multicultural awareness* (2nd ed.). Alexandria, VA: American Counseling Association.

Pedersen, P. B., & Locke, D. C. (1996). *Cultural and diversity issues in counseling.* Alexandria, VA: ERIC/CASS.

Vacc, N., Devaney, S., & Wittmer, J. (1995). *Experiencing and counseling multicultural and diverse populations* (3rd ed.). Philadelphia: Taylor & Francis.

Wehrly, B. (1996). *Counseling interracial individuals and families.* Alexandria, VA: American Counseling Association.

Videotapes

All of the following videotapes are available from Microtraining Associates, Inc., Box 9641, North Amherst, MA 01059-9641; phone (413) 549-2630; fax (413) 549-0212.

Arredondo, P. *Latina/Latino counseling and psychotherapy: Tape 1. Cultural considerations for working more effectively with Latin Americans.*

Arredondo, P. *Latina/Latino counseling and psychotherapy: Tape 2. Specifics of practice for counseling with Latina/os.*

Davis, D. P., Prieto, L., Reynolds, A. L., & Vazquez, L. A. *Multicultural counseling: Issues of diversity.*

Davis, D. P., Stone, G., Sue, D. W., & Vazquez, L. A. *Multiculturalism: Issues in counseling and education.*

Giordano, J. *Ethnic sharing—valuing diversity.*

Hardiman, R., with Cross, W. *White identity theory: Origins and prospects.*

LaFromboise, T. *Counseling and therapy with Native American Indians.*

Parham, T. *African-American counseling and psychotherapy: Tape 1. Issues in counseling African-American clients.*

Parham, T. *African-American counseling and psychotherapy: Tape 2. Managing therapeutic issues with African-American clients.*

Pedersen, P. *Developing multicultural awareness.*

Sue, D. W. *Guidelines for counseling Asian-American clients.*

16

Women and Addiction

Objectives

- Appreciate the history of women and addiction in the United States.
- Acknowledge the great disparity between women's needs and the services provided.
- Articulate a philosophy of treatment for women.
- Implement effective treatment with women.
- Grasp the significance of Women for Sobriety's New Life program.
- Recognize the special needs of pregnant addicts.
- Identify treatment goals for perinatal addiction.

Outline

- **Women and Addiction**
  - Historical Background
  - Needs and Services
  - Pregnant Addicts
- **Treatment with Women**
  - Treatment Philosophy
  - Effective Treatment
  - Women for Sobriety
- **Treatment for Perinatal Addiction**
- **Summary**
- **Related Skills Checklist**
- **Special Topics for Further Study**
- **Addiction Practice 2000**

Women and Addiction

Historical Background

In the United States, drinking, smoking, gambling, and using drugs have long been associated with men and male lifestyles. Much less visible and less acceptable have been the drinking, smoking, gambling, or drug-using habits of women. Yet it has been suggested that during the 19th century the majority of morphine and opium addicts were women. In his classic book *Substance and Shadow* (1996), Stephen Kandall chronicles the history of women and addiction in the United States. He relates that it was common practice in the 1780s for the women of Nantucket Island to take a "dose of opium every morning" (p. 3). Alcohol, opium, and morphine were the primary ingredients in patent medicines. Mass-circulation magazines and mail-order catalogs brought these "cures" to women from all walks of life who lived in cities, towns, and remote rural areas. Drug use by women was generally considered acceptable. However, according to Kandall, from the 1880s to the turn of the century, the use of drugs by members of minority groups, the association of cocaine with heightened sexuality, and an increase in drug-related urban crime (including prostitution) contributed to the unacceptability of drug use by "proper" women.

Zero tolerance became public policy, and laws were passed to control and eliminate alcohol and drug use, most notably the Harrison Anti-Narcotic Act of 1914 and the Volstead Act, which enforced prohibition of the manufacture, sale, and transportation of intoxicating liquors under the 18th Amendment to the U.S. Constitution, proposed in 1917 and ratified in 1919. Many federal and state drug laws were passed during the next 50 years. Major federal legislation included the Comprehensive Drug Abuse Prevention and Control Act (1970), which established five schedules of controlled substances based on potential for abuse, and the Anti-Drug Abuse Act (1988), the goal of which was a drug-free America by 1995 (for more on this topic, see Chapter 2).

According to Kandall (1996), limited numbers of women received treatment in drug maintenance clinics (1919 to 1923), through the federal programs at Lexington and Fort Worth (1935 to the early 1970s), and through methadone maintenance programs introduced in the 1960s. The women's movement of the 1970s drew attention to women's substance use, yet during the 1980s and 1990s, most women received treatment through traditional inpatient and outpatient programs. And although the number of specialized treatment programs for women has increased slightly in the past 25 years, it has been estimated that only 14% of women who need treatment receive it.

Needs and Services

In *Substance Abuse and the American Woman,* a report published by the National Center on Addiction and Substance Abuse at Columbia University, Reid (1996) documents the shrinking gap between men's and women's substance abuse. According to Reid's findings, there is no gender gap among adolescent substance abusers; roughly equal numbers of adolescent boys and girls are beginning to smoke, drink, and use illicit drugs. Adolescent girls today are 15 times more likely to begin using illegal drugs by the age of 15 than their mothers were. Teenage girls who drink are more likely to have unprotected sex than are girls who do not drink.

Alcohol is the substance most commonly abused by women. One in five women abuses alcohol or drugs at some point in her life, compared with one in three men. Caucasian women drink slightly more alcohol than African American women and much more than Latino women. Women use fewer illicit drugs than do men; however, an estimated 40% of crack cocaine users are women. In some regions, heroin is the number one drug of choice among incarcerated women. Twice as many women as men use prescription drugs. Women are more likely than men to be addicted to prescription drugs in combination with alcohol.

There are physiological differences between men and women who abuse alcohol and other drugs. Women get drunk faster, become addicted sooner, and develop related diseases earlier than men. Female alcoholics are twice as likely to die as same-age male alcoholics. Sexually transmitted diseases (STDs) have more frequent and severe long-term consequences in female substance abusers. The incidence of HIV/AIDS is increasing in heterosexual women. Almost 70% of women in addiction treatment, compared with 12% of men, were sexually abused as children (it should be noted that addiction practitioners suggest that such abuse is underreported by men).

Pregnant Addicts

Pregnant addicts and alcoholics need to know that public policy reflects a trend toward criminalization of substance abuse during pregnancy, mandatory treatment of perinatal addiction, possible loss of child custody, and a potential threat to their rights as women. Addiction clinicians must advocate for pregnant addicts in their dealings with other human service providers, the legal system, legislators, and the lay community. Pregnant addicts need services and support, not punishment within the criminal justice system. Pregnancy may motivate some women addicts to change—to stop using and begin the recovery process. A comprehensive program for pregnant and postpartum women and their infants who have been exposed to alcohol and other drugs includes prevention and education, early identification through outreach, screening and assessment, treatment, maintenance, and follow-up.

The medical consequences of the use of alcohol and other drugs for pregnant women are substance specific. General effects include spontaneous abortion, placental abruption and bleeding, and premature labor. Labor and delivery complications include premature labor, prolonged or arrested delivery, and abnormal bleeding. Fetal and infant effects are likely.

Treatment With Women

Treatment Philosophy

A philosophy to guide the treatment of women who abuse alcohol and other drugs has been expressed by the Center for Substance Abuse Treatment (1994, p. 3). This philosophy challenges addiction clinicians to do the following:

- Engender hope and empowerment in their clients.

- Ensure safe, secure, and supportive environments.

- Provide advocacy in accessing all services needed.

- Promote self-responsibility, self-sufficiency, and interdependence.

- Strive for gender-specific and culturally relevant client-driven services.

- Eliminate labeling of women and their children in all respects.

- Build the effective linkages and networking required for model women's programs.

Effective Treatment

Effective addiction treatment for women includes medical intervention, counseling, support groups, health education, life skills, and social services as needed. Continuing care and follow-up, case management, and outreach for high-risk populations are critical treatment elements.

Medical intervention with women emphasizes testing and treatment for infectious diseases, including hepatitis, tuberculosis, HIV, and STDs. Screening and treatment of general health problems—including anemia and poor nutrition, hypertension, diabetes, cancer, liver disorders, eating disorders, dental and vision problems, and poor hygiene—is critical. Obstetrical and gynecological services must be included, emphasizing family planning, breast cancer screening, and periodic gynecological screening, such as Pap smears. Many women require health services for their infants and children, especially primary and acute health care, developmental assessment, immunizations, nutrition services, and determination of eligibility for the Women, Infants, and Children supplemental food program.

Substance abuse counseling and psychological counseling with women address the use and abuse of substances directly, as well as other issues, which may include low self-esteem; race and ethnicity issues; gender-specific issues; disability-related issues; family relationships; unhealthy interpersonal relationships; violence, including incest, rape, and other abuse; eating disorders; sexuality; grief related to loss of children, other family members, or partners; sexual orientation; and responsibility for one's feelings, including shame, guilt, and anger. Parenting counseling includes information on child development, child safety, injury prevention, and child abuse prevention. Relapse prevention must be a discrete component of each phase of a woman's recovery.

Support groups especially for women include self-help groups such as Women for Sobriety, gender-specific Alcoholics Anonymous and Narcotics Anonymous meetings, and groups whose aims are to strengthen recovery and help prevent relapse. *Health education and prevention activities* with women address HIV/AIDS, the physiology and transmission of STDs, reproductive health, preconception care, prenatal care, childbirth, female sexuality, childhood safety and injury prevention, physical and sexual abuse prevention, nutrition, smoking cessation, and general health.

Life skills critical for women include education in practical life skills, vocational evaluation, financial management, negotiating access to services, stress management and coping skills, and personal image building. Many women require training in parenting skills, including infant/child nutrition, child development, and child-parent relationships. Education, training, and remedial services help women access local education or GED programs and other services identified and needed; these may include English-language competency and literacy assessment programs as well as job counseling, training, and referral, with case-managed and/or coordinated referrals to community programs.

Women may need *social services* to help them with transportation to substance abuse treatment and related community services, child care, legal services, and housing. *Continuing care* and *follow-up* with women emphasize relapse prevention, address core issues, and promote recovery. *Case management* that is sound and sensitive is an essential component of treatment for women. Gender-specific outcome evaluation is needed. (It should also be noted that treatment providers need to develop policies to prevent intentional and unintentional sexual harassment of female clients.)

Effective treatment for women must include *outreach* to all women, especially to high-risk populations, including victims of childhood trauma or domestic violence; pregnant addicts, incarcerated women, and homeless women;

women with dual disorders, HIV/AIDS, or disabilities; minority women; women residing in rural areas; adolescent girls and older women; and lesbian women and lesbian parents. The barriers to treatment for such women are legion.

Women for Sobriety

Women for Sobriety (WFS) grew out of the search for sobriety by Jean Kirkpatrick, Ph.D., and her landmark book *Turnabout: Help for a New Life* (1977). WFS is both an organization and a self-help program for women alcoholics, with self-help groups throughout the United States and the world. In addition, WFS produces and distributes literature written specifically for women alcoholics. According to Dr. Kirkpatrick, since WFS started in 1976, the New Life program has been adapted for other addictions. In addition, many men have shown interest in the program, and Men for Sobriety groups have begun in the United States and Canada.

WFS's statement of purpose may be paraphrased as follows: Women for Sobriety is an organization whose purpose is to help all women recover from problem drinking through the discovery of self, gained by sharing experiences, hopes, and encouragement with other women in similar circumstances. WFS is an organization of women for women. It recognizes woman's emerging role and the necessity of self-esteem and self-discovery. WFS is not affiliated with Alcoholics Anonymous, although WFS members often belong to both organizations. WFS believes that women begin drinking to overcome stress, loneliness, frustration, emotional deprivation, or harassment. Dependence and addiction result. WFS believes that the physiological addiction can be overcome only through abstinence. Mental and emotional addiction are overcome with the knowledge of self gained through membership in Women for Sobriety. Members of WFS live by this philosophy: Forget the past, plan for tomorrow, and live today. Membership in WFS requires a desire to stop drinking and a sincere desire for a new life.

Women for Sobriety is based upon a 13-statement program of positivity that encourages emotional and spiritual growth: the New Life acceptance program. The 13 statements are reprinted here by permission of Women for Sobriety:

1. I have a life-threatening problem that once had me.

2. Negative thoughts destroy only myself.

3. Happiness is a habit I will develop.

4. Problems bother me only to the degree I permit them to.

5. I am what I think.

6. Life can be ordinary or it can be great.

7. Love can change the course of my world.

8. The fundamental object of life is emotional and spiritual growth.

9. The past is gone forever.

10. All love given returns.

11. Enthusiasm is my daily exercise.

12. I am a competent woman and have much to give life.

13. I am responsible for myself and my actions.

Treatment for Perinatal Addiction

The primary goal of perinatal care is a healthy pregnancy that results in a healthy mother and a viable, healthy newborn. Ideally, pregnant women from intact families with no alcohol or other drugs problems voluntarily seek perinatal care. These women share goals with perinatal care providers and, to the best of their abilities, comply fully with perinatal care regimens. In contrast, alcohol/drug-dependent women often deny their addiction, refuse care, and/or comply poorly with care regimens, with harmful consequences for mother, fetus, and newborn.

It is best for a woman to abstain from all alcohol and other drugs as well as other deleterious substances prior to becoming pregnant and throughout pregnancy. However, many women do not know they are pregnant until they have missed a second menstrual period, and they continue to drink, smoke, or use other drugs in the first trimester of pregnancy. Alcohol and other drugs have profound effects on maternal health, placental integrity, and fetal development. For women who are HIV-positive, early treatment is critical.

Some women stop their use of *all* potentially harmful substances during pregnancy. Many women stop using street drugs when pregnant, yet continue to drink and smoke. The U.S. Food and Drug Administration has identified the actual and potential fetal harm that various prescription medications can cause.

Many alcohol/drug-dependent women can stop drinking or using, but have much more difficulty changing their alcohol/drug-related lifestyles. Because of fear of losing custody of their children, many women may avoid care altogether, deny their substance abuse, or minimize their use. Family and social supports for such women may be minimal or lacking altogether. On a daily basis, pregnant addicts confront basic survival and life management crises related to transportation, housing, employment, and child care. Depression, guilt, and shame are common.

Follow-up and continuing care are essential for mother and infant. The majority of pregnant addicts were victims of physical or sexual abuse as children; frequently they are in battering relationships. As such, they are at high risk to neglect or abuse their own children. Rigorous, sensitive parenting education is needed to break this destructive intergenerational cycle. Some women pride themselves on being drug-free during pregnancy and reward themselves by using after their babies are born. Effective perinatal treatment is a complex process of coordination and collaboration among many community agencies and clinicians. Federal confidentiality laws sometimes complicate the necessary communication among providers.

Summary

In the United States, drinking, smoking, gambling, and using drugs have been associated with men and male lifestyles. Today, equal numbers of adolescent boys and girls smoke, drink, and use illicit drugs. Women get drunk faster, become dependent sooner, and develop related diseases earlier than men. Twice as many women as men use prescription drugs. An estimated 40% of crack cocaine users are women. It is estimated that only 14% of the women who need addiction treatment receive it. Some 70% of women who receive substance abuse treatment were sexually abused as children. Effective treatment with women builds upon a philosophy of treatment for women. Women for Sobriety, an organization and self-help program for women, advances the New Life acceptance program of recovery. Public policy reflects a trend toward ever-harsher penalties for substance abuse among pregnant women. Many infants and children are innocent victims of perinatal addiction.

Related Skills Checklist

Practitioner skills related to addiction treatment for women include the ability to do the following:

- Engender hope and empowerment in clients.
- Ensure safe, secure, and supportive environments.
- Provide advocacy in accessing all services needed.
- Promote self-responsibility, self-sufficiency, and interdependence.
- Strive for gender-specific and culturally relevant client-driven services.

- Eliminate labeling of women and their children in all respects.

- Build the effective linkages and networking required for model women's programs.

(These skills are laid out in the treatment philosophy expressed by the Center for Substance Abuse Treatment, 1994, p. 3, as noted above.)

Special Topics for Further Study

What theories or models of addiction help explain addiction in women? What treatment methods are especially useful with women clients? Outline an outreach program that welcomes women into treatment. Discuss prevailing public attitudes toward pregnant addicts. Should such women be punished or treated? Given the fact that as many young girls as boys "smoke, drink, and use," how realistic are prevention efforts with young women? Draft an early intervention program for women with addiction problems.

Addiction Practice 2000

Addiction practice 2000 requires gender-sensitive treatment of clients. Addiction clinicians must demonstrate treatment efficacy with women. Public policy and funding must support research and programs aimed at preventing and managing perinatal addiction.

References

Center for Substance Abuse Treatment. (1994). *Practical approaches in the treatment of women who abuse alcohol and other drugs* (DHHS Publication No. SMA 94-3006). Rockville, MD: Author.

Kandall, S. R. (1996). *Substance and shadow: Women and addiction in the United States.* Cambridge, MA: Harvard University Press.

Kirkpatrick, J. (1977). *Turnabout: Help for a new life.* Garden City, NY: Doubleday.

Reid, J. (1996). *Substance abuse and the American woman.* New York: Columbia University, National Center on Addiction and Substance Abuse.

Other Sources

Abbott, A. A. (1994). A feminist approach to substance abuse treatment and service delivery. *Social Work in Health Care, 19,* 67-83.

Bepko, C. (1992). *Feminism and addiction.* New York: Haworth.

Blechman, E. A., Lowell, E. S., & Garrett, J. (1999). Prosocial coping and substance use during pregnancy. *Addictive Behaviors, 24,* 99-109.

Blume, S. B. (1992). Alcohol and other drug problems in women. In J. H. Lowinson, R. B. Millman, & J. G. Langrod (Eds.), *Substance abuse: A comprehensive textbook* (2nd ed.). Baltimore: Williams & Wilkins.

Burman, S. (1992). A model for women's alcohol/drug treatment. *Alcoholism Treatment Quarterly, 9,* 87-99.

Center for Substance Abuse Prevention. (1993). *Pregnancy and exposure to alcohol and other drug use* (DHHS Publication No. SMA 93-2040). Rockville, MD: Author.

Center for Substance Abuse Prevention. (1993). *Toward preventing perinatal abuse of alcohol, tobacco, and other drugs* (DHHS Publication No. SMA 93-2052). Rockville, MD: Author.

Center for Substance Abuse Prevention. (1996). *A guide for implementing perinatal addiction prevention and treatment programs* (DHHS Publication No. SMA 96-3109). Rockville, MD: Author.

Center for Substance Abuse Treatment. (1993). *Improving treatment for drug-exposed infants* (DHHS Publication No. SMA 93-2011). Rockville, MD: Author.

Center for Substance Abuse Treatment. (1995). *Pregnant, substance-using women* (DHHS Publication No. SMA 95-3056). Rockville, MD: Author.

Cooper, E. F. (1991). *Alcohol use and abuse.* Washington, DC: Library of Congress.

Covington, S. (1999). *Helping women recover: A program for treating addiction.* San Francisco: Jossey-Bass.

Daley, M., Argeriou, M., & McCarty, D. (1998). Substance abuse treatment for pregnant women: A window of opportunity? *Addictive Behaviors, 23,* 239-249.

Eber, C. (1995). *Women and alcohol in a highland Maya town.* Austin: University of Texas Press.

Ettoree, B. (1992). *Women and substance use.* New Brunswick, NJ: Rutgers University Press.

Gilligan, C. (1982). *In a different voice: Psychological theory and women's development.* Cambridge, MA: Harvard University Press.

Gomberg, E. S. L., & Nirenberg, T. D. (Eds.). (1993). *Women and substance abuse.* Norwood, NJ: Ablex.

Haack, M. R. (Ed.). (1997). *Drug-dependent mothers and their children: Issues in public policy and public health.* New York: Springer.

Kaufman, E. (1996). Diagnosis and treatment of drug and alcohol abuse in women. *American Journal of Obstetrics and Gynecology, 174,* 21-27.

Lather, P., & Smithies, C. (1997). *Troubling the angels: Women living with HIV/AIDS.* Boulder, CO: Westview.

Mahan, S. (1996). *Crack cocaine, crime, and women: Legal, social, and treatment issues.* Thousand Oaks, CA: Sage.

Marecek, M. (1999). *Breaking free from partner abuse: Voices of battered women caught in the cycle of domestic violence.* Buena Park, CA: Morning Glory.

Miller, J. (1976). *Toward a new psychology of women.* Boston: Beacon.

National Institute on Alcohol Abuse and Alcoholism. (1999). *Bibliography on alcohol and pregnancy.* Bethesda, MD: Author.

National Institute on Drug Abuse. (1994). *Women and drug abuse* (NIH Publication No. 94-3732). Rockville, MD: Author.

National Institute on Drug Abuse. (1996). *Treatment for drug-exposed women and their children: Advances in research methodology* (NIH Publication No. 96-3632). Rockville, MD: Author.

Pagliaro, A. M., & Pagliaro, L. A. (1999). *Substance use among women.* Philadelphia: Brunner/Mazel.

Reid, J. (1998). *Under the rug: Substance abuse and the mature woman.* New York: Columbia University, National Center on Addiction and Substance Abuse.

Sherman, B. R. (1998). *Addiction and pregnancy.* Westport, CT: Praeger.

Snyder, L. (Ed.). (1994). *Fetal alcohol syndrome resource guide* (IHS Publication No. IHS001). Rockville, MD: National Clearinghouse for Alcohol and Drug Information.

Statman, J. B. (1995). *The battered woman's survival guide: Breaking the cycle.* Dallas, TX: Taylor.

Svikis, D. S., Gorenstein, S., Paluzzi, P., & Fingerhood, M. (1998). Personality characteristics of treatment-seeking HIV+ pregnant drug dependent women. *Journal of Addictive Diseases, 17,* 91-111.

Thompson, M. P., & Kingree, J. B. (1998). Frequency and impact of violent trauma among pregnant substance abusers. *Addictive Behaviors, 23,* 257-262.

Wagner, C. L., Katikaneni, L. D., Cox, T. H., & Ryan, F. M. (1998). Impact of prenatal drug exposure on the neonate. *Obstetrics and Gynecology Clinics of North America, 15,* 169-194.

Watson, R. E. (Ed.). (1994). *Addictive behaviors in women.* Totowa, NJ: Humana.

Ybarra, S. (1991). Women and AIDS: Implications for counseling. *Journal of Counseling and Development, 69,* 285-287.

17

Gay and Lesbian Clients

Objectives

- Identify the characteristics of gay and lesbian individuals with addictive disorders.
- Offer sensitive treatment for gay and lesbian clients.
- Advocate for gender-specific studies and services.
- Recognize the high incidence of substance abuse and related problems in gay and lesbian youth.
- Accept the challenge of addiction prevention and early intervention with gay and lesbian youth.

Outline

- **Background**
- **Alcohol and Drug Abuse**
  - General Considerations
  - Gender-Specific Studies and Services
  - Needs of Transgender and Bisexual Clients
- **Treatment Sensitivity**
- **Gay and Lesbian Youth**
  - Risk Factors
  - Prevention and Early Intervention
- **Summary**
- **Related Skills Checklist**
- **Special Topics for Further Study**
- **Addiction Practice 2000**

Background

Homosexuals who were held in Nazi concentration camps were forced to wear pink triangles on their clothing to set them apart from other inmates. Ironically, when the Allied forces liberated the camps in 1945, they treated those wearing pink triangles as criminals and undesirables and transferred them to civilian prison cells. Today, stigmatization and discrimination still dominate beliefs about homosexuality. American society accepts heterosexuality as the norm and the natural order; homosexuality, by contrast, is seen by many as unnatural and abnormal. In a society where cultural homophobia is rampant, lesbians and gay men may use alcohol and other drugs to cope with dissonance, discrimination, depression, and despair.

Alcohol and Drug Abuse

General Considerations

It is estimated that 25-35% of lesbians and gay men have serious problems with alcohol, rates higher than are found in the general population. Of course, gays and lesbians represent many different racial, ethnic, and class backgrounds. Polydrug use is high, and abuse of other drugs in combination with alcohol is high. Gays and lesbians with addictive disorders face two major problems: their addictions and societal homophobia. The phenomenon of the "gay bar," a social center for many gays and lesbians, contributes to substance abuse. A lifestyle of isolation and loneliness also places many gay and lesbian adults at risk to drink or use. Lesbians consume fewer drugs and less alcohol than gay men, and substance use for both men and women declines with age. Yet there are few treatment providers or programs that are sensitive to the special needs and problems of this diverse population. A stress-vulnerability model helps explain the high rates of substance abuse and suicide among gay men and lesbians. Suicide rates are even higher among gay men who are also members of minority groups. According to a report by the National Coalition of Anti-Violence Programs and the Violence Recovery Program of Fenway Community Health Center in Boston, hate crimes committed against lesbian, gay, bisexual, transgender, and HIV-positive persons continue to rise throughout the United States, despite dramatic decreases in overall violent crime (Fenway Community Health Center, 1998).

Gays and lesbians may use alcohol and other drugs to manage painful feelings of shame, guilt, alienation, isolation, and loneliness. Substance use also helps reduce inhibitions to engage in sex and contributes to unsafe sexual practices by gay men and lesbians. Alcohol and drug use eases the pain gays and lesbians experience in their struggle for group and individual identity.

Gays and lesbians who are adult children of alcoholics in all likelihood grew up in shame-based family systems and are used to high levels of stress and intolerance. Continuing dysfunctional relationships lead to feelings of fear, alienation, and loneliness. Gay and lesbian parents often lose custody of their children. The children of gay and lesbian parents are often subjected to the homophobic remarks of other children. It is a challenge for same-sex partners with children to maintain their relationship; child rearing in such families can be very demanding.

Like heterosexual men and women, gays and lesbians who share needles in their drug use or engage in unsafe sex are at high risk for HIV. Substance abuse by gays and lesbians who are HIV-positive may exacerbate their already compromised immune systems. Substance use may cause disinhibition and noncompliance with risk-reduction behaviors, leading to infection of others and resulting in progressive deterioration of quality of life for gays and lesbians.

Gay and lesbian clients who may present with additional addiction treatment needs and problems include adolescents, incest survivors, victims of battering and abuse, clients with dual disorders, and those who are HIV-positive.

Gender-Specific Studies and Services

As Hughes and Wilsnack (1997) observe, few studies have systematically explored the use and abuse of alcohol and other drugs by lesbians. In their extensive review of the literature on the prevalence of alcohol use by lesbians, these authors found a paucity of research, and the studies they did find exhibited many design and methodological problems. They caution against generalization from studies of gay men to lesbian women. For example, risk factors most frequently cited in the literature include reliance on gay bars for socialization and stress related to homophobic attitudes and discrimination. Hughes and Wilsnack note, "We cannot expect to understand lesbians' experience with alcohol by focusing on research findings from gay men" (p. 33).

Although the life experiences of heterosexual women and lesbians differ, Hughes and Wilsnack hypothesized that a comparison of these two groups, as opposed to the study of gay men, might provide data about risk factors more specific to lesbians and in turn prompt more gender-sensitive specialized services. They studied the risk factors of age, employment, multiple role, marital status, psychological, and interpersonal factors. They found that lesbians have rates of alcohol consumption and other problems that are significantly higher than those of heterosexual women. Lesbians share many risk factors for drinking with heterosexual women; however, whereas traditional roles and responsibilities such as marriage and child rearing may protect heterosexual women, these factors do not operate in the same way for lesbians. Discrimination and harassment, as well as family, kinship, and friendship networks differ between lesbians and hetero-sexual women. Hughes and Wilsnack advocate for the development of more ap-propriate theoretical perspectives to ground population-specific research. These studies can in turn guide more gender-sensitive specialized services for gay and lesbian clients and for heterosexual men and women.

Needs of Transgender and Bisexual Clients

The sexuality of transgender and bisexual persons increases their risk for sub-stance abuse, but research with such persons is limited. Rarely do they receive adequate treatment. In addition, their access to treatment is hindered because service providers themselves are often stigmatized if they render services to these special populations. This discrimination creates a climate of secrecy, backdoor health care services, and a medical ghetto for transgender and bisexual individuals. *The New England Transgender Resource and Service Guide* pro-vides information for clinicians and clients about health care centers and medi-cal providers who work with transgender and bisexual individuals (JRI Health & Massachusetts Department of Health, 1999). The guide identifies organiza-tions and support groups for gay, lesbian, bisexual, and transgender individuals. It also provides information about legal assistance, violence recovery programs, housing, education, and employment.

Treatment Sensitivity

Outreach and sensitive treatment are critical for gay, lesbian, bisexual and transgender substance abusers. Agencies, providers, and clinicians need special training to develop the sensitivity and skills they need to work effectively with these high-risk populations. Effective treatment is holistic, involves the family, and addresses codependency issues. Recovery programs based on a 12-step model may be useful. In such programs, for example, Step 1 may be for clients to accept both their addictions and their sexual orientation. Clients may be in vari-ous stages of "coming out" during treatment.

Treatment goals emphasize the transformation of two stigmatized identities, that of being an addict and that of being gay or lesbian, into a positive, affirming individual identity. McNally and Finnegan (1992) describe the identity transfor-mation that follows recovery when two subidentities, those of lesbian and alco-holic, transform into a single, distinct identity of a lesbian recovering alcoholic. Similarly, in a publication of the Center for Substance Abuse Prevention (1994), a lesbian client is quoted:

I was different, alone, and afraid. I drank to cope with being a lesbian, but ended up being an alcoholic. I became a recovering alcoholic: sobriety saved my life. I accepted my lesbian identity in sobriety. I am a lesbian recovering alcoholic. (p. 18)

There is evidence that before alcoholic gay men and lesbians become sober, they view being gay or lesbian as negative. After choosing sobriety and living sober, they accept being gay or lesbian as a positive aspect of self (Kus, 1988).

Gay/Lesbian Youth

The incidence of alcohol and other drug use is three times greater in gay and lesbian adolescents than in straight youth. Gay and lesbian adolescents often begin to drink and use drugs to reduce confusion, anxiety, pain, and feelings of isolation when they become aware of their sexual orientation. These young people struggle with acceptance of their sexual orientation and identity, decisions to come out or not, and family and community acceptance. Suicide is three times higher in gay and lesbian youth than in heterosexual peers. These problems are even greater for gay and lesbian youth who are also members of minority groups.

Gay and lesbian youth may use drugs to decrease the feelings associated with the stigma they experience in discovering and developing their homosexual identity. They self-medicate to manage anxiety, decrease depression and dissonance, discharge sexual impulses more comfortably, and escape the pain of exclusion, ridicule, and rejection by peers and family. Alcohol and other drug use gives them a sense of power, belonging, and identity.

Risk Factors

The risk factors that contribute to substance abuse by gay and lesbian youth include a history of family addiction, a lack of healthy role models, and physical, emotional, and/or sexual abuse and victimization. Low self-esteem and self-efficacy, lack of support by schools, inadequate social services, and pro-use norms in the community contribute to the risk to abuse alcohol or other drugs. Dropping out of school, becoming homeless, and attempting suicide are associated with substance abuse by gay and lesbian youth.

Group homes, emergency shelters, residential facilities, and juvenile detention facilities are dangerous places for gay and lesbian youth; frequently they are blamed by staff when sexual or other assaults take place. Among teenage lesbians, pregnancy is sometimes a problem; for some girls, becoming pregnant is a way to conceal their sexual orientation.

Prevention and Early Intervention

Informed, concerned, and involved families can help gay and lesbian youth to develop healthy identities and reduce their risk of substance abuse; so, too, can informed, concerned, and involved schools and communities. Addiction treatment for these young people emphasizes early intervention. Parents, teachers, and service providers need to understand and examine their own beliefs and practices concerning homosexuality and homophobia. Education is needed to change community attitudes. Communities can help by supporting telephone hot lines that gay and lesbian teens and their families can call for information and service numbers. Gay and lesbian youth need to have available to them alcohol-free and other drug-free activities and events, especially programs that increase the visibility and promote the image of healthy, substance-free youth. Straight parents and gay/lesbian role models can develop advocacy and prevention programs to address issues of homophobia and raise community consciousness about gay and lesbian youth, especially their high risk for substance abuse and suicide.

Gay and lesbian youth need safe schools. They fear discovery, lack role models, and desperately want affirmation and acceptance. Teachers, guidance and adjustment counselors, and other school staff need to be educated about homosexuality and should receive sensitivity training about homophobia and preparation for crisis intervention. All students, especially student leaders, need to learn about gay and lesbian issues. Role models and other resource people need to be visible and accessible. Does the school philosophy promote inclusion? Does the school have policies to protect gay and lesbian students from discrimination, harassment, and violence? Does the school library have information available about homosexuality and homophobia? Does the curriculum address gay and lesbian subjects? Does the school have support groups for gay and lesbian students, especially those with substance abuse problems?

Summary

Gay men and lesbians have higher rates of substance abuse than the general population. Addiction clinicians need to offer sensitive treatment for gay and lesbian clients. The incidence of alcohol and other drug use in gay/lesbian youth is three times greater than in straight youth. Parents and teachers, schools, and the community must accept responsibility for addiction prevention and early intervention with these youth.

Related Skills Checklist

Practitioner skills related to addiction treatment with gay and lesbian clients include the ability to do the following:

- Consider client sexual orientation when interpreting standardized assessment data.
- Collect additional assessment client data as necessary.
- Develop treatment goals and outcomes that reflect clients' special needs or problems.
- Select interventions that recognize client strengths and preferences.
- Evaluate treatment outcomes and goal achievement with regard for clients' values, beliefs, and practices.

Special Topics for Further Study

Search the literature to determine whether separate or general treatment programs are more effective with gay and lesbian clients. Identify mutual self-help support groups for gay, lesbian, bisexual, and transgender clients in your geographic area. Determine the need for substance abuse prevention and early intervention for gay and lesbian youth in your community.

Addiction Practice 2000

Addiction practice 2000 requires responsible public and professional commitment to early intervention with gay and lesbian clients. Addiction practitioners must support gay and lesbian youth in their efforts to cope positively with their sexual orientation.

References

Center for Substance Abuse Prevention. (1994). *Lesbians, gay men, and bisexuals* (DHHS Publication No. SMA 94-2097). Rockville, MD: Author.

Fenway Community Health Center. (1998). *Anti-lesbian, gay, and transgender violence in 1997.* Boston: Fenway Community Health Center.

Hughes, T. L., & Wilsnack, S. C. (1997). Use of alcohol among lesbians: Research and clinical implications. *American Journal of Orthopsychiatry, 67,* 20-36.

JRI Health & Massachusetts Department of Public Health. (1999). *The New England transgender resource and service guide.* Boston: Author.

Kus, R. J. (1988). Alcoholism and non-acceptance of gay self: The critical link. *Journal of Homosexuality, 15*(1-2), 25-41.

McNally, E. G., & Finnegan, D. C. (1992). Lesbian recovering alcoholics: A qualitative study of identity transformation. *Journal of Chemical Dependency Treatment, 5,* 93-103.

Other Sources

Alcoholism Center for Women. (1993). *Creating visibility: Providing lesbian-sensitive and lesbian-specific alcoholism recovery services* (a training curriculum project of the Alcoholism Center for Women). Los Angeles: Author.

Alexander, C. J. (1998). *Gay and lesbian mental health: A sourcebook for practitioners.* New York: Haworth.

Bloomfield, K. (1993). A comparison of alcohol consumption between lesbians and heterosexual women in an urban population. *Drug and Alcohol Dependence, 33,* 257-269.

Cadwell, S. A., Burnham, R. A., & Forstein, M. (1995). *Therapists on the front line: Psychotherapy with gay men in the age of AIDS.* Washington, DC: American Psychiatric Association.

DeCrescenzo, T. (1994). *Helping gay and lesbian youth: New policies, new programs, new practice.* New York: Haworth.

Doyle, I. (1996). *What are the risk factors associated with substance abuse in the homosexual community?* Unpublished master's thesis, Cambridge College.

Cornett, C. (1993). *Affirmative dynamic psychotherapy with gay men.* Northvale, NJ: Jason Aronson.

Green, B., & Herek, G. M. (Eds.). (1994). *Lesbian and gay psychology: Theory, research, and clinical applications.* Thousand Oaks, CA: Sage.

Harbeck, K. M. (1992). *Coming out of the classroom closet: Gay and lesbian students, teachers, and curricula.* New York: Haworth.

Hellman, R. E. (1992). Dual diagnosis issues with homosexual persons. *Journal of Chemical Dependency Treatment, 5,* 105-117.

Kelly, J. (1994). *Preventing alcohol and other drug problems in the lesbian and gay community.* Sacramento: California Department of Alcohol and Drug Programs.

Klein, C. (1991). *Counseling our own: Lesbian/gay subculture meets the mental health system* (2nd ed.). Seattle, WA: Consultant Services Network.

Kus, R. J. (1995). *Addiction and recovery in gay and lesbian persons.* New York: Haworth.

Marshall, J. L. (1997). *Counseling lesbian partners.* Louisville, KY: Westminster John Knox.

Martinez, M. C., & White, J. C. (1997). *The lesbian health book: Caring for ourselves.* Seattle, WA: Seal.

Penn, R. E. (1997). *The gay men's wellness guide: The National Lesbian and Gay Health Association's complete book for physical, emotional, and mental health and well-being for every gay male.* New York: Henry Holt.

Ryan, C., & Futterman, D. (1998). *Lesbian and gay youth: Care and counseling.* New York: Columbia University Press.

Segal, J. (1994, January/February). Gay parents in addictions treatment. *Counselor,* pp. 26-27.

Shalit, P. (1998). *Living well: The gay man's essential health guide.* Los Angeles: Allyson.

Shifrin, F., & Solis, M. (1992). Chemical dependency in gay and lesbian youth. *Journal of Chemical Dependency Treatment, 5,* 67-76.

Silverstein, C. (1991). *Gays, lesbians, and their therapists.* New York: W. W. Norton.

Skinner, W. F. (1994). The prevalence and demographic predictors of illicit/licit drug use among lesbians and gay men: The Trilogy Project. *American Journal of Public Health, 84,* 1307-1310.

Solarz, A. L. (Ed.). (1999). *Lesbian health: Current assessment and directions for the future.* Washington, DC: National Academy Press.

Stall, R., Barret, D., & Paul, J. (n.d.). *Changes in drug and alcohol use patterns among gay men in San Francisco: The San Francisco Men's Health Study.* Sacramento, CA: EMT Group.

Tasker, F. L., & Golombok, S. (1997). *Growing up in a lesbian family: Effects on child development.* New York: Guilford.

Teague, J. B. (1992). Issues relating to the treatment of adolescent lesbians and homosexuals. *Journal of Mental Health Counseling, 14,* 422-439.

Unks, G. (1995). *The gay teen: Education practice and theory for lesbian, gay, and bisexual adolescents.* New York: Routledge.

Warren, B. E. (1993, February/March). Transsexuality, identity, and empowerment: A view from the front lines. *SIECUS Report,* pp. 14-16.

Weinstein, D. L. (1993). *Lesbians and gay men: Chemical dependency treatment issues.* New York: Haworth.

Wilton, T. (1997). *Good for you: A handbook on lesbian health and wellbeing.* Washington, DC: Cassell.

Part V

Treatment Collaboration for Coexisting Medical, Psychological, and Social Problems

18

Medical Conditions

Objectives

- Assess coexisting client medical conditions.
- Identify the adverse effects of alcohol on body organs and systems.
- Note the higher incidence of cancer in clients who abuse alcohol.
- Examine the indications and contraindications of moderate drinking to lessen the risk for heart disease.
- Recognize the adverse medical effects of drug abuse.
- Understand that substance abuse compromises the health of clients who are HIV-positive or have AIDS.
- Recognize the risk of substance abuse in clients with pain.
- Acknowledge that individuals with physical disabilities have a higher incidence of substance use disorders.
- Collaborate with health and human service providers and professionals to treat clients with coexisting medical conditions.

Outline

- **Assessment of Coexisting Medical Conditions**
- **Alcohol-Related Medical Problems**
  - Liver Disease and Other Gastrointestinal Problems
  - Cardiovascular Problems
  - Brain and Other Neurological Problems

- – Musculoskeletal Problems
- – Respiratory Problems
- – Endocrine and Reproductive Problems
- – Immune System Problems
- – Cancer
- – Treatment Collaboration
- ■ **Adverse Medical Effects of Drug Abuse**
  - – CNS Depressants
  - – CNS Stimulants
  - – Opioids
  - – Hallucinogens
  - – Marijuana
  - – Inhalants
  - – Anabolic Steroids
  - – Designer Drugs
  - – Herbs
- ■ **HIV/AIDS**
  - – Background
  - – High-Risk Behavior
  - – Treatment Collaboration
  - – Harm Reduction
  - – Prevention
- ■ **Pain**
  - – Acute Pain
  - – Chronic Pain
  - – Treatment Collaboration
    - Assessment
    - Pain Management
    - Children and Older Adults
- ■ **Physical Disabilities**
  - – Treatment Collaboration
  - – Americans With Disabilities Act
  - – Prevention
- ■ **Summary**
- ■ **Related Skills Checklist**
- ■ **Special Topics for Further Study**
- ■ **Addiction Practice 2000**

Assessment of Coexisting Medical Conditions

It has been estimated that 30-60% of adults who are hospitalized for medical or surgical problems abuse alcohol or other drugs. Unfortunately, medical and surgical staff often fail to identify or treat these coexisting addictions. And what about the millions of clients with medical conditions who visit physicians, nurse practitioners, and other health professionals as outpatients or who receive home care? In addition, the majority of clients who seek help for addictive disorders have concomitant medical conditions or complications. Yet how skilled are addiction clinicians at recognizing client medical conditions and collaborating with colleagues for client treatment?

Medical problems often coexist with or contribute to addiction severity, and, concomitantly, addiction causes many medical conditions and complications. Assessment of clients with addictive disorders includes a health history and physical examination to identify medical problems. Axis III of *DSM-IV* reports current general medical conditions that are relevant to understanding the primary disorder (American Psychiatric Association, 1994). The Addiction Severity Index addresses medical problems, and Dimension 2 *ASAM PPC-2* criteria assess biomedical conditions and complications (American Society of Addiction Medicine, 1996). Addiction clinicians collaborate with health and human service providers to treat clients with coexisting medical conditions.

Alcohol-Related Medical Problems

Heavy, chronic drinking of alcohol can harm every organ and system of the body.

Liver Disease and Other Gastrointestinal Problems

Because the liver is the primary site for alcohol metabolism, it is particularly vulnerable to the development of fatty liver, hepatitis and fibrosis, and cirrhosis. Other serious gastrointestinal problems related to alcoholism include nutritional deficits with serious fluid and electrolyte imbalances, metabolic disorders, malnutrition, esophagitis and varices, gastritis and ulceration, and pancreatitis. Hemorrhage from esophageal varices or gastric ulceration can cause death.

Cardiovascular Problems

Alcohol can have harmful effects on the cardiovascular system, including cardiomyopathy, hypertension, weakened heart muscle, and increased risk of stroke. Arrhythmias account for the high incidence of sudden death in many alcoholics. Chronic, heavy drinking, together with poor nutrition and liver damage, affects the blood: red blood cells, white blood cells, and platelets. Anemia, lower resistance to infection, and a tendency to bruise and bleed are common in alcoholics.

According to the American Heart Association, moderate drinking may lessen the risk for coronary heart disease, especially in older adults, who as a group have high rates of cardiovascular disease. Alcohol seems to increase the level of high-density lipoprotein, the "good kind of cholesterol" that removes plaque from arterial walls. This reduces atherosclerosis, the hardening and narrowing of the coronary arteries than can cause blockage and heart attack. Alcohol may reduce the stickiness of the blood and interfere with the formation of clots, thus preventing thrombosis. Alcohol may enhance estrogen levels in postmenopausal women and in this way reduce the risk of heart disease. Moderate drinking is *not recommended* for anyone with an actual or potential problem with alcohol or other drugs. Moderate alcohol consumption means one drink a day for women and two for men, with one drink defined as 5 ounces of wine, 12 ounces of beer, or 1.5 ounces of spirits (Foreman, 1999a). (For more on moderate drinking, see Chapter 7.)

Brain and Other Neurological Problems

Acute and chronic drinking affects the brain and nervous system. Alcohol intoxication or withdrawal may be fatal. Seizures occur. Brain injury due to trauma is common. Chronic drinking can cause Wernicke-Korsakoff syndrome, which is characterized by confusion, impaired memory, visual disturbances, and difficulty standing and walking.

Alcohol can cause brain atrophy with major cognitive and motor impairments. Alcoholics frequently experience polyneuropathy, a diminished sensation of pain and temperature with tingling, burning, and numbing of the extremities. Brain damage from alcohol may be irreversible.

Musculoskeletal Problems

Alcoholics have a higher incidence of injuries from accidents, including injuries sustained in fights, than is found in the population as a whole. Consequently, they sustain a high incidence of broken bones. In addition, alcohol causes myopathy, a progressive muscular weakness. Women who drink are at increased risk for osteoporosis.

Respiratory Problems

Alcoholics have a higher incidence than other groups of chronic obstructive pulmonary disease, pneumonia, and tuberculosis. Large doses of alcohol can cause death from respiratory arrest. Smoking, which has its own negative health consequences, is twice as common in people who drink as it is in the general public. Emphysema and cancer are serious respiratory problems directly related to smoking.

Endocrine and Reproductive Problems

Alcohol has harmful effects on endocrine and reproductive functions. Drinking while taking oral diabetic medications adversely affects blood sugar. Drinking when taking insulin can cause a marked drop in blood sugar with mental impairment or even death. Alcohol can suppress testosterone levels in men, and chronic alcohol use can disturb the menstrual cycle in women. Alcohol may impair fertility by preventing pregnancy or increasing the risk of spontaneous abortion. Alcohol crosses the placental barrier, with many adverse effects on fetal and postnatal development. (See also the discussion of perinatal addiction in Chapter 14.)

Immune System Problems

Chronic alcohol abuse depresses the immune system, thereby placing heavy drinkers at increased risk for infectious disease. This is especially significant for people who are infected with the human immunodeficiency virus, or HIV (see the section on HIV/AIDS below for more on this topic).

Upper respiratory infections are common among alcoholics and, as I have noted, alcoholics have a high incidence of pneumonia and tuberculosis. "Wine sores" are superficial infected areas of the skin often seen in alcoholics with poor personal hygiene.

Cancer

Alcoholics have a higher incidence than other populations of cancers of the mouth, tongue, throat, esophagus, stomach, colon and rectum, liver and pancreas, lungs, urinary tract, prostate, and possibly breast. Alcoholic clients with cancer have a poorer chance of survival and a greater chance of metastasis than do nonalcoholic clients with the same cancer. Smoking and drinking act together to increase the risk of many cancers. The American Cancer Society recommends limiting alcohol consumption or abstaining, because even a moderate intake may increase the risk of cancer in some people.

Treatment Collaboration

Treatment collaboration for coexisting alcohol-related medical conditions is an essential element of effective case management for clients with addictive disorders. Addiction clinicians assess all clients for alcohol-related medical conditions and complications. Acute, life-threatening medical conditions are treated prior to or in conjunction with addiction treatment, most often in an acute-care level of service. When alcohol-related medical conditions are not life threatening or acute, clinicians refer clients appropriately and coordinate medical management with addiction treatment. Addressing alcohol-related medical conditions may be an important client goal for aftercare. Failure to address client medical conditions may contribute to relapse. Resolution or improvement of biomedical conditions and complications is an important evaluation outcome indicator.

Clients who drink while taking medications can impair the effectiveness of their treatment regimens. They may experience serious adverse effects, including death. Clinicians need to obtain thorough drug histories, including all prescription drugs, over-the-counter (OTC) drugs and herbs, alcohol, and all illicit substances being used. For heavy drinkers, nonprescription painkillers can be hazardous. Clinicians must educate clients about all potentially dangerous alcohol and medication interactions.

Adverse Medical Effects of Drug Abuse

See Chapter 3 for a discussion of drug properties and desired effects as well as signs and symptoms of substance abuse, especially intoxication and withdrawal.

CNS Depressants

Chronic use of sedatives, hypnotics, and anxiolytic drugs can cause malnutrition with weight loss. Clients may experience cardiovascular or respiratory depression followed by convulsions, coma, shock, and death. Barbiturates combined with alcohol or narcotics are often lethal. Overdose with this combination is a common form of suicide.

CNS Stimulants

Medical conditions associated with chronic cocaine/crack use include scars and abscesses, perforated nasal septum, insomnia or hypersomnia, and fatigue. Clients exhibit psychomotor retardation or agitation and complain of severe headaches. Decreased sexual performance is common. Chronic cocaine use is associated with increased risk for HIV/AIDS.

Adverse effects from chronic use of amphetamines include cardiac irregularities and respiratory problems. Irreversible damage to blood vessels in the brain can lead to stroke. Clients neglect nutrition and lose weight; they develop anorexia. Intravenous amphetamine use can cause sudden increase in blood pressure, very high fever, stroke, or cardiovascular collapse and death.

Nicotine is an extremely toxic substance; it irritates lung tissue, constricts blood vessels, and increases blood pressure and heart rate. Chronic nicotine use is associated with cancers of the mouth, throat, larynx, lungs, esophagus, breast, bladder, pancreas, and kidney. Smokers experience more chronic obstructive lung diseases, such as emphysema and chronic bronchitis. Smokeless tobacco is a direct cause of oral cancer. Careless smoking habits and fires cause accidental injury and death. Smokers experience a higher incidence of gastrointestinal problems, such as gastric ulcers and cirrhosis. There is an increased risk of cerebral hemorrhage (stroke) in women over 35 who smoke and take birth control pills. Medicaid expenditures for smoking-related health care costs are significant.

Excessive caffeine consumption can cause heart palpitations, tachycardia, cardiac arrhythmias, and hypotension, with an increased incidence of angina and myocardial infarction. Clients may experience difficulty breathing and flushing and may complain of headache, light-headedness, dizziness, ringing in the ears, and visual flashes of light. Intraocular pressure increases in clients with unregulated glaucoma. Caffeine is associated with gastrointestinal disturbances, including nausea, acid indigestion, gastric irritation, peptic ulcer, pain, and diarrhea. Caffeine increases plasma glucose and lipid levels. Insomnia with periods of exhaustion is common. Clients may experience reflex hyperexcitability, muscle twitching, and psychomotor agitation. Rambling flow of thoughts and speech, apprehension, the jitters, restlessness, nervousness, irritability, excitement, and excessive sensibility characterize chronic caffeine use.

Opioids

Chronic opioid users often experience malnutrition, constipation, dermatitis, and abscesses. Cellulitis and other vascular complications often accompany intravenous drug use, and IV drug users are at higher risk for bacterial endocarditis, hepatitis, tetanus, and HIV/AIDS. Other serious conditions include hypoglycemia, pulmonary emboli, renal failure, and cardiac arrest. Slow and shallow breathing with clammy skin is common. Respiratory depression and failure, seizures, coma, and death may occur.

Hallucinogens

Adverse effects are associated with chronic or heavy use of hallucinogens. With PCP, there is a drop in blood pressure, pulse, and respiratory rates. Individuals may experience nausea and vomiting, chills and tremors, blurred vision, dizziness, loss of balance, and drooling. When hallucinogens are used with CNS depressants such as alcohol or benzodiazepines, clients may experience convulsions, coma, and/or heart and lung failure. Chronic users are at increased risk for HIV/AIDS. The effects of chronic LSD use are highly individual; common physical problems include nausea, chills, and tremors.

Marijuana

Marijuana irritates lung tissues and damages the respiratory system because pot smokers usually inhale unfiltered smoke deeply and hold it in their lungs as long as possible. Marijuana smoke contains more carcinogens than tobacco smoke. Male users may experience decreased sperm count, lowered testosterone levels, and enlarged breasts. Persistent menstrual irregularities are common in female users.

Inhalants

Inhalants can cause cardiopulmonary arrest with death from asphyxiation. Reversible effects from inhalant use include nausea and vomiting with weight loss, chest pain, fatigue, and muscular and joint pain. Inhalant use can produce electrolyte imbalance and blood oxygen depletion. Liver and kidney damage may occur. Irreversible effects from specific substances include hearing loss, peripheral neuropathies, bone marrow depression, and permanent damage to the brain and other nervous system structures. Inhalants can cause stupor, unconsciousness, coma, and death.

Anabolic Steroids

Adverse effects from use of anabolic steroids range in severity from acne and trembling to liver cancer and homicide. Some serious effects appear quickly, whereas others—such as heart attack, stroke, and hemorrhagic liver disease—may not be evident for years. People who inject steroids run the added risk of contracting or transmitting hepatitis or HIV. Steroids have their most adverse effects on the cardiovascular and reproductive systems. Men may experience shrinking of the testicles, impotence, reduced sperm count, infertility, baldness, and development of breasts. Women may experience growth of facial hair, changes in or cessation of the menstrual cycle, breast reduction, enlargement of the clitoris, and deepened voice. In adolescents, growth may be halted through premature skeletal maturation and accelerated puberty. Other serious effects include jaundice, fluid retention, and liver tumors. High blood pressure is common in steroid users.

Designer Drugs

Because designer drugs can be several hundred times stronger than the drugs they are designed to imitate, adverse effects can develop quickly and be quite severe. Medical conditions and complications associated with designer drugs mimic the psychoactive effects of the parent drugs. For example, fentanyl (a synthetic opioid analgesic) can cause respiratory paralysis and death. Adverse effects from meperidine (Demerol) analogs resemble Parkinson symptoms: uncontrollable tremors, drooling, impaired speech, paralysis, and irreversible brain damage. Both MDA and MDMA can be neurotoxic.

Herbs

Adverse effects from chronic use of herbs are substance specific and highly individual. Clinicians need to assess herbal use, abuse, or dependence. A comprehensive history of all substance use, including alcohol, OTC medications, licit and illicit drugs, and herbs helps clinicians identify actual and potential drug interactions.

HIV/AIDS

Background

Addiction clinicians work with significant numbers of clients who are HIV-positive or who have acquired immunodeficiency syndrome, or AIDS. They also work with many more clients who demonstrate behaviors that place them at high risk to contract HIV, which causes AIDS. HIV is transmitted primarily through sexual contact or through exposure to blood and blood products; infected mothers of newborns can transmit HIV to their infants through breast milk. The greatest concentrations of the virus are found in blood, semen, cerebrospinal fluids, and cervical/vaginal secretions. HIV is not transmitted through casual contact. HIV infection is detected through the presence of antibodies to HIV in the blood.

HIV/AIDS is actually a series of stages along a continuum from asymptomatic HIV to the development of a debilitating, terminal condition. Approximately 70% of HIV-infected individuals develop AIDS within 10 years following infection, with a life expectancy of 10 to 15 years. Since 1995, however, deaths from AIDS in the United States have decreased, and there are more asymptomatic survivors. It should be noted, however, that the rate of HIV transmission is on the rise among women and minorities. In the mid-1990s, it was projected that by the year 2000 a million people in the United States would be infected with HIV. The spread of HIV is rampant in many African countries and in Southeast Asia.

High-Risk Behavior

In the early 1980s, many gay men who had unsafe anal receptive sex with multiple partners acquired HIV. Today, intravenous drugs users who share needles and individuals who engage in unsafe heterosexual sex account for most new cases of HIV infection. At high risk to acquire the virus are addicts who share needles or trade sex for drugs, people who use alcohol or other drugs and then engage in unsafe sex, and people who have sex with multiple partners. These behaviors also increase the risk of contracting hepatitis C (HCV) and other sexually transmitted diseases, which in turn suppress the immune system and contribute to higher risk for contracting HIV. For example, HIV-positive mothers who are also infected with HCV are nearly twice as likely to transmit HIV to their babies as are HIV-infected women without HCV.

Homeless and runaway youth often abuse alcohol and other drugs, fall prey to abusive relationships, and exchange sex for shelter or drugs, putting them at risk for HIV. Childhood sexual abuse predicts high-risk sexual behavior in adult gay and bisexual men.

Being tattooed with nonsterile needles and receiving acupuncture treatment from providers who reuse needles also increase the risk of HIV infection.

Treatment Collaboration

Remaining alcohol- and drug-free is a key part of treatment for HIV/AIDS clients. Substance abuse compromises such clients' health and increases the likelihood they will infect others.

Pregnant women at risk for HIV should be tested; if HIV-positive, they should receive medication during pregnancy to reduce the risk of HIV infection in their infants. In some cases, treatment of infants after delivery is effective. In most states, pregnant women have a choice as to whether or not they are tested for HIV. Clinicians need to present testing options in a respectful way, emphasizing the positive aspects of testing for mother and baby. Clinicians must advocate for treatment, not punishment, for pregnant addicts. Harm reduction and prevention are treatment goals for women who are not HIV-positive.

Specific medications have been shown to slow the progression of AIDS. Other drugs strengthen the immune system, and anti-infective and antineoplastic drugs combat opportunistic infections and associated cancers. New treatment protocols combine two or more drugs to produce maximum benefit with the fewest adverse reactions. Combination therapy also helps inhibit the production of mutant HIV strains resistant to particular drugs.

Nucleoside analogs were the first effective class of antiretroviral drugs. These drugs act by incorporating themselves into the DNA of the virus and thereby stopping the building process. The resulting DNA is incomplete and cannot create a new virus. Nucleoside analogs include the following:

- Zidovudine, also known as ZDV or AZT (Retrovir)

- Lamivudine, also known as 3TC (Epivir)

- Zalcitabine, also known as ddC (Hivid)

- Didanosine, also known as ddI (Videx)

- Zalcitabine, also known as ddC (Hivid)

- Stavudine, also known as d4T (Zerit)

Protease inhibitors work at the last stage of the virus reproduction cycle. These drugs prevent HIV from being assembled and released from the infected CD4+ cell. Protease inhibitors include the following:

- Saquinavir mesylate (Invirase)

- Indinavir (Crixivan)

- Ritonavir (Norvir)

- Nelfinavir mesylate (Viracept)

The newest class of antiretroviral agents, nonnucleoside reverse transcriptase inhibitors (NNRTIs), stop HIV production by binding directly onto reverse transcriptase and preventing the conversion of RNA to DNA. These drugs are called nonnucleoside inhibitors, because even though they work at the same stage as nucleoside analogs, they act in a completely different way. Examples of NNRTIs are nevirapine (Viramune) and delavirdine mesylate (Rescriptor).

In addition to medication, HIV/AIDS clients require adequate nutrition, pain management, personal support, and social services, including housing. Many clinicians serve as case managers for HIV/AIDS clients. Terminally ill clients may choose hospice care. To date, there is no vaccine to prevent HIV, nor are there any effective medications to cure AIDS. Ethnocultural factors and socioeconomic conditions contribute to an uneven rate of incidence and treatment in the United States. Many individuals are uneducated about cause, risk factors, and treatment. Some people are too poor to access available treatment.

Harm Reduction

Needle exchange programs for intravenous drug users are a classic example of harm reduction. In 1996, 75% of IV drug users in Australia were using needle exchange programs. In 1997, the Catholic Church advocated for needle exchanges to prevent the spread of HIV in Australian prisons. Despite the evidence that such programs reduce the spread of HIV and do not increase drug use, the United States has been slow to embrace them, even though the concept of needle exchange is supported by the Centers for Disease Control and Prevention, the American Medical Association, the National Institutes of Health, the National Academy of Sciences, the American Public Health Association, and the American Bar Association. Cleaning needles with chlorine bleach also reduces the risk of spreading the virus.

Prevention

Addiction clinicians play a vital role in the education of individuals, couples, and community groups about HIV/AIDS. Outreach to high-risk populations is a public health mandate. In some states, HIV/AIDS education is a required part of all substance abuse treatment.

Education regarding safe sex should be part of an overall program of education, support, and counseling. Safe sex is defined as 100% condom use for vaginal or anal sex. Safe sex also includes avoiding alcohol and other drugs (especially cocaine) prior to sex. Teens and young adults are urged to limit their numbers of sexual partners.

Peer education is especially effective with teens and minority populations. Gay men at high risk are best exposed to such education through outreach at bars, at community events, and at other venues where gay men socialize. Structured programs that may compromise anonymity are not well received. Indigenous paraprofessionals are effective in HIV/AIDS outreach education. Empowerment groups motivate individuals to change their behavior. Clinicians need to recognize the strong influence of ethnocultural factors, especially traditional gender roles, when teaching about the spread of HIV through heterosexual sex in Latino and African American communities. Knowledge alone rarely changes behavior.

Pain

The International Association for the Study of Pain defines pain as an unpleasant sensory and emotional experience arising from actual or potential tissue damage. Injury or disease is usually the source of pain, although stress and other psychological factors can precipitate and maintain pain. Nerve endings at the pain source send signals to a control center in the spinal cord and then to the brain. The brain evaluates the signal and may send back a signal to the spinal cord to mute the body's response to the pain or to perceive the pain. Pain includes the perception of uncomfortable stimuli as well as the response to that perception. Acute pain is a warning.

Half of all people who seek medical help do so because of pain. Yet pain is poorly managed, especially in children, the elderly, and many persons who are members of minority groups. Pain is one of the primary reasons that some individuals who are terminally ill ask their physicians for help in committing suicide. Many Americans support the legalization of physician-assisted suicide because they fear an agonizing, painful death.

Responses to pain are highly individual and are influenced by age, emotional state, situational factors, and ethnocultural variables. Present health status, including fatigue, sleep deprivation, anxiety, and depression, affects responses to pain. The meaning of pain varies greatly from client to client. Unrelieved pain heightens anxiety and causes physical and mental exhaustion. Many people in pain self-medicate with alcohol, as well as with licit and illicit drugs, in their attempts to manage their pain. Pharmacological researchers are working on the development of medications that will interrupt the relays to the brain as a way to manage pain. Individuals who experience pain as intolerable and uncontrollable often attempt suicide.

Acute Pain

Acute pain has an identifiable, immediate onset and is usually of short, limited, and predictable duration (less than 6 months). Every year in the United States, 155 million people experience at least one episode of acute pain; not surprisingly, pain management is big business.

Acute pain is a warning, an indicator to the individual that something is wrong—for example, chest pain may signal a heart attack. Acute pain motivates the individual to seek relief. Significant signs of pain include increased heart rate, elevated blood pressure, dilated pupils, sweaty palms, hyperventilation, hypomotility, escape behavior, and anxiety state.

Chronic Pain

Chronic pain is pain that persists beyond the expected time required for healing of an injury or the resolution of an acute problem. Pain is usually considered chronic when it lasts more than 3 months and has no foreseeable end except for very slow healing or death. According to Dr. Russell Portenoy, head of the American Pain Society, chronic pain affects 35 to 40 million Americans. In the United States, workers lose an estimated 700 million workdays annually because of chronic pain, at a cost of $60 billion.

Chronic pain often has an identifiable cause, but it is much more difficult to manage than acute pain. Chronic pain often goes untreated because some physicians do not believe their patients (see Foreman, 1999b). Chronic, intractable pain may be caused by cancer, neurological disorders, mental disorders, and terminal illness. Chronic pain serves no useful purpose, such as a warning to the individual of an impending heart attack. Signs and symptoms of chronic pain include decreased pain tolerance, irritability, appetite disturbance, constipation, psychomotor retardation, mental depression, sleep disturbance, insomnia, and chronic fatigue. Some individuals become preoccupied with their pain; their lives are characterized by drastic restrictions in the activities of daily living, extreme psychological stress, and social withdrawal. Substance dependence is common among people suffering from chronic pain. Chronic pain greatly compromises client functioning, lifestyle, and quality of life. Suicide offers relief for many people with chronic pain.

Treatment Collaboration

Assessment

The client's self-report is the single most reliable indicator of the existence and intensity of pain. Self-report measurement scales with numerical or adjective ratings are useful. For example, "On a scale of 1 to 10, with 1 being *no pain* and 10 being the *worst possible pain,* how would you rate your pain?" Or, "Using a continuum of *no pain, mild pain, moderate pain, severe pain, worst possible pain,* please describe your pain." The tools used must be appropriate for the client's developmental, physical, emotional, and cognitive status. The American Pain Society, an organization of physicians, nurses, psychologists, dentists, basic scientists, pharmacologists, therapists, and social workers, has published guidelines for pain management in its *Principles of Analgesic Use in the Treat-*

ment of Acute Pain and Cancer Pain (1999). This reference guide offers concise descriptions of appropriate drug selection, variations in dosages among patients, rapid treatment of breakthrough pain, and minimization of side effects. The society recommends that an interdisciplinary committee monitor and evaluate the implementation and effectiveness of pain treatment.

Pain Management

In order to manage the client's pain, clinicians strive to identify the underlying causes, remove the causes, and decrease the intensity of the pain. Clinicians employ any and all measures to divert or distract the client from the pain, alleviate fear and anxiety, eliminate discomfort, and promote adequate rest and sleep. Nonpharmacological measures include application of heat or cold, manipulation, and immobilization. Progressive relaxation, guided imagery, rhythmic breathing, biofeedback, hypnosis, acupressure, and acupuncture may also be used to treat pain. Some clients respond favorably to transcutaneous electrical nerve stimulation. Invasive procedures such as intraspinal analgesia may be required.

Pain management often includes medications appropriate for the severity and type of pain. Scientists have traced the paths of pain from the sites of diseases or injuries to the brain. Analgesics are drugs that decrease the intensity of pain or relieve the pain itself. Common OTC medications, especially nonsteroidal anti-inflammatory drugs such as acetylsalicylic acid (aspirin) and ibuprofen (Motrin, Advil), as well as acetaminophen (Tylenol), should be tried first.

Narcotics are the most effective analgesics; morphine works especially well because it taps into the body's own pain relief system. Opioid analgesics are routinely given to patients in acute, temporary pain. Patient-controlled analgesia with an intravenous pump or by mouth is an effective way to manage pain postoperatively or when pain is continuous. Commonly prescribed opioid analgesics include morphine (MSO_4, MS Contin), codeine (Paveral), meperidine (Demerol), methadone (Dolophine, Methadose), hydromorphone (Dilaudid), propoxyphene (Darvon), fentanyl (Sublimaze), and levophanol (Levo-Dromoran, Levorphan), as well as oxycodone (Oxycontin), oxycodone/acetaminophen (Percocet), and oxycodone/aspirin (Percodan).

Many clinicians and clients use narcotics sparingly in cases of chronic pain or with terminal illness. Physicians are cautious about prescribing narcotics as needed by clients for fear they will be prosecuted for dispensing too many controlled substances. Clients fear they may become addicted and dread the stigma associated with addiction. Yet studies with cancer patients have found that the incidence of addiction is very low. When patients are medicated appropriately with oral morphine or through use of a skin patch, the drug is absorbed slowly and does not provide the "rush" that addicts crave. Many AIDS patients with severe pain are undermedicated.

Children and Older Adults

Pain is real for infants and children. Clinicians need to assess and manage pain judiciously for these vulnerable populations. Pain is common in older adults due to the many physiological and psychological changes associated with normal aging, the presence of chronic health problems, and terminal illness. Unfortunately, many health care providers and clients alike consider pain a normal part of aging. Ethnocultural norms influence responses to pain in older adults, some of whom attempt to be very stoic in reporting pain or believe that their pain cannot be relieved. The frail elderly (usually adults over 85) are at particular risk for undertreatment of pain. Opioids are safe and effective when prescribed carefully and monitored closely. The elderly are more sensitive than younger adults to the analgesic effects of opioid drugs; they experience higher peak effect and longer duration of pain relief.

Addiction clinicians may be part of hospice teams. Hospice is a program of palliative care and supportive services that addresses the physical, spiritual, and social needs of terminally ill individuals and their families. Palliative care involves dealing with the pain, psychological distress, and fears of dying of patients and their families. Such care may be provided in clients' homes or at hospice centers.

Physical Disabilities

Approximately 49 million individuals in the United States have one or more physical or mental disabilities. This number is increasing as the population grows older and as medical advances allow people to live longer after serious injury. In addition to mental illness and mental retardation, disabilities include attention deficit disorders, blindness and visual impairments, deafness and hearing loss, learning disabilities, mobility limitations, spinal cord injuries, traumatic brain injuries, and other "hidden" disabilities. Yet substance abuse among the disabled is generally ignored by clinicians. Most often, when an individual has a physical disability and a substance abuse problem, the physical disability is viewed as primary and the substance abuse as secondary.

Studies indicate that 15-30% of people with disabilities may have an alcohol or other drug problem. Helwig and Holicky (1994) found that 68% of the clients they studied resumed drinking while undergoing rehabilitation, 49% of persons with spinal cord injury demonstrated alcoholic symptomatology, and 62% of vocational rehabilitation clients reported symptoms of alcohol abuse. In a sample of clients who were physically impaired, 53% reported alcohol or other drug problems as a "substantial or great" concern.

People with disabilities are at increased risk for substance abuse. The risks specific to this population include the following:

- *Health and medical risks:* health concerns; chronic pain; misuse of medications; lack of knowledge about substance use, abuse, and dependence and disability

- *Psychological risks:* enabling of substance use by family, friends, and health professionals; increased stress on family life; unhealthy coping with disability

- *Social risks:* peer-group differences, fewer social supports, poorly developed social skills, and isolation; negative societal attitudes toward the disabled; myths regarding the relationship between disability and substance abuse (e.g., "Disability causes substance abuse"; "All client problems are caused by disability")

- *Economic and employment risks:* underemployment or unemployment; financial concerns

- *Access:* lack of access to adequate treatment services, providers, and recourse

Treatment Collaboration

Treatment programs for individuals with physical disabilities and substance abuse problems are woefully lacking. Cross-training helps rehabilitation staff and substance abuse staff to identify and coordinate treatment for both problems. Indicators of substance abuse in persons with disabilities include frequent intoxication, intentional heavy use, belligerence, symptomatic drinking, and psychological dependence. Disabled individuals with related health, employment, financial, and legal problems are at risk for substance abuse. Isolation and other atypical social experiences, problems with family members or friends, and "handicapism" may indicate actual or potential substance abuse (see Ford & Moore, 1992).

Treatment for clients with disabilities and substance abuse includes individual, family, and education counseling. Mutual self-help groups for clients and families support treatment. Counseling with the client addresses grief and loss issues related to the disability and the addiction; major life changes; loss of privacy in areas of self-care; devaluing, enabling, or patronizing social attitudes; loss of control or self-determination; and the incredible stress that the presence of a disability can place on the family and support systems. Family counseling deals with grief, anger, loss, depression, guilt, and frustration. Family members and friends may find support through Al-Anon or through self-help groups for adult children of alcoholics/addicts or other groups. Education with the client emphasizes learning about use and abuse of prescription medication, including medications that contain alcohol. Educational counseling helps clients learn alternative ways to manage their disabilities and their many chronic effects without abusing substances (see Helwig & Holicky, 1994, pp. 229-230).

Americans With Disabilities Act

The Americans With Disabilities Act (ADA) extends civil rights protections to persons with disabilities. The act provides protection in five key areas: employment, transportation, public accommodations, state and local government operations, and telecommunications. Many people who are disabled receive Social Security Disability Insurance or supplemental security income.

The ADA recognizes drug addiction and alcoholism as disabilities. For employment purposes, alcoholics and addicts are not protected under the act if they are currently using alcohol or other drugs. Since March 1995, new requirements have applied to clients who are disabled because of an Axis I *DSM-IV* substance use diagnosis:

1. Their benefits must be paid to "representative payees."

2. They must undergo and make progress in appropriate treatment for their drug addiction and/or alcoholism, if it is available.

3. They can receive disability benefits on the basis of their drug addiction and/or alcoholism for no more than 36 months.

Prevention

Because the incidence of substance abuse by people with disabilities may be as high as 30%, compared with 10% for the general population, research and prevention specialists are studying the risk factors that contribute to this coexisting condition as well as the protective factors that deter disabled persons from abusing alcohol and other drugs. The Resource Center on Substance Abuse Prevention and Disability plays a leadership role in prevention programming, products, and services for people with disabilities as well as other individuals and organizations involved with the disabled community.

Summary

Addiction causes many medical problems, and medical conditions coexist with and contribute to addiction severity. Alcohol abuse causes liver disease and other gastrointestinal problems, cardiovascular problems, brain and other neurological problems, musculoskeletal problems, and respiratory problems, as well as problems with the endocrine, reproductive, and immune systems.

Compared with the general population, alcoholics have a higher incidence of many kinds of cancer. Smoking and drinking act together to increase the risk of many cancers. Drugs other than alcohol can have serious adverse effects, most often as the result of chronic or heavy use. Cardiovascular or respiratory depression followed by coma and death can and does happen. Substance abuse compromises the health of clients who are HIV-positive or have AIDS. Needle exchange programs and safe sex education can reduce the spread of HIV among substance users. Many people with pain, especially chronic pain, self-medicate with alcohol and other licit or illicit drugs. Unfortunately, individuals with severe, chronic pain are often undermedicated because they fear addiction and because many health professionals administer narcotics sparingly. Many nonpharmacological measures are effective for treating pain. Addiction clinicians may be part of pain management teams. People with physical disabilities, such as attention deficit disorders, blindness or other visual impairments, deafness or other hearing loss, learning disabilities, mobility limitations, spinal cord injuries, traumatic brain injuries, and other "hidden" disabilities, have a higher incidence of substance use disorders than is found in the population as a whole. Addiction clinicians collaborate with health and human service providers and professionals to treatment clients with coexisting medical conditions.

Related Skills Checklist

Practitioner skills related to the treatment collaboration needed for clients with medical conditions include the ability to do the following:

- Assess addiction clients for coexisting medical conditions.

- Factor medical conditions into addiction severity.

- Educate clients about the adverse effects of alcohol and other drugs on body organs and systems.

- Advise clients about the higher incidence of cancer in people who abuse alcohol.

- Develop relapse prevention plans for clients who are HIV-positive or have AIDS.

- Consult with pain management experts to help clients with acute and chronic pain.

- Collaborate with rehabilitation colleagues to manage clients with physical disabilities and addictive disorders.

- Collaborate with health and human service providers and professionals to prioritize and treat clients with coexisting medical conditions.

- Integrate medical conditions into relapse prevention plans.

Special Topics for Further Study

Evidence suggests that treating addiction improves overall client and family health. Addiction treatment reduces individual and family utilization of health insurance benefits for medical and psychiatric problems. Given these findings, why are public and private benefits for addiction treatment so limited? Why is there little or no funding for early intervention with addiction clients?

Addiction Practice 2000

Addiction practice 2000 demands outreach, case finding, and client consultation to medical treatment providers and professionals to better meet the needs of clients with coexisting medical concerns and complications. Links between addiction treatment and primary health care are critical (D'Aunno, 1997).

References

American Pain Society. (1999). *Principles of analgesic use in the treatment of acute pain and cancer pain* (4th ed.). Glenview, IL: Author.

American Psychiatric Association. (1994). *Diagnostic and statistical manual of mental disorders* (4th ed.). Washington, DC: Author.

American Society of Addiction Medicine. (1996). *Patient placement criteria for the treatment of substance-related disorders* (2nd ed.). Chevy Chase, MD: Author.

D'Aunno, T. (1997). Linking substance-abuse treatment and primary health care. In J. A. Egertson, D. M. Fox, & A. I. Leshner (Eds.), *Treating drug abusers effectively* (pp. 311-331). Malden, MA: Blackwell.

Ford, J. A., & Moore, D. (1992). Identifying substance abuse in persons with disabilities. In *SARDI Training Manual for Professionals* (Vol. 4, pp. 8-9). Dayton, OH: Wright State University, School of Medicine, SARDI Program.

Foreman, J. (1999a, November 15). Here's to your health: The benefits of drinking outweigh the risks, but only within limits. *Boston Globe,* pp. F1, F3.

Foreman, J. (1999b, March 22). Ow! Ow! Ow! *Boston Globe,* pp. E1, E4.

Helwig, A. A., & Holicky, R. (1994). Substance abuse in persons with disabilities: Treatment considerations. *Journal of Counseling and Development, 72,* 227-233.

Other Sources

Acute Pain Management Guideline Panel. (1991). *Acute pain management: Operative or medical procedures and trauma* (Clinical Practice Guideline No. 92-0032). Rockville, MD: Agency for Health Care Policy and Research, Public Health Service.

Center for Substance Abuse Prevention. (1993). *People with disabilities* (DHHS Publication No. SMA 94-2066). Rockville, MD: Author.

Center for Substance Abuse Treatment. (1995). *Treatment for HIV-infected alcohol and other drug abusers* (DHHS Publication No. SMA 95-3038). Rockville, MD: Author.

Center for Substance Abuse Treatment. (1995). *The tuberculosis epidemic: Legal and ethical issues for alcohol and other drug abuse treatment providers* (DHHS Publication No. SMA 95-3047). Rockville, MD: Author.

Fischl, M. A. (1998). *Clinician's manual on the management of HIV* (2nd ed.). Research Triangle Park, NC: Current Medicine.

Grinstead, S. F., & Gorski, T. T. (1997). *Addiction-free pain management.* Independence, MO: Herald House/Independence.

Heinemann, A. (Ed.). (1993). *Substance abuse and physical disability.* New York: Haworth.

Kelly, J. A. (1998). Group psychotherapy for persons with HIV and AIDS-related illnesses. *International Journal of Group Psychotherapy, 28,* 143-163.

Levin, F. R., & Kleber, H. D. (1995). Attention-deficit hyperactivity disorder and substance abuse: Relationships and implications for treatment. *Harvard Review of Psychiatry, 1,* 246-258.

McDaniel, S. H. (1995). *Counseling families with chronic illness.* Alexandria, VA: American Counseling Association.

Miller, D., & Blum, K. (1996). *Overload: Attention deficit disorders and the addictive brain.* Kansas City, MO: Andres & McMeel.

Resource Center on Substance Abuse Prevention and Disability. (1995). [Information package]. Washington, DC: Author.

Social Security Administration. (1995). *Disability based on drug addiction or alcoholism* (SSA Publication No. 05-10047). Washington, DC: Author.

Stimmel, B. (1997). *Pain and its relief without addiction: Clinical issues in the use of opioids and other analgesics.* New York: Haworth Medical.

U.S. Department of Health and Human Services. (1994). *Alcohol and health* (NIH Publication No. 94-3699). Alexandria, VA: Author.

Winiarski, M. G. (Ed.). (1997). *HIV mental health for the 21st century.* New York: New York University Press.

19

Dual Disorders

Objectives

- Recognize that individuals with addictive disorders are at increased risk for mental disorders.
- Recognize that individuals with mental disorders are at increased risk for addictive disorders.
- Be familiar with the prevalence of dual disorders.
- Assess the adverse psychological effects of client substance abuse.
- Assess clients with Axis I DSM-IV symptoms of mood disorders, anxiety disorders, and psychotic disorders.
- Assess clients with Axis II DSM-IV symptoms of personality disorders or mental retardation.
- Realize that complex client needs, separate treatment systems, and clinicians' differing treatment philosophies challenge treatment.
- Participate in sequential, parallel, or integrated treatment.
- Collaborate with health and human service providers and professionals to treat clients with dual disorders.

Outline

- **Dual Disorders**
- **Prevalence**
- **Adverse Psychological Effects of Drug Abuse**
  - CNS Depressants

Dual Disorders

Addictive disorders often coexist with other psychiatric disorders. In addition to an Axis I *DSM-IV* substance-related diagnosis, many clients have other Axis I diagnoses as well as Axis II psychopathology (American Psychiatric Association, 1994). Addictive disorders cause, exacerbate, mimic, or mask many psychiatric symptoms and disorders, and vice versa. Clients with addictive disorders are at increased risk for mental disorders, and individuals with mental disorders are at increased risk for addictive disorders. Compared to clients with a single Axis I diagnosis, clients with dual disorders experience more severe and chronic medical and social problems. They relapse with alcohol and other drugs more frequently, decompensate psychiatrically more often, have more crises, and progress more slowly in treatment. Failure to diagnose dual disorders accurately and to initiate responsive treatment constitutes irresponsible, incompetent care. Clients with dual disorders challenge addiction clinicians and the entire health and human services provider system.

Prevalence

More than half of the people who abuse alcohol or other drugs experience psychiatric symptoms significant enough to fulfill diagnostic criteria for a psychiatric disorder. About one-third of individuals who have psychiatric disorders also abuse alcohol and other drugs—about twice the rate of people without psychiatric disorders. Clinicians use assessment tools such as the Addiction Severity Index to screen for psychiatric problems as well as Dimension 3 of *ASAM PPC-2* to recognize emotional/behavioral conditions and complications associated with substance use (American Society of Addiction Medicine, 1996).

Clinicians need *DSM-IV* competence in order to assess and diagnose dual disorders. Addiction clinicians must be thoroughly familiar with Axis I *DSM-IV* criteria for mood disorders, anxiety disorders, and psychotic disorders, as well as Axis II diagnoses of personality disorders and mental retardation. Mental health practitioners must be knowledgeable about the signs and symptoms of substance-related disorders, including use, dependence, intoxication, and withdrawal.

Adverse Psychological Effects of Drug Abuse

Many drugs cause psychiatric symptoms when used or when withdrawn. (See Chapter 3 for a discussion of drug properties and desired effects as well as signs and symptoms of substance abuse, especially intoxication and withdrawal.)

CNS Depressants

Individuals who consume alcohol and other CNS depressants often demonstrate impaired judgment, mood lability, and impaired attention or memory. They may exhibit inappropriate sexual or aggressive behavior; dysfunctional social or occupational behavior is common. High anxiety usually accompanies alcohol withdrawal, and clients may experience visual, tactile, or auditory hallucinations or illusions.

CNS Stimulants

Chronic cocaine users often experience vivid, unpleasant dreams; paranoid delusions and hallucinations persist. Clients report high stress and demonstrate dysfunction related to neglect of health, family, and work. Chronic amphetamine use may lead to impulsive assaultive behavior; clients may experience paranoia, delusions, and hallucinations. Depression and fatigue, together with severe anxiety and panic, contribute to the use of alcohol and other CNS depressant drugs to induce sleep.

Hallucinogens

Adverse psychological effects associated with chronic or heavy use of hallucinogens include rapid mood swings with very labile behavior. Impulsive behavior with anxiety and panic is common. Clients may demonstrate bizarre, violent behavior with aggressive acts toward self and others. Clients may exhibit regressive behavior, such as public masturbation. Chronic use often mimics symptoms of schizophrenia, such as paranoia, visual delusions and hallucinations, flashbacks, mental turmoil, and a sense of distance and estrangement from one's environment. Loss of pain sensation, incoherent thoughts and speech, and depression may occur.

Marijuana

Marijuana use causes many adverse psychological effects: moodiness, irritability, anxiety, impaired short-term memory and comprehension, decreased attention span, and slowed speech and thought patterns. Motivation and cognition may be altered, making acquisition of new information difficult. Users may demonstrate distorted concepts of time and space, reduced ability to perform tasks requiring concentration, and impaired psychomotor coordination, such as that needed to drive a car or operate machinery.

Chronic users may experience lethargy and anhedonia. Marijuana can produce disorientation, disorganized thought processes, paranoia and fear of insanity, hallucinations, and psychosis.

Inhalants, Anabolic Steroids, Designer Drugs, and Herbs

Inhalant use may cause memory impairment as well as visual and auditory hallucinations. Anabolic steroid use can lead to persistent negative feelings, including extreme irritability, jealousy, and delusions. Steroid users often experience depression when they stop using and often continue to use to counteract this negative feeling. Wild mood swings, including manic symptoms, together with impaired judgment arising from feelings of invincibility can lead to violent, even homicidal episodes. The adverse psychological effects of designer drugs mimic the psychoactive effects of the drugs they imitate. Psychological effects from abuse of herbs are substance specific and highly individual.

Mood Disorders

Mood disorders are characterized by disturbances in physical, emotional, and behavioral responses ranging from excessive elation and agitation to extreme depression with serious potential for suicide. Mood disorders include depressive disorders and bipolar disorders as well as mood disturbances due to medical conditions or induced by substances. All psychoactive drugs alter normal mood; this is the major reason people use drugs, especially CNS depressants, CNS stimulants, and hallucinogens. Drug-induced mood changes can last from hours to days. Depression may last for months or years.

Depression is the most common mental health problem in the United States. It affects some 11 million Americans, yet an estimated two-thirds of the depressed people in this country go undiagnosed and untreated. Dysfunction of certain serotonergic neurons has been linked with depression. Levels of the neurotransmitters norepinephrine, serotonin, acetylcholine, and dopamine have been found to be deficient in depressed people and elevated in individuals experiencing manic episodes. The biological basis of depression helps us to understand the tendency of many people to "self-medicate" with substances as well as the usefulness of antidepressant medications.

Women who drink, heroin addicts and clients maintained on methadone, persons with HIV/AIDS, older individuals, and Native Americans commonly experience depression. General medical conditions (Axis III *DSM-IV*) and psychosocial and environmental factors (Axis IV *DSM-IV*) can precipitate depression.

Depression greatly reduces the functional capacities of clients (Axis V *DSM-IV*). Untreated depression impairs psychological, social, and occupational functioning; greatly compromises quality of life; and often triggers relapse.

Symptoms of depression include depressed mood, diminished interest or pleasure in daily activities, weight loss or gain, insomnia or hypersomnia, psychomotor agitation or retardation, fatigue, diminished sexual desire, feelings of worthlessness, excessive or inappropriate guilt, diminished ability to think or concentrate, and recurrent thoughts of death. Symptoms associated with manic episodes include inflated self-esteem, decreased need for sleep, excessive talking, flight of ideas, distractibility, psychomotor agitation, increase in goal-directed activities, and an excess of pleasurable activities with high potential for negative consequences. Clients in early recovery often live with guilt and shame that they associate with their addiction and fail to recognize as true clinical depression.

Assessment of depression requires a thorough health history and a chronology of the onset and development of both the psychiatric and substance use symptoms. The Beck Depression Inventory is a short screening tool that helps clinicians identify the presence and severity of depression. Clinicians utilize Axis I *DSM-IV* diagnostic criteria to differentiate between mood disorders and substance intoxication, withdrawal, or physiological dependence. Clinicians use data from Axes II, III, IV, and V, and questions about emotional/behavioral conditions and complications (Dimension 3 *ASAM PPC-2*), to determine addiction severity. Genograms can help clinicians identify family patterns of depression and substance use.

Treatment goals and intervention vary with acute and chronic conditions. Is the client a danger to self or others? If so, the client should be admitted to a secure psychiatric facility. Are there any medical conditions, trauma, or medications causing the mood disorder? Medical problems should be addressed immediately. When the client is safe, detoxification proceeds, followed by active treatment for both conditions. Depressive symptoms may dissipate following acute withdrawal. If symptoms persist during early full remission, it is more than likely that the client has a concomitant depressive disorder.

Increasingly, antidepressant medications are being prescribed early in recovery to help prevent relapse, enhance overall functioning, and improve quality of life. Tricyclic antidepressants include amitriptyline (Elavil), desipramine (Norpramin), doxepin (Sinequan), imipramine (Tofranil), and nortriptyline (Pamelor). Monoamine oxidase inhibitors include phenelzine (Nardil) and tranylcypromine (Parnate). Many dual-disorder clients respond well to selective serotonin reuptake inhibitors such as fluozetine (Prozac), fluvoxamine (Luvox), paroxetine (Paxil), and sertraline (Zoloft). Other antidepressants include bupropion (Wellbutrin), nefazodone (Serzone), venlafaxine (Effexor), and trazodone (Desyrel, Trazon). Lithium carboneate is effective for treating acute manic and hypomanic episodes. Carbamazepine (Tegretol) controls bipolar symptoms in people who do not respond to lithium.

Anxiety Disorders

Anxiety symptoms are the most common psychiatric symptoms seen in clients who abuse alcohol or other drugs. An estimated 60% of clients with substance abuse problems have coexisting anxiety disorders. Anxiety disorders include anxiety, panic, and phobias. Obsessive-compulsive disorder (OCD) and post-traumatic stress disorder (PTSD) are classified as anxiety disorders. Anxiety disorders are more prevalent in women than in men. Domestic violence causes acute stress and chronic anxiety for many clients. Clients with addictive disorders do not tolerate anxiety well. Anxiety drives individuals to seek immediate relief, often through self-medication with alcohol or licit or illicit drugs.

Anxiety

Anxiety may be caused by general medical conditions or situational factors, or it may be substance induced. Cocaine, amphetamines, and high doses of hallucinogens can cause anxiety and panic. Anxiety accompanies withdrawal from alcohol, sedative-hypnotic drugs, and opioids.

Anxiety develops abruptly and is characterized by intense discomfort or fear. Symptoms include palpitations, chest pain, hyperventilation, dizziness, sweating, trembling, shaking, nausea, choking, experience of unreality and depersonalization, and fear of losing control, going crazy, or dying. Anxiety, especially a panic attack, often mimics a heart attack, and clients may present at an emergency room. Once staff rule out a heart attack, they frequently discharge the client with benzodiazepine medication to manage symptoms. Yet clients with coexisting anxiety, depression, and substance abuse are at high risk to harm themselves or others. It is possible that clients who present with anxiety are drug seeking. Clinicians need to evaluate anxiety very carefully and inventory the many medical conditions, situational factors, and substances used that could cause anxiety and then plan treatment accordingly.

Treatment for clients with anxiety and substance abuse avoids almost all anxiolytic or antianxiety medications, especially the benzodiazepines, because they are highly addictive. Medications such as alprazolam (Xanax), chlordiazepoxide (Librium), clonazepam (Klonopin), clorazepate (Tranxene), diazepam (Valium), flunitrazepam (Rohypnol), flurazepam (Dalmane), lorazepam (Ativan), miazolam (Versed), oxazepam (Serax), temazepam (Restoril), and triazolam (Halcion) should not be used. In addition, barbiturates and antihistamines such as hydroxyzine (Vistaril) relieve anxiety but are addictive and should be avoided.

Intervention begins with calm, confident reassurance on the part of clinicians to the client that the uncomfortable, frightening symptoms will subside shortly. Clinicians help the client learn a variety of mind-body techniques to reduce anxiety, such as breathing exercises, progressive relaxation, visualization, meditation, and self-hypnosis. Cognitive-behavioral techniques such as thought stopping and self-talk are also useful. Stress management is an integral part of the client treatment plan. Long-term goals may address lifestyle modifications such as consuming less caffeine, chocolate, and sugar; stopping smoking; getting adequate rest and sleep; and exercising regularly. Certain medications, such as fluoxetine (Prozac) and sertaline (Zoloft), are useful for treating both anxiety and depression. Buspirone (BuSpar) relieves anxiety and does not appear to cause physical or psychological dependence or tolerance. The herb kava is being used increasingly to manage anxiety.

Obsessive-Compulsive Disorders

Obsessions are recurrent and persistent thoughts, impulses, or images that cause clients anxiety or distress; obsessions are intrusive, inappropriate, and extreme, in contrast to everyday concerns or worries about real-life problems. Clinicians should encourage clients to try to ignore or suppress obsessions or try to neutralize them with some other thoughts or actions. Clinicians should help clients to recognize that obsessions are products of their own minds.

Compulsions are repetitive behaviors or mental acts that an individual feels he or she must perform in response to an obsession. Compulsions often follow rigid rules, such as washing hands exactly nine times after going to the bathroom, clicking all locks exactly five times whenever one comes in or goes out, checking and rechecking the stove visually and then touching all burners lightly. Compulsions prevent or reduce stress, even though the persons performing these behaviors recognize that their compulsions, and the obsessions that stimulate them, are excessive or unreasonable. Obsessions and compulsions cause distress because they consume considerable time and interfere markedly with individuals' normal psychological, social, and occupational functioning.

Many addictive disorders exhibit elements of OCD, such as drug-seeking thoughts and behaviors, preoccupation with food or sex, compulsive shopping, and addiction to the Internet. Pathological gambling is characterized by persistent and recurrent problem gambling.

Domestic Violence

Domestic violence is a pattern of coercive control used by one person to exert power and control over another person within the context of an intimate relationship. This pattern is allowed to persist by societal and cultural attitudes, institutions, and laws that are inconsistent in naming such violence as wrong. There is a higher prevalence of substance abuse among both victims and perpetrators of domestic violence than is found in the population as a whole.

Incidents of domestic violence, or battering, follow a predictable cycle of three stages:

1. *Tension building:* criticism, yelling, swearing, using angry gestures, coercion, threats

2. *Violence:* actual physical and sexual attacks

3. *Seduction/honeymoon:* apologies, blaming, promises to change, gifts

Love, hope, and fear keep the cycle going and make it very difficult for the abused person to end the violent relationship. A woman loves her partner ("The relationship has its good points; it's not all bad"), hopes that he will change ("The relationship didn't begin like this"), and fears that her abuser's threats to kill her or her children will become a reality. The failure of clinicians to identify and address the presence of domestic violence in their clients' lives invites revictimization and triggers relapse.

Posttraumatic Stress Disorder

Addiction, domestic violence, and childhood trauma often coexist. Failure to recognize and treat this syndrome triggers relapse, invites revictimization, and activates PTSD. An estimated 70% of women who abuse alcohol and other drugs have been abused. Clinicians interview all clients in a sensitive, thorough manner to obtain information about emotional, physical, and sexual abuse in childhood as well as adulthood.

PTSD is a very serious anxiety syndrome that is caused by exposure to traumatic events. When people witness or experience actual or potentially serious injury or death, or threats to the integrity of self or others, these experiences may elicit intense fear, helplessness, and horror. Clients with PTSD experience stress because they persistently relive traumatic events through thoughts, perceptions, dreams, illusions, hallucinations, and flashbacks. Cues that symbolize the traumatic events trigger acute physiological reactions and severe psychological stress. Clients with PTSD avoid stimuli associated with the traumatic events. They numb themselves to avoid thoughts, feelings, and actions associated with the trauma. They dissociate and demonstrate a deadening of general responsiveness characterized by a restricted range of affect, detachment or estrangement from others, a diminished interest in the world around them, and a sense of foreboding about the future. Such clients have difficulty sleeping; they experience hypervigilance with an exaggerated startle response. They report difficulty concentrating, and irritability and angry outbursts may occur. There is marked impairment in these clients' psychological, social, and occupational areas of functioning.

In children, disorganized or agitated behavior may indicate PTSD. Children may reexperience traumatic events through repetitive play, in nonspecific frightening dreams, or through trauma-specific reenactment.

Clinicians recognize and assess addiction, domestic violence, and childhood trauma. They initiate crisis intervention, with safety as the treatment goal. Intervention may emphasize detoxification, shelter, or inpatient psychiatric care. Following stabilization, clinicians implement early treatment to address addiction. Abstinence is the most appropriate treatment goal. Treatment for battering emphasizes personal development of a sense of self and self-in-relation. Ongoing intervention to address childhood trauma promotes healing through trust, remembering and grieving, and re-creation and reconnection. Effective treatment prevents relapse, revictimization, and retraumatization and helps clients to continue their recovery, personal development, and healing. Thought field therapy has shown promise in work with clients diagnosed with PTSD (see especially the pioneering work of Callahan, 1996).

Psychotic Disorders

Psychotic disorders are characterized by disintegration of thought processes and inability to distinguish external reality from internal fantasy. Psychosis is a common feature of schizophrenia, schizophreniform disorder, schizoaffective disorder, delusional disorder, and brief psychotic disorder. Clients may have mood disorders with psychotic features; medical conditions, trauma, and substances can induce psychosis. It has been estimated that 1% of the general population has a schizophrenic disorder. Some 47% of schizophrenic clients have coexisting substance use disorders. Clients with diagnoses of schizophrenia and substance use are twice as likely as others to engage in violence or attempt suicide.

Acute schizophrenia is characterized by *positive symptoms* such as hallucinations, delusions, excitement, disorganized speech motor manifestations such as agitated behavior or catatonia, relatively minor thought disturbances, and positive response to neuroleptic medication. Chronic schizophrenia is characterized by *negative symptoms* such as anhedonia, apathy, flat affect, social isolation, socially deviant behavior, conspicuous thought disturbances, evidence of cerebral atrophy, and generally poor response to neuroleptics.

Initial Assessment and Acute Management

Initial assessment and acute management of clients with psychotic disorders address high-risk biological, psychological, and social conditions: life-threatening medical problems; violent and impulsive behaviors; and basic needs and life support. Biological or medical issues are usually stabilized in a hospital-based setting. High-risk psychological conditions with danger to self or others and other violent and impulsive behavior may require involuntary psychiatric hospitalization for stabilization of symptoms. High-risk social conditions such as homelessness, housing instability, victimization, and unmet basic needs require aggressive social crisis intervention.

Comprehensive Assessment and Long-Term Management

During comprehensive assessment, clinicians evaluate more fully the onset and development of the client's psychotic disorder and substance abuse. History of treatment, including medication noncompliance, and identification of patterns of decompensation, relapse, and crises are especially useful for planning long-term management. Substance use increases noncompliance, and noncompliance triggers substance use.

Clinicians, clients, clients' families, and society must embrace a proactive long-term care perspective. Long-term management goals emphasize (a) collaborative treatment with clients for both their psychiatric disorders and their substance use disorders and (b) a wide array of health and human services to address biopsychosocial issues. A skilled, dedicated treatment team provides dual-focused treatment. Staff engage clients in the treatment process, and family support and involvement are critical. Assertive case management assures personalized service planning. Medication, relapse prevention, and group therapy are primary interventions. Treatment plans address associated psychosocial needs, such as housing, health care, and vocational services.

Personality Disorders

Clients with an Axis I *DSM-IV* substance use diagnosis may also have an Axis II personality disorder diagnosis. Personality disorders are rigid, inflexible, and maladaptive behavior patterns that are severe enough to cause significant internal distress or impair psychological, social, and occupational functioning. Personality disorders are enduring and persistent styles of behavior and thought. Alcohol-induced and other drug-induced states can mimic personality disorders. The course and severity of personality disorders are worsened by substance use. People with personality disorders use substances for purposes that relate to their particular disorders. The presence of Axis I psychiatric problems such as mood, anxiety, and psychotic disorders greatly increases dual-disorder severity in clients with Axis II diagnoses.

Borderline Personality Disorder

Clients with borderline personality disorder exhibit a pattern of instability of mood, self-image, and interpersonal relationships. They display extremes of idealization and devaluation. Impulsive spending, unsafe sex, binge eating, or substance abuse may be self-damaging. Recurrent suicidal threats, gestures, and behaviors are common. Clients may experience paranoid ideation and dissociative symptoms.

People with borderline personality disorder tend to use substances in chaotic and unpredictable, polydrug ways. They often self-medicate with alcohol and other sedative-hypnotic drugs. They frequently abuse benzodiazepines that have been prescribed for anxiety; this often leads to relapse with their primary drugs of choice.

Assessment of borderline personality includes a history of previous treatment, including medication; information about sexual abuse, dissociative experiences, fugue states, and psychotic-like thinking; and assessment of suicidality. A neurological consultation may be helpful. Treatment addresses both the addiction and borderline personality. Dialectical behavioral therapy has shown promise in work with clients with borderline personality diagnoses (see especially the work of Linehan, 1993a, 1993b).

Antisocial Personality Disorder

Antisocial personality disorder involves a history of chronic antisocial behavior that begins before age 15 and continues into adulthood. Clients demonstrate a pattern of impulsive, irresponsible, rebellious, and reckless behavior, as evidenced by academic failure, poor job performance, and illegal activities. Clients experience dysphoria and demonstrate diminished capacity for intimacy. They do not tolerate boredom well and feel victimized. A high number of clients with substance abuse and antisocial personality disorder end up in the criminal justice system.

Many people with antisocial personality disorder use substances in a poly-drug pattern involving alcohol, marijuana, heroin, cocaine, and methamphet-amine. The illegal drug culture corresponds with their view of the world as fast paced and dramatic and supports their need for a heightened self-image. They may be involved in crime and other sensation-seeking, high-risk behaviors. Indi-viduals with extreme antisocial symptoms tend to prefer stimulants such as co-caine and amphetamines. Rapists with severe antisocial personality disorder of-ten use alcohol to justify their "conquests." People with less severe antisocial personality disorder tend to use heroin and alcohol to diminish feelings of de-pression and rage.

Assessment includes a thorough family history; information about whether or not the client set fires as a child, abused animals, or was a bed wetter; a thor-ough sexual history that includes questions about animals and objects; infor-mation about the client's ability to bond with others; questions about possible parasitic relationships; and history of head injuries, fighting, and being hit. Neuropsychological testing may be useful, and HIV testing is recommended. Assessment should consider criminal thinking patterns, such as rationalization and justification for maladaptive behaviors. Treatment addresses both the addic-tion and antisocial personality.

Narcissistic Personality Disorder

Narcissistic personality disorder involves a recurring cycle of grandiosity, lack of empathy, and hypersensitivity to evaluation by others. People with narcissis-tic personality disorder are often polydrug users with a preference for stimu-lants. Alcohol has disinhibiting effects on such individuals and may help to di-minish symptoms of anxiety and depression. Socially awkward or withdrawn people with narcissistic personality disorder may be heavy marijuana users. Some people with narcissistic personality disorder use anabolic steroids to build up a sense of physical perfection. When not using substances, people with nar-cissistic personality disorder may feel that others are hypercritical of them or do not sufficiently appreciate their work, talents, and generosity. During a crisis, in-dividuals with narcissistic personality disorder may become upset or severely depressed.

Assessment for narcissistic personality disorder includes information about the client's early childhood beliefs with regard to his or her looks, behaviors, and thoughts; a sexual history to identify the ability to be empathic with partners is useful. Treatment addresses both the addiction and narcissistic personality disorder.

Passive-Aggressive Personality Disorder

Passive-aggressive personality disorder involves a pervasive pattern of negative attitudes and passive resistance to demands for adequate performance in social and occupational situations. Such clients lack adaptive or assertive social skills, especially with regard to authority figures. They generally fail to connect their passive-resistant behavior with their feelings of resentfulness and hostility toward others.

Drug preferences among people with passive-aggressive personality disorder often vary according to gender. Women prefer alcohol and other sedative-hypnotic drugs to sedate negative feelings such as anxiety and depression. Although men may use these substances too, they usually choose stimulants to disinhibit aggressive or risk-taking behaviors. People with passive-aggressive personality disorder often complain of somatic problems such as migraines, muscle aches, and ulcers. They often seek over-the-counter (OTC) medications as well as cocaine and amphetamines to relieve somatic symptoms.

Assessment with narcissistic clients includes a thorough history and assessment of use and abuse of alcohol and other drugs; OTC drugs such as NyQuil, Dexatrim, Benadryl, laxatives, vitamins, minerals, and herbs; as well as antidepressant and antianxiety medications. Assessment of self-care and survival skills and identification of the client's typical passive-aggressive maneuvers or "scripts" are useful. Collateral information from other health and human service professionals aids in diagnosis and treatment planning. Treatment addresses both the addiction and passive-aggressive personality disorder.

Treatment for Personality Disorders

Treatment for clients with substance abuse and personality disorders requires special attention to issues such as violence to self or others, post-acute withdrawal syndrome, symptom substitution, and many somatic complaints. Transference and countertransference are common; treatment resistance is high. Treatment contracts emphasize clear boundaries and changing roles.

Initial treatment is a process of engagement, assessment, and crisis stabilization. Longer-term care includes individual counseling, group therapy, and mutual self-help groups, with a dynamic aftercare plan to prevent relapse and minimize psychiatric crises.

Clients with personality disorders will make excuses, minimize, manipulate, redefine, intellectualize, justify, lie, blame, power play, victim play, ingratiate, somatize, seek drugs, self-mutilate, and split staff. *Step Study Counseling With the Dual Disordered Client,* by Evans and Sullivan (1990), is a useful guide for working with these special clients. Clinicians need to be mindful of their own well-being, which can be compromised when they work with clients who have both substance abuse and personality disorders. Adequate supervision, peer support, and self-care help maintain and promote clinician well-being.

Mental Retardation

Mental retardation renders people especially vulnerable to substance abuse and other addictive behaviors. According to *DSM-IV,* mental retardation describes clients with significantly subaverage intellectual functioning, an IQ of approximately 70 or below, an onset before age 18, and concurrent deficits or impairments in adaptive functioning. *Adaptive functioning* refers to how effectively individuals manage activities of daily living, cope with common life demands, and meet the standards of personal independence expected of persons in their particular age group, sociocultural background, and community setting. The recognized levels of severity of mental retardation include mild (IQ of 50-55 to approximately 70), moderate (IQ of 35-40 to 50-55), severe (IQ of 20-25 to 35-40), and profound (IQ below 20-25).

Substance abuse and other addictive disorders greatly confound functioning for individuals with an Axis II *DSM-IV* diagnosis of mental retardation. People who are mildly retarded, and thus are more likely than moderately to profoundly retarded individuals to live in the community, have easy access to alcohol and other drugs. Misuse of prescription medications is common. Problem gambling is increasing: Daily lottery and scratcher tickets are available at corner convenience stores, and bingo is a social activity. Compulsive overeating is common. Clinicians assess and treat both the addiction and mental retardation.

Disorders of Childhood and Adolescence

Substance use compromises functioning and development for children and adolescents with learning disorders, motor skills disorders, communication disorders, pervasive developmental disorders, tic disorders, and attention-deficit and disruptive behavior disorders. (Note that if a general medical condition or sensory deficit is present with a disorder, clinicians code the disorder on Axis III.)

Attention deficit disorder is common in children and teens who abuse substances. The academic problems of such young people are legion. Conduct disorder and oppositional defiant disorder frequently accompany adolescent drug abuse, other addictive behaviors, and related self-destructive unsafe behaviors.

Clinicians with expertise in working with children assess and treat clients with both addiction and disorders of childhood and adolescence. (See Chapter 14 for a discussion of the impacts of addiction on children and adolescents.)

Treatment Challenges

Complex Client Needs

Dual-disorder clients exhibit many health and human services problems and require more resources than clients with one diagnosis. Dual-disorder clients have higher acute-care utilization rates with more frequent and longer hospitalizations. An estimated 60% of homeless people meet dual-disorder diagnostic criteria, and 50% of incarcerated men and women have histories of substance abuse plus other psychiatric problems. Dual-disorder clients and their families make up approximately 40% of the open caseloads of social and welfare agencies.

The medical system is the single largest point of contact for clients with dual disorders. Unfortunately, many practitioners, emergency room personnel, and hospital staff fail to diagnose dual disorders or to recognize drug-seeking behavior. Most often they treat the symptoms, not the client. Clients receive anti-anxiety or analgesic medications, the majority of which are addictive.

The services and systems required to treat clients with dual disorders effectively include the following:

- Substance abuse treatment services

- Mental health treatment services

- Acute medical care services

- Social and welfare services

- Housing services

- Homeless shelters

- Child and adult protective services

- General health services

- HIV/AIDS prevention and treatment services

- Educational services

- Vocational rehabilitation programs

- Criminal justice system services

Yet dual-disorder clients often can access these kinds of services only with great difficulty. And unfortunately, when dual clients fall through the cracks, there is a tendency for providers and other professionals to "blame the clients" for poor treatment outcomes.

Separate Treatment Systems

Specialization characterizes the health care delivery system in the United States, and this fragmentation limits access for clients with dual disorders. Until very recently, most substance abuse treatment centers had a single focus and were not prepared to treat clients with other psychiatric diagnoses. Most psychiatric facilities did not treat alcoholics or addicts. This rigid model of health care has been slow to change. Many states have departments of mental health, but responsibility for substance abuse treatment often resides in separate health departments or substance abuse divisions. Insurance companies split mental health and substance abuse benefits. Clients with two Axis I *DSM-IV* diagnoses may be treated in two different inpatient facilities or may see two different outpatient counselors. Treatment providers may receive more reimbursement if clinicians record the Axis I psychiatric disorder as primary, rather than the substance use diagnosis. It is easier for clients to receive disability benefits with an Axis I psychiatric diagnosis than with a substance use diagnosis.

Although treatment outcome studies have demonstrated the clinical and financial value of treating both problems, the development of dual-disorder services has been slow. Ignorance, bias, and professional turf battles have obstructed dual-disorder treatment. There has been a general lack of "ownership" and overall lack of willingness to take responsibility concerning dual-disorder clients among providers and other professionals. Whose problem? Not mine! Whose solution? Theirs! Other barriers to dual services include lack of cross-trained staff, insufficient resources, inflexible state licensing regulations, and complex accreditation standards. There are no federal mandates for a case management model for substance abuse clients. Dual-disorder clients and their families do not constitute a vocal consumer group, nor has there been any groundswell of public advocacy for this special population. Homelessness and incarceration serve as sites for services for many dual-disorder clients. The needs for well-informed policy, program incentives, and equitable reimbursement are great.

Differing Treatment Philosophies

The treatment philosophies of mental health practitioners and addiction treatment providers often differ. Mental health treatment utilizes a case management model and attempts to engage, link, and support clients along a continuum of community mental health services. Mental health treatment addresses past and developmental issues with clients. Psychopharmacological intervention is central to most mental health treatment regimens.

Addiction treatment emphasizes individual responsibility and focuses on the here and now. Abstinence is a common treatment goal. Addiction clinicians use medication very cautiously. Yet for clients with dual disorders, abstinence may be an unrealistic goal. Harm reduction with incremental steps to reduce the amount and frequency of drug use may be more appropriate. Psychotropic medication may augment treatment.

Pharmacological management can be therapeutic or detrimental for clients with dual disorders. Addiction may occur. Many psychiatric medications are psychoactive and cause rapid changes in mood, thought, and psychomotor performance. Because so many clients with psychiatric symptoms self-medicate with alcohol and other drugs, dual-disorder clients require very precise pharmacological management. Sound principles of medication management with dual-disorder clients dictate that clinicians (a) try a nonpharmacological approach, (b) add nonpsychoactive medication if necessary, and (c) add psychoactive medication *only* if the first two steps are unsuccessful.

Treatment Collaboration

Dual-disorder treatment may be sequential, parallel, or integrated.

Sequential Treatment

In sequential treatment, clients with dual disorders receive treatment by one system—addiction or mental health—followed by treatment by the other system. Specific problem severity determines which service comes first. For example, Keith M. acknowledges an alcohol, marijuana, and cocaine problem; he has a $40,000 gambling debt. He attempted to kill himself and was admitted to the surgical unit at Riverside Hospital with a self-inflicted gunshot wound. Consulting psychiatric staff met with Keith and he contracted for safety. Keith was discharged and referred to the Liberty Street Substance Abuse Treatment Center for day treatment. Ellen M. was diagnosed with alcohol dependence; she is also depressed. Ellen and her clinician have developed a treatment plan that identifies abstinence as goal number one. Ellen has agreed to wait and see if her depression "lifts" once she stops drinking. Her clinician assures her that if the depression persists during remission, she will refer Ellen to a psychiatrist for evaluation and possibly an antidepressant medication.

Parallel Treatment

Parallel treatment involves the client in both mental health and addiction treatment simultaneously. For example, Bill H. is sober 6 months; his depression is responding well to paroxetine (Paxil). Bill participates in a weekly early recovery group offered by Liberty Street Substance Abuse Treatment Center. He attends four A.A. meetings a week and sees a psychiatric clinical nurse specialist once a month at Tri-City Community Mental Health Center for medication monitoring.

Integrated Treatment

Integrated treatment for clients with dual disorders combines mental health and addiction services in one unified, comprehensive treatment program. Clinicians are cross-trained in both mental health and addiction disciplines. Staff and system accommodate clients with both problems. Dual Recovery Anonymous is a 12-step self-help program for clients with dual disorders. Carl F. is a 42-year-old single man with a diagnosis of paranoid schizophrenia. Carl lives with his mother in subsidized housing. Increasingly, he has become verbally abusive and destructive of their apartment. The local police apprehended Carl while he was drunk and brought him to the emergency room at Ashland City Hospital. Carl was admitted to one of the detoxification beds on the 24-bed dual-diagnosis treatment unit. Following a safe, medically managed detoxification, Carl was transferred to an active treatment bed on the unit. There counselors and nurses worked with him and others individually and in small groups to review their medication regimens and practice "drinking refusal behaviors." Carl attended a daily A.A. meeting on site with other clients. A social worker met with Carl and his mother to assess his recovery environment, and following 6 days of active inpatient treatment, Carl was discharged home. Carl returned to the unit 5 days a week to participate in the Progressive Partial Hospitalization Program; transportation was provided. When Carl achieved his treatment objectives, staff helped him enroll in Promises, a recovery club in the community. A visiting nurse with expertise in working with dual-disorder clients visits Carl weekly to help him comply with his medication regimen, support his abstinence from alcohol, talk with his mother, and assess his overall functioning.

Summary

More than half of the people who abuse substances experience psychiatric symptoms. One-third of individuals with mood disorders, anxiety disorders, psychotic disorders, personality disorders, and mental retardation also have substance abuse disorders. Clients with dual disorders experience more severe and chronic medical and social problems than do other substance abusers. They relapse with alcohol and other drugs more frequently, decompensate psychiatrically more often, have more crises, and progress more slowly in treatment. Access to appropriate treatment is difficult, and there is a tendency for providers and professionals to "blame the client" for poor treatment outcomes. Separate treatment systems, clinicians' differing treatment philosophies, and lack of treatment collaboration by providers and professionals compromise treatment for dual-disorder clients. Dual-disorder treatment may be sequential, parallel, or integrated.

Related Skills Checklist

Practitioner skills related to the treatment of dual-disorder clients include the ability to do the following:

- Assess addiction clients for symptoms of mood disorders, anxiety disorders, and psychotic disorders.
- Assess addiction clients for symptoms of personality disorders or mental retardation.
- Diagnose dual disorders.
- Develop comprehensive treatment plans to address the complex needs of clients with dual disorders.
- Educate clients about desired effects as well as adverse reactions and side effects of different antidepressant medications.
- Teach clients a variety of nonpharmacological ways to reduce anxiety.
- Provide treatment for clients with dual disorders in sequential, parallel, or integrated treatment settings.

Selected Topics for Further Study

In relation to clients with dual disorders, explore the concept of vulnerability. Discuss the concepts of addiction severity and treatment intensity. What treatment methods are especially effective with dual-disorder clients? Evaluate the clinical efficacy of new, emerging therapies such as thought field therapy and dialectical behavioral therapy. Examine blocks and barriers to effective treatment for clients with dual disorders, including separate treatment systems, clinicians' differing treatment philosophies, and lack of collaboration among providers and professionals.

Addiction Practice 2000

Addiction practice 2000 urges clinicians to press for integrated treatment for clients with dual disorders. Collaboration among colleagues must transcend different treatment philosophies. There is a great need for clinicians to articulate separate treatment programs to respond to client needs.

References

American Psychiatric Association. (1994). *Diagnostic and statistical manual of mental disorders* (4th ed.). Washington, DC: Author.

American Society of Addiction Medicine. (1996). *Patient placement criteria for the treatment of substance-related disorders* (2nd ed.). Chevy Chase, MD: Author.

Callahan, R. (1996). *Thought field therapy (TFT) and trauma: Treatment and theory.* Indian Wells, CA: Thought Field Training Center.

Evans, K., & Sullivan, J. M. (1990). *Step study counseling with the dual-disordered client.* Center City, MN: Hazelden.

Linehan, M. M. (1993a). *Cognitive-behavioral treatment of borderline personality disorder.* New York: Guilford.

Linehan, M. M. (1993b). *Skills training manual for treating borderline personality disorder.* New York: Guilford.

Other Sources

Bass, E., & Davis, L. (1986). *The courage to heal: A guide for women survivors of child sexual abuse.* New York: Harper & Row.

Berkowitz, L. (1993). *Aggression: Its causes, consequences, and control.* New York: McGraw-Hill.

Brady, K. T., & Roberts, J. M. (1995). The pharmacotherapy of dual diagnosis. *Psychiatric Annals, 26,* 344-352.

Brems, C., & Johnson, M. E. (1997). Clinical implications of the co-occurrence of substance use and other psychiatric disorders. *Professional Psychology Research and Practice, 28,* 437-447.

Center for Substance Abuse Prevention. (1995). *Coordination of alcohol, drug abuse, and mental health services* (DHHS Publication No. SMA 95-3069). Rockville, MD: Author.

Center for Substance Abuse Treatment. (1993). *Assessment and treatment of patients with coexisting mental illness and alcohol and other drug abuse* (DHHS Publication No. SMA 94-2078). Rockville, MD: Author.

Center for Substance Abuse Treatment. (1996). *Approaches in the treatment of adolescents with emotional and substance abuse problems* (DHHS Publication No. SMA 96-3093). Rockville, MD: Author.

Daley, D. C., Moss, H. B., & Campbell, F. (1993). *Dual disorders: Counseling clients with chemical dependency and mental illness* (2nd ed.). Center City, MN: Hazelden.

Davidson, K. M., & Ritson, E. B. (1993). The relationship between alcohol dependence and depression. *Alcohol and Alcoholism, 28,* 147-155.

Evans, K., & Sullivan, J. M. (1991). *Understanding depression and addiction.* Center City, MN: Hazelden.

Evans, K., & Sullivan, J. M. (1995). *Treating addicted survivors of trauma.* New York: Guilford.

Fields, R., & Vandenbelt, R. (1992). *Understanding personality problems and addiction.* Center City, MN: Hazelden.

Glover, N. M., Janikowski, T. P., & Benshoff, J. M. (1995). The incidence of incest histories among clients receiving substance abuse treatment. *Journal of Counseling and Development, 73,* 475-476,

Gold, M. S., & Slaby, A. E. (1993). *Dual diagnosis in substance abuse.* New York: Marcel Dekker.

Hamilton, T., & Samples, P. (1995). *The twelve steps and dual disorders.* Center City, MN: Hazelden.

Hazelden Foundation. (1993). *The dual disorders recovery book: A twelve step program for those of us with addiction and an emotional or psychiatric illness.* Center City, MN: Hazelden.

Jody, N. (1992). *Understanding bipolar disorder and addiction.* Center City, MN: Hazelden.

Khantzian, R. J. (1997). The self-medication hypothesis of addictive disorders. In D. L. Yalisove (Ed.), *Essential papers on addiction.* New York: New York University Press.

Lew, M. (1988). *Victims no longer: Men recovering from incest and other sexual child abuse.* New York: Harper & Row.

Manley, A. (1992). Comorbidity of mental and addictive disorders. *Journal of Health Care for the Poor and Underserved, 3,* 60-72.

Marecek, M. (1999). *Breaking free from partner abuse: Voices of battered women caught in the cycle of domestic violence.* Buena Park, CA: Morning Glory.

Miller, K. (1998). *Thought field therapy: Treatment of post traumatic stress disorder with individuals and families.* Unpublished master's thesis, Cambridge College.

Miller, N. S. (Ed.). (1994). *Treating coexisting psychiatric and addictive disorders.* Center City, MN: Hazelden.

Miller, N. S., Klamen, D., Hoffmann, N. G., & Flaherty, J. A. (1996). Prevalence of depression and alcohol and other drug dependence in addictions treatment populations. *Journal of Psychoactive Drugs, 28,* 111-124.

Minkoff, K., & Drake, R. E. (1991). *Dual diagnosis of major mental illness and substance disorder.* San Francisco: Jossey-Bass.

National Institute on Drug Abuse. (1994). *Mental health assessment and diagnosis of substance abusers* (NIH Publication No. 94-3846). Rockville, MD: Author.

National Institute on Drug Abuse. (1997). *Treatment of drug-dependent individuals with comorbid mental disorders* (NIH Publication No. 97-4172). Rockville, MD: Author.

Ortman, D. C. (1997). *The dually diagnosed: A therapist's guide to helping the substance abusing psychologically disturbed patient.* Northvale, NJ: Jason Aronson.

Peace at Home. (1995). *Domestic violence: The facts.* Boston: Author.

Polcin, D. L. (1992). Issues in the treatment of dual diagnosis clients who have chronic mental illness. *Professional Psychology Research and Practice, 23,* 30-37.

Ries, R. (1994). *Assessment and treatment of patients with coexisting mental illness and alcohol and other drug abuse.* Rockville, MD: Center for Substance Abuse Treatment.

Ryglewicz, H., & Pepper, B. (1996). *Lives at risk: Understanding and treating young people with dual disorders.* New York: Free Press.

Santoro, J., & Cohen, R. J. (1997). *The angry heart: Overcoming borderline and addictive disorders.* Oakland, CA: New Harbinger.

Sheehan, M. F. (1993). Dual diagnosis. *Psychiatric Quarterly, 64,* 107-137.

Statman, J. B. (1995). *The battered woman's survival guide: Breaking the cycle.* Dallas, TX: Taylor.

Substance Abuse and Mental Health Services Administration. (1995). *Substance abuse and mental health statistics sourcebook* (DHHS Publication No. SMA 95-3064). Washington, DC: Author.

Tracy, J. I., Josiassen, R. C., & Black, A. S. (1995). Neuropsychology of dual diagnosis: Understanding the combined effects of schizophrenia and substance use disorders. *Clinical Psychology Review, 15,* 67-97.

Turnbull, J. M., & Roszell, D. K. (1993). Dual diagnosis. *Primary Care, 20,* 181-190.

Weiss, R. D., & Mirsin, S. M. (1997). Substance abuse as an attempt at self-medication. In D. L. Yalisove (Ed.), *Essential papers on addiction.* New York: New York University Press.

Winter, A. C. (1990). *When self-help isn't enough: Overcoming addiction and psychiatric disorders.* Center City, MN: Hazelden.

20

Social Problems

Objectives

- Recognize the influence of social problems on the development, treatment, and outcomes of addictive disorders.
- Address the problems caused by worker alcohol and drug use.
- Acknowledge the relationships among education, unemployment, and addiction.
- Recognize the impacts that poverty and excess can have on addiction.
- Identify the impacts of housing problems such as homelessness and unsafe neighborhoods on addiction.
- Acknowledge the high correlation between addictive disorders and legal problems.
- Consider social problems when developing treatment goals and aftercare plans with clients.
- Identify actual and potential social strengths in the client recovery environment.
- Collaborate with other health and human service providers and professionals to treat clients and families who are adversely affected by social problems.
- Advocate for prevention of social problems that contribute to addiction.
- Accept the challenge of addiction practice 2000.

Outline

- **Assessment**
- **Occupational Problems**
  - Worker Alcohol and Drug Use
  - Employee Assistance Programs
    - Origins and Development
    - Intervention
- **Education and Economic Problems**
  - Education
  - Unemployment
  - Poverty
  - Excess
- **Housing Problems**
  - Homelessness
  - Unsafe Neighborhoods
  - Rural America
- **Legal Problems**
  - Addiction and Crime
  - Drunk Drinking
  - Treatment and the Criminal Justice System
    - Treatment Planning
    - Substance Abuse Treatment With Intermediate Sanctions
    - Drug Courts
    - Relapse Prevention
- **Summary**
- **Related Skills Checklist**
- **Special Topics for Further Study**
- **Addiction Practice 2000**
- **Epilogue**

Assessment

Because social problems contribute to the development of addictive disorders, influence treatment planning, and have strong impacts on recovery, addiction clinicians must collect data to assess their weight. If clinicians use the Addiction Severity Index (ASI) to assess clients, questions about employment/support status and legal status can help them gather information about social problems:

Employment/Support Status: The client is asked about years of education and training, sources of income, number of dependents, and work history. The client also is asked whether he or she has a current driver's license and owns or has access to a car. The client is asked to use the rating scale to rate the level of concern over employment problems, and whether it is important to get counseling for these problems now. These questions identify the client's resources for developing a drug-free life and deficiencies (such as a lack of marketable skills) that could contribute to relapse.

Legal Status: The client is asked about arrests, charges, and convictions for a variety of offenses ranging from shoplifting to homicide. There are also questions about public intoxication and motor vehicle violations related to drug use (for example, driving while intoxicated, reckless driving, or driving without a license). The client uses the rating scale to indicate the level of concern over legal problems and whether counseling or referral is desired. (National Institute on Drug Abuse, 1995, pp. 3-4)

In Axis IV *DSM-IV,* clinicians report psychosocial problems that may affect treatment and outcomes of various addictive disorders (American Psychiatric Association, 1994). In addition, Axis IV includes problems relating to the context or environment in which the addictive disorder has developed. Major categories of environmental problems include educational, occupational, economic, housing, and legal problems.

Dimension 6 of *ASAM PPC-2* addresses the "recovery environment":

Are there any dangerous family, significant others, living or school/working situations threatening treatment engagement and success? Does the patient have supportive friendship, financial or educational/vocational resources to improve the likelihood of successful treatment? Are there legal, vocational, social service agency or criminal justice mandates that may enhance motivation for engagement into treatment? (American Society of Addiction Medicine, 1996, p. 3)

Occupational Problems

Worker Alcohol and Drug Use

As of 1996, according to the U.S. Department of Labor (1996), 75% of substance users in the United States were employed. Workplace alcohol-, tobacco-, and other drug-related problems cost companies more than $100 billion each year in decreased productivity and increased health care costs. The costs to the impaired employees and their families far exceed this dollar figure.

Studies show that employees who abuse alcohol and other drugs are less productive than other workers, use three times as many sick days, are more likely to injure themselves or someone else, and are five times more likely to file worker's compensation claims. Family members of substance-abusing employees experience more health problems and have higher-than-average health care claims.

However, as problematic as these findings are is the fact that 70% of substance abusers ages 18 to 49 work full-time in a variety of occupations. According to a recent study conducted by the Substance Abuse and Mental Health Services Administration (SAMHSA, 1999a), 6.3 million full-time workers are illicit drug users and 6.2 million are heavy alcohol users; 1.6 million are both heavy alcohol and illicit drug users. The overall rate of illicit drug use among full-time employees fell from 17.5% in 1985 to a low point of 7.4% in 1992, and then remained steady at 7.7% through 1997.

The types of drugs that workers reported using in the SAMHSA study included the following:

- Marijuana (81.1%)

- Cocaine (11.9%)

- Prescription stimulants (18.5%)

- Hallucinogens, such as LSD and PCP (10.5%)

- Heroin (2.7%)

- Inhalants (4.1%)

- Marijuana only (62.3%)

The rates of illicit drug and heavy alcohol use are highest among 18- to 25-year-olds, males, Whites, and those with less than a high school education. Whereas 8% of full-time workers ages 18 to 49 in the SAMHSA sample reported using illicit drugs, employees in four of the occupational categories studied reported current illicit drug use at or above 10%. These included food preparation workers, waiters, waitresses, and bartenders (19%); construction workers (14%); other services workers (13%); and transportation and material moving workers (10%). Whereas nearly 8% of all full-time workers ages 18 to 49 in the sample reported heavy alcohol use, rates were significantly higher among food preparation workers, waiters, and bartenders (15%); handlers, helpers, and laborers (14%); and construction workers (12%).

Addiction practitioners need to understand the patterns of alcohol and other drug use among workers in the United States to identify high-risk occupations and industries. These work sites can then be targeted by prevention programs and practitioners can tailor treatment efforts for those employees most affected by illicit drug and heavy alcohol use.

During the 1990s, the practice of employee drug testing increased, especially in the transportation, utilities and sanitary, grocery, and public order industries. Several occupations and related industries with high rates of illicit use rarely participate in drug testing; these include food preparation and servers as well as entertainers and writers. Small businesses are particularly vulnerable to problems with substance abuse, in part because alcohol and drug users often seek work at such companies, reasoning that the likelihood of drug testing is slim.

It is worth noting that when indigent clients in Washington State completed an alcohol and drug treatment program, they worked more and earned significantly more. Length of treatment was related to employment outcomes for clients in both intensive inpatient and outpatient treatment, but the magnitude of effect was greater for inpatient clients. The benefits of treatment in terms of enhanced earnings offset the costs of treatment (SAMHSA, 1997).

Employee Assistance Programs

Origins and Development

Employee assistance programs (EAPs) began in the mid-1920s at the Western Electric Company, the manufacturing division of Bell Telephone. The company brought social workers into the firm's plant in Hawthorne, Illinois, in an attempt to increase production. Each time the social workers changed the work environment, there was a corresponding increase in productivity. For instance, productivity increased when the lighting in the work area was enhanced, but productivity also increased when the lighting was decreased and then again when it was returned to normal. When the social workers questioned the employees about the changes in their performance, it became clear that the workers had responded each time to the feeling that someone was paying attention to them and to their work. The Bell System then began a modest effort of involving workers in the process of defining and changing their work environment.

In the late 1940s, New England Telephone combined this employee-employer joint decision-making process with its Occupational Alcoholism Program (OAP). By the late 1940s, there were many sober alcoholics within the workforce. (Note that Alcoholics Anonymous had been founded in 1935, the "Big Book" was published in 1939, and in 1941 a *Saturday Evening Post* article on Alcoholics Anonymous by Jack Alexander had propelled A.A. into the mainstream of American life.) In the workplace, medical departments and personnel departments began to utilize recovering workers in an informal way to assist other employees who had drinking problems. Throughout the 1950s and the 1960s, EAPs flourished in large companies. In 1964, New England Telephone hired two recovering individuals for full-time management positions in its OAP. By now, some employees had begun illicit drug use.

In the late 1960s, the federal government appointed a commission to study the problems of alcohol and drug use in the workplace. This initiative led to the formation of the Association of Labor and Management Administrators and Consultants on Alcoholism (ALMACA). By 1975, ALMACA had broadened its mission to include drug abuse as well as other emotional and mental health problems. In the mid-1980s, ALMACA became the Employee Assistance Professionals Association. Separate member assistance programs (MAPs) developed. Unfortunately, what had started as a venture of equal partnership between labor and management now had become two separate kinds of organizations. Together, both EAPs and MAPs emphasize prevention, early intervention, treatment when necessary, and support for workforce reentry.

Numerous studies have demonstrated the value of EAPs, which are cost-effective for business and industry and contribute to the improved health and well-being of employees and their families. Sadly, with the advent of managed care, many industries have contracted outside individual companies for EAP services. What was once a very personal on-site service between employees and staff now often takes the form of a series of questions and answers over a toll-free phone line on a touch-tone telephone.

The SAMHSA (1999a) study mentioned above found that workplace policies and programs make a difference. Some 44% of all illicit drug-using employees work for small establishments with fewer than 25 employees, 43% work for medium-sized establishments (25 to 499 employees), and 13% work for large establishments (500 or more employees). Employees in occupations with the lowest rates of drug use (protective services, mining and electronic equipment assemblers, and administrative support) are also among the employees in the four occupations with the highest rates of drug information and policies in the workplace. Employees in occupations with high rates of drug use (food preparation, bartenders, and construction) have the lowest amounts of drug information and policies in the workplace.

Intervention

Addiction clinicians, especially social workers and nurses, are often employed by business and industry and work directly with employees and their families to prevent and treat addiction problems. As the U.S. Department of Labor states in a 1996 publication:

> If substance abuse could be contributing to an employee's deteriorating performance, ignoring the situation won't help. It may be the employee who has an alcohol or drug problem or it may be a family member. No matter who has a problem, it will likely only get worse and have costly—and possibly disastrous—consequences for everyone unless some action is taken.

Clinical assessment and diagnosis of an addictive disorder is *not* the job of most work-site supervisors. However, addiction clinicians often train supervisors to recognize employee performance and behavior that could indicate addiction problems, such as the following:

- Performance
  - Inconsistent work quality
  - Poor concentration
  - Lowered productivity
  - Increased absenteeism
  - Unexplained disappearances from the job site
  - Carelessness, mistakes
  - Errors in judgment
  - Needless risk taking
  - Disregard for safety
  - Extended lunch periods and early departure
- Behavior
  - Frequent financial problems
  - Avoidance of friends and colleagues
  - Blaming others for own problems and shortcomings
  - Complaints about problems at home
  - Deterioration in personal appearance
  - Complaints and excuses of vaguely defined illnesses

Whenever employees' performance begins to deteriorate or their behavior deviates from acceptable work protocols, supervisors have the right and responsibility to intervene. The following sound principles guide effective intervention by supervisors:

1. Maintain control of the conversation.
   Stick to the facts as they affect work performance.
   Have all supporting documents and records available.
   Do not discuss substance use, gambling, or other addictions.

2. Be clear and firm.
   Stick to company policy concerning performance.
   Explain company policy related to substance, use, gambling, or other unacceptable addictive behaviors.
   Explain the consequences if performance expectations are not met.

3. Be supportive but avoid emotional involvement.

Offer help in resolving performance problems.

Identify resources for help in addressing personal problems.

Education and Economic Problems

Limited education, unemployment, and poverty are socioeconomic factors that contribute to substance abuse, affect access to treatment, and determine treatment outcomes. Education reflects personal achievement and contributes to self-worth. Educational level is directly related to household income. Money is a critical variable for clients with pathological gambling or compulsive shopping problems. Axis IV *DSM-IV* identifies education, inadequate finances, insufficient welfare support, and extreme poverty as socioeconomic problems that affect diagnosis, treatment, and prognosis. Excess characterizes addictive behaviors, and economic excess and privilege may increase risk for addiction.

Education

Axis IV *DSM-IV* lists education problems as one category of psychosocial and environmental problems that affect diagnosis, treatment, and prognosis of addiction and other mental problems. This category includes illiteracy, academic problems, discord with teacher or classmates, and inadequate school environment. Education is best viewed as a cluster of attributes associated with risk and resilience, and not as a single property. People with limited education can get clean and sober, and individuals with Harvard Ph.D.s may continue to abuse substances or engage in other self-destructive addictive behaviors.

Academic problems, including failure, truancy, and school dropout, frequently accompany teen substance abuse. Education problems often cue teachers and parents that students may be using drugs. Students with learning problems have higher rates of substance use. Learning about addiction, relapse, and recovery is an important ingredient of addiction treatment. Clients can participate more fully in their treatment if they are able to read and write. Education is fundamental for successful employment and career advancement. As noted above, education reflects personal achievement and contributes to a sense of self-worth. Educational level correlates with household income, and limited education is associated with unemployment, criminality, and homelessness.

Unemployment

Studies have shown that unemployed individuals consistently have the highest rates of illicit drug and heavy alcohol use when compared with part-time and full-time employees. Unemployed individuals thus constitute a population at high risk for substance use problems. Problem gambling is also high among unemployed people. SAMHSA (1999b) has examined the prevalence of alcohol and illicit drug use/dependence and other mental health concerns among the working-age U.S. population. That study's findings include the following (SAMHSA, 1999b, pp. 1-2):

■ Education and income

In the study sample, the unemployed and those not in the labor force were generally less educated (more than one-fourth had not graduated from high school, compared with 12% of full-time workers and 14% of part-time workers), had lower annual household incomes (more than 40% had annual family incomes of less than $20,000, compared with 14% of full-time workers and 29% of part-time workers), and were more likely to receive government assistance (e.g., 26% of the unemployed and 18% of those not in the labor force received food stamps, compared with 4% of full-time workers and 9% of part-time workers).

■ Substance use

The unemployed were the most likely to report lifetime, past-year, and past-month illicit drug use. For example, 13% of the unemployed reported past-year illicit drug use, whereas 7% of part-time workers and 5% of full-time workers and those not in the labor force reported illicit drug use in the past year.

Full-time workers were more likely than part-time workers, the unemployed, and those not in the labor force to report lifetime, past-year, and past-month alcohol use.

Among current alcohol users, however, the unemployed generally consumed larger quantities of alcohol than those employed full-time. Among past-month alcohol users, the unemployed reported higher rates of binge drinking (46%) and heavy drinking (19%) than full-time workers (35% and 12%, respectively), part-time workers (29% and 11%), and those not in the labor force (30% and 12%). Rates of binge drinking and heavy drinking were high among two subsets of the labor force population—nonworking students (50% and 22%, respectively) and the disabled (40% and 26%).

■ Substance dependence

Consistent with the finding of a higher prevalence of illicit drug use for the unemployed, the prevalence of illicit drug dependence was also higher for the unemployed (5%) than for full-time workers (1%), part-time workers (2%), and those not in the labor force (2%).

Consistent with the finding of a higher prevalence of binge and heavy drinking among the unemployed, the unemployed had a higher prevalence of alcohol dependence (8%) than did full-time workers (5%), part-time workers (5%), and those not in the labor force (3%).

In all employment categories, there was a higher prevalence of substance dependence (34% with alcohol dependence, and 9% with illicit drug dependence) among
those who reported past-month heavy drinking.

- Other mental health concerns

  The unemployed and those not in the labor force were more likely than those employed full-time or part-time to report mental health symptoms consistent with
  probable diagnoses for a major depressive episode, a general anxiety disorder, ag-
  oraphobia, and panic attacks.

  In particular, the unemployed and those not in the labor force were substantially
  more likely to report a major depressive episode in the past year (11% in each
  group) than full-time workers (6%) and part-time workers (8%). Among those not
  in the labor force, this syndrome was particularly common for the disabled (22%).

Poverty

Poverty rarely exists as a single, random variable. For example, clients at increased risk for addictive disorders include poor street youth, low-income pregnant women, low-income urban African American males, and poor elderly. As
discussed above, unemployed individuals and part-time workers have higher
rates of drug use and heavy drinking than do persons working full-time. Illicit
drug use is higher among recipients of aid to families with dependent children
(AFDC) than among the working-age population as a whole; overall, drinking is
lower among AFDC recipients, but "high" on the days they drink. According to
the SAMHSA (1999b, p. 2) study report:

- There was a higher prevalence of illicit drug use, excluding marijuana use, among
  AFDC recipients ages 18 to 64 (28% lifetime, 9% past year, 5% past month) than in
  the overall working-age population (23% lifetime, 6% past year, 3% past month).

- By contrast, AFDC recipients, compared with the overall working-age population,
  did not have a higher prevalence of past-month alcohol use (54% versus 64% for
  full-time workers, 59% versus 59% for part-time workers, 53% versus 60% for the
  unemployed, and 40% versus 43% for those not in the labor force).

- AFDC recipients not in the labor force were more likely than non-AFDC recipients not in the labor force to report having two or more drinks per day on the days
  they drank (70% versus 59%).

- There was a high prevalence of substance dependence (8%) and other mental
  health diagnoses (24%) among AFDC recipients compared with the overall working-age population (5% and 11%, respectively).

Dire poverty in the home may prompt youth to work the streets to support
themselves or supplement family income. Street youth often survive by dealing

drugs, selling sex, or committing crimes. Alcohol and drug use characterizes this high-risk lifestyle. Poverty, low educational achievement, family instability, homelessness, and lack of prenatal care increase the risk for substance abuse by pregnant women and the high likelihood of damage to the developing fetus and newborn.

Black and Ricardo (1994) examined relationships among drug use, drug trafficking, and weapon carrying among low-income, urban African American boys in early adolescence. Boys who were involved in drug activities or weapon carrying exhibited more school failure and expulsion; effective communication with parents was limited. These boys reported high rates of drug involvement by their family members, friends, and community. Personal values regarding economics predicted drug trafficking. Psychological and interpersonal factors were better predictors of individual risk activity than were community or family variables. Black and Ricardo recommend community-level interventions to alter the myth that drug involvement and weapon carrying are normative; they suggest the promotion of images that are less materialistic and more supportive of education and future-oriented activities.

In a similar study, Whitehead, Peterson, and Kaljee (1994) examined socioeconomic deprivation, urban drug trafficking, low income, and African American male gender identity. These authors identify two core constructs of masculine identity in the United States: the capacity to support one's family and the ability to achieve a sense of status, respect, and reputation among peers. They note that the historical and worsening inequities in access to economic resources and power by African American males have significantly reduced the opportunities of members of this group for economic success through social and legal enterprises. The pursuit of nonmainstream activities, such as drug trafficking, offers opportunities for economic advancement and for establishing a power base to those who have been denied access to the mainstream.

Most older people live on fixed incomes that are considerably smaller than their previous employment earnings. Aging, chronic illness, and personal losses, together with limited income, increase the risks that older people may cope with their lot in life by abusing substances or engaging in addictive behaviors. Over-the-counter drugs and bingo become the friends of many poor elderly people.

Excess

The lives of the rich and famous often reflect overindulgence and excess, which are defining characteristics of addiction: drinking until drunk, polysubstance abuse, binge eating, pathological gambling, compulsive shopping, many sexual addictions. Clients meeting diagnostic criteria for substance dependence usually demonstrate tolerance—that is, a need for markedly increased amounts of alcohol or other drugs to achieve the desired effects or a markedly diminished effect with continued use of the same amounts of alcohol or other drugs. Clients consume more alcohol, use more drugs, engage in more addictive behaviors or for a longer time than intended. And there is never enough "wine, women, and song."

Excess has been glamorized in the popular media, especially in films and music videos. Many teens and young adults attempt to mimic the "sex, drugs, and rock and roll" lifestyles they see on MTV, even though it is widely known that many successful authors, film and television stars, and recording artists have died prematurely from alcohol abuse or overdose, eating disorders, or related suicide; the lengthy list includes John Cheever, F. Scott Fitzgerald, Ernest Hemingway, John Belushi, Chris Farley, Judy Garland, Marilyn Monroe, River Phoenix, Karen Carpenter, Kurt Cobain, Jerry Garcia, Jimi Hendrix, Janis Joplin, Jim Morrison, and Elvis Presley.

Housing Problems

Rates of alcohol and other drug use are higher among homeless people than among the general population. People with histories of chronic homelessness are more likely to have coexisting substance abuse problems than are the short-term homeless. Who are the homeless? The members of this hidden population, who would benefit greatly from treatment and prevention, by definition have no fixed addresses. Thus it is difficult, if not impossible, for epidemiologists, researchers, and clinicians to find, study, and treat these persons. The homeless population includes many unemployed and low-income adults, people with chronic mental illness, runaway youth who have left home and dropped out of school, individuals who have been incarcerated, undocumented aliens, and women with children.

Affordable housing is scarce for many people, and competition for low-income housing is challenging. People with addictive disorders, especially those with dual disorders, are less likely to find adequate housing and more likely to find themselves on the streets. Deinstitutionalization increased the number of mentally ill people who are homeless. Access to substances is easier on the street. There are limited numbers of residential homes for people with mental illness or mental retardation. Noncompliance with psychotropic medication is common among the homeless, who also have a tendency to self-medicate with alcohol or other drugs. In 1996, federal legislation (P.L. 104-121) curtailed supplemental security income and Social Security Disability Insurance benefits for individuals whose primary diagnosis is substance abuse. These benefits often meant the difference between housing and homelessness, as well as access to health care through Medicaid. Now more people with substance abuse problems are homeless; consequently, demands on homeless service providers and the indigent substance abuse treatment system are increasing.

Less than half of homeless people who need treatment for substance dependence receive treatment. Addiction severity in this population, as evaluated by the ASI, is usually high in all categories: medical status, employment and support status, drug/alcohol use, legal status, family history, social relationships, and psychiatric status. Homeless clients, assessed by *DSM-IV* criteria, often present with two or more Axis I diagnoses; dual disorders are common. Homeless clients often display Axis II criteria; homeless men who have been incarcerated often exhibit antisocial personality characteristics; homeless women may exhibit borderline personality characteristics. Axis III general medical conditions and Axis IV psychosocial and environment problems are legion. Although they may survive from day to day, homeless clients usually demonstrate serious impairment in Axis V global functioning with a current score on the Global Assessment of Functioning Scale of 50 or lower. Relapse potential (Dimension 5 *ASAM PPC-2*) is high because of lack of a supportive recovery environment (Dimension 6 *ASAM PPC-2*). Housing stability is essential for successful treatment and sustained recovery. Without a secure place to live, many people can never achieve recovery.

Most shelters for the homeless provide food and a bed. In urban areas, a bus or van may cruise the streets, pick up the homeless, and take them to a shelter, where they are given an evening meal and a place to sleep. After breakfast the next day, the bus drops them back on the street. We see them every day in our parks and public libraries. Sometimes they panhandle or scavenge. When the weather is inclement, we encounter them in doorways or in ATM cubicles or see them huddled near heating vents or under piles of cardboard. "Wet shelters" admit people who are under the influence of alcohol and other drugs *if* they are not a danger to themselves and others. These shelters provide spaces to sit, but no beds. The worst fear of many homeless people is being barred from a shelter because of dangerous or destructive behavior. Some shelters guarantee individuals a bed if they enroll in a substance abuse treatment program. Some shelters for women and children allow 24-hour occupancy, but the demand far exceeds available space. Although federal funding aimed at addressing the problems of homelessness (from the U.S. Department of Housing and Urban Development, or HUD) has increased markedly in recent years, the numbers of homeless and their complex problems continue. According to the National Law Center on Homelessness and Poverty, increasing numbers of cities are using aggressive policing to remove the homeless from certain sections of town, sometimes charging homeless persons with criminal offenses in order to take them into custody.

Unsafe Neighborhoods

Living in a neighborhood where drug trafficking is frequent increases individuals' risk for use. The relationship between access and addiction is significant. According to Skogan and Annan (1994), residents of public housing are highly vulnerable to drug trafficking and other drug-related crime. Rates of property and violent crime are often high in public housing projects. Residents who qualify for public housing are generally old and/or poor. Most nonelderly public housing residents are single, unemployed women with children. In many cities, members of racial and cultural minority groups make up a disproportionate number of the residents of public housing. Security is difficult in high-rise public housing complexes and in low-rise complexes with multiple access points. Residents often distrust the local housing authority and fear the police. Police must deal with both law-abiding citizens and offenders within the same neighborhoods. Citizen coalitions to fight drugs, reduce crime, and increase public safety in high-crime neighborhoods show promise.

In 1996, President Clinton announced a "One strike and you're out" policy under which public housing tenants can be evicted if they or their guests are arrested—no conviction required—for alleged drug activity. Nationwide, 3,847 public housing tenants were ousted in the policy's first 6 months, an increase of 84% over the number evicted for drugs and other crimes in the previous 6 months. Yet tenants' rights groups question whether anything meaningful is accomplished by a policy that would throw an 85-year-old great-grandmother out of her apartment. In this particular case, police found a kilogram of cocaine and a scale in the woman's apartment; they arrested her grandson and two of his friends on drug charges. Grant money from HUD, dispensed through programs such as the Low-Income Housing Drug Elimination Grant Program, helps many public housing authorities combat drug-related crimes.

Rural America

About 25% of the U.S. population lives in rural regions. Research data show that total substance abuse rates in these areas are similar to those in nonrural areas. Alcohol is by far the most widely abused substance in rural America, and smoking and use of smokeless tobacco are high. Prevalence for some drugs, such as cocaine and heroin, appears to be lower than in the general population, but rates for other drugs, such as inhalants, are higher. The incidence of cocaine and heroin use is currently increasing in rural areas. Arrest rates for substance abuse violations are as high as those in nonrural areas; most of those incarcerated have abused alcohol, other drugs, or both.

In rural areas, the prevalence of substance abuse problems far exceeds any available treatment (see National Institute on Drug Abuse, 1997). Although the addiction problems are similar to those in urban areas, addiction treatment and prevention programs are limited. Factors endemic to rural America—geographic isolation, transportation difficulties, and limited health and social services—account for this disparity. Addiction programs are underfunded, there are few rural-specific programs, and there is a paucity of trained and experienced staff. People who live in rural areas are often more reluctant than their urban and suburban counterparts to seek help for personal problems, at least in part because of the relative lack of anonymity in small communities. Rural school boards, administrators, teachers, and parents often resist offering alcohol and drug prevention programs. All of the problems noted above are even more complex in poor rural areas and for minority populations living in rural America.

Rural areas also have many strong protective factors working against substance abuse, including supportive family relationships and extended families as well as community networks that revolve around churches and schools.

Legal Problems

Addiction and Crime

According to a 1997 report by the National Center on Addiction and Substance Abuse at Columbia University (CASA), 80% of the adults held in U.S. prisons are there because of criminal activity linked to drug and alcohol abuse. The tripling of America's prison population, from 500,000 in 1980 to 1.7 million in 1997, is due mainly to criminal acts that were influenced by drugs and/or alcohol. The CASA report urges federal and state governments to spend more money to help some 1.4 million inmates kick their habits before returning to society. State prisons house more than 1 million inmates, and approximately 6% of them are enrolled in substance treatment programs (see Bart, 1999). In 1999, the Justice Policy Institute projected that by February 2000, the prison population in the United States would reach 2 million (see Shaw, 1999).

The relationship between addiction and crime is strong and very complex. Some people use illicit drugs; other people sell drugs. Still others commit crimes to obtain alcohol or drugs or to gamble. And many people commit crimes against persons or property while under the influence of alcohol or other drugs. For example, Craig L. buys and uses heroin daily. Ellen M. works as a prostitute to support her crack cocaine habit. Franklin R. controls the drug distribution network in the South End; he employs a staff of 30 young men and women in the field and delivers to known regulars. Laura B. defends her right to drink even though she was just arrested for a third time for driving under the influence (DUI).

Eric, Mickey, and Sal, ages 13 to 15, wanted money for alcohol and drugs. Armed with baseball bats, they plundered two apartments in a senior citizens' housing center, injured three residents, and stole as many personal items as they could carry. They are arraigned in juvenile court on charges of armed assault with intent to rob, assault and battery on persons over 65, malicious destruction of property, and grand larceny. At exactly 6:30 P.M. on Friday night, Kevin places a call to his bookie to place his bets on the weekend college football games. Kevin "borrowed" money from an account at work, but knows he will win big this time and pay everything back. Wendy calls the police because "Joe just went crazy when I burned the chops. He trashed the room. Then he beat and bloodied me something terrible. He broke my right arm, knocked out four teeth, and then left." Wendy and Joe appear together in court holding hands. Wendy refuses to testify against Joe because "he just gets that way when he drinks too much."

Drunk Driving

For several weeks in the late summer of 1997, the world acknowledged the role that drunken driving played in the death of Princess Diana. In the United States, two out of five people will be involved in alcohol-related vehicle crashes during their lives.

In all, 41,480 people were killed on U.S. highways in 1998, down from 42,103 in 1977. In 1979, 51,093 people were killed on the nation's highways; fatalities reached a record low in 1992, when 39,250 people were killed in highway accidents. Alcohol was involved in 15,936 traffic fatalities in 1998, or 38.4% of total highway deaths. In 1997, alcohol was a factor in 16,189 traffic fatalities, or 38.5% of the total. Even though the number of licensed drivers has increased, the current trend in traffic deaths is downward; the U.S. Bureau of Justice Statistics attributes the decline in part to the aging of drivers. The older the driver over age 21, the lower the rate of drunken driving arrests. Teen drinking and driving, and related accidents and deaths, continue to be a major public health problem.

Drinking impairs alertness, judgment, and the skills an individual needs to drive safely. The proportion of alcohol to blood in the body is expressed as the blood alcohol concentration (BAC) or blood alcohol level (BAL). State laws stipulate driver BAC/BAL limits. The limit for drivers age 21 and older is 0.10% in most states, although an increasing number of states have reduced the limit to 0.08%. Because young drivers lack experience with both drinking and driving, some states have set BAC/BAL limits for them at 0.02% or lower (referred to as the "zero-tolerance law"). Raising the legal drinking age to 21 and reducing the BAC/BAL limit for young drivers has prevented traffic deaths. Legal sanctions such as suspension of a driver's license and court-ordered alcoholism treatment are designed to deter drinking and driving. These sanctions are also likely to reduce rearrest for driving under the influence of alcohol or other substances.

DUI offenders with less severe drinking problems benefit most from short-term educational programs that emphasize modifying drinking behavior. Participants in such programs often decide to accept the admonition "Don't drink and drive." They may embrace the designated driver concept. For repeat offenders or those with more severe drinking problems, treatment includes education, individual counseling, and follow-up for at least 12 months. Today, public acceptance of drinking and driving is decreasing, and states are demonstrating a growing willingness to develop public policies to prevent alcohol-related injuries and deaths and to enforce legal sanctions against drinking drivers. But Americans' love affair with the automobile is long and strong, and drinking and driving remains a rite of passage for many teens.

Treatment and the Criminal Justice System

Treatment reduces substance abuse; however, substance abuse treatment alone is not enough to prevent relapse and recidivism with inmate clients. In addition to treatment, most inmates need to develop new psychological and social skills, such as new ways to manage anger and communicate without violence. Occupational skills are woefully lacking among incarcerated clients. Effective rehabilitation offers literacy training, GED completion, and vocational education. Values clarification, with a major paradigm shift from criminal thinking and behavior to responsibility and accountability for self and family, grounds effective rehabilitation and return to the community. Opportunities for spiritual growth and development are needed.

Treatment Planning

Ideally, in the criminal justice system, substance abuse treatment begins with the arrest of an individual and continues to the successful completion of the justice mandate. Key times to monitor progress include at the pretrial hearing and at the presentencing hearing (plea) or trial/sentencing. Treatment continues during incarceration and parole. Criminal justice system treatment programs reflect coordinated strategies for substance abuse treatment interventions at every stage: pretrial, jail, trial, sentencing, probation, corrections, and parole. Sound and safe classification, treatment, and case management from arrest to release are essential for linkage between treatment and corrections.

Substance Abuse Treatment With Intermediate Sanctions

In response to the burgeoning number of offenders with substance abuse problems, more criminal justice systems are managing and treating these offenders through use of intermediate sanctions with a substance abuse treatment component. *Sanctions* are legally binding orders of the court or paroling authority that deprive or restrict offender liberty or property. An *intermediate sanction* is any sanction that is more rigorous (unpleasant, intrusive, or controlling) than traditional probation but less restrictive than total incarceration. With the creation of the federal Law Enforcement Assistance Administration in the early 1970s, more money became available to develop and operate community-based offender treatment and training programs. During the 1980s, many states created community corrections programs. Intermediate sanctions include means-based fines (also called day fines); community service, or restitution; placement in outpatient or residential substance abuse treatment centers; requirement to report to day centers or residential centers for other types of treatment or training; intensive-supervision probation; curfew or house arrest (with or without electronic monitoring); placement in halfway houses or work release centers, or boot camps; and placement in other special needs probation programs or caseloads (Center for Substance Abuse Treatment, 1994, pp. 4-5).

To be successful, combining substance abuse treatment and intermediate sanctions requires flexible services, mutual understanding, good information, and well-informed collaboration. For example, criminal justice system personnel must understand the importance of the continuation of treatment and avoid unilateral action that disrupts treatment unless such action is absolutely necessary. Treatment providers must be responsible for reporting critical incidents to the criminal justice system. Treatment is usually more demanding than just doing time, because offender clients are expected to work actively and participate fully in creating change. The aim of the criminal justice system is a safer community, whereas treatment providers want healthier individuals. Substance abuse treatment is an effective way to protect society by addressing individual problems that lead to crime.

Drug Courts

Drug courts are similar to diversion programs, but are more formalized. Janet Reno developed the first drug court in the United States in 1989 when she was Florida's state attorney for Dade County. As attorney general of the United States, she championed the establishment of federal support of drug courts through the 1994 Crime Law. According to Bart (1999), there are now drug court programs in 39 states, the District of Columbia, and Puerto Rico, with programs planned or about to be implemented in Guam and nine additional U.S. states, including several Native American tribal courts. There were 258 adult drug courts and 43 juvenile and family drug courts as of 1999. High retention, decrease in substance abuse, low recidivism, and financial savings characterize drug courts. The U.S. Department of Justice has reported that more than 70% of the 100,000 offenders assigned to drug courts are still enrolled or have successfully completed treatment. A 1998 evaluation by the National Center on Addiction and Substance Abuse at Columbia University found that drug courts substantially reduce drug use and criminal behavior while the offender is under the court's jurisdiction (see Bart, 1999). In addition, recidivism decreases for drug court participants after they leave the program. The Department of Justice estimates savings of at least $5,000 in jail bed days alone for each participant. (For a description of the key components of a drug court program, see Exhibit P in the appendix.)

Relapse Prevention

Formerly incarcerated clients are especially vulnerable to relapse. Factors associated with this group that contribute to relapse with alcohol and other drugs include the following (Center for Substance Abuse Treatment, 1995, p. 14):

- Inadequate skills to deal with the social pressure to use
- Frequent exposure to "high-risk" situations that have led to drug or alcohol use in the past
- Physical or psychological reminders of past drug use, such as drug paraphernalia, drug-using friends, and money
- Inadequate skills to deal with interpersonal conflict or negative emotions
- Desire to test their personal control over drug use
- Recurrent thoughts or physical desire to use drugs
- Other stressors related to their return to the community and placement under criminal justice supervision

Effective substance abuse treatment with offender clients emphasizes relapse prevention. Clients learn to identify and monitor high-risk situations and warning signs. They rehearse strategies and role-play situations to learn to manage lapses successfully. Clients learn to identify and modify self-statements that lead to negative emotions or to rationalization to use alcohol or other drugs. They learn how to identify urges and cues to use; this phenomenon is called BUDDING—building up to drink or drug. They learn to recognize and control the thoughts, feelings, and behaviors associated with their using. Treatment techniques that help offender clients to manage stress and redirect anger, communicate effectively, and solve problems successfully can prevent relapse. In addition, solution-focused techniques can help offender clients identify situations when they did not drink or use and why. Mandated aftercare is critical to prevent relapse and facilitate successful reentry into the community.

Perhaps it is an indictment of our current health care system, or possibly wisdom on the part of an enlightened criminal justice system, but some of the most responsive, creative, and intensive addiction treatment today is taking place in prison, drug court, and community corrections programs.

Summary

Social problems such as occupational drug use, unemployment, poverty, homelessness, and unsafe neighborhoods contribute to the development of addictive disorders, influence treatment planning, and have strong impacts on rates of recovery. Addiction clinicians address client social problems when they develop treatment goals and aftercare plans. Clinicians collaborate with other health and human services providers to help clients and their families who are adversely affected by social problems. Clinicians advocate actively for the prevention of social problems that contribute to addiction.

Related Skills Checklist

Practitioner skills related to treatment of addiction clients with social problems include the ability to do the following:

- Assess employment/support status and legal status using the ASI.
- Collect data about educational, occupational, economic, housing, and legal problems using *DSM-IV* Axis IV.
- Assess the strengths and limitations of the client recovery environment (Dimension 6 *ASAM PPC-2*).
- Include social needs and problems in treatment plan goals and outcomes.
- Select interventions that include social supports and resources.
- Develop relapse prevention plans that recognize social assets and liabilities.

Special Topics for Further Study

How do social problems influence addiction severity and treatment intensity? What supports and resources in the client environment promote recovery? What social factors in the client environment threaten recovery and contribute to re-lapse? Role-play confronting a work colleague about performance and behavior that could indicate an addiction problem. Evaluate the effectiveness of sub-stance abuse treatment programs for homeless clients. Compare and contrast legal sanctions for drunk driving in the United States with those in other countries. Determine public attitudes toward addiction treatment within the criminal justice system.

Addiction Practice 2000

Addiction practice 2000 demands support for broad-based social engineering initiatives to correct social problems that have impacts on addiction, such as un-employment, poverty, homelessness, violence, and crime.

Epilogue

Addiction jeopardizes the health and well-being of individuals, families, and communities. Addiction theory and research ground and guide effective preven-tion and quality treatment. Addiction practitioners affirm and advance addiction practice 2000. Accept the challenge!

References

American Psychiatric Association. (1994). *Diagnostic and statistical manual of mental disorders* (4th ed.). Washington, DC: Author.

American Society of Addiction Medicine. (1996). *Patient placement criteria for the treatment of substance-related disorders* (2nd ed.). Chevy Chase, MD: Author.

Bart, M. (1999, January). Drug courts found effective in curbing substance abuse, crime. *Counseling Today,* pp. 1, 18, 20

Black, M. M., & Ricardo, I. B. (1994). Drug use, drug trafficking, and weapon carrying among low-income African-American, early adolescent boys. *Pediatrics, 93,* 1065-1072.

Center for Substance Abuse Treatment. (1994). *Combining substance abuse treatment with intermediate sanctions for adults in the criminal justice system* (DHHS Publica-tion No. SMA 94-3003). Rockville, MD: Author.

Center for Substance Abuse Treatment. (1995). *Relapse prevention and the substance-abusing offender* (DHHS Publication No. SMA 95-3071). Rockville, MD: Author.

National Institute on Drug Abuse. (1995). *Assessing client needs using the ASI: Resource manual* (NIH Publication No. 95-3620). Rockville, MD: Author.

National Institute on Drug Abuse. (1997). *Rural substance abuse: State of knowledge and issues* (NIH Publication No. 97-4177). Rockville, MD: Author.

Shaw, G. (1999, December 29). Inmate total nears 2 million. *Boston Globe,* p. 16.

Skogan, W. G., & Annan, S. O. (1994). Drugs and public housing: Toward an effective police response. In D. L. MacKenzie & C. D. Uchida (Eds.), *Drugs and crime: Evaluating public policy initiatives.* Thousand Oaks, CA: Sage.

Substance Abuse and Mental Health Services Administration. (1997). *Employment outcomes of indigent clients receiving alcohol and drug treatment in Washington State* (DHHS Publication No. SMA 97-3129). Rockville, MD: Author.

Substance Abuse and Mental Health Services Administration. (1999a). *An analysis of worker drug use and workplace policies and programs: Results from the 1994 and 1997 National Household Survey on Drug Abuse, Policies and Programs* (DHHS Publication No. SMA 99-3352). Rockville, MD: Author.

Substance Abuse and Mental Health Services Administration. (1999b). *Substance use and mental health characteristics by employment status* (DHHS Publication No. 99-3311). Rockville, MD: Author.

U.S. Department of Labor. (1996). *Working partners: Substance abuse in the workplace.* Washington, DC: Government Printing Office.

Whitehead, T. L., Peterson, J., & Kaljee, L. (1994). The "hustle": Socioeconomic deprivation, urban drug trafficking, and low-income, African-American male gender identity. *Pediatrics, 93,* 1050-1054.

Other Sources

Bayle-Lissick, S., & Jahns, E. M. (1990). *Resolving conflicts on the job.* Center City, MN: Hazelden.

Center for Substance Abuse Prevention. (1994). *Rural communities* (DHHS Publication No. SMA 94-2087). Rockville, MD: Author.

Center for Substance Abuse Prevention. (1995). *Cost-effectiveness and preventive implications of employee assistance programs* (DHHS Publication No. SMA 95-3305). Rockville, MD: Author.

Center for Substance Abuse Prevention. (1996). *Violence* (NCADI MS451). Rockville, MD: Author.

Center for Substance Abuse Prevention. (1996). *Youth in low income environments* (NCADI MS446). Rockville, MD: Author.

Center for Substance Abuse Treatment. (1994). *Impaired driving* (DHHS Publication No. SMA 94-2070). Rockville, MD: Author.

Center for Substance Abuse Treatment. (1994). *Juvenile justice treatment planning chart* (DHHS Publication No. SMA 94-2091). Rockville, MD: Author.

Center for Substance Abuse Treatment. (1996). *Counselor's manual for relapse prevention with chemically dependent criminal offenders* (DHHS Publication No. SMA 96-3115). Rockville, MD: Author.

Center for Substance Abuse Treatment. (1996). *Critical elements in developing effective jail-based drug treatment programming.* Washington, DC: Government Printing Office.

Center for Substance Abuse Treatment. (1996). *Treatment drug courts: Integrating substance abuse treatment with legal case processing* (DHHS Publication No. SMA 96-311). Rockville, MD: Author.

Center for Substance Abuse Treatment. (1997). *Substance abuse treatment planning guide and checklist for treatment-based drug courts* (DHHS Publication No. SMA 97-3146). Rockville, MD: Author.

Covington, S. S. (1999). *Helping women recover: Special edition for use in the criminal justice system.* San Francisco: Jossey-Bass.

Dutton, D. (1995). *The batterer: A psychological profile.* New York: HarperCollins.

Herman, D. B., & Susser, E. S. (Eds.). (1998). *Homelessness in America.* Washington, DC: American Public Health Association.

Jones, A. (1994). *Next time she'll be dead: Battering and how to stop it.* Boston: Beacon.

MacKenzie, D. L., & Uchida, C. D. (Eds.). (1994). *Drugs and crime: Evaluating public policy initiatives.* Thousand Oaks, CA: Sage.

McDonough, J. (1998). *Total immersion program: Manual for treating violent offenders with substance (a combined effort of the Gavin House Staff, the Massachusetts Office of the Commissioner of Probation, and South Boston District Court).* Unpublished master's thesis, Cambridge College.

National Coalition for the Homeless. (1999, April). *Addiction disorders and homelessness* (NCH Fact Sheet 6) [On-line]. Available Internet: http://nch.ari.net/addict.html

National Institute on Alcohol Abuse and Alcoholism. (1996). *Drinking and driving: Alcohol alert* (NIAAA Publication No. 31 PH362). Bethesda. MD: Author.

National Institute on Drug Abuse. (1991). *The collection and interpretation of data from hidden populations* (DHHS Publication No. ADM 90-1678). Rockville, MD: Author.

National Institute on Drug Abuse. (1991). *Drugs in the workplace: Research and working data* (Vol. 2) (DHHS Publication No. ADM 91-1730). Rockville, MD: Author.

National Institute on Drug Abuse. (1992). *Drug abuse treatment in prisons and jails* (DHHS Publication No. ADM 92-1884). Rockville, MD: Author.

National Institute on Drug Abuse. (1994). *Drugs and violence: Causes, correlates, and consequences* (NIH Publication No. 94-3633). Rockville, MD: Author.

Office for Substance Abuse Prevention. (1992). *Employee assistance programs* (NCASI MS439). Rockville, MD: Author.

Ragghianti, M., & Glenn, T. (1991). *Breaking down the walls: Steps to freedom for addicted inmates.* Center City: MN: Hazelden.

Smith, C. C. (1989). *Who needs to know? Anonymity in the workplace.* Center City, MN: Hazelden.

Substance Abuse and Mental Health Services Administration. (1997). *Bringing excellence to substance abuse services in rural and frontier America* (DHHS Publication No. SMA 97-3134). Rockville, MD: Author.

Wanberg, K. W., & Milkman, H. B. (1998). *Criminal conduct and substance abuse treatment.* Thousand Oaks, CA: Sage.

Ward, R. I. (1984). *When you go back to work: The transition from treatment to work.* Center City, MN: Hazelden.

Appendix: Exhibits

Exhibit A Treatment Costs for Mental Health and Substance Abuse Problems

The majority of treatment costs for mental health and substance abuse problems are paid for by federal, state, and local governments. According to a study by the Substance Abuse and Mental Health Services Administration (SAMHSA), more than $79 billion was spent on treatment for mental health and substance abuse problems in 1996. Of this total, $66.7 billion was spent on the treatment of mental illness, $5 billion on the treatment of alcohol abuse, and $7.6 billion on the treatment of other drug abuse. Government funding (including Medicare, Medicaid, and other federal, state, and local government programs) paid for the majority of all three types of treatment. Treatment for other drug abuse had the highest proportion of government funding (66%), and treatment for mental illness had the lowest (53%).

In 1996, treatment costs for mental illness, alcohol, and other drug abuse, by payer, were as follows:

- Mental illness ($66.7 billion)

  Private, 47%

  Government, 53%

- Alcohol abuse (includes patients with primary alcohol problems) ($5.0 billion)

  Private, 43%

  Government, 58%

- Other drug abuse (includes patients with primary drug disorders and patients with combined drug and alcohol disorders) ($7.6 billion)

  Private, 34%

  Government, 66%

Government in the above list includes Medicaid, Medicare, and other local, state, and federal government sources. *Private* includes private insurance, out-of-pocket expenses, and other private sources.

SOURCE: Based on *CSAT by Fax*, December 16, 1998. Adapted by the Center for Substance Abuse Research from Tami Mark et al., *National Expenditures for Mental Health, Alcohol and Other Drug Abuse Treatment, 1996*, September 1998. Prepared by the MEDSTAT Group for the Substance Abuse and Mental Health Services Administration. Copies of the report are available on-line at http://www.health.org/mhaod/spending/htm.

Exhibit B   Definition of Alcoholism

The Joint Committee to Study the Definition and Criteria Diagnosis of Alcoholism of the National Council on Alcoholism and Drug Dependence (NCADD) and the American Society of Addiction Medicine (ASAM) have developed a definition of alcoholism. The following statement was prepared by the NCADD.

Alcoholism is a *primary,* chronic *disease* with genetic, psychosocial, and environmental factors influencing its development and manifestations. The disease is *often progressive and fatal.* It is characterized by continuous or periodic: *impaired control* over drinking, *preoccupation* with the drug alcohol, use of alcohol despite *adverse consequences,* and distortions in thinking, most notably *denial.*

- *Primary* refers to the nature of alcoholism as a disease entity in addition to and separate from other pathophysiologic states which may be associated with it. Primary suggests that alcoholism, as an addiction, is not a symptom of an underlying disease state.

- *Disease* means an involuntary disability. It represents the sum of the abnormal phenomena displayed by a group of individuals. These phenomena are associated with a specified common set of characteristics by which these individuals differ from the norm, and which places them at a disadvantage.

- *Often progressive and fatal* means that the disease persists over time and that physical, emotional, and social changes are often cumulative and may progress as drinking continues. Alcoholism causes premature death through overdose, organic complications involving the brain, liver, heart, and many other organs, and by contributing to suicide, homicide, motor vehicle crashes, and other traumatic events.

- *Impaired control* means the inability to limit alcohol use or to consistently limit on any drinking occasion the duration of the episode, the quantity consumed, and/or the behavioral consequences of drinking.

- *Preoccupation* in association with alcohol use indicates excessive, focused attention given to the drug alcohol, its effects, and/or its use. The relative value thus assigned to alcohol by the individual often leads to a diversion of energies away from important life concerns.

- *Adverse consequences* are alcohol-related problems or impairments in such areas as: physical health (e.g. alcohol withdrawal syndromes, liver disease, gastritis, anemia, neurological disorders); psychological functioning (e.g. impairments in cognition, changes in mood and behavior); interpersonal functioning (e.g. marital problems and child abuse, impaired social relationships); occupational functioning (e.g. scholastic or job problems); legal, financial, or spiritual problems.

- *Denial* is used here not only in the psychoanalytic sense of a single psychological defense mechanism disavowing the significance of events, but more broadly to include a range of psychological maneuvers designed to reduce awareness of the fact that alcohol use is the cause of an individual's problems rather than a solution to those problems. Denial becomes an integral part of the disease and a major obstacle to recovery.

For more information about alcoholism as a disease, call the Council's 24-Hour Information & Referral Helpline. We have general pamphlets on alcoholism and articles which discuss the advances science is making in identifying the biological and environmental elements which seem to play a role in the development of alcoholism. Call 1-800-622-2255 or 1-800-475-4673.

Exhibit C Do You Have a Gambling Problem?

Gamblers Anonymous offers the following 20 questions to individuals who are questioning whether they might have a gambling problem. According to G.A., "Most compulsive gamblers will answer yes to at least seven of these questions."

1. Did you ever lose time from work or school due to gambling?

2. Has gambling ever made your home life unhappy?

3. Did gambling affect your reputation?

4. Have you ever felt remorse after gambling?

5. Did you ever gamble to get money with which to pay debts or otherwise solve financial difficulties?

6. Did gambling cause a decrease in your ambition or efficiency?

7. After losing did you feel you must return as soon as possible and win back your losses?

8. After a win did you have a strong urge to return and win more?

9. Did you often gamble until your last dollar was gone?

10. Did you ever borrow to finance your gambling?

11. Have you ever sold anything to finance gambling?

12. Were you reluctant to use "gambling money" for normal expenditures?

13. Did gambling make you careless of the welfare of yourself or your family?

14. Did you ever gamble longer than you had planned?

15. Have you ever gambled to escape worry or trouble?

16. Have you ever committed, or considered committing, an illegal act to finance gambling?

17. Did gambling cause you to have difficulty in sleeping?

18. Do arguments, disappointments, or frustrations create within you an urge to gamble?

19. Did you ever have an urge to celebrate any good fortune by a few hours of gambling?

20. Have you ever considered self-destruction as a result of your gambling?

Exhibit D Substance Abuse by Nurses

Nurses who abuse alcohol and other drugs jeopardize public safety, stigmatize the nursing profession, and diminish their own personal health and well-being. Loss of control in the work setting, overwhelming personal demands, and access to addictive substances increase the risk of substance abuse by nurses. A public health agent-host-environment model can help us to address this serious problem.

Environment. Increasingly, job security for nurses is fraught with uncertainty. Layoffs inevitably follow mergers, and some nurses find themselves competing with colleagues and applying for the same positions they have held for years. Because reimbursement determines services and patient census dictates staffing, many nurses hold several part-time or per diem positions, usually without benefits. Job satisfaction from direct patient care has disappeared for many nurses, who instead find themselves lost in paperwork. Despite higher patient acuity, an increasing number of unlicensed personnel care for patients.

Work stress increases the risk of substance abuse by nurses; thus reducing that work stress decreases the likelihood that nurses will abuse drugs. Organized nursing must work tirelessly to promote working conditions that assure greater job security and increase job satisfaction.

Host. Nurses exemplify the Type "E" personality: "everything for everybody." Personal responsibilities for most working nurses are legion. Nurses work full-time or more. They are parents, sometimes single parents. Or they may juggle the challenges of a two-career family. Often they assume responsibility for aging parents. In their spare time, nurses continue their own educations and advance their careers.

Nurses may self-medicate with alcohol or other drugs to manage personal stress. When nurses relinquish their "super-person" syndrome and develop a "self-care" lifestyle, they can manage personal stress more effectively and without chemicals.

Agent. Access to drugs, be it free beer at a fraternity party or medications in a patient's kitchen cupboard, invites use. Nurses are among the very few health professionals who administer medications to patients. In the "old days" of stock drugs, it was fairly easy for nurses to self-diagnose and self-medicate. Today, nurses find ways to hide their drug use with the unit dose system until chart audits, patient and family complaints, or impaired nursing practice prompt an investigation. We can truly recognize the "insanity of addiction" when nurses divert drugs, knowing it is only a matter of time before a computerized medication system identifies a pattern of "excessive administration of controlled substances" by particular nurses.

Because nurses will continue to administer medications, access to drugs remains a risk factor. All nurses need to understand substance abuse and that substance abuse by nurses is a very serious personal, professional, and public safety problem. Schools of nursing curricula, as well as continuing education hours for all nurses who renew their licenses, must include substance abuse education for nurses.

When nurses abuse alcohol or other drugs, early intervention, intensive treatment, and extensive rehabilitation are required to protect the public and help the impaired nurses. The Massachusetts Board of Registration in Nursing recognizes the seriousness of this problem. To protect public safety and help impaired nurses, the board offers the Substance Abuse Rehabilitation Program for nurses who meet admission criteria.

SOURCE: Adapted from Sandra Rasmussen, "Substance Abuse by Nurses," to appear in *Nursing Board News* (Massachusetts Board of Registration in Nursing).

Exhibit E   Code of Ethics of the American Academy of Health Care Providers in the Addictive Disorders

Since Hippocrates wrote his oath more than 2000 years ago, health care providers have sought to establish standards for ethical and competent medical and psychological treatment. The American Academy itself was created to establish such a standard in the field of addiction treatment, which it succeeded doing with the creation of the Certified Addiction Specialist (C.A.S.) credential. The C.A.S. credential reflects the highest and most comprehensive standard in the field today, a standard that is based both on the acquisition and demonstration of a body of knowledge in the area of addiction treatment and on the adherence to the strict ethical standards set forth below.

The Academy's membership is comprised of clinicians from a variety of disciplines and treatment modalities who include nurses, doctors, psychologists, psychiatrists, social workers, forensic counselors and counselors, unified in their commitment to providing the highest quality of health care to individuals suffering from addiction. Our diverse membership is also unified in their recognition of the ethical standards and considerations that are specific to this field.

This code is meant to provide only a very general outline of the principles for those health care providers specifically treating the addictions and is in no way exhaustive of the ethical responsibilities of our membership. Since our members come from a variety of disciplines and may carry multiple credentials, the principles set forth here should not be viewed as in any way supervening or abrogating other ethical codes that our members might be bound to. On the contrary, the Academy's code is meant to supplement or complement other standards, both legal and ethical, while setting forth a code of conduct that addresses the issues that are unique to working with individuals with addictions. This code is also meant to serve notice to the public as to the standards of health care and treatment that they can expect from Academy members.

Academy members are bound by the Academy's ethical code and will be held to the letter and spirit of this code. The membership of those violating this code will be subject to inquiry and review, and the credential could be suspended or revoked.

It is important to note that addiction treatment has historically been an area in which professional standards have been inconsistent; this code is meant to set forth a crucial, consistent, ethical standard.

Principles of Conduct

I. Competence

Academy members recognize both the strengths and limitations of their ability to treat addictions. They continually seek to stay abreast of innovations in the understanding and treatment of addiction. They also only treat addictions that they are knowledgeable about and capable of treating. As a corollary to this, they only offer treatment services which are within their realm of competence (competence which is determined on the basis of their education, clinical supervision, and experience).

II. Maintenance of Competence

Because of the continual changes in the field of addiction treatment, Academy members strive to maintain the awareness of research findings and changes in treatment techniques and approaches that is necessary to maintain their competence in the field.

III. Nondiscrimination

In their work in the addictions, members of the Academy do not discriminate against their clients or co-workers on the basis of race, gender, religion, sexual orientation, age, disability, ethnicity, socioeconomic status, or national origin. They also do not unfairly discriminate on the basis of addiction or the medical complications of the addiction. While alcoholism and drug addiction are recognized by the federal government to be disabilities and individuals suffering from such addictions are protected from discrimination under the Federal Rehabilitation Act, Academy members do not restrict their nondiscrimination practices to these individuals but extend them to all people suffering from addiction, recognizing that all such addictions are debilitating.

   a. Academy members are knowledgeable about the unique or special issues that face the individuals that they are treating both on the basis of their individual situations and on the basis of the addiction from which they suffer.

   b. Academy members are able to recognize instances in which individual differences between themselves and their client affect their ability to provide the highest quality health care. In such cases, Academy members either take the necessary steps to become competent in these areas or they make referrals to agencies or individuals who can best address their client's needs.

c. Academy members recognize those personal issues and conflicts that might affect their ability to provide their clients with the best possible health care. In such instances, they will refer the patient to someone better able to deal with him/her or will refrain from treating the patient until the Academy member has adequately resolved these issues.

d. Academy members recognize that there are individuals who suffer from multiple addictions. In such cases, Academy members will only treat the addictions that they are competent to treat. With regard to the other addictions, they will either take the steps necessary to become competent in these areas or will make referrals to agencies or individuals who can best address them.

e. Academy members recognize that many clients suffering from addiction, suffer from other mental disorders as well. Academy members treat only the problems that they are competent to treat. In complicated cases, cases in which several disorders must be treated simultaneously, Academy members will seek the requisite support and consultation and, if this is not available, will refer the client to the appropriate agency or clinician.

f. Academy members recognize that many clients seeking treatment for addiction may also suffer from medical complications and/or viral infections e.g., HIV, TB or hepatitis that eventuate from their addiction. If they are not competent to work with such clients, they will either take the necessary steps to become competent, or will consult with others and make referrals to the agencies or individuals who can best address the client's needs.

IV. Harassment

Academy members do not engage in any type of harassment, sexual or otherwise, in the work place.

a. The Academy considers sexual harassment to be any activity that demands or creates a hostile environment for an individual through sexual behavior or language. This includes unwelcome or unwanted advances of a sexual nature, verbal and non-verbal behavior of a sexual nature that would be deemed inappropriate by a reasonable person, and soliciting sex within the context of one's professional responsibilities.

b. Academy members do not engage in any other forms of harassment in the work place. This includes activities that involve the exploitation, denigration of others or that, otherwise, create a hostile work environment for others.

V. Conflicts of Interest

Because of the potential legal conflicts inherent in treating addiction, Academy members are familiar with the laws concerning their responsibilities and are able to anticipate those responsibilities that might potentially conflict with their role as health care provider. In cases in which the conflicts might be too great, the Academy member does his/her best to avoid such dual-roles.

VI. Confidentiality

Because of the popular stigmatization of addiction and of the legal implications that it often has, Academy members take the patient-client confidentiality agreement very seriously and take considerable precautions to ensure it. Because of the potential limitations on confidentiality (as suggested in Principle V), Academy members are careful to apprise their clients of the limits of confidentiality.

VII. Clients Receiving Services Elsewhere

Individuals being treated for an addiction often receive health services from other sites. In considering whether to treat such individuals, Academy members consult these other services and determine whether the client is best served in this manner. Academy members also anticipate and attempt to resolve potential conflicts that might arise from this arrangement.

VIII. Making Referrals

In making referrals, Academy members consider the best possible placement for their clients. Such referrals are always based on the best interests of the client and never on the financial interests of the clinician. Academy members attempt to familiarize themselves with a particular treatment site before making a referral to that site.

IX. Assessment Tools

Because definitions of addiction have changed radically in the past several years, Academy members are careful to use up-to-date assessment tools, tools that are compatible with contemporary theories of addiction, when diagnosing addiction.

X. Relapse

Since relapse is a critical part of addiction, Academy members are familiar with the facts concerning relapse and include relapse prevention as part of their treatment approach.

XI. Impaired Professionals

As a corollary to Principle I, but one worth mentioning in its own right, Academy members who develop their own addiction-related difficulties will refrain from providing treatment until such time as they have adequately addressed and resolved these difficulties and are again able to provide competent treatment.

SOURCE: Reprinted by permission of the American Academy of Health Care Providers in the Addictive Disorders.

Exhibit F Organizations, Associations, and Other Resources Related to Addiction Treatment

Government Web Sites

Center for Substance Abuse Prevention
www.samhsa.gov

Center for Substance Abuse Treatment
www.samhsa.gov

Drug Enforcement Administration
www.usdoj.gov/dea

Indian Health Service
www.tucson.ihs.gov

National Institute of Mental Health
www.nimh.nih.gov

National Institute on Alcohol Abuse and Alcoholism
www.niaaa.nih.gov

National Institute on Drug Abuse
www.nida.nih.gov

National Institutes of Health
www.nih.gov

National Library of Medicine
www.nlm.nih.gov

Office of Minority Health Resource Center
www.omhrc.gov

Office of National Drug Control Policy
www.whitehousedrugpolicy.gov

Substance Abuse and Mental Health Services Administration
www.samhsa.gov

U.S. Department of Health and Human Services
www.os.dhhs.gov

Addiction and Related Organizations

American Anorexia/Bulimia Association
Regeant Hospital
425 East 61st Street, 6th Floor
New York, NY 10021
phone: (212) 575-6200

American Medical Association, Office of Alcohol and Other Drug Abuse
515 North State Street
Chicago, IL 60610
phone: (312) 464-4202

American Methadone Treatment Association
217 Broadway, Suite 304
New York, NY 10007
phone: (212) 566-5555

American Society of Addiction Medicine
4601 North Park Avenue, Suite 101
Chevy Chase, MD 20815
phone: (301) 656-3920

Association of Halfway House Alcoholism Programs of North America
Rural Route 2, Box 415
Kerhonkson, NY 12446
phone: (914) 626-1684

Entertainment Industries Council
500 South Buena Vista Street
Burbank, CA 91521
phone: (818) 560-4231

Faith Partners Against Substance Abuse
1406 Ethridge Avenue
Austin, TX 78703
phone: (512) 476-2896

International Community Corrections Association
3903 Gresham Place
Alexandria, VA 22305
phone: (703) 836-0279

International Council on Alcohol and Addiction
Case postale 189

1001 Lausanne Switzerland
phone: 011 41 21 320 9865

Mothers Against Drunk Driving
511 East John Carpenter Freeway, Suite 700
Irving, TX 75062-8187
on-line: www.madd.org

National Association for Children of Alcoholics
11426 Rockville Pike, Suite 100
Rockville, MD 20852
phone: (888) 554-2627; (301) 468-0985
on-line: www.health.org/nacoa

National Association of Anorexia Nervosa and Associated Disorders
P.O. Box 7
Highland Park, IL 60035
phone: (708) 433-4632

National Coalition for the Homeless
1012 14th Street NW
Washington, DC 20036
phone: (202) 387-5000

National Council on Alcoholism and Drug Dependence
1511 K Street NW, Suite 433
Washington, DC 20005
phone: (202) 737-8122
on-line: www.ncadd.org

National Council on Compulsive Gambling
444 West 56th Street, Room 3207S
New York, NY 10019
phone: (202) 765-3833

National Organization on Fetal Alcohol Syndrome
1815 H Street NW, Suite 750
Washington, DC, 20006
phone: (202) 785-4585
on-line: www.nofas.org

Partnership for a Drug-Free America
405 Lexington Avenue, 16th Floor
New York, NY 10174
phone: (212) 922-1560
on-line: www.drugfreeamerica.org

Partnership for Recovery
601 13th Street NW, Suite 410 South
Washington, DC 20503
phone: (202) 737-0100

Students Against Destructive Decisions
P.O. Box 800
Marlboro, MA 01752
phone: (800) 787-5777
on-line: www.saddonline.com

Therapeutic Communities of America
1611 Connecticut Avenue NW, Suite 4-B
Washington, DC 20009
phone: (202) 296-3503

Professional Associations

American Academy of Health Care Providers in the Addictive Disorders
767C Concord Avenue
Cambridge, MA 02138
phone: (617) 661-6248

American Bar Association, Standing Committee on Substance Abuse
740 15th Street NW
Washington, DC 20005
phone: (202) 662-1785

American Counseling Association
5999 Stevenson Avenue
Alexandria, VA 22304
phone: (703) 823-9800

American Psychiatric Association
1400 K Street NW
Washington, DC 20002
phone: (202) 682-6326

American Psychological Association
750 First Street NE
Washington, DC, 20002
phone: (202) 336-5857

American Public Health Association
14405 Briarwood Terrace
Rockville, MD 20853
phone: (301) 460-4185

Employee Assistance Professionals Association
2101 Wilson Boulevard, Suite 500
Arlington, VA 22201
phone: (703) 522-6272
on-line: www.eap.association.com

International Certification and Reciprocity Consortium
120 First Flight Lane
Morrisville, NC 27560
phone: (919) 572-6823

National Association of Addiction Treatment Providers
501 Randolph Drive
Litz, PA 17543
phone: (717) 581-1901

National Association of Alcoholism and Drug Abuse Counselors
1911 North Fort Meyer Drive, Suite 900
Arlington, VA 22209
phone: (800) 548-0487
on-line: www.naadac.org

National Association of Social Workers
750 First Street NE, Suite 700
Washington, DC 20002
phone: (202) 408-8600

National Association of State Alcohol and Drug Abuse Directors
808 17th Street NW, Suite 410
Washington, DC 20006
phone: (202) 293-0090
on-line: www.nasadad.org

National Nurses Society on Addiction
4101 Lake Boone Trail, Suite 201
Raleigh, NC 27607
phone: (919) 783-5871
on-line: www.nnsa.org

Educational Resources

Hazelden Publishing and Education
P.O. Box 176
Center City, MN 55012
phone: (800) 328-9000
on-line: www.hazelden.org

Johnson Institute
7205 Ohmn Lane
Minneapolis, MN 55439
phone: (800) 231-5165
on-line: www.johnsoninstitute.com

National Clearinghouse for Alcohol and Drug Information
P.O. Box 2345
Rockville, MD 20847
phone: (800) 729-6686
on-line: www.health.org

National Women's Resource Center
515 King Street, Suite 410
Alexandria, VA 22314
phone: (800) 354-8824
on-line: www.nwrc.org

Substance Abuse Librarians and Information Specialists
P.O. Box 9513
Berkeley, CA 94709-0513
phone: (510) 642-5208
on-line: www.salis.org

Research Institutions

Betty Ford Center
3900 Bob Hope Drive
Rancho Mirage, CA 92270
phone: (800) 854-9211; (760) 773-4100
on-line: www.bettyfordcenter.com

Center for Alcohol and Addiction Studies
Brown University
Box G-BH

Providence, RI 02912
phone: (401) 444-1818
on-line: www.caas.brown.edu

Center for Science in the Public Interest
1875 Connecticut Avenue NW, Suite 300
Washington, DC 20009
phone: (202) 332-9110
on-line: www.cspinet.org

Christopher D. Smithers Foundation
P.O. Box 67
Mill Neck, NY 11765
phone: (516) 676-0067
on-line: http://aaw.com/smithers

Harvard Medical School, Division of Addictions
220 Longwood Avenue
Goldenson Building 231, Room 523
Boston, MA 02115
phone: (617) 432-0058
on-line: www.hms.harvard.edu/doa

Hazelden Foundation
P.O. Box 11
Center City, MN 55012
phone: (612) 257-4010
on-line: www.hazelden.org

Johnson Institute Foundation
2909 Wayzata Boulevard
Minneapolis, MN 55405
phone: (612) 374-9100

National Association for Responsible Gaming
P.O. Box 25366
Kansas City, MO 64119
phone: (816) 453-9964
on-line: www.ncrg.org

National Center on Addiction and Substance Abuse at Columbia University
152 West 57th Street
New York, NY 10019
(212) 841-5200
on-line: www.casacolumbia.org

Robert Wood Johnson Foundation
Route 1 and College Road East
P.O. Box 2316
Princeton, NJ 08543
phone: (609) 452-8701
on-line: www.rwjf.org

Rutgers University Center of Alcohol Studies
Smithers Hall, Busch Campus
Piscataway, NJ 08855
phone: (732) 445-4442
on-line: www.rci.rutgers.edu

Multicultural Resources

Latino Council on Alcohol and Tobacco
1015 15th Street NW, Suite 409
Washington, DC 20005
phone: (202) 371-1186

National Asian Pacific American Families Against Substance Abuse
300 West Cesar Chavez Avenue, Suite B
Los Angeles, CA 90012
phone: (213) 625-5795

National Black Alcoholism Council
1101 14th Street NW, Suite 802
Washington, DC 20005
phone: (202) 296-2696

National Coalition of Hispanic Health and Service Organizations
1501 16th Street NW
Washington, DC 20036
phone: (202) 387-5000
on-line: www.cossmho.org

Self-Help Organizations

Adult Children of Alcoholics
World Service Organization
P.O. Box 3216

Torrance, CA 90510
phone: (310) 534-1815

Al-Anon/Alateen Family Group Headquarters
1600 Corporate Landing Parkway
Virginia Beach, VA 23454
phone: (757) 563-1600
on-line: www.al-anon.alateen.org

Alcoholics Anonymous
General Service Office
475 Riverside Drive
New York, NY 10115
phone: (212) 870-3400
on-line: www.aa.org

Anorexia and Bulimia Support, Inc.
432 West Onondaga Street
Syracuse, NY 13202
phone: (315) 474-7011

Cocaine Anonymous
World Service Organization
P.O. Box 2000
Los Angeles, CA 90049
phone: (310) 559-5833
on-line: www.ca.org

Gam-Anon International Service Office, Inc.
P.O. Box 157
Whitestone, NY 11357
phone: (718) 352-1671

Gamblers Anonymous
World Service Office
P.O. Box 17173
Los Angeles, CA 90017
phone: (213) 386-8789
on-line: www.gamblersanonymous.org

Jewish Alcoholics, Chemically Dependent Persons and Significant Others
426 West 58th Street
New York, NY 10019
phone: (212) 397-4197
on-line: www.jacsnet.org

Nar-Anon Family Group Headquarters, Inc.
P.O. Box 2562
Palos Verdes, CA 90274
phone: (310) 547-5800

Narcotics Anonymous
World Service Office
P.O. Box 9999
Van Nuys, CA 91409
phone: (818) 773-9999
on-line: www.wsoinc.com

National Self-Help Clearinghouse
25 West 43rd Street, Room 620
New York, NY 10036
phone: (212) 354-8525
on-line: www.selfhelpweb.org

Recovery Network
1411 Fifth Street, Suite 200
Santa Monica, CA 90401
phone: (310) 393-3979
on-line: www.recoverynetwork.com

Sex and Love Addicts Anonymous
Fellowship-Wide Services, Inc.
P.O. Box 199, New Town Branch
Boston, MA 02258
phone: (617) 332-1845

Women for Sobriety
P.O. Box 618
Quakertown, PA 18951
phone: (215) 536-8026
on-line: www.mediapulse.com/wfs

Exhibit G Alcoholics Anonymous: How It Works and Twelve Steps

Rarely have we seen a person fall who has thoroughly followed our path. Those who do not recover are people who cannot or will not completely give themselves to this simple program, usually men and women who are constitutionally incapable of being honest with themselves. There are such unfortunates. They are not at fault; they seem to have been born that way. They are naturally incapable of grasping and developing a manner of living which demands rigorous honesty. Their chances are less than average. There are those, too, who suffer from grave emotional and mental disorders, but many of them do recover if they have the capacity to be honest.

Our stories disclose in a general way what we used to be like, what happened, and what we are like now. If you have decided you want what we have and are willing to go to any length to get it—then you are ready to take certain steps.

At some of these we balked. We thought we could find an easier, softer way. But we could not. With all the earnestness at our command, we beg of you to be fearless and thorough from the very start. Some of us have tried to hold on to our old ideas and the result was nil until we let go absolutely.

Remember that we deal with alcohol—cunning, baffling, powerful! Without help it is too much for us. But there is One who has all power—that One is God. May you find Him now!

Half measures availed us nothing. We stood at the turning point. We asked His protection and care with complete abandon.

Here are the steps we took, which are suggested as a program of recovery.

1. We admitted we were powerless over alcohol—that our lives had become unmanageable.

2. Came to believe that a Power greater than ourselves could restore us to sanity.

3. Made a decision to turn our will and our lives over to the care of God as we understood Him.

4. Made a searching and fearless moral inventory of ourselves.

5. Admitted to God, to ourselves, and to another human being the exact nature of our wrongs.

6. Were entirely ready to have God remove all these defects of character.

7. Humbly asked Him to remove our shortcomings.

8. Made a list of all persons we had harmed, and became willing to make amends to them all.

9. Made direct amends to such people wherever possible, except when to do so would injure them or others.

10. Continued to take personal inventory and when we were wrong promptly admitted it.

11. Sought through prayer and meditation to improve our conscious contact with God as we understood Him, praying only for knowledge of His will for us and the power to carry that out.

12. Having had a spiritual awakening as the result of these steps, we tried to carry this message to alcoholics, and to practice these principles in all our affairs.

Many of us exclaimed, "What an order! I can't go through with it." Do not be discouraged. No one among us has been able to maintain anything like perfect adherence to these principles. We are not saints. The point is that we are willing to grow along spiritual lines. The principles we have set down are guides to progress. We claim spiritual progress rather than spiritual perfection.

Our description of the alcoholic, the chapter to the agnostic, and our personal adventures before and after make clear three pertinent ideas:

a. That we were alcoholic and could not manage our own lives.

b. That probably no human power could have relieved our alcoholism.

c. That God could and would if He were sought.

NOTE: The Twelve Steps of Alcoholics Anonymous and "How It Works" (excerpted from Chapter 5 of the book *Alcoholics Anonymous*) are reprinted with the permission of Alcoholics Anonymous World Services, Inc. (A.A.W.S.). Permission to reprint and adapt the Twelve Steps does not mean that Alcoholics Anonymous is affiliated with any program discussed in this volume. A.A. is a program of recovery from alcoholism *only*—use of the Steps, or an adapted version of the Steps, in connection with programs and activities which are patterned after A.A., but which address other problems, or use in any other non-A.A. context, does not imply otherwise.

Exhibit H Clinical Institute Withdrawal Assessment for Alcohol (CIWA-Ar)

Patient _____   Pulse _____

CIWA Total Score _____

Date _____   Blood pressure _____

Rater's Initials _____

Time _____

Nausea and vomiting: Ask, "Do you feel sick to your stomach? Have you vomited?" Observe.

  0 no nausea and no vomiting
  1 mild nausea with no vomiting
  2
  3
  4 intermittent nausea with dry heaves
  5
  6
  7 constant nausea, frequent dry heaves and vomiting

Tremor: Arms extended and fingers spread apart. Observe.

  0 no tremor
  1 not visible, but can be felt fingertip to fingertip
  2
  3
  4 moderate, with patient's arms extended
  5
  6
  7 severe, even with arms not extended

Paroxysmal sweats: Observe.

  0 no sweat visible
  1 barely perceptible sweating, palms moist
  2
  3
  4 beads of sweat obvious on forehead
  5
  6
  7 drenching sweats

Anxiety: Ask, "Do you feel nervous?" Observe.

    0 no anxiety, at ease
    1 mildly anxious
    2
    3
    4 moderately anxious; guarded with anxiety inferred
    5
    6
    7 equivalent to acute panic states, as seen in severe delirium or acute schizophrenic reactions

Agitation: Observe.

    0 normal activity
    1 somewhat more than normal activity
    2
    3
    4 moderately fidgety and restless
    5
    6
    7 paces back and forth during most of the interview, or constantly thrashes about

Tactile disturbances: Ask, "Have you any itching, pins and needles sensations, any burning, any numbness or do you feel bugs crawling on or under your skin?" Observe.

    0 none
    1 very mild itching, pins and needles, burning or numbness
    2 mild itching, pins and needles, burning or numbness
    3 moderate itching, pins and needles, burning or numbness
    4 moderately severe hallucinations
    5 severe hallucinations
    6 extremely severe hallucinations
    7 continuous hallucinations

Auditory disturbances: Ask, "Are you more aware of sounds around you? Are they harsh? Do they frighten you? Are you hearing anything that is disturbing you? Are you hearing things you know are not there?" Observe.

    0 not present
    1 very mild harshness or ability to frighten
    2 mild harshness or ability to frighten
    3 moderate harshness or ability to frighten
    4 moderately severe hallucinations

5 severe hallucinations

6 extremely severe hallucinations

7 continuous hallucinations

Visual disturbances: Ask, "Does the light appear to be too bright? Is the color different? Does it hurt your eyes? Are you seeing anything that is disturbing to you? Are you seeing things you know are not there?" Observe.

0 not present

1 very mild sensitivity

2 mild sensitivity

3 moderate sensitivity

4 moderately severe hallucinations

5 severe hallucinations

6 extremely severe hallucinations

7 continuous hallucinations

Headache, fullness in head: Ask, "Does your head feel different? Does it feel like there is a band around your head?" Do not rate dizziness or light-headedness. Otherwise, rate severity.

0 not present

1 very mild

2 mild

3 moderate

4 moderately severe

5 severe

6 very severe

7 extremely severe

Orientation and clouding of sensorium: Ask, "What day is this? Where are you? Who am I?" Observe.

0 oriented and can do serial additions

1 cannot do serial additions or is uncertain about date

2 disoriented for date by no more than 2 calendar days

3 disoriented for date by more than 2 calendar days

4 disoriented for place and/or person

Score (subject to agency policy)

<25 = minimal to mild withdrawal

$20-25$ = moderate withdrawal

>25 = severe withdrawal

Exhibit I Clinical Institute Narcotic Assessment (CINA)

Patient _____   Pulse _____

CINA Total Score _____

Date _____   Blood pressure _____

Rater's Initials _____

Time _____

Abdominal changes: Ask, "Do you have any pains in your abdomen?" Listen.

0 no abdominal complaints, normal bowel sounds
1 reports waves of abdominal crampy pain
2 reports crampy abdominal pain, diarrhea movements, active bowel sounds

Gooseflesh: Observe.

0 no gooseflesh visible
1 occasional gooseflesh but not elicited by touch; not permanent
2 prominent gooseflesh, in waves and elicited by touch
3 constant gooseflesh over flesh and arms

Changes in temperature: Ask, "Do you feel hot or cold?"

0 no report of temperature change
1 reports feeling cold, hands cold and clammy to touch
2 uncontrolled shivering

Nasal congestion: Observe.

0 no nasal congestion, sniffling
1 frequent sniffling
2 constant sniffling with watery discharge

Restlessness: Observe.

0 normal activity
1 somewhat more than normal activity, moves legs up and down, shifts position occasionally
2 moderately fidgety and restless, shifting positions frequently
3 gross movements most of the time or constantly thrashes about

Tremor: Arms extended and fingers apart. Observe.

    0 no tremor
    1 not visible but can be felt fingertip to fingertip
    2 moderate with patient's arms extended
    3 severe even if arms not extended

Nausea and vomiting: Ask, "Do you feel sick to your stomach? Have you vomited?"

    0 no nausea, no vomiting
    2 mild nausea with no retching or vomiting
    4 intermittent nausea with dry heaves
    6 constant nausea, frequent dry heaves and/or vomiting

Lacrimentation: Observe.

    0 no lacrimentation
    1 eyes watering, tears at corners of eyes
    2 profuse tearing from eyes over face

Muscle aches: Ask, "Do you have any muscle cramps?"

    0 no muscle aching reported, arm and neck muscles soft at rest
    1 mild muscle pains
    3 reports severe muscle pains, muscle of legs, arms and neck or constant
       state of contraction

Sweating: Observe.

    0 no sweat visible
    1 barely perceptible sweating, palms more
    2 beads of sweat obvious on forehead
    3 drenching sweat over face and chest

Yawning: Observe.

    0 no yawning
    1 frequent yawning
    2 constant uncontrolled yawning

Scoring subject to agency policy

SOURCE: Adapted from *Recovery Manual,* copyright 1998 by the UniQual Network of Addiction Medicine. Used with permission.

Exhibit J   AUDIT (Alcohol Use Disorder Identification Test)

AUDIT is a brief structured interview, developed by the World Health Organization, that can be incorporated into a medical history. It contains questions about recent alcohol consumption, dependence symptoms, and alcohol-related problems.

Begin the AUDIT by saying, "Now I am going to ask you some questions about your use of alcoholic beverages during the past year." Explain what is meant by alcoholic beverages: beer, wine, liquor (vodka, whiskey, brandy, etc.).

Record the score for each question in the brackets on the right side of the question.

1. How often do you have a drink containing alcohol?

   _____ Never   (0)   [ ]
   _____ Monthly or less   (1)
   _____ 2 to 4 times a month   (2)
   _____ 2 to 3 times a week   (3)
   _____ 4 or more times a week   (4)

2. How many drinks containing alcohol do you have on a typical day when you are drinking?

   _____ None   (0)   [ ]
   _____ 1 or 2   (1)
   _____ 3 or 4   (2)
   _____ 5 or 6   (3)
   _____ 7 or 9   (4)
   _____ 10 or more   (5)

3. How often do you have six or more drinks on one occasion?

   _____ Never   (0)   [ ]
   _____ Less than monthly   (1)
   _____ Monthly   (2)
   _____ Weekly   (3)
   _____ Daily or almost daily   (4)

4. How often during the last year have you found that you were unable to stop drinking once you had started?

   _____ Never   (0)   [ ]
   _____ Less than monthly   (1)
   _____ Monthly   (2)
   _____ Weekly   (3)
   _____ Daily or almost daily   (4)

5. How often during the last year have you failed to do what was normally expected from you because of drinking?

_____ Never	(0)	[ ]
_____ Less than monthly	(1)	
_____ Monthly	(2)	
_____ Weekly	(3)	
_____ Daily or almost daily	(4)	

6. How often during the last year have you needed a first drink in the morning to get yourself going after a heavy drinking session?

_____ Never	(0)	[ ]
_____ Less than monthly	(1)	
_____ Monthly	(2)	
_____ Weekly	(3)	
_____ Daily or almost daily	(4)	

7. How often during the last year have you had a feeling of guilt or remorse after drinking?

_____ Never	(0)	[ ]
_____ Less than monthly	(1)	
_____ Monthly	(2)	
_____ Weekly	(3)	
_____ Daily or almost daily	(4)	

8. How often during the last year have you been unable to remember what happened the night before because you had been drinking?

_____ Never	(0)	[ ]
_____ Less than monthly	(1)	
_____ Monthly	(2)	
_____ Weekly	(3)	
_____ Daily or almost daily	(4)	

9. Have you or has someone else been injured as the result of your drinking?

_____ Never	(0)	[ ]
_____ Less than monthly	(1)	
_____ Monthly	(2)	
_____ Weekly	(3)	
_____ Daily or almost daily	(4)	

10. How often has a relative, friend, or a doctor or other health worker expressed concern about your drinking or suggested you cut down?

_____ Never   (0)   [ ]
_____ Less than monthly   (1)
_____ Monthly   (2)
_____ Weekly   (3)
_____ Daily or almost daily   (4)

Record the total of the specific items.   [ ]

A score of 8 or greater may indicate the need for a more in-depth assessment.

Exhibit K   Example of a Client Health History and Physical Exam

<u>NAME:</u>

<u>DOA:</u> 12/26/99   <u>ROOM:</u> 322

<u>CHIEF COMPLAINT:</u> Opioid dependence

<u>HISTORY OF PRESENT ILLNESS:</u> This is the second AdCare admission for this 41-year-old white, married female admitted with a 15-year history of opioid dependence. Using 10 bags a day intranasally and intravenously for the past 3 weeks. She experiences muscle cramps, abdominal cramps, aches, chills, sleep disturbance, anxiety and depression, sweats, nausea, vomiting and diarrhea in withdrawal. Currently complaining of feeling shaky and having chills. She has a past history for both alcohol and barbiturate dependence. Nothing current.

<u>TREATMENT HISTORY:</u> Includes AdCare 5/99 for 4 days with no clean time. She went to Brookside in June 1999, again with no clean time. Returned home in July 1999 and stayed clean for a 4-month period, relapsing 3 weeks ago. She has continued in outpatient counseling through Arbour Hospital since July 1999. She had a 10-year clean period from 1987 to 1997. She was attending A.A./N.A. meetings, approximately 3 times a week. Stopped listening. Her last meeting was 1 week ago.

<u>PAST MEDICAL HISTORY:</u> HIV-positive. T-cell count 184, viral load less than 400 (undetectable). S/p PCP in 1997. On Viracept, Zerit, Bactrim, Viramune, and Fortivase. She also has fibromyalgia for which she takes Elavil. She had a D&C in 1984. Skin graft to her right lower leg in 1987 secondary to a motor vehicle accident. Hepatitis C. Hypercholesterolmia at 287. Smokes 1-2 ppd.

<u>PSYCHIATRIC HISTORY:</u> Depression/anxiety. She has been on multiple antidepressants and continues only on Xanax 0.5 mg qam, 1 mg qhs. Also Elavil 20 mg.

<u>MEDICATIONS:</u> Viracept, Zerit, Bactrim, Viramune, Fortivase; Elavil and Xanax.

<u>ALLERGIES:</u> No known drug allergies.

<u>SOCIAL HISTORY:</u> She has a lot of family support. She lives with her husband and 15-year-old son. She has a sponsor. No legal issues. Unemployed.

<u>FAMILY HISTORY:</u> Mother sober in A.A. for 2 years. Father OD heroin 3 years ago.

<u>REVIEW OF SYSTEMS:</u> She has had a 7-pound weight loss with this most recent relapse. Otherwise, mild withdrawal symptoms as above.

<u>PHYSICAL EXAMINATION:</u>

BP: 126/84   T: 99.1   P: 84   R: 22

HEIGHT: 5'4"

WEIGHT: 135 lbs.

INTOX: 00

<u>GENERAL STATEMENT:</u> Pleasant female in mild distress. Cooperative.

<u>SKIN:</u> Slightly moist.

<u>HEENT:</u> Normocephalic, atraumatic. Extraocular movements intact. Pupils dilated. Conjunctivae clear. No nystagmus. EARS: hearing acuity normal and adequate. NOSE/THROAT/OROPHARYNX: Unremarkable.

<u>NECK:</u> Supple, no thyromegaly, carotids are normal. Trachea is in the midline. No nodes.

<u>LUNGS:</u> Clear to auscultation, bilaterally.

<u>CHEST:</u> Normal excursions.

<u>BREASTS:</u> Exam deferred.

<u>HEART:</u> Regular rhythm without murmur, gallop or rub. S1, S2 normal.

<u>ABDOMEN:</u> Benign. No hepatomegaly. No surgical scars. No masses, bruits, guarding, or tenderness. Bowel sounds were present.

<u>MUSCULOSKELETAL EXAM:</u> No deformities or limitations.

<u>CARDIOVASCULAR:</u> Pulses were within normal limits. No lymphadenopathy.

EXTREMITIES: No cyanosis, clubbing, or edema.

NEUROLOGICAL: DTRs within normal limits and equal. CN II-XII intact. Motor and sensory examination within normal limits. Cerebellar: Heal to shin within normal limits. Finger to nose within normal limits. Romberg negative. Babinski: toes downgoing.

MENTAL STATUS: The patient is oriented in three spheres with good eye contact, fluent speech, and appropriate behavior. Memory: recent and remote intact. There is no thought disorder, hallucinations, nor are there any suicidal or homicidal ideations. The patient's judgment is appropriate.

IMPRESSION:

    opioid dependence
    history of alcohol dependence
    history of barbiturate dependence
    HIV-positive
    fibromyalgia
    hepatitis C
    hypercholesterolemia
    depression/anxiety
    s/p PCP

PLAN: To detoxify the patient in a safe environment and monitor for medical and psychiatric complications. Further treatment needs to be assessed as the withdrawal proceeds.

AMY WILSON, RN-C, NP DICTATING FOR DAVID M. CHISHOLM, D.O.

D: 12/27/99   T: 12/18/99   maf

SOURCE: Reprinted by permission of AdCare Hospital of Worcester, Inc.

Exhibit L Sample Genogram Forms

GENOGRAM

Symbols for Genogram

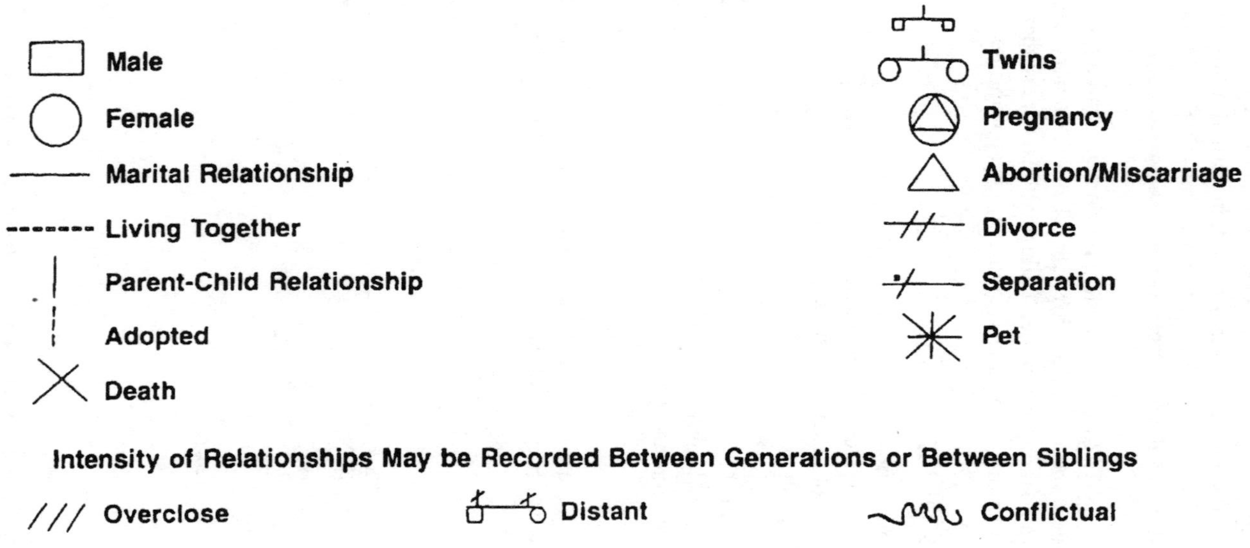

Male

Female

Marital Relationship

Living Together

Parent-Child Relationship

Adopted

Death

Twins

Pregnancy

Abortion/Miscarriage

Divorce

Separation

Pet

Intensity of Relationships May be Recorded Between Generations or Between Siblings

/// Overclose

Distant

Conflictual

Exhibit L Continued

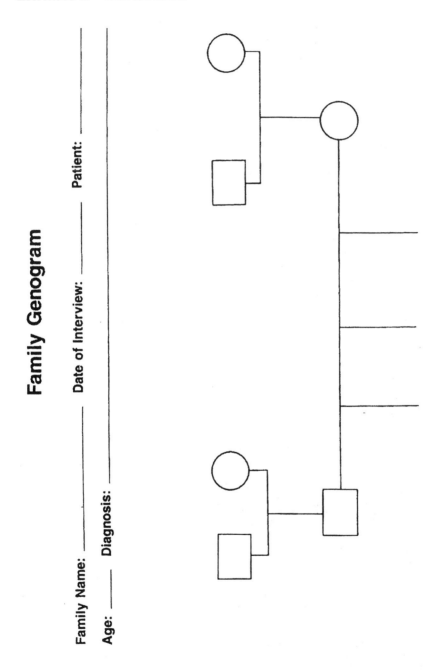

Family Genogram

Family Name: _____ Date of Interview: _____ Patient: _____

Age: _____ Diagnosis: _____

Exhibit M   Example of an Admissions/Intake Assessment Form

Note: ALL ITEMS MUST BE COMPLETED.

AdCare Hospital of Worcester, Inc.
Admissions Intake/Assessment

Date:_____ Projected Date: _____ Interviewer: _____

Patient Name: _____ Account#: _____

Referred for Admission By: Dr. _____ On Date: _____

To: Observ. _____ Inpt.Detox _____ Inpt.Rehab. _____ Op.Detox _____ Op.Tx _____

EAP Involvment: Yes _____ No _____ Name _____

Telephone#: _____ Address: _____

1. ACUTE INTOXICATION/WITHDRAWAL POTENTIAL

Substance	Type	Frequency/ Amount	Route	Last Use	Total	Duration* This Episode	Staff Comments
Alcohol							
Benzo							
Barb.							
Cocaine							
Opiates							
Marijuana							
Inhalants							
Methadone							

Clinic _____ To be Maintained _____

Detoxed _____ Administrative _____ Voluntary _____

Other_____

WITHDRAWAL SYMPTOMS

Present	History	Present	History	Present	History
Tremors	___	Muscle Cramps	___	Chest Pain	___
Sweats	___	Abd. Cramps	___	Shortness of Breath	___
N/V/D	___	Aching	___	Palpitations	___
B/O's	___	Chills	___	Paranoia	___
Haluc. A/V/T	___	Sleep Disturbance	___	Weight Loss	___
History of DT's	___	Anxiety	___	Depression	___

Are you using more to get the effect? Yes____No____Which drug?_____

Have you tried to stop on your own? Yes____ No____
Do you use alcohol/drugs to stop feeling sick? Yes____ No____
Does patient report any medical or psychiatrical complications during past inpatient Tx
(i.e., seizures, hallucinations, DT, suicidal thoughts) transfer to medical or psychiatric facilities?
Yes____No_____ Specify _____
If seizures, relate to Substance w/d? Yes ____No_____
Date of Last Seizure: _____
Was medication Prescribed? Yes _____ No_____ Last Dose _____

Notes: _____
_____
_____

Reprinted by permission of AdCare Hospital of Worcester, Inc.

Exhibit M Continued

Note: ALL ITEMS MUST BE COMPLETED.

AdCare Hospital of Worcester, Inc.
Admissions Intake/Assessment

Staff Comments

Family/Realtionship: Intact _____ Disrupted _____ Supportive _____ Explain: _____

_____

Contact Name/Telephone# _____
Does your present partner have a problem with alcohol or drugs? Yes _____ No _____
Do you have anyone close to you in recovery? Yes _____ No _____ If yes, who?

Do you have a family history of chemical dependency? Yes _____ No _____

If yes, who? _____
Any minor children? Yes _____ No _____ If yes, ages _____
Who is presently the caretaker of the children (Name & Number) _____

Employment/School Difficulties

Absenteeism? Yes ____ No ____ Explain _____

In jeopardy? Yes ____ No ____ Explain _____

Loss of? Yes ____ No ____ Explain _____

EAP? Yes ____ No ____ Explain _____

What is your occupation?
How long have you worked at this job?
Legal History: Current Pending Charges? Yes _____ No _____ What? _____

Pending Court Date? Yes ____ No ____ Date(s) _____

D.U.I. Arrests? Yes ____ No ____ How many? _____ Date(s) _____

Past arrests? Yes ____ No ____ What? _____

Protective Custody? Yes ____ No ____ How many times? _____ The most recent _____

Probation/Parole Officer? Yes _____ No _____ Name & Number _____

Restraining Order? Yes _____ No _____ If yes, when _____

II. BIOMEDICAL CONDITIONS/COMPLICATIONS
Is client Pregnant? Yes _____ No _____ How many months? _____
Physician's Name _____ Telephone #: _____
(Complete Pregnancy Appendix)

NOTES _____
_____
_____
_____
_____
_____
_____
_____
_____
_____

Exhibit M Continued

Note: ALL ITEMS MUST BE COMPLETED.

AdCare Hospital of Worcester, Inc.
Admissions Intake/Assessment

MEDICAL HISTORY   Staff Comments
Have you ever been teste for T.B.? Yes_____ No_____ Result? Pos._____ Neg._____ Date_____
Have you ever been treated for T.B.? Yes_____No_____ Dates_____ Meds._____
Do you have: __ a cough   __ a fever   __ shortness of breath
              __ night sweats   __ bloody sputum   __ chest pain
Medical Problems_____

Medications (type.dose)_____

Are you taking your medication as prescribed? Yes_____ No_____
Recent Accidents/Injuries_____

Physical Disabilities/Limit Medical Hospitilization (past year): Yes_____ No_____ Hospital_____

Diagnosis_____

Primary Care Physician:_____

Address:_____

III. EMOTIONAL/BEHAVIORIAL CONDITIONS & COMPLICATIONS
Psychological/Emotional Difficulties? Yes_____ No_____ If yes, explain:_____

Medications? (type/dose)_____

Are you taking your medications as prescribed? Yes_____ No_____
History of Suicide Attempt(s)? Yes_____ No_____ Date(s)_____

While Intoxicated? Yes_____ No_____
Have you thought about killing yourself? Yes_____ No_____ Past_____ Present_____
Explain_____

Have you thought about killing anyone else? Yes_____ No_____ Past_____ Present_____
Explain_____

Have you suffered any major losses? Yes_____ No_____ What?_____
How are you feeling right now?_____

Inpatient/Psychiatric Treatment? Yes_____ No_____
Dates   Hospital   Reason for Admission
_____ _____ _____

_____ _____ _____

_____ _____ _____

Outpatient/Psychiatric? Yes   No   Last Contact
Dates   Therapist/Psychiatrist (Name & Tele.)   May Contact?
_____ _____ Yes_____ No_____
_____ _____ Yes_____ No_____
_____ _____ Yes_____ No_____
NOTES: _____

Exhibit M Continued

Note: ALL ITEMS MUST BE COMPLETED.

AdCare Hospital of Worcester, Inc.
Admissions Intake/Assessment

Staff Comments

IV. TREAMENT ACCEPTANCE/RESISTANCE

What motivated you to call at this time?_____

Involvement in 12 step program? Yes _____ No _____ Past _____ Present _____
AA   NA   CA   Frequency?
Last meeting attended?_____ Sponsor? Yes _____ No _____ Home Group? _____

V. RELAPSE POTENTIAL

Prior treatment for chemical dependency   Yes _____ No _____

Inpatient

From	To	Program/Tx Center	LOS	Detox or Rehab	Period of Abstinence

Outpatient

From	To	Program/Tx Center	LOS	Detox or Rehab	Period of Abstinence

Methadone Clinic

From	To	Program/Tx Center	LOS	Detox or Rehab	Period of Abstinence

Residential

From	To	Program/Tx Center	LOS	Detox or Rehab	Period of Abstinence

What were the past Tx recommendations? _____

Did you follow up?_____

Longest sobriety ever _____ Date _____

How maintained?_____

Longest period of sobriety in last 6 months _____ Date _____

How maintained? _____

NOTES:_____
_____
_____
_____
_____

Exhibit M Continued

Note: ALL ITEMS MUST BE COMPLETED

AdCare Hospital of Worcester, Inc.
Admissions Intake/Assessment

VI. RECOVERY ENVIRONMENT   Staff Comments

With whom are you living?_____   _____

Is that person supportive of you seeking treatment?_____   _____

Are you able to return to there? Yes ____ No ____ If not, why?_____   _____

Is there drug/alcohol use in the home? Yes ____ No ____ If yes, by whom?_____   _____

_____   _____

Is there physical/sexual/emotional abuse in the current environement? Yes ____ No ____   _____

If yes, explain _____   _____

_____   _____

Are you willing to change your living situation if necessary for recovery? Yes ____ No ____   _____

Staff Comments _____   _____

_____   _____

Would you be interested in learning more about Revia? Yes ____ No ____

Notes: _____

_____

_____

_____

_____

_____

_____

Nurse Review _____   Counselor Review _____

Date _____   Date _____

Revised: 8/96
Revised: 2/97
Revised: 4/97
Revised: 11/97
Revised: 1/28/98

Exhibit N Example of a Treatment Outcome Follow-Up Questionnaire

Medical Record # _____ Name: _____

Status of follow-up:

    __ refused
    __ unable to contact
    __ deceased
    __ cannot participate

Admission date: _____ Discharge date: _____

Discharge status: _____ Follow-up #: __ 1 mo. __ 6 mos. __ 12 mos.

Interviewer initials: _____ Completed follow-up date: _____

Note to the interviewer: Establish rapport with the patient before proceeding with questions. Assure the patient of the confidentiality of his or her responses and that the information will not be shared with his or her insurance company or employer.

1. Are you alcohol- and drug-free at this time? __ Yes __ No

2. Since discharge, have you been alcohol- and drug-free? __ Yes __ No

(Note to interviewer: If client says he or she is and has been substance-free since discharge, skip to Q. 5.)

3. How often have you used any substance in the past 30 days?

    _____ once
    _____ once a week
    _____ more than once a week
    _____ daily
    _____ not in the past 30 days
    _____ no response/don't know

4. How does your current use of substances compare with your use before you were treated at AdCare?

    _____ less than prior to admission
    _____ about the same
    _____ more than prior to admission
    _____ no response/don't know

5. How often do you attend self-help meetings?

_____ daily
_____ three or more times a week
_____ weekly
_____ less than weekly
_____ not at all

6. If you are attending self-help, what groups are you attending? (Check all that apply.)

_____ A.A.
_____ N.A.
_____ C.A.
_____ G.A.
_____ Other groups (please specify): _____

7. Do you have a sponsor?   __ Yes __ No

(Note to interviewer: Ask about joining a group or speaking at a meeting only after 30-day follow-up.)

8. Have you joined a group?   __ Yes __ No

9. Have you spoken at a meeting?   __ Yes __ No

10. Have you chaired a meeting?   __ Yes __ No

11. What is your employment status? (Check only one.)

_____ employed full-time
_____ employed part-time
_____ retired
_____ homemaker
_____ unemployed

(Note to interviewer: If patient answered retired, homemaker, or unemployed, skip to Q. 13.)

12. Thinking back over the past 30 days, how many days were you unable to go to work because of your substance abuse problems?

_____ days

13. Thinking back over the past 30 days, in general, how many days would you say you functioned at much less than your best due to your substance abuse problems?

_____ days

14. In the past 30 days, on average, how many packs of cigarettes would you say you smoked per day?

    _____ packs

15. In the past 30 days, how many times were you arrested on substance abuse-related charges?

    _____ times

16. Thinking back over the past 30 days, please tell me about any medical or substance abuse services you have received.

Yes	No	Treatment	No. of Admissions	Length of Treatment
1	2	Outpatient Substance Abuse Services		__ Visits/Last 30 Days
1	2	Inpatient Services for Substance Abuse	__ Admissions/ Last 30 Days	__ Days/Last 30 Days
1	2	Inpatient Services for Emotional/Mental Health Problems	__ Admissions/ Last 30 Days	__ Days/Last 30 Days
1	2	Outpatient Counseling With a Mental Health Professional		__ Visits/Last 30 days

17. Thinking back over the past 30 days, please tell me about any medical services you have received.

Yes	No	Treatment	No. of Admissions	Length of Treatment
1	2	Visits to Medical Doctors	__ Visits/Last 30 Days	
1	2	Emergency Room/ Urgent Care	__ Visits/Last 30 Days	
1	2	Medical or Surgical Hospitalizations	__ Admissions/ Last 30 Days	__ Nights in Hospital/Last 30 Days

18. How helpful would you say the services you received at AdCare Hospital were in helping you to keep your job?

    _____ very helpful
    _____ fairly helpful
    _____ not at all
    _____ not applicable (person is unemployed)
    _____ no response/don't know

19. Other than self-help groups, what other support activities are you regularly participating in?

   _____ outpatient counseling for substance abuse problems
   _____ outpatient counseling for emotional problems
   _____ aftercare support group
   _____ residential program/halfway house/sober house
   _____ medication management by a psychiatrist
   _____ urinalysis
   _____ other support activities (please specify): _____

20. How helpful was AdCare Hospital in the development of your discharge plan?

   _____ very helpful
   _____ fairly helpful
   _____ not at all
   _____ no response/don't know

21. What were your goals when you left treatment? (Check all that apply.)

   _____ to remain completely alcohol- and drug-free
   _____ to control my alcohol and drug use
   _____ to return to methadone maintenance
   _____ no response/don't know

22. Overall, to what extent did you meet your goals?

   _____ completely
   _____ somewhat
   _____ not at all

Note to interviewer: If "not at all," ask why not _____

_____

23. How satisfied are you with your employment status?

   _____ very satisfied
   _____ mostly satisfied
   _____ dissatisfied
   _____ no response/don't know

24. How satisfied are you with your present life situation?

   _____ very satisfied
   _____ mostly satisfied
   _____ dissatisfied
   _____ no response/don't know

25. How satisfied are you with your present relationship with your spouse or partner?

_____ very satisfied
_____ mostly satisfied
_____ not in a relationship
_____ dissatisfied
_____ no response/don't know

26. How satisfied are you with your relationship with your children?

_____ very satisfied
_____ mostly satisfied
_____ not applicable (no children)
_____ dissatisfied
_____ no response/don't know

27. How satisfied are you with your relationship with your friends?

_____ very satisfied
_____ mostly satisfied
_____ not applicable (no friends)
_____ dissatisfied
_____ no response/don't know

28. Taken all things together, how would you say things are these days—would you say you are:

_____ very happy
_____ pretty happy
_____ not too happy
_____ no response/don't know

29. Overall, how well would you say you're coping with life these days?

_____ coping very well
_____ managing day-to-day
_____ barely coping

30. Thank you for your time. Is there anything else you would like to comment on?

_____

_____

I am willing for AdCare to contact me in 30 days to see how I am doing?

___ Yes ___ No

Thank you for participating in this survey.

SOURCE: Reprinted by permission of AdCare Hospital of Worcester, Inc.

Exhibit O Example of a Program Outcome Service Satisfaction Questionnaire (Rehabilitation Version)

Medical Record # _____

Date _____   Staff Initials _____

Directions: Below are several questions about your satisfaction with the services you received here at AdCare. Please read each question carefully. Answer as honestly as possible. Your answers will allow us to improve our services. Please circle only one number.

1. The admissions staff were courteous and helpful to me.

Strongly Agree   Agree   Disagree   Strongly Disagree
        1   2   3   4

2. My counselor seemed to understand me and my individual needs.

Strongly Agree   Agree   Disagree   Strongly Disagree
        1   2   3   4

3. The services I've received have helped me to understand why I may have relapsed in the past and to make specific plans to avoid relapse in the future.

Strongly Agree   Agree   Disagree   Strongly Disagree
        1   2   3   4

4. The treatment surroundings were clean and comfortable.

Strongly Agree   Agree   Disagree   Strongly Disagree
        1   2   3   4

5. I participated in developing my Treatment Plan.

Strongly Agree   Agree   Disagree   Strongly Disagree
        1   2   3   4

6. The staff helped me to deal with problems related to my living situation.

Strongly Agree   Agree   Disagree   Strongly Disagree   Not Applicable
        1   2   3   4   5

7. I learned how to use a sponsor and phone numbers for AA or NA.

Strongly Agree   Agree   Disagree   Strongly Disagree
        1   2   3   4

8. The nursing staff helped me to stay as comfortable as possible during my treatment.

Strongly Agree	Agree	Disagree	Strongly Disagree	Not Applicable
1	2	3	4	5

9. My physician answered any questions I had about my treatment.

Strongly Agree	Agree	Disagree	Strongly Disagree
1	2	3	4

10. The staff here treated me with courtesy and respect.

Strongly Agree	Agree	Disagree	Strongly Disagree
1	2	3	4

11. It felt safe while I was here.

Strongly Agree	Agree	Disagree	Strongly Disagree
1	2	3	4

12. I think the staff has had the right amount of contact with my family or significant others.

Strongly Agree	Agree	Disagree	Strongly Disagree	Not Applicable
1	2	3	4	5

13. I think the staff has had the right amount of contact with my employer or Employee Assistance Program.

Strongly Agree	Agree	Disagree	Strongly Disagree	Not Applicable
1	2	3	4	5

14. The staff here helped to motivate me to become clean and sober.

Strongly Agree	Agree	Disagree	Strongly Disagree
1	2	3	4

15. I understand what my next steps should be in my recovery.

Strongly Agree	Agree	Disagree	Strongly Disagree
1	2	3	4

16. I feel more able to handle my day-to-day responsibilities now than when I began to receive services here.

Strongly Agree	Agree	Disagree	Strongly Disagree
1	2	3	4

17. The services I have received have helped me make a commitment to get actively involved in self-help (for example, AA).

Strongly Agree	Agree	Disagree	Strongly Disagree
1	2	3	4

18. I would recommend these services to friends if they needed this kind of help.

Strongly Agree	Agree	Disagree	Strongly Disagree
1	2	3	4

19. Overall, how satisfied have you been with our services?

Strongly Agree	Agree	Disagree	Strongly Disagree
1	2	3	4

20. In your opinion, is there anything we can do to make our services even better? Please explain.

_____

_____

_____

_____

_____

Thank you for participating in this survey.

SOURCE: Reprinted by permission of AdCare Hospital of Worcester, Inc.

Exhibit P: Key Components of a Drug Court Program

Although drug court programs vary based on community needs and resources, the National Association of Drug Court Professionals (NADCP) brought together a group of drug court practitioners and other experts from across the country to develop an outline of what they believe to be the key components. The committee included representatives from courts, prosecution, public defense, treatment, pretrial services, case management, probation, court administration, and academia and others with drug court experience. The following 10 components:

1. Drug courts integrate alcohol and other drug treatment services with justice system case processing.

2. Using a nonadversarial approach, prosecution and defense counsel promote public safety while protecting participants' due process rights.

3. Eligible participants are identified early and promptly placed in the drug court program.

4. Drug courts provide access to a continuum of alcohol, drug, and other related treatment and rehabilitation services.

5. Abstinence is monitored by frequent alcohol and other drug testing.

6. A coordinated strategy governs drug court responses to participants' compliance.

7. Ongoing judicial interaction with each drug court participant is essential.

8. Monitoring and evaluation measure the achievement of program goals and gauge effectiveness.

9. Continuing interdisciplinary education promotes effective drug court planning, implementation, and operations.

10. Forgoing partnerships among drug courts, public agencies, and community-based organizations generates local support and enhances drug court effectiveness.

Source: Defining Drug Courts: The Key Components. Drug Courts Program Office, Office of Justice Programs, January 1997

Index

About the Author

Sandra Rasmussen, Ph.D., R.N., L.M.H.C., C.A.S., teaches psychiatric/mental health nursing at Rhode Island College. She has also taught for more than 10 years in the Graduate Program in Counseling Psychology at Cambridge College, where she coordinates the Addiction Studies Program. In addition, she is a faculty mentor in the Professional Psychology Doctoral Program for Walden University. She currently works as an addiction clinician for AdCare Hospital; she provides clinical supervision for AdCare Recovery Services corrections treatment staff. She is a member of the board of directors of the Massachusetts Council on Compulsive Gambling and serves on the Substance Abuse Rehabilitation Evaluation Committee of the Massachusetts Board of Registration in Nursing. She facilitates a weekly addiction support group for nurses and other health professionals.

Dr. Rasmussen was previously Director of Counseling, then Executive Director, of the NORCAP Center for Addictions of Southwood Community Hospital. NORCAP provided multiple levels of treatment via a network of inpatient and outpatient facilities throughout southeastern Massachusetts. She was also engaged by Brown University Center for Alcohol and Addiction Studies as a collaborating investigator with Project MATCH. She served as site coordinator for the GAMMA Project. In her current research, she is investigating the relationship between developmental tasks and treatment outcome with young adult clients.

Dr. Rasmussen received her Ph.D. in clinical psychology and public practice from Harvard University. She holds graduate degrees in child development and nursing management and an undergraduate degree in nursing. She is a registered nurse, licensed mental health counselor, and certified addiction specialist.